COYOTE RUIN, NA 6654,
A PRESCOTT-AREA COMMUNITY

by

Mary Spall

YAVAPAI CHAPTER AAS CONTRIBUTORS

Robert Beck
Andrew L. Christenson
Joanne S. Cline
Elizabeth S. Higgins

Ginger Johnson
Scott M. Kwiatkowski
Judy Stoycheff

ADDITIONAL CONTRIBUTORS

Beverley A. Everson
Wayne Ranney
M. Steven Shackley
Sharon F. Urban

EDITORIAL ASSISTANCE

Andrew L. Christenson
Ginger Johnson
Mary I. S. Moore

Arizona Archaeological Society
December 2013

The cover photograph is a fly's-eye-view of an intact *Glycymeris* shell valve pendant carved in the shape of a frog or toad. It measures approximately 4.8 cm long, and was recovered from Room 40 at the Coyote Ruin.

Alan Ferg, Series Editor

Kenneth J. Zoll, Series Production Manager

© 2013 Arizona Archaeological Society, Inc.

ISBN 9780939071746

Published by the Arizona Archaeological Society, Inc.

P.O. Box 9665

Phoenix, AZ 85068-9665

www.AzArchSoc.org

Members of the Arizona Archaeological Society, at the time of publication, have the option of receiving either a free hardcopy or PDF version of the *Arizona Archaeologist*. PDF versions of most previous editions are available to members at any time on the "Members Only" page of the Society's website.

ABSTRACT

This report documents the archaeological work conducted at Coyote Ruin (NA 6654), a Prescott Culture site located northeast of Prescott Valley, Arizona. The field work for this project involved survey, mapping, excavation, and recording of rock art, followed by extensive analysis and write-up of the features and artifacts. Work began in November 1998 and concluded in April 2004 using volunteers from the Yavapai Chapter of the Arizona Archaeological Society.

Data recovered indicates Coyote Ruin represents a record of human occupation from perhaps the A.D. 900s until after 1300. Excavations at the site in the late 1920s are the earliest in the Prescott area for which we have documentation. Included herein is the account of J. W. Simmons who worked at the site starting in 1927. The Yavapai Chapter conducted excavations at 11 of the 26 masonry rooms, 2 of the 10 pit structures, and documented many of the agricultural and water-control features. Ceramics recovered included Prescott Gray Ware, Verde Brown, and a range of tradewares mostly from the Kayenta and lower Colorado River areas. The abundance of projectile points and bones from deer, antelope, elk, and small mammals indicated the importance of hunting for the inhabitants. Archaeobotanical analysis documented consumption of maize, harvesting of a variety of seeds, and use of agave.

The concluding chapter of the report places the pueblo into a context of 13th to 14th century occupation in the Prescott area, discusses how the Prescott Culture was organized in this period, and provides some hypotheses that need to be examined with future research.

MARY SPALL

After growing up on a ranch near Greeley, Colorado and spending her adult years in the military (Navy, WAVES, and U. S. Marine Corps), Mary Spall moved to Prescott, Arizona and fulfilled her lifelong interest in archaeology by joining the Yavapai Chapter of the Arizona Archeological Society where she later served on the Chapter's Board of Directors and as Vice President. Under the auspices of the AAS she took certification courses and learned to excavate and record rock art.

Mary worked with the chapter on excavations at the Neural Site (NA 20788), the PCE site (NA 25516), and the Stricklin Forest Park site (AZ N:7:63 - ASM).

She was interested in and tried to explore all the ramifications of the area in which she was working. For instance, as site director she incorporated into her report on the excavation of the Hillebrand site (AZ N:6:23 - ASM; NA 25726 - MNA) a general survey of hilltop sites which comprised almost half of her report.

She was site director for the recording of Inscription Canyon (NA 5352 - MNA) which contained 1220 petroglyphs on 123 boulders, and the Cooley site (NA 13518 - MNA) which had 1226 pecked images on 230 boulders. She was also active in photographing the Blue Hills Petroglyph site, although no publication has resulted from that project. Her archaeological reports are listed below.

Then in 1998 she began work as site director of the large Coyote Ruin (NA 6654 - MNA). Excavation continued for six years, interrupted only for excavating the small Evans Site (NA 26289 - MNA). Before the analysis of Coyote Ruin was complete she assisted in the development of an exhibition, *The Puzzle of Ancient Prescott: Pieces from Coyote Ruin,* at the Smoki Museum of Indian Art and Culture. Here many of the site's finest artifacts were placed on display for more than a year so that members of the community could learn about the site. At the time of Mary's death, although Coyote Ruin excavation work had ceased, the analysis of artifacts was completed, and the artifacts either returned to the site, placed in storage (because construction at Sharlot Hall Museum required that our entire lab be moved), or returned to the property owners, the report remained incomplete. It has been the editors' task to pull together the "pieces of the puzzle" and complete the report as a fitting memorial to a dedicated member of the chapter and archaeological community.

1995 *Inscription Canyon Site: NA 5352.* Yavapai Chapter, Arizona Archaeological Society, Prescott.

1997 *The Cooley Site: NA 13518.* Yavapai Chapter, Arizona Archaeological Society, Prescott.

1997 *The Hillebrand Site: NA 25726 (AZ N:6:23).* Yavapai Chapter, Arizona Archaeological Society, Prescott.

2009 *The Evans Site: NA 26289.* Yavapai Chapter, Arizona Archaeological Society, Prescott.

Mary Spall giving a tour of Coyote Ruin to visitors, 1999.
Photograph by A. L. Christenson.

ACKNOWLEDGMENTS

Writing this report involved numerous people, and I am grateful to all of you for your input. I have attempted to thank certain individuals for their time and effort to make this report possible. I will inadvertently leave someone off the list, and for this I ask for forgiveness.

I wish to express my gratitude to Rita and Herm Peck, owners of the property, for giving us permission to investigate the site, and to members of the Yavapai Chapter, AAS, who contributed large amounts of time in the field and in the laboratory to make this report possible. Special thanks to Ginger Johnson, Mary Moore, and Susan Ford for their compilation and editing work. Special thanks to Dick Lord for his photography of the site, the rooms and the artifacts, and to Mary Moore, Pete Lepescu, Joe Vogel, Sue Sheffield and Jim Steinke for their general photography. Special thanks also to Vern Neal, Jim Roberts, and Sue Sheffield for excavation work, and to Winn Law, Mark Ziem, Jim Roberts and Sheila DeWoskin for mapping and surveying in wind, heat, snow and rain. Thanks to Andy Christenson for his guidance and encouragement as our chapter advisor. I also thank those persons who spent many hours providing special expertise, for which I am grateful. This includes Bob Beck (lithic analysis), Andrew Christenson (ceramic attribute, projectile point, petrographic, and microartifact analyses), Joanne Cline (faunal analysis), Betty Higgins (ceramic analysis), Scott Kwiatkowski (flotation analysis), Wayne Ranney (geology), Judy Stoycheff (historic artifacts), and Sharon Urban (shell analysis).

Many, many thanks!

Mary Spall
Coyote Ruin Site Director

TABLE OF CONTENTS

LIST OF FIGURES

LIST OF TABLES

CHAPTER 1
INTRODUCTION
Mary Spall

Coyote Ruin has probably been known from nearly the earliest arrival of miners, teamsters, and cattlemen in the area (Figure 1). The earliest wagon road to Jerome came from Ash Fork, by Coyote Springs, to Yeager Canyon and then up the canyon and over to Jerome. The first digging at the site apparently was done by a miner looking for gold. The first archaeological excavation in the Prescott area for which we have documentation was done by J. W. Simmons at the site in the late 1920s (see below) who gave it the designation Jerome:8:5 (Gila Pueblo). Later, Museum of Northern Arizona archaeologists recorded the site as NA 3810 and NA 6654 (David A. Breternitz and Milton Wetherill) and described the site as a masonry pueblo (Pueblo III) consisting of 29 plus rooms. As part of his hilltop site survey, Ken Austin, who was not aware of Simmons' work, recorded the site in 1976 as NA 14549, renaming it the Emilienne site (Appendix F). He described it as a hilltop pueblo at least two stories high with a two-foot causeway on the east side. There were twelve rooms in the pueblo and eleven outlying rooms, probably one story high. In 1979 Austin filed information on the Paula site, consisting of petroglyphs on the south end of the hilltop. Recently, the site was also given the number AZ N:7:293 (ASM) so it would be included in the AZSITE system.

Figure 1. Aerial photograph of house mound and mid-level rooms. View to west.
Selected room numbers indicated. Photograph by Joe Vogel.

Along with Fitzmaurice Ruin, Coyote Ruin was one of the early sites Simmons called the "Black on Grey Culture," (Simmons 1931) after the distinctive decorated type present on late sites of what is now called the Prescott Culture or Tradition (see discussion in Chapter 14).

The land on which the site was located was subdivided in 1987 as part of the Prescott Ridge housing development. The site is privately owned and is not open for visitation. In 1998, the Yavapai Chapter of the AAS was approached by the lot owners Robert H. and Chloe R. (Rita) Peck about the possibility of excavating the site, which had been subject to sever vandalism in recent years. A research design was prepared for work at the site and an agreement was signed with the Pecks in September of 1998. Work at the site began at that time under the direction of Mary Spall, and extended until 2004 (see Appendix J for list of project participants). Specialized analyses were begun at this time and most of those were completed by 2008. Unfortunately, Mary died that year and so was not able to see the report to completion. Editing of the report was taken up by several members of the Chapter (see list on title page). Andrew L. Christenson took on the task of putting the site into a regional context which is done in Chapter 14. Mary Spall wrote the chapters and sections not identified as to author. All dates are A. D. unless indicated otherwise.

SITE LOCATION AND DESCRIPTION

Coyote Ruin is located in Township 15N Range 1E Section 9 (Prescott Valley North 7.5 min. Quadrangle) of Yavapai County, Arizona (Figure 2). The site elevation ranges from 5460 ft. at the top of the house mound to 5380 ft. in the southwest corner (see cross-section insert in Figure 29). The site is at the edge of Lonesome Valley, and is among a series of granite hills that form the divide between the Agua Fria River drainage and the Verde River drainage.

Other ceramic period sites in Lonesome Valley are Brady's Fort (a.k.a. Aiken; NA 3809, NA 14548), Yeager (a.k.a. Stansel; NA 11358), Lonesome Valley Ruin (NA 1139) (Barnett 1973), the Henderson Site (Weed and Ward 1970), and Fitzmaurice Ruin (NA 4031) (Barnett 1974).

When J. W. Simmons worked at Coyote he called the masonry pueblo on the hill "New Coyote" and a series of pit houses in an open area about 120 m southwest "Old Coyote" (see Chapter 2), although both areas certainly overlapped in occupation. The Old Coyote part of the site has five shallow, rock-lined pit houses, a garden plot, and burials located in or near the pit houses. The "New" part of the site has about 26 masonry rooms on and around a hilltop and nearby are scattered garden plots, bedrock grinding features, petroglyphs, and water control features. A few additional pit houses and other features are located elsewhere in the nearly 18 acres that the site encompasses. The Chapter's work at the site was concentrated in the upper area.

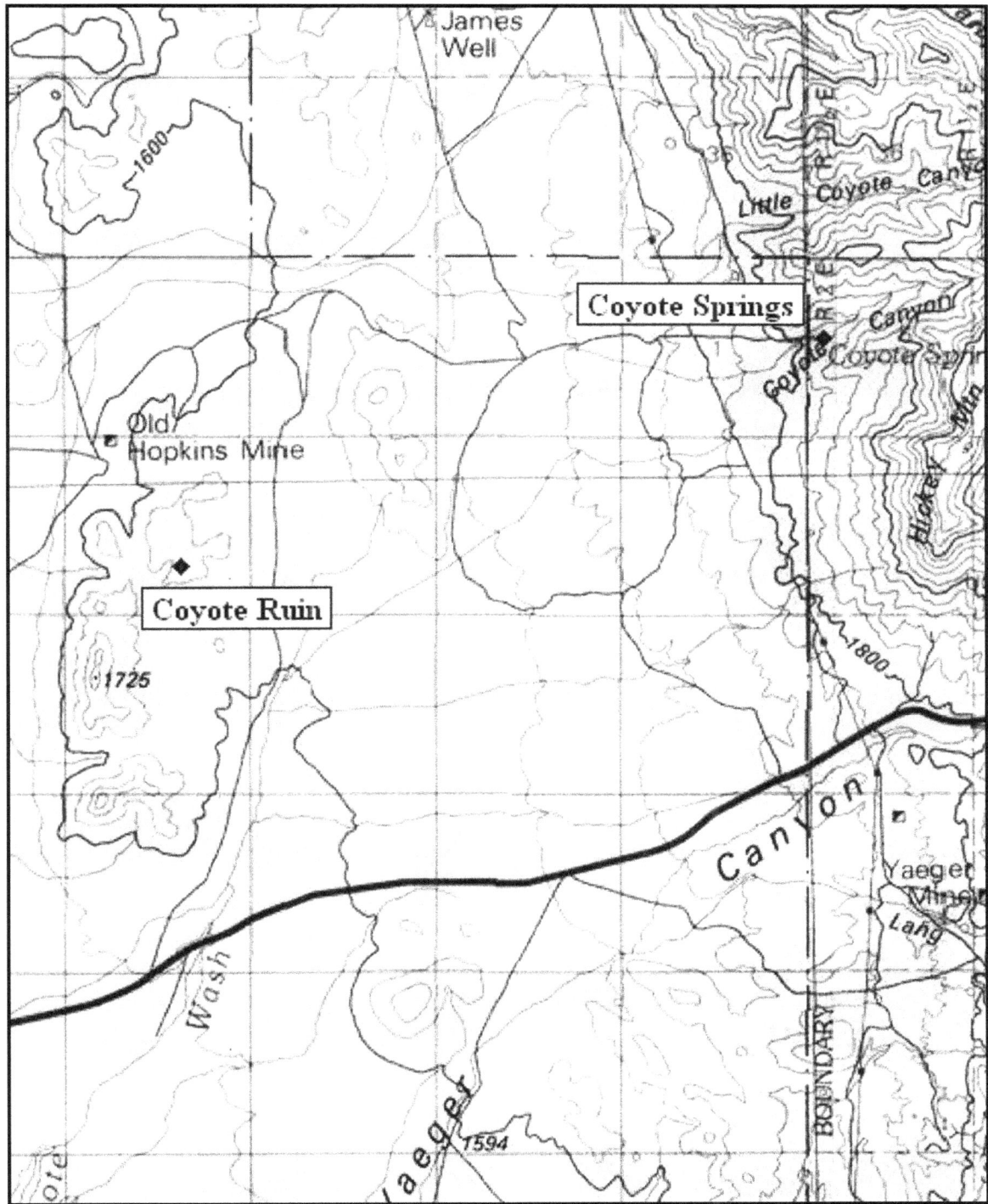

Figure 2. Location of Coyote Ruin and Coyote Springs. Highway 89A (Prescott-Jerome Highway) runs diagonally to the south of the site. Grid units are one mile sections.

ENVIRONMENT

Geology
Wayne Ranney

A geologic examination of the Coyote Ruin site was undertaken by myself and Mary Spall on the morning of November 18, 2003. Coyote Ruin is located on the northeast side of Prescott Valley and sits on top of one of a series of erosional remnants composed of Precambrian-age granite. The ruin site is located within the Transition Zone Province of the state of Arizona. The Black Hills and Mingus Mountain are located about 3 miles to the east. The Black Hills are composed of Precambrian volcanic and sedimentary rocks, unconformably overlain by Paleozoic sedimentary rocks, which are in turn overlain by late-Tertiary age volcanic rocks belonging to the Hickey Formation. Preliminary identification of the granite suggests that it is part of the widespread 1.7 billion year-old granite suite of northern Arizona (Zoroaster Granite Suite in the Grand Canyon). Most likely, it is not part of the 1.45 billion year-old Granite Dells granite located nearby but further to the west.

Many lithologies within the Black Hills could have been used by the occupants of the Coyote Ruin for domestic uses. Numerous green-colored stones that appear to have been shaped somewhat are found among the lithics at the base of the hill. Preliminary identification suggests that these stones may have been obtained from exposures of the Grapevine Gulch Formation in the Black Hills (see Appendix C for more information). The rock is a fine-grained meta-siltstone and the possible use by these people is unknown. It is the only local rock type that could be the source for these lithics. The black basalt rocks could have come from the Black Hills or more likely from nearby volcanic flows on the valley floor. Obsidian is also found, and good sources of this material are obtained from the San Francisco Volcanic Field to the north of the site. The gray obsidian is most likely from the Partridge Creek source area north of the site. Red and dark jasper may be from the Redwall Limestone that crops out in the Black Hills and to the west, north of Paulden. Yellow chert may originate from the Kaibab Formation, the closest outcrop being along the Mogollon Rim near Sycamore Canyon.

The granite upon which the ruin is located has a distinct northwest-southeast joint pattern. This joint pattern is common in the northeast side of the Transition Zone and represents a time when the crust in this area was first compressed (about 70 million years ago) and subsequently extended (about 17 million years ago). The jointing, when weathered, creates thin upright slabs of granite that would have provided excellent slabs of building material in the construction and maintenance of the community.

A curious aspect of this site is trying to ascertain why the builders chose this particular hill rather than any of the others that surround it. The Coyote Ruin sits at an elevation of 5439 feet but is not the tallest of the erosional remnants nearby. Views to the southwest and northwest are partially obstructed by higher landforms that contain larger sub-horizontal surfaces (which would seem to be better building surfaces). To understand why these people would have chosen this site, we must temporarily attempt to "think" as they might have in selecting a site.

First, this particular hill is the only one in the area that has bedrock outcrops of granite. The other hills are covered with soil and vegetation. For this reason the Coyote Ruin contains more available building materials. This alone could be the reason for the specific location, as the size of the site demands large quantities of stone. However, a mature Hackberry tree is growing out of an overhung niche among other water-loving shrubs on the southeast side. This suggests that in times past a source of spring water may also have been present. This certainly would have been reason enough to locate here. Additionally, the bedrock nature of this hill affords many eroded pockets within the granite, where runoff could accumulate after a storm. The other landforms would not collect this ephemeral source of water. Numerous worn-down grinding surfaces on the granite are found in close proximity to these pockets.

The Coyote Ruin is a spectacular site that is fortunately being protected and studied. Understanding its geologic setting helps us to better know how the people interacted with the landscape. It is likely that much thought was given in choosing a building site. The presence of naturally shaped slabs of granite, possible spring water, and surface pools of runoff probably helped determine the location.

Climate

The climate in the Prescott area is moderate, given the elevation range from 5,000 to 6,300 feet above sea level. Extreme temperatures range from –2 F during winter to 105 F during the summer. Normal temperatures range from 30-50 F during winter and 50-90 F during summer. The area averages 140 frost-free days per year.

Precipitation averages 18 inches per year, with one third falling in July, August and September, one third during December, January and February, and the remainder spread over the other six months. Because of the many micro-environments and altitude levels, precipitation can be very scattered, with some areas getting record amounts while others get none.

The vegetation in the Coyote Ruin area is primarily pinion/juniper woodland grading to high desert grassland, and reflects an environment of dry, moderate temperatures and warm breezes, possibly enhanced by a rain-shadow effect from the mountains to the west.

Water

Coyote Ruin is located in the arid high desert of north central Arizona. Water is generally available from underground streams that give rise to springs in some areas and from seasonal precipitation in summer (monsoon rains) and in winter (snow and rain). That dry farming in this area was possible during prehistoric times is evidenced by the presence of garden plots near the site, as well as small associated buildings that may have been used to house workers during farming season. Sufficient water must have been available to make these efforts fruitful. Included in the garden area were several check dams and catchments that were designed to direct water flow and to store water after rainfall and snowstorms. As noted above, there is a possibility that there was a spring at the site. Otherwise, the nearest permanent water is Coyote Springs three miles northeast.

Flora and Fauna

The following list reflects an inventory of current vegetation found in the area. A flotation analysis of plant remains in the site deposits is found in Chapter 10.

COMMON NAME	SCIENTIFIC NAME
Agave	*Agave parryi*
Aster	*Leucelena* sp.
Barberry	*Berberis* sp.
Beards tongue	*Penstemon* sp.
Cliff-rose	*Cowania mexicana*
Dandelion	*Taraxacum* sp.
Evening primrose	*Oenothera* sp.
Four o'clock	*Mirabilis* sp.
Globe-mallow	*Malva* sp.
Gourd	*Cucurbita* sp.
Grasses	various
Hackberry	*Celtis reticulata*
Horehound	*Marrubium* sp.
Jimsonweed	*Datura meteloides*
Juniper	*Juniperus* sp.
Manzanita	*Arctostaphylos* sp.
Mountain-mahogany	*Cercocarpus montanus*
Oak	*Quercus* sp.
Prickly pear	*Opuntia* sp.
Rabbitbrush	*Chrysothamnus* sp.
Sagebrush	*Artemisia* sp.
Squawbush	*Rhus trilobata*
Wolfberry	*Lycium* sp.
Yarrow	*Achillea millefolium*
Yucca	*Yucca* sp.

Presence of the following fauna was observed during work at the site. Analysis of excavated faunal material is found in Chapter 11.

Mammals

Bobcat	*Felis rufus*
Coyote	*Canis latrans*
Mule Deer	*Odocoileus hemionus*
Elk	*Cervus elaphus*
Javelina	*Pecari tajacu*
Gopher	*Geomys bursarius*
Pronghorn	*Antilocapra americana*
Mouse	*Peromyscus maniculatus*
Woodrat	*Neotoma cinerea*

Cottontail	*Sylvilagus floridanus*
Jackrabbit	*Lepus californicus*
Squirrel	*Sciurus casrolinensis*

Birds

Ground Dove	*Columbina passerina*
Mourning Dove	*Zenaida macroura*
Eagle	*Aquila chrysaetos*
Swainson Hawk	*Buteo swainsoni*
Red-Tailed Hawk	*Buteo jamaicenses*
Anna's Hummingbird	*Calpte anna*
Rufous Hummingbird	*Selasphorus rufus*
Scrub Jay	*Aphelocoma coerulescens*
Mockingbird	*Mimus polyglottos*
Gambel's Quail	*Callipepla gambelii*
Roadrunner	*Geococcys californianus*
Raven	*Corvus corax*
Rock Wren	*Salpinctes obsoletus*
Turkey Vulture	*Cathartes aura*

In addition, snakes, lizards, centipedes, scorpions, tarantulas and various ants, bees, beetles, butterflies, flies, gnats, grasshoppers, and wasps were observed.

CHAPTER 2
COYOTE RUIN, LONESOME VALLEY
J. W. Simmons

[Preface: Coyote Ruin is the first site excavated in the Prescott region for which we have documentation. J. W. Simmons began work here in 1927, but returned many times. In 1931 he brought A. V. Kidder to the site as part of a tour of Prescott-area archaeology. Simmons' extensive involvement in central Arizona archaeology is detailed elsewhere (Christenson 2005d).

Simmons sold his Coyote Ruin collection along with his other early collections to Gila Pueblo in 1933. Most of that collection was transferred to the Arizona State Museum (ASM) in 1951. His photographs and manuscripts are also at the Museum. Appendix H lists the artifacts from Coyote Ruin in the ASM database and Appendix I summarizes information on the Old Coyote burials contained in another manuscript.

What follows is from a typed manuscript by J. W. Simmons in the Arizona State Museum Archives (Folder A-36:86-118). A date of "Feb. 12, 1937" is written on it and it is probably one of many Arizona site descriptions he wrote while working for the WPA Arizona Writers' Project. Spelling has been corrected and a punctuation mark occasionally added but everything else remains as Simmons' typed it. A few clarifying words and comments have been added in square brackets and figure numbers have been added. Alan Ferg of the ASM Library and Archives made arrangements for reproduction of this manuscript.]

LONESOME VALLEY, YAVAPAI COUNTY, ARIZONA

Lonesome Valley consists of an oblong rolling plain especially adapted to the raising of cattle. From south to north the valley is approximately 15 miles long by 11 miles wide. To east the plain is bordered by the towering Mingus Mt. Range; to south by Lynx Creek and the Bradshaw Mts; to the west by Granite Creek, the Santa Fe railway, and Highway 89, respectively; and on the north by cedar studded hills which separate the valley from the Verde River.

In the south end the plain is bisected, generally east-west, by Highway 79 [now 89A]. In the central part the valley is about equally divided by a broken chain of ridges oriented north and south. On the east side of these broken hills the drainage is into Coyote Wash—the north fork of the Agua Fria River, which flows southward. On the west side of these ridges the run-off is into Granite Creek, which flows northward and eventually into the Verde River.

The Lonesome Valley Ruins

The five principal ruins of the Lonesome Valley series are: the Fitzmaurice Ruin, on Lynx Creek; Yaeger Canyon Ruin, at the mouth of Yaeger Canyon; Coyote Ruin, midway in the east half of the valley; Brady's Fort, in the northeast corner of the plain, and the Windmill Ruin [a.k.a. Porter Ranch; Argillite Pueblo], on lower Granite Creek—in the northwest corner of the valley.

Prehistoric Agriculture

Adequate evidence can clearly be seen at all of the Lonesome Valley series of ruins that these people practiced agriculture. The evidence they left for us to see consists of numerous small plots so placed and arranged that the run-off from any moderate shower would find its way to these family-size gardens. Because these rather backward people were in contact with their more advanced neighbors (to north, east, and south as seen by intrusive ceramics), it can be assumed that they had corn, squash, etc. But in addition to what their gardens might yield, they had access to acorns, pinyon nuts, prickly pear, wild vegetables, and an abundance of meat in the form of deer, antelope, and small game.

Location of the Ruins

All of the major sites in the Lonesome Valley Series are located at defensive or strategic points. The Fitzmaurice Ruin, Yaeger Canyon Ruin, and Brady's Fort are defendable. The Coyote Ruin [is] to a certain extent, while the Windmill Ruin lies on a knoll-like terrace [and] could have been approached from the west with a minimum of trouble. The fact remains, however, that any one member of the series could have communicated with another one by smoke signals and thereby spread general alarm in case of aggression.

Coyote—Water—Ruin

As some of the ravines and deep gullies among the broken chain of hills have granitic bottoms or small pot holes, some water could have been stored by throwing up small dams. And in case of a severe drought water could have been had at a live spring along the west base of the Mingus Mt. Range, northeast of there. But it was a long, long walk. [Figure 2]

Brady's Fort: The only apparent means that the people at this ruin has of obtaining water was to wait for rains to start the gullies flowing and store as much as possible. Of course, they also could have gone to the live spring southeast of there. But that, too, was a long, long walk.

Fitzmaurice Ruin lies on a live stream; Yaeger Canyon Ruin has a live spring near its southeast base, and the Windmill Ruin has large pot holes in Granite Creek, a short distance north of the site.

Foreword to Coyote Ruin

The author grew up in a region at one time inhabited by Indians. That this fact was obvious was seen in village sites which were more like sherd and chipped stone areas. These sites were found on the high banks of creeks or knolls, or along small rivers. Other evidence consisted of the plowing up of an occasional spearhead. And if I ever heard the term "archaeology" I fail to remember it. And if I had I would not have known what it denoted.

For a part of 1926 I happened to live in Flagstaff, Arizona. And while there heard some people talk about Indian graves being dug up a short distance east of the town. So, on our first day of leisure I drove out to Elden Pueblo, located at the junction of Highways 66-89. And it was there that I met the venerable Dr. J. W. Fewkes, Chief of the Bureau of Ethnology, Smithsonian Institution, Washington, D. C. and his most capable assistant Dr. J. P. Harrington.

Being camera wise I was given the privilege of photographing the ruin and some of the uncovered skeletons (See *Smithsonian Miscellaneous Collections,* Vol. 78, 1926) [Fewkes (1927: Figures 209, 213-215) published four of Simmons' photographs]. In addition, I had an opportunity to observe Dr. Harrington "work" (examine) the recovered pottery specimens and stone artifacts, and catalogue them.

After Dr. Fewkes had returned to Washington, he sent me a number of Vols. dealing with archaeological explorations. Among them was the 28th Annual Report on the "Antiquities of the Upper Verde River and Walnut Creek Valleys, Arizona." Some time later Dr. Harrington sent me the Report on his explorations of the Burton Mound Santa Barbara, Calif.

It is with deep feeling of gratitude when I recount in detail the help that these two good men were to me. For they put my feet on the right trail and to honor them I have tried my best to keep them there. (If this tribute to these men should seem a bit maudlin, I'm not ashamed of it.)

Coyote Ruin in the Yavapai Black-on-grey Culture, Yavapai County, Arizona

The winter of 1926-27 was spent in Phoenix, and while there met the late Dr. Omar A. Turney, at that time the city archaeologist. He invited me to visit his private museum containing many specimens of the Hohokam culture. In the course of time I became acquainted with numerous parties who were either digging in ruins for profit or to establish a collection of their own. As most of the ruins within the Phoenix area had been dug over a number of times, I confined my efforts to surface hunting the ruins for arrow points, beads, and other lost trinkets. In the spring of 1927 I moved to Prescott.

Having read the Fewkes report on the Upper Verde and Walnut Creek, caused me to inquire about ruins not so far distant. Through these inquiries I learned that there were numerous small sites within a mile or so of the city, and larger ones in Lonesome Valley – one in particular on the Coyote [Springs] Ranch, owned by Mr. Jack Stanley.

After becoming oriented in Prescott I visited Mr. Stanley at his ranch. And not until then did I learn that the cattle ranch derived its name from a live spring along the west base of Mingus Mt. Range. Mr. Stanley volunteered to guide me to the spring and also point out some "shaped stones" left there by Indians. While Coyote Spring always has a flow it has its ups and downs like many others in Arizona. But at that a mile or more long pipe line to the corral near his home flows most of the time.

The evidence of "shaped" stones consisted of fragmentary metates, manos, and hammerstones – indicating the area to have been used as a camp site by migrating peoples, and very likely by those from Coyote Ruin, about 1 ½ mile southwest, and those of Brady's Fort – a walled in site, a similar distance to the northwest of the spring. As these two ruins lie on high, rocky points it is quite possible that a water shortage troubled them occasionally.

That Coyote Springs was known to the peoples of the Tusayan area, is seen by the fact that an isolated burial, accompanied by northern mortuary offerings, was washed out in a gully about 1 mi. south of the spring. As a search of the surroundings failed to show any evidence of a permanent or even of a camp site, it may be taken for granted that a death occurred among a group bent on trade or migration. That the local people accepted increments from the north has been well established in the area. For I have uncovered a number of graves which contained only Tusayan ceramics and ceremonial paraphernalia mostly found in the northern region.

When on our way back to the ranch home and had reached the broad and long slope before it fans out into flat land, a series of stone outlines, flush with the surface, were observed. They were not continuous but seemed to crop up here and there but always on a line with the mountain range. Mr. Stanley said that he had never noticed them before. But that may have been because he always had a saddle under him. This time he walked or strolled because it being Sunday his pony was in the pasture. (It was not until I had become acquainted with Coyote Ruin that it dawned on me what the stone outlines, east of the Stanley home, stood for. They were water retention checks to step down the flood water for irrigation purposes. Of course, years of erosion on the upper slopes almost had obliterated them. No telling how large that field was at one time.)

The Top, West Side, and North End of the Structure

At the south end is an explored and demolished room the dimensions of which cannot be ascertained as only a part of the east wall stands. To the north of it – but detached, lies a roughly oval room with meandering wall conforming to the shape of the underlying rocky formation. The room [Room 2 in this report] lies 15 feet northeast-southwest, 11' 6" wide in the center, 9 feet at the northeast and 8 feet at the southwest end. The narrowing south end is partitioned off into a storage room, 4 feet wide at the west end, 3' in the center, and 1 foot at the east end [Figure 3]. The variations in width were due to a large, fixed boulder in the south wall and the base of which projected into the bin.

In cleaning out the bin it was found that the partition wall rested, at a depth of 3', on a hard packed culture strata 16" deep. Along the west wall was about a bushel of carbonized pinon nuts. Along the south wall were two ¾-gooved axes, 5 and 7" long. respectively. One was of diorite and the other of syenite(?). The diorite had a fair polish. One shaped arrow polisher with one groove—6" long, a scraper or knife of basalt 7" long, 3" wide at one end, and pointed at the other. A cache in a niche on the east side of the boulder contained a Pueblo III bowl nested in a smudged culinary bowl. The Pueblo III bowl was 4" [Figure 24] and the plain bowl 5" in diameter. (Main room a blank.)

Southwest and West Side

Possibly two rooms had been demolished at the south end of the west side slope around 1910-15 by Brady, a prospector camping near "Brady's Fort." "Supposed to have recovered a carved shell frog," Jack Stanley – quoted. (For the debris from this/or these rooms see Figure 26.)

The first room explored, lying north of the demolished ones, contained two crude metates, several common-place manos, and two stone posts with a saddle in the wide end and notched near the top. They were not in service but were lying near the metates. A second room adjoining it, on the north, was not examined. (Walls: Vertical base, walls laid on top [of] them.)

Rooms at the North End

There are two rooms at the north end, and one, not well defined, at the northwest corner. However, all three adjoin each other.

The northeast corner room contained one metate of lava and one of fine-grained sandstone. Two, of several manos, were of dark colored sandstone, though well worn, as symmetrical as if machine made. Other objects consisted of two types of pestles/or paint grinders, several stone hoes, and a number of ruin-run[?] bone awls.

One of the paint grinders was of the Elden Pueblo type: This type has hand-knob. The one of the local type was 2 ½" tall, 3" at the base, and 2 ½" at the top. It was better than the average specimen from this culture. (The two rooms to the west were not examined.)

Old Coyote

(Old Coyote lies in the flat southwest of the house mound – see Figure 26. The stone outline is visible in the print and is indicated by two [circles].)

Approximately 300 yards to west-southwest is the inception of a narrow fertile meadow [Figure 4]. At its upper (north) end were the boulder outlines of two small contiguous plots; and a broken circular outline, about 3' across, lay 7' north of the eastside plot. From west of the double outline a row of boulders stretched westward across the narrow neck of the shallow dip-like meadow. This row of stones appeared to be a water retention check and served a twofold purpose. It retained the water and also the washed-down surface soil – the makings of a garden patch.

The circular outline proved to be a shallow roasting pit. It contained ash mixed with soil and heat-fractured stones.

Next, the area enclosed by boulders (the west side one of the two) was examined. The skeleton of an adult was uncovered along the eastside natural earth wall, with the skull almost in the southeast corner. Near the left foot was the half of a black-on-gray bowl carrying an intricate design – which later proved to be of type shape but a very early period design. No tools were found in this pit house. The house was 8x10 feet, oriented north-south. It was 27" deep at the north end and 20" at the south end. The difference in depth was due to the sloping ground.

The house on the east side was of the same dimensions but only 22" deep. This house appeared to have been excavated after the other had been abandoned, and filled in with soil and house rubbish as very few sherds were in the fill – all plain reddish. The reason for assuming that the house was of a later date is because the boulder outline of the west side of the house overlapped the deeper house by 8". I did not know it at the time but that's the reason why I had to remove the row of boul[ders] to undress the skeleton. Evidently the house was abandoned after the occupant had died and had been allowed to remain in the position that death had occurred.

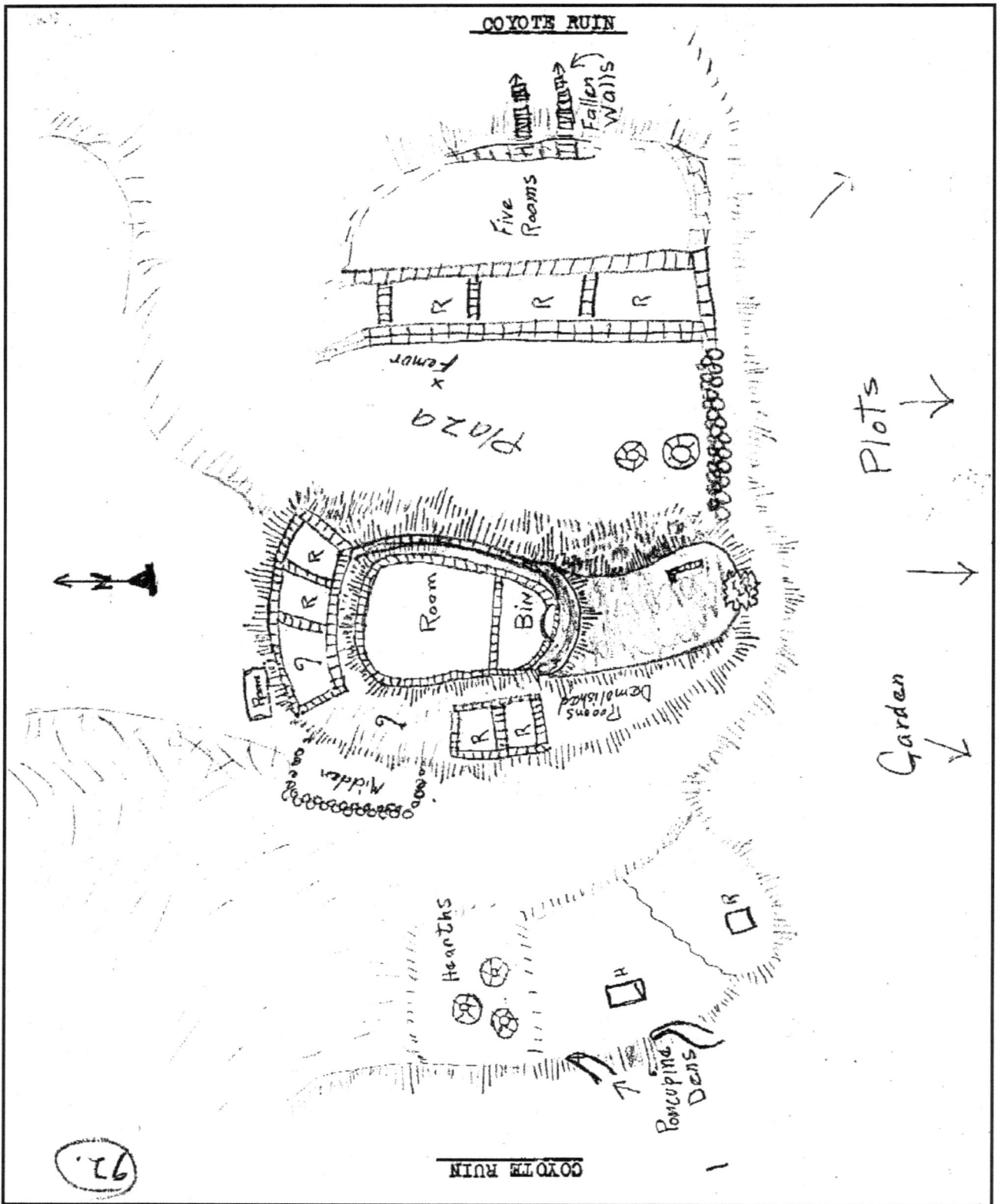

Figure 3. Plan of central part of site. See also Appendix K.

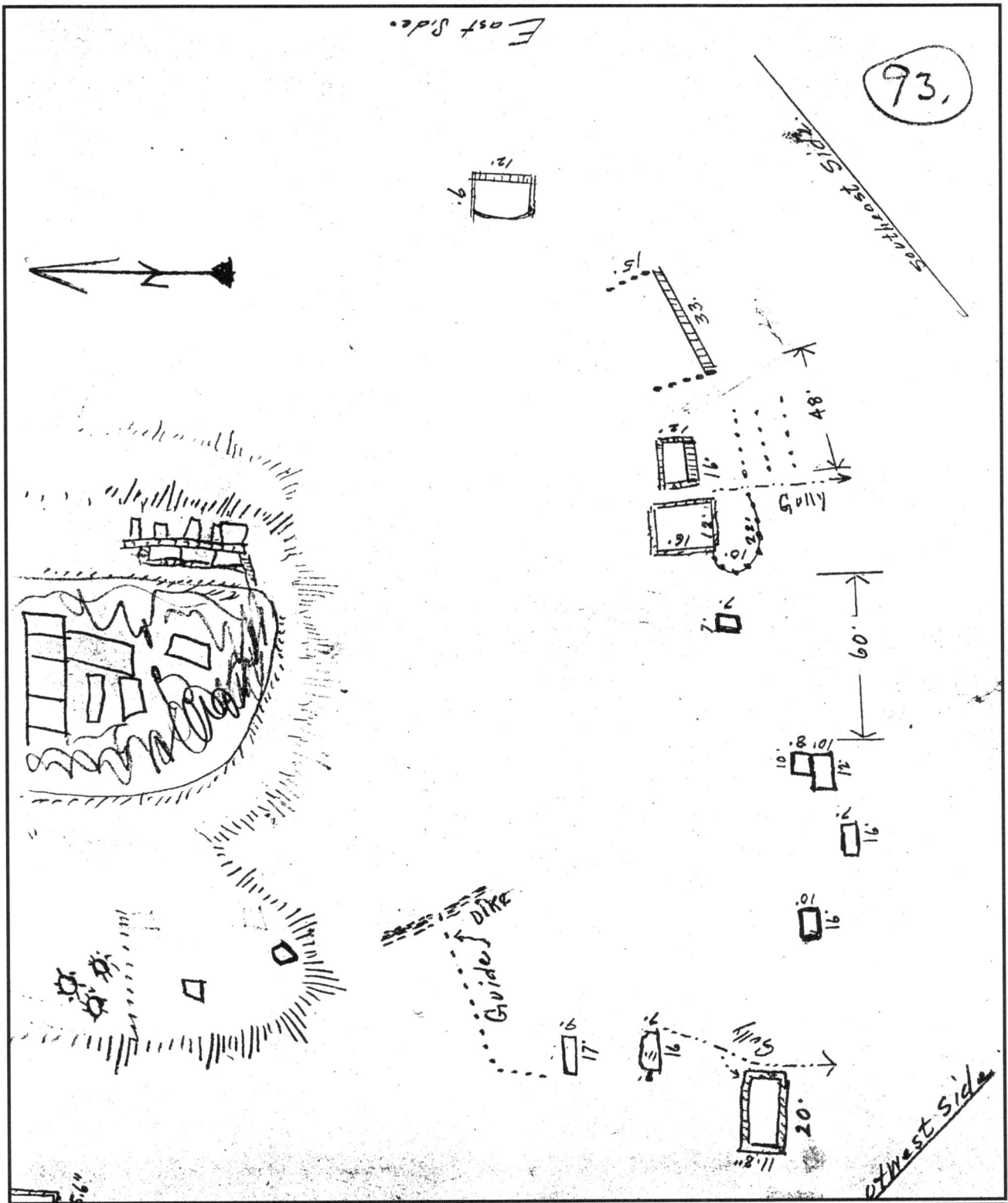

Figure 4. Plan of southern part of site. See also Appendix K.

Old Coyote's Burial Ground

At about 75' down the gentle slope of the meadow-like draw there is a flat cove on the east side. A masonry structure lies a little back of the draw, and adjacent to the east and north of it are a number of rectangular plots outlined with large boulder[s] and of some slabs set on end.

The masonry structure was 25' long, 11 feet wide and divided by a masonry partition which was flush with the debris in the room. According to the lay of the fallen wall, the west side of the house stood about 3' above the surrounding surface. A test pit in the north end of the house revealed a packed floor at a depth of 3 feet. According to this evidence, head-room was close to 6 feet.

About midway on the east side of the structure and joined to the wall was what appeared to be a storage bin. As the walls of the bin were only flush with the ground and no fallen material lay nearby, it appeared that that also had been its original height. The length was 2 ½' (approx.), 1 ½ feet wide and of the same depth.

Almost adjoining the west side of the house a few large stones were projecting from the ground or lying at an angle almost covered with soil. While they were in small groups – from two to three or more, they covered an area about 25 feet square. The plot proved to be a burial ground containing five adults and two children.

The first grave uncovered lay a few feet west of the southwest corner of the house. The block and slab-like stones continued down to within a few inches of the burial. The skeleton of an adult lay with head to east and at an angle across the breast lay an infant with head to the northeast. The only evidence of a mortuary gift was a ceremonial fire offering, covered with a plain sherd, near the infant's head. (The fetish of giving fire offerings to the dead in this culture culminated in its highest form at the King Bros., Pueblo II & III ruin, on the Big Chino, about 40 mi. northwest of Coyote.)

While several of the graves contained one or two culinary bowls, only one stood out in the group: this grave contained one black-on-grey bowl; one symmetrical arrow point of obsidian; thirty-five turquoise flakes and a thin red stone, the remains of a mosaic laid on wood. The black-on-grey bowl was not of the later type shape because of its shallowness and flare rim, nor the design because nothing has so far been reported to compare with it. The only feature about the vessel was that the same paste remained constant in the culture (see Figure 27).

One feature showed up in the graves which later also was noted (but in only a few instances) at the Fitzmaurice Ruin, 6 mi. east of Prescott. This feature was that flat stones had been placed over the arms or legs – or both. In my notes I spoke of it as "anchoring" the dead. (Was this feature a hang-over from a time when these people lived in caves and buried their dead on the steep slope, anchored (weighted) down with rocks?)

About 150 yards below Old Coyote and on the west side of the (by now) wide dip, lay a rectangular pile of stones about one foot high. Because I had found stone in connection with other graves, they were removed and eventually the skeleton of an adult uncovered. It was found as the others: with the head to the east. As no pottery protruded on a level with the bones and no other evidence had been found to indicate it an Indian burial, the thought came that it might be the grave of some prospector as a gold bearing shaft lay only a short distance away. Nevertheless, the skeleton was cleaned up and four small and rather crude bowls were uncovered near the feet (for the location of this grave see Figure 10).

About this time, Tony, the handy-man at the ranch, remarked about some "Indian pottery" near the inception of a gully along the west base of the Mingus Mt. Range – almost due east of Coyote Ruin. As he agreed to point out the place we cut across the valley as I was anxious to see if a site was nearby. A thorough search of the area failed to find any such evidence. Nor did the spot he indicated show the least sign of a washed-out grave along the gully.

Feeling somewhat dubious about the specimens and place of their supposed origin, I returned the next day and, commencing along the gully, turned over a plot about 8 feet square, garden fashion. The result was amazing. Enough ash, charcoal, and bones were uncovered to establish the fact that the body of an adult had been cremated there. Furthermore, the only partly consumed bones and charcoal pointed to a hurried burial rite.

On our next visit to the Stanley ranch home the "water jar" and bones (recovered at the same time) were photographed (see Figure 28 for the water jar). To sum it up: A Tusayan family, or contingent, migrating south to the Yeager Canyon Ruin – about one mile gen[erally] south, or to the large Fitzmaurice Ruin – about 4 mi. southwest, lost a member by death and stopped only long enough to perform a hasty burial.

The East Side of the House Mound

The east side of the house mound is paralleled by a plaza 32 feet wide – on an average [Figure 3]. At the south end it is bounded by a boulder wall 2 ½ feet high by 3 feet wide, while on the east side it consists of a rough-coursed masonry wall. The apparent reason for this better wall is because it also served as the west wall for three or four rooms lying north and south on a slightly lower level. A second series of rooms lie, contiguous to the upper tier, to the east.

Two of the rooms in the upper tier (partly excavated) appear to be 16 feet long by 10 feet wide. The one at the north end, however, is nearer 10 feet long by 6 or 7 feet wide. Two of the rooms in the lower series are 18-22 feet long, 10-14 feet wide, respectively. While the lower (east side) walls have fallen down the slope they show to have consisted of twelve courses of masonry. One room in the southeast corner, though damaged, appears to be 16 feet by 12 feet wide.

Tests in the Plaza

(Decorated sherds found on the surface, and the black-on-grey bowl recovered in the burial ground, were of an unknown pottery type to me.) [Simmons means that the designs were unfamiliar.]

Several tests in the south end of the plaza revealed that it was a filled-in area. It consisted of ash; fractured stones; pot sherds, and debris from the rooms and the site. This fill rested on a decomposed granitic base with a pronounced slope to the east. Along the east side and at the south end the fill was 2 ½ feet deep but rising gradually to the surface at the north end.

The pot sherds recovered in the tests were a revelation. While the culinary sherds were of a course reddish paste, those decorated had a course grey paste carrying a black or faded blackish design. Some of the painted sherds had such a pronounced zigzag pattern that it resembled a series of oversize V's. A few of the large sherds carried as much as three unrelated elements.

The culinary sherds were thinner on the average than those decorated but all had rough interiors – ridges, finger marks etc. All sherds showed that the exterior had received better treatment than the interior. The temper consisted of mica, feldspar, and large grains of granite.

Other specimens recovered consisted of animal bones, fragments of human skelet[on] and the complete femur of an adult. Whether Brady, the prospector, had worked the plaza, or if the occupants themselves had disturbed the area could not be ascertained. The disturbance might also indicate that when the rooms adjacent to the plaza were built that some graves had been disturbed and the bones buried in the plaza. At the south end several hearths were uncovered, enclosed by stone slabs set on edge. But it appeared that they were of an early date as they lay from one to two feet below the surface.

West Side

(With the exception of one point the west has been covered in the discussion of Figure 26.)

A terraced enclosure lies at the northwest base of the house mound. At a glance it appears to be a garden plot. A considerable test, however, showed it to be more of midden. Ash impregnated soil, a few smudged stones, and numerous animal bones of the deer or antelope were its contents. This, however, does not preclude its original use as a garden plot. It lies well situated for such a purpose.

Coyote Ruin, Lonesome Valley (Supplement).

Figures 5 through 13.

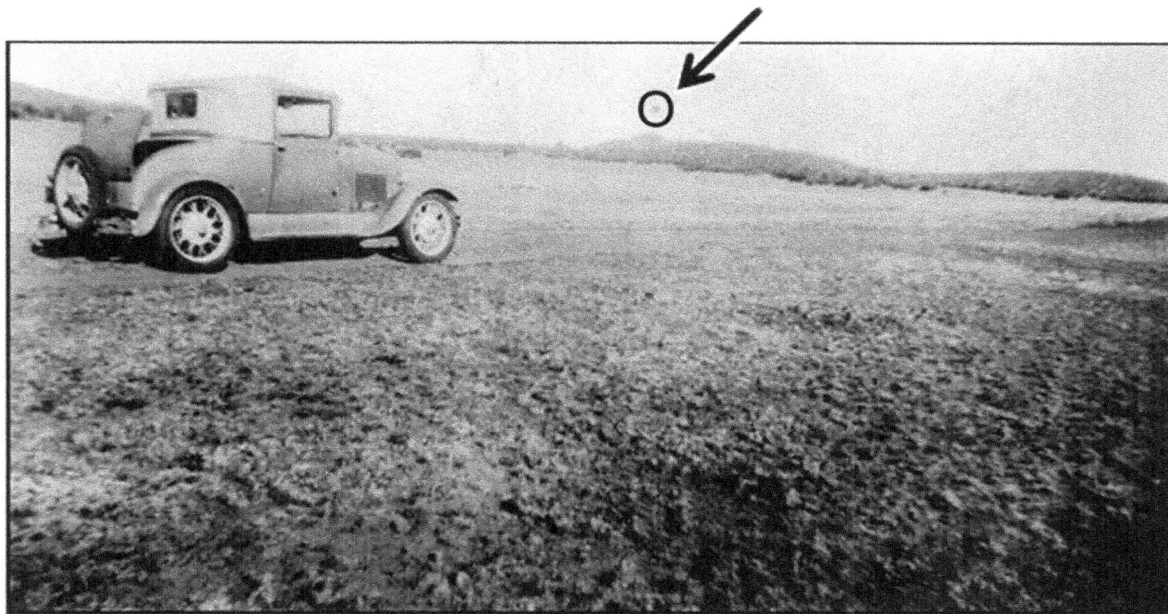

Figure 5. View northwest.

(The ruin is reached over Highway 79 to a point where the Coyote Ranch Road branches off to the north, on the west side of the north fork of the Agua Fria River.)

A distant view of the ruin from the Coyote Ranch Road. With the exception of the upper part of the main structure [below the circle], the site is obscured by a brush covered knoll. The ruin is accessible by car to within one hundred fifty yards.

Figure 6. A close-up from the south side.

Two large rooms are situated on the low, crumbling ledge. A demolished structure lies in a saddle between the highest point of the house mound and of the granitic outcrop [at the white circle].

Figure 7. View to the south.

The view shows the garden plots scattered among oak brush south of the site. Only a few can be seen.

Figure 8. One hundred fifty yards to the ruin. View northwest.

A long series of terraced gardens, which begin with only one on the east side, extend around the south, west and the north side of the site. A terrace, 33 feet long by 15 wide, lies at the rear of the car. Evidence of others can be seen in the form of scattered stones to L.

20

Figure 9. View north.

A small garden plot outlined with stones lies in the foreground. Similar ones occur among the oak brush to the left. The remains of dwellings occur on the high ledge to the left, and contiguous rooms on the central mound. Quite a series of them are found on the right shoulder of the house mound.

Figure 10. View northeast.

A "lonesome" grave lies in the foreground. A rectangular outcropping of placed stones led to its discovery. It was also one of the earliest burials at the site – according to the pottery offerings in the grave. All of it – four pieces – was crude in paste and workmanship – a coarse redware. Old Coyote is [located below the] dot on the far side of the draw.

Figure 11. View east-southeast.

Coyote as seen from the broken chain of hills which run parallel to the ruin three-quarter mile to the west. There are indications that Coyote rests on an outcropping very similar to the lower, blackish ridge.

The Yaeger Canyon Ruin (at the mouth of Yaeger Canyon) lies directly in line over Coyote. And the Mingus Mt. Range, which skirts the valley along the east side, shows itself as a natural barrier which separated the Verde-Oak Creek culture, from that of the Lonesome Valley-Chino Basin culture.

Figure 12. View south-southwest.

Two rooms lie near the south end of the rising ledge. Large depressions in this ledge made suitable rain basins. Only one mortar hole was noted. Fire pits lined with slabs set on edge are indicated by [the black circle] to left of ledge. A terraced enclosure filled with midden trash, is shown by [the white circle] along the base of the structure.

22

Figure 13. View south-southwest.

A plaza, 32 feet wide, follows the length of the structure. Three, and possibly four, rooms lie below but contiguous to the plaza. And five rooms lie below but adjoining the upper tier. Several stone marked outlines occur on the small flat between the north end of the structure and the brushy bush in the foreground.

Coyote and Its Terraced Garden Plots

Figure 14. Garden plot view 1.

The stone, marked with the figure 1 [inside the black circle], lies at the southeast corner of an odd-shape plot, 22 feet long by 10 wide. A well enclosed plot, adjacent on the upper side, lies oriented up the slope, 16 feet by 12 W. An enclosed tract among the bushes to the right is 16 feet long by 12 wide. Single terraces, but not well defined, occur for some distance, down the slope below this tract. The west ends of the terraces have been damaged by a gully, which begins at this point.

23

Figure 15. Garden plot view 2.

The lower garden is 12 feet long by 10 wide. The one laying a few above, 10 feet long by 8 wide.

Figure 16. Garden plot view 3.

The lower plot is 12 feet long by 7 wide. The one along the edges of the bushes above, 16 feet long by 10 wide. Others in the open to the right have been damaged by erosion.

Figure 17. Garden plot view 4.

Due to the rocky terrain #4 is of an odd shape, 16 feet long by 7 feet wide on the east, 8 at the west end and a maximum diameter of 11 feet in the west end center. Diggers have damaged the structure. An enclosed plot at 40 feet above #4 is 17 feet long by quite 9 feet wide. A line of boulders, 25 feet above the structure and 30 feet below the base of the high ledge, diverted an excess run-off to a point near the northwest end of the garden.

Figure 18. Garden plot view 5.

#5 lies between the brush and the gap in the rocky point. As can be seen, a gully which has its inception directly below #4, has built up a pile of debris on the far side of #5. Probably due to the area receiving a large volume of the run-off, that the foundation of the structure consists of large slabs set on edge. Were it not that the structure is oriented east and west, the size of it might lead one to think it a house. But a test pit shows only rich soil but not a trace of a sherd. It is 20 feet long by 11' 8" W.

25

Figure 19. Garden plot view 6.

#6 lies on the west slope of the site, 50 feet northwest of the north end of the outcropping ledge. It is a husky built structure oriented up the slope, 21 feet by quite 15 feet wide. Quite a number of gardens occur on the west slope, father north, left of #6.

The Coyote House Mound

Figure 20. House mound, view northeast. Room at northeast corner.

A glance at the three views [of the Coyote House Mound] (Figures 8-10) will, approximately, indicate how the two rooms on the top, those on the west side, and three at the north end are situated. From the northeast corner of the room (at the northeast corner of the structure) to the vertical south end, the length is 78 feet. Due to a bowing in to the west at a point 28 feet from the northeast corner, the rooms at the north end lie oriented northeast-southwest. From the 28-foot point the top runs 50 feet a little east of south. The room at the northeast corner is 15 feet long, 11 at the southwest end, and 12 at the northeast end. A room of about the same size adjoins it on the west, and a third, not so well defined, ends the northside series. The [white circle] in the north end center of the room points out a cedar post, 8 inches in diameter.

26

Figure 21. House mound, view south-southwest from northeast corner.

The rising top of the [house mound] structure can be seen beyond the far, shaded wall.

Figure 22. View northeast from the corner room of the house mound.

A view to the northeast from the corner room. Brady's Fort, a fortified village atop a malapai butte, 2.5 miles generally north of Coyote, is indicated by a dot [in black circle] on its long slope. Perkinsville, on the Verde River, lies beyond the deepest part of the distant Mt. Range. Just a trace of the San Francisco Mt. Peaks is visible just over the deep saddle.

(From Brady's Fort, the road swings to the northwest and toward the lower, north end of Lonesome Valley to the Stillman Windmill ruin just a few miles short of the Verde River.)

27

Figure 23. House mound, view generally south.

Figure 23 shows the central room on top of the mound. While it does not show the complete room, the chief aim was to focus on the bin in the south end of it. Note the large boulder incorporated in the south end of the bin's wall [white circle]. It was at the base and to the left of the boulder where the pottery specimens were contained in a niche in the wall [Figure 24]. The stone bordered walk on the left is of modern origin.

Figure 24. The decorated bowl from the pottery cache.

The south end of the mound, with a demolished house on it, lies below a five-foot slope below the bush growing out of the wall at the southeast corner. From that point on there is just a perceptible fall for 45 feet to the south end of the mound.

Two excavated rooms occur on the west side and opposite the central room. They lie just above the base of the mound and are 15 by 8 feet wide, approximately. One of them shows base stones set on edge over which the wall was carried.

All of the southwest end of the slope – possibly two rooms – was demolished by a prospector named Brady. It occurred about 1910-15. The author recovered the half of a carved shell frog in the debris, and Brady is supposed to have found a complete specimen.

Figure 25. Rooms adjoining the plaza.

A view of some of the rooms adjoining the plaza from the top at the south end of the house mound [Figure 25]. The foreground shows a test pit in the south end of the plaza. [Above that is] the south-end room (partly excavated) in the first (upper tier) row of rooms below the plaza. [Circles] below the probed room point out the second tier of rooms, which lie on lower ground and whose east walls have fallen down the slope. An outcrop of large granite boulders is seen in the upper right corner of the view.

Figure 26. West side, view southwest.

A view of the broken, granite ledge on the west side of the house mound. The view was taken from the upper slope of the big structure. Building stone and room debris from the rooms, demolished by Brady, lies in the foreground. The open area is littered with broken manos and metates. A metate of such size it had to be loaded on a wagon by skids came from the demolished rooms – quoting Mr. Stanley. A large room or house lies on the broken down point – indicated by [black circle at left center]. The deep shadow along the higher part of the ledge is a test pit in the southwest corner of a large house. Just below the tested house is a flat in which considerable outdoor activities were carried on. Several hearths, sunk into the decomposed granite, were bordered with stone slabs set on edge (not on end).

The site of Old Coyote is indicated by two [side-by-side black circles at center] in the open draw southwest of the ledge. It is so named because seven inhumations were uncovered just a few feet west of the house; and that the only decorated, black-on-grey bowl, had a design bordering on a Basketmaker III pattern – according to Dr. Roberts, of the Smithsonian [Figure 27].

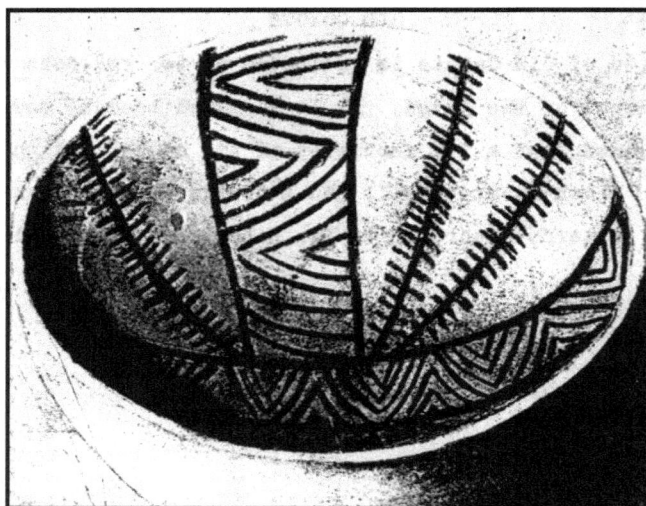

Figure 27. Prescott Black-on-gray bowl from Old Coyote.

Figure 28. The "water jar" from the cremation near Coyote
[midway between Coyote Ruin and Yeager Canyon].

CHAPTER 3
YAVAPAI CHAPTER EXCAVATION
Mary Spall

The investigation of Coyote Ruin included mapping, surface collection, photo documentation, excavation, and maintenance of a daily journal.

MAPPING

First, a walking survey was made to determine the site boundaries. Second, a permanent datum was established at the highest point of the mound (Figure 30). Third, the Yavapai County Engineering Department provided a crew and equipment to lay out a network of thirty-meter grids, establishing a datum in the northwest corner of each grid to locate points by use of coordinates.

When a structure was selected for excavation, the thirty-meter grids were further divided into ten-meter grids. A one by two-meter string grid system, based on true north, was used for actual excavation. The reference point for excavation of each of these grids was the northwest corner. This was also referenced back to the site datum.

The master map (Figure 29 and Appendix K) and other maps included in this report of the site have been hand-drawn by Jim Roberts.

SURFACE SURVEY

Surface collections were made at the site, and artifact counts are reflected in the various sections of the report.

EXCAVATION METHODS

To standardize recording and to insure that no important observations were overlooked, each worker kept a series of forms to supplement the daily journal. There were separate forms for each excavation level, features, recovered artifacts, burials, notes, drawings, and photographs. Location of all artifacts and features was carefully measured and recorded and, when necessary, photographed.

All excavated dirt and fill was sifted through a ¼-inch screen. Artifacts collected were noted on the required form, then placed in a paper bag with the location, square number, depth at which artifact was found, and description of artifact written on the bag. A bag list was kept daily. The list included bag number, contents, grid, room, square, level, unit size, name of excavator, and date excavated.

Artifacts were transported to the Yavapai Chapter's laboratory for analysis. Excavations were backfilled in order to provide some protection. The collections from the Ruin reside in several locations. Most of the surface-collected artifacts were returned to the site. Most of the smaller artifacts and special items are in possession of the land owner. The bulk of the ceramics and lithics, and all of the notes and photographs are held by the Yavapai Chapter, AAS.

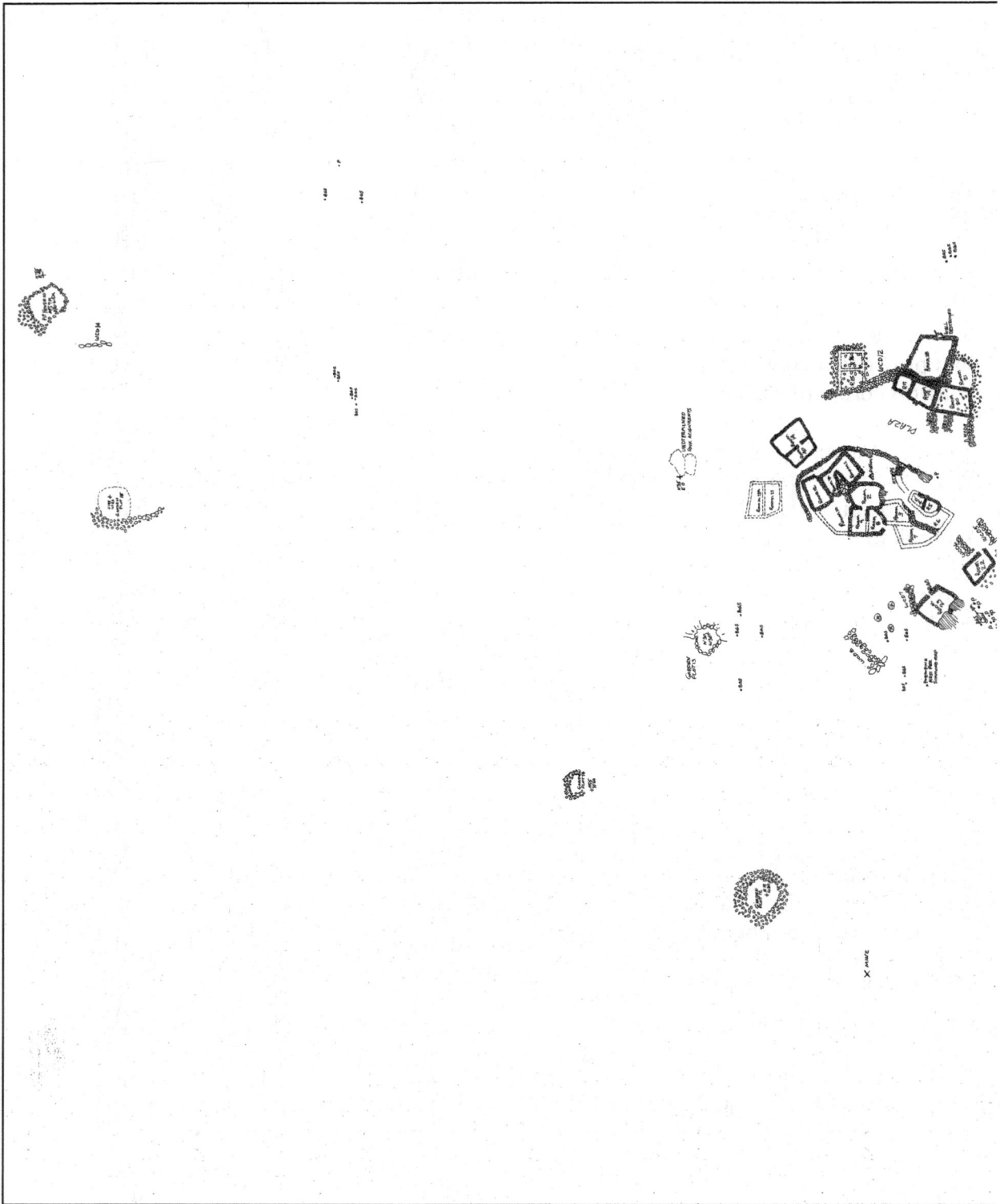

Figure 29. Site map north half. Scale (on facing page) is 10 m. See also Appendix K.

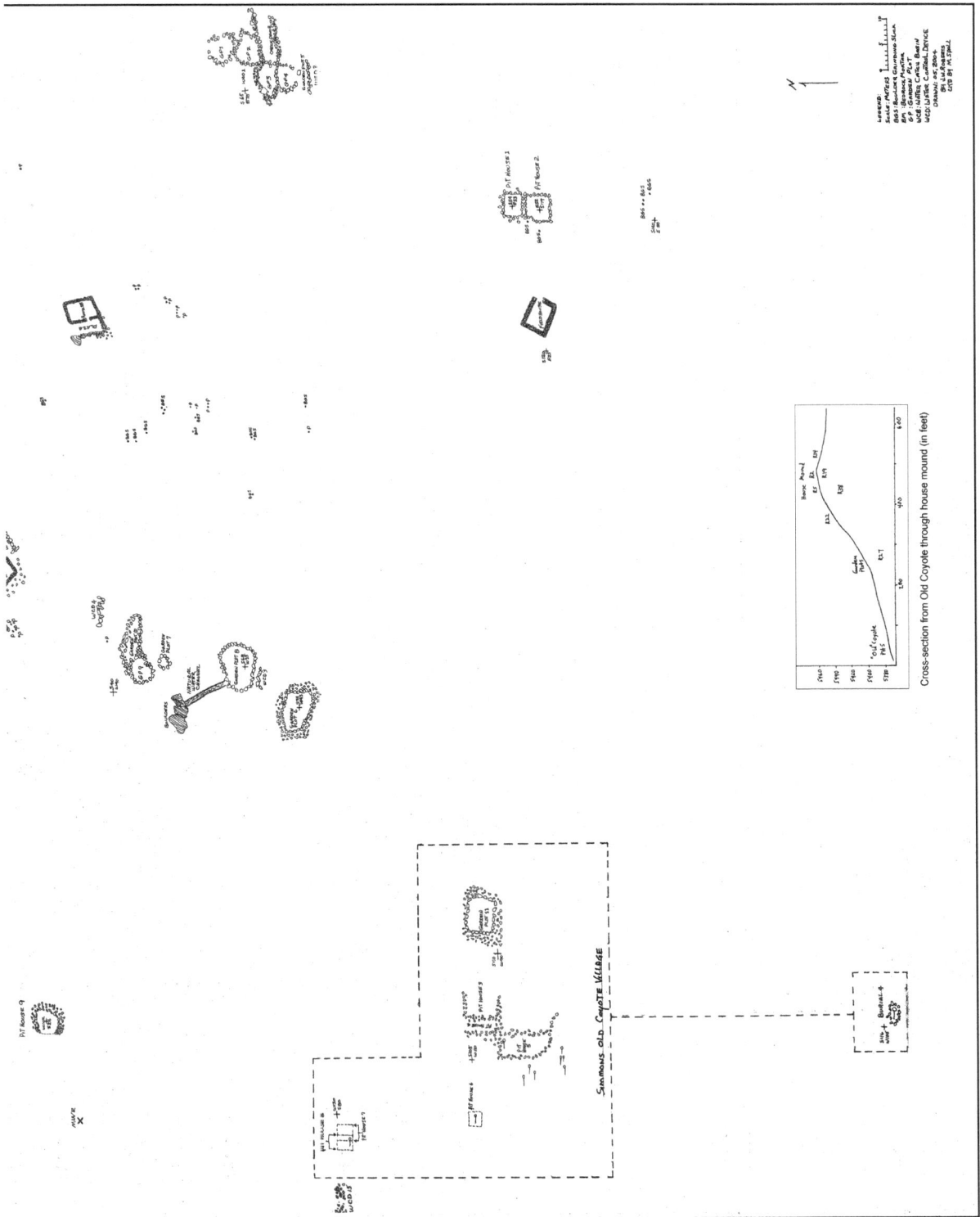

Figure 29. Site map, south half. Scale is 10 m. Room 27 is labelled "Fieldhouse." See also Appendix K.

ARCHITECTURE

The architecture at Coyote Ruin included masonry blocks of contiguous structures, clusters of structures, subterranean structures, and pit houses. Evidence of steps was found in some room entrances. These entrances faced north, east or west, or access was gained through the roof. There was no evidence of consistency of entrance orientation. Roof supports were not detected. Most hearths were circular and in the center of the room. Some of them were lined with clay. Some rooms had doorways connecting adjacent rooms (e.g., Rooms 14 and 40). Masonry room configurations were rectangular, with rooms contiguous or separated.

Pit Houses

Ten shallow rock-lined pit houses were present (Table 1). Pit houses numbered 3-8 were in a shallow drainage in the "Old Coyote" part of the site, approximately 120 meters southwest of the pueblo mound. Pit houses 1 and 2 (Room 28/28A), 9 and 10 were located as shown on the map in Figure 29. The results of excavation of Pit houses 1 and 2 are given below.

Table 1. Pit House information.

No.	Location	Size (ft.)	Depth	Notes
1 (Room 28A)	SE of house mound			excavated by YCAAS
2 (Room 28)	"			"
3	"Old Coyote"			
4	"			
5	"	25x11	several feet	Simmons' House I, called "low-walled masonry house"; excavation started by Simmons but never completed; burials to west
6	"			burial
7	"	8x10	22"	excavated by Simmons
8	"	8x10	20-27"	excavated by Simmons; burial
9	W of house mound			see Figure 29
10	"			"

Masonry Structures

What we will refer to as the "house mound" is the hilltop mound visible from a distance. Excavation of masonry structures was focused on this mound and the slopes around it. Figure 30 shows the rooms at the top of the mound, and Figure 31 shows the rooms found at mid-level on the eastern slope of the mound. Table 2 lists information on all of the masonry rooms located at the site.

The Yavapai Chapter conducted work on Rooms 2, 5, 14, 17, 18, 19, 22, 23, 27, 28/28a (called pit houses), 38 and 40. Excavation was done in an area called Room 41, but it is unclear that this was in fact a room. No further discussion is done of this feature. Excavation of the above rooms totaled 3,483 hours.

Table 2. Masonry structure information. Sizes are approximate.

No.	Location	Size (m)	Notes
1/1A	house mound	5.7x4.5	
2	"	5x3	excavated by Simmons & YCAAS
[3]	"	-	on Austin's map, see Appendix F; not identified by YCAAS
4	"	-	
5	"	2.2x2.1	
6-7	"	-	demolished by Brady according to Simmons
8	"	4.7x3.5	excavated by Simmons?; 2 notched slabs present
9	"	4.7x3.5	
10	"	-	
11	N of house mound	3.9x3.1	location differs from Austin's map
11A	"	3.6x3.1	
12	"	5x3.3	
[13]	"	-	on Austin's map, see Appendix F; not identified by YCAAS
14	E of house mound	5.8x3.5	
15	"	-	
16	"	-	
17	SE of house mound	4.9x2.6	
18	"	7.2x5.5	
19	"	4.7x3.4	
20	"	-	
21	"	-	
22	SW of house mound	4.6x3.9	
23	"	4.8x3.9	
27		4x3	field house?
28/28A			see Pit houses 1 and 2 in Table 1
38		4x3	
40	E of house mound	5.8x2.8	
41	N. of R38	-	probably not a room

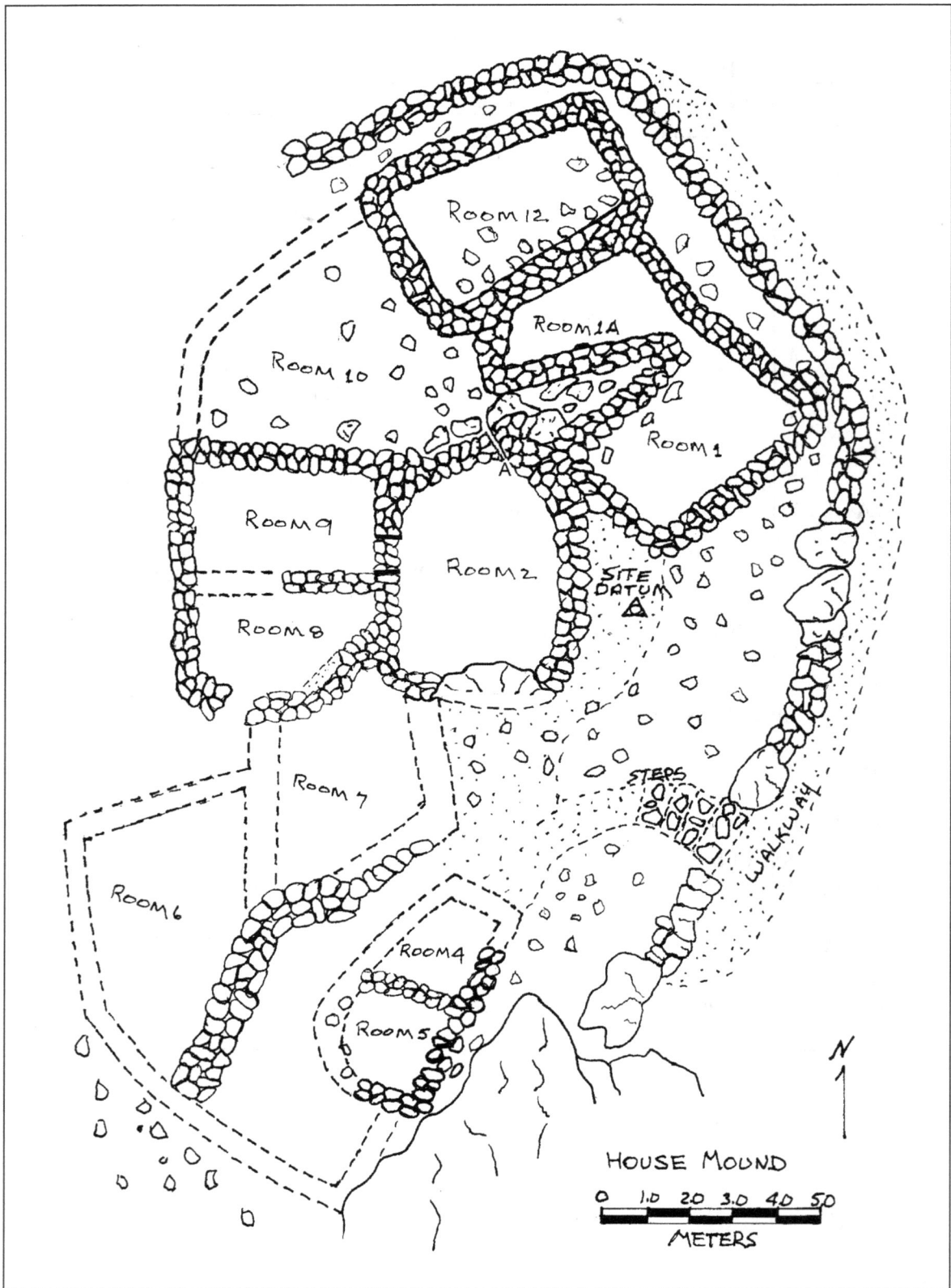

Figure 30. Plan of house mound rooms. "A" in Room 2 indicates abutted wall. Scale is 5 m long.

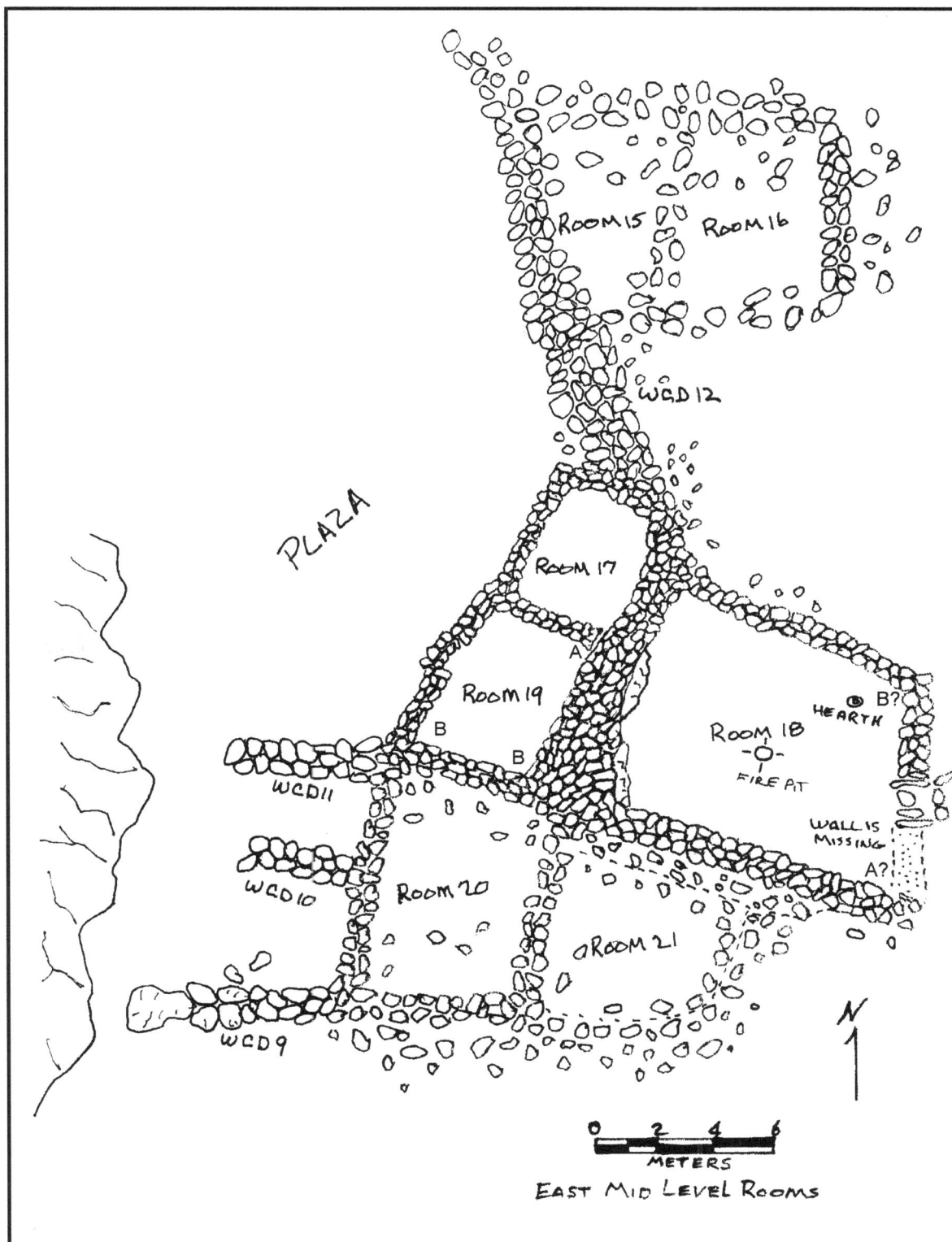

Figure 31. Plan of mid-level rooms east of house mound. "A" indicates abutted wall; "B?" indicates a probable bonded corner. "WCD" indicates water control devices.

Room 2

Room 2 is located at the top of the mound (Figures 30, 32) and shares a common wall with Rooms 8 and 9 to the west and with Room 1 to the north. This room differs from others that were excavated, as it has 5 wall sections and is the only room that was plastered. The plaster ranges from 1.0 to 3.8 cm in thickness, and originally filled and covered crevices, cracks, joints and flat-surfaced rocks. The corners of the walls were rounded, with the exception of the northeast corner that abuts the common wall of Room 1 (Figure 30).

Figure 32. Room 2, northwest corner. Note blackened wall.

Interior wall dimensions are as follows: east wall 7 meters; south wall 3.1 meters (this wall is actually the face of a boulder); west wall 4.3 meters; northeast wall 2.1 meters; and northwest wall, 2.7 meters. A considerable amount of wall fall was removed before excavation could begin. Vandalism and weathering made it difficult to establish wall heights. The room appeared to have been consumed by fire twice. Wall rocks were burned to shades of gray and black at heights 20-52 cm from what was defined as a floor. A doorway 63 cm wide was found in the west wall leading to Room 9. It was sealed after the room was burned the first time, as rocks and boulders used to seal it had no signs of ash or charcoal and did not have the plaster found on the rest of the walls. The large chunks of charcoal and ashes found throughout the fill and especially near the floor indicated a second burning of the room. A radiocarbon date from wood charcoal in levels 4 or 5 or in a wall trench gave a date of 550+/-60 years bp (corrected 95% confidence interval of A.D. 1295-1444) (see discussion in Chapter 14). Artifacts found on the floor indicated an entryway between rooms 1 and 2. The floor surface was leveled by filling in the bedrock depressions. Manos, polishing stones, a bone needle, tabular knives, obsidian points, and a metate were found on the leveled surface. Fragments of human remains were found in this room. Simmons worked in this room

(Figure 23) and found a pottery cache in a "bin" in the south wall; the "bin" was not found in our re-excavation of the room. He also noted that an east-west dividing wall to the room, no longer visible, was built on an older level of trash. Excavation hours = 248.5.

Room 5

Room 5 is a small rectangular room located on the southeast corner of the mound (Figure 30). It was the smallest room excavated, measuring only 2.1 by 2.2 meters. The floor was quite flat and made of a hard packed clay surface. A scatter of charcoal and ashes with a decomposed granite mixture was found just above the floor. Four hundred fifty-five animal bones (splintered and burned) indicate the room may have been used for trash. Excavation hours = 47.5.

Room 14

Room 14 is located at mid-level near the top on the northeast side of the mound (Figure 29). It shares a common wall and doorway with Room 40 (Figure 33). The room is about 3.8 by 3.7 m. The original opening set in the 67 cm thick wall was closed with the use of large angular granite rocks set in rough courses with a mixture of dirt, clay and decomposed granite applied between these rocks. The opening measured 67 cm wide and contained a granite boulder 67 cm in length and 20 cm high that served as a step where the floor differential was a factor. The wall corners of the opening were squared on both sides (Figure 33). The surface of the floor was uneven, consisting of areas of protruding bedrock. The occupants filled in natural depressions in the bedrock with trash and soil prior to leveling a compact surface then covering it with clay. Heavy disturbance by vandals and rodent activity obliterated any evidence of floor in the southeast corner. The structure may have burned, as pockets of ash and charcoal were found throughout the room.

A clay-lined hearth was located about 1.2 meters from the northeast wall, 1.55 meters equidistant from walls in the east portion of the room, measuring 24 cm in diameter and 12 cm deep.

The southeast wall is 55 cm wide and exhibits fine masonry work evident in the hand-chipped fitted stones. A ventilator shaft was found in this wall. It measured 13 cm wide and 18 cm high. The base is 32 cm above the floor, 45 cm from the top of the wall, and 1.04 meters from the northeast wall. It appeared that this wall was constructed at a later time, probably replacing an earlier wall (Figure 34).

Sherds with a curvature indicating large vessels were recovered. Tabular knives, scrapers, saws, hammerstones, hoes and bone awls were found on or near the floor. Perhaps preparation of both plant and animal foods took place in this room. Fragments of human bone were also found in this room. Excavation hours = 220.

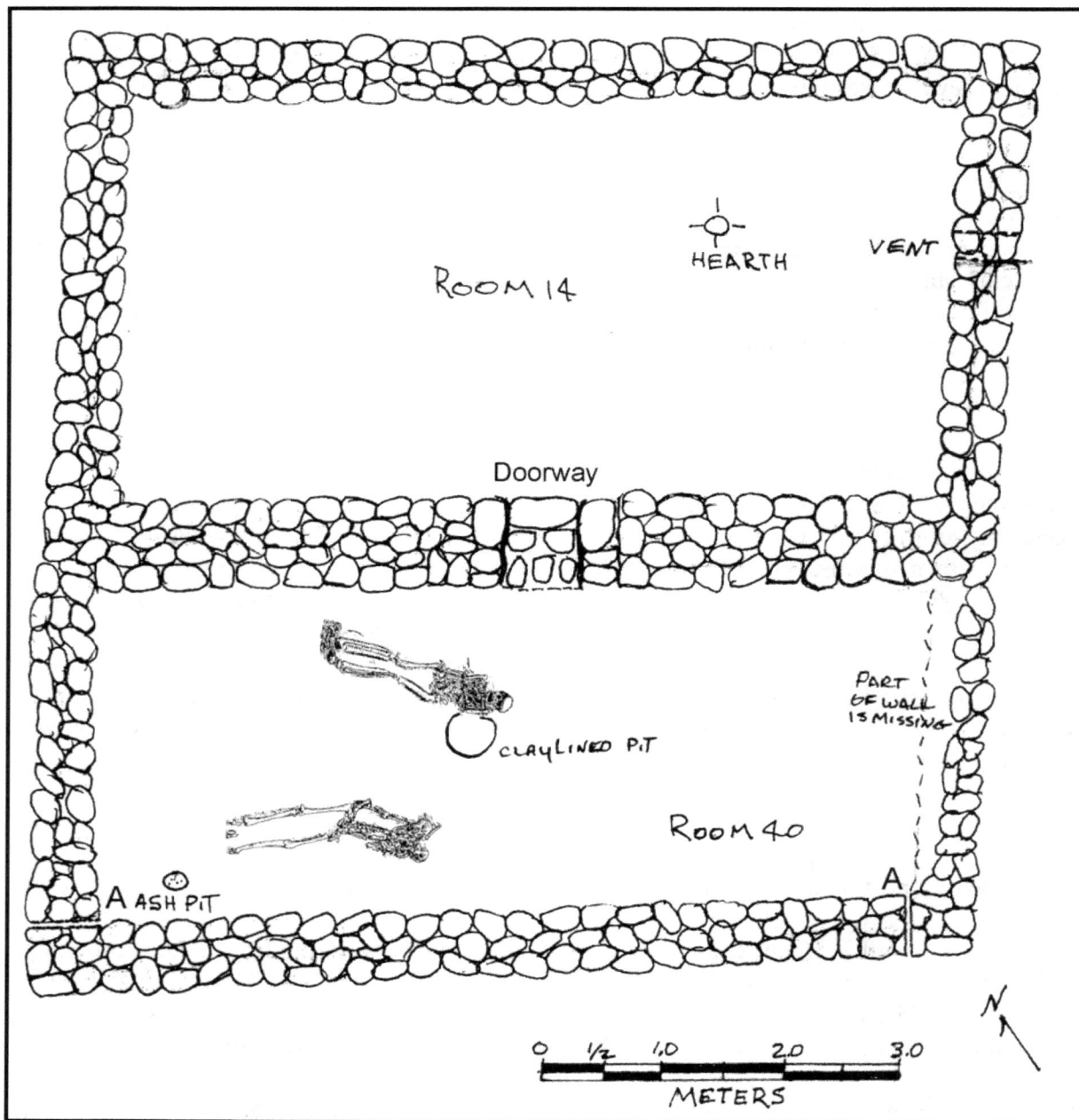

Figure 33. Plan of Room 14 and Room 40. Burial in southwest corner of Room 40 is adult male in fill. Burial inside doorway is adult female under lower floor. One subadult and two infant burials not shown. "A" indicates abutted wall.

Figure 34. Room 14, southeast wall with ventilator shaft.

Room 40

Room 40 is located at mid-level on the slope of the northeast side of the mound (Figure 29), and it had not been vandalized. Hundreds of large rocks that rolled down the steep hillside through the centuries had to be removed before excavation began. A trench defining the walls was dug, and a trench was put across the room. The room was rectangular, with interior dimensions measuring: northeast wall 6.2 meters, southwest wall 5.35 meters, southeast wall 2.7 meters, and northeast wall 2.95 meters (Figure 33).

The height of the southwest wall measured from 1.90 m to 2.10 m (measured from the floor to the top of the existing walls). The northeast wall measures 70 cm in height, and is a common wall with Room 14, nearly a meter thick. The northwest and southwest walls measured 70 cm to 1.9 cm, and exhibited fine craftsmanship of granite masonry. The southeast wall, partially collapsed, was constructed of rocks varying in size and randomly fitted together. In the other walls the rock courses were bound together by clay. The interior facing flat surfaces of the rocks brought a neat appearance to the room.

A doorway in the middle of the northeast wall measured 67 cm wide. It was sealed, making it difficult to distinguish it from the rest of the southwest wall of Room 14 (Figures 33, 35).

Room 40 had two floor levels, with about 14 cm between them. The first 3 cm of the first (upper) "floor" was loose soil with charcoal, ash, broken pieces of pottery, and a few lithics. The last 11 cm of floor fill above the 2nd floor contained flake stone, marine shell, sherds, animal bones, broken figurines, burned corn cobs, walnut shells, pinion nuts, metate and mano fragments, projectile points, and jewelry items.

A 1 x 2 meter grid was excavated until sterile soil was found, after which the remainder of the room was excavated to that level. The lower floor was a hard packed or plastered surface upon which rested burned wood, charcoal, ashes and small flat rocks. In the west corner there were 2 large metates with the working surface face up, 2 grinding stones and a large ash pit. Near the northeast wall and close to the doorway were 6 manos, 4 hammerstones, an abrader, and a clay-lined pit (hearth?) that measured 49 cm in diameter and was 23 cm deep. Five burials were found in the room. They are discussed in Chapter 12. Excavation hours = 301.

Figure 35. Looking southwest, across Room 14, at Room 40. Note abutted back wall on left side.

Room 17

Room 17 shares a common wall with Room 19 to the south that measures 70 cm wide, and a wall that abuts part of Room 18 to the east (Figure 31). Rooms 18 and 19 have doorways, but Room 17 must have been entered from the roof, as no entryway was found. The roof had burned. Burned clay, charcoal and ash pockets, and small flat rocks were found in the level 15 cm above the floor, or 90 cm below the present ground surface.

The interior wall measurements for the walls are east wall 5.20 m, west wall 4.6 m, north wall 2.55 m and south wall 2.62 m. The depths of the walls varied from 1.10 to 1.25 m below present ground surface. With the exception of the north wall, bowed in the middle due to poor construction, the interior walls stand almost vertical and were set directly on a hard packed soil surface. There is no evidence of a foundation or other footing for the wall construction. The walls are constructed of granite rocks of various sizes, laid up with mortar of local clay, with the flat rock surfaces oriented so as to create a smooth wall face.

The floor was a hard packed clay surface that was defined by the presence of hammerstones, hand grinders, bifacial manos, and finished tools. A round storage (?) pit was present in the floor. Fragments of human remains were found during excavation. A rare artifact found was a miniature carved deer hoof (Figure 65). It is similar to larger, carved hooves found in the Flagstaff area and associated with the Motswimi Society (McGregor 1943: 287, Plate III, 2-3), but the Coyote Ruin carved hoof is much too small to be one of the wands of the Motswimi Society. Perhaps it was used as a hairpin by a local member of that society. Excavation hours = 171.

Room 18

This room shares a common wall with Room 17 and Room 19 to the west (Figures 31, 36). The size of the room and the artifacts found in it indicated it might have been used as a community room. It is the largest room excavated. Interior wall dimensions are: north wall 6.80 m, south wall 7.7 m, east wall 5.40 m, and west wall 5.60 m. A portion of the room was vandalized, destroying part of the east wall and part of the doorway. A large depression extended approximately 20 cm below the east and south walls. The floor surface was uneven and consisted of areas of protruding bedrock. Further excavation showed the room had been trash filled to level sharp drops in the bedrock surface. After leveling, a hard packed clay surface existed and was defined as the floor. An ash lens of 1 to 2 cm covered the debris.

Figure 36. Room 18, view west.

A doorway was located in the east wall. The north side of the doorway consisted of flat upright slabs, but vandals, leaving only one upright slab, destroyed the south side of the doorway. The opening was 65 cm wide and flat rock slabs for steps. The angular granite rocks used in the wall were local material. A mixture of earth and clay was used as mortar. The upper portion of the north wall bowed in the middle.

Two features were found in this room. A fire pit, 66 cm long, by 65 cm wide and 45 cm deep, was located near the east wall. Rocks appeared to have been carefully placed in the saucer-shaped depression. Two wedge-shaped granite firedogs, 18 and 22 cm long, were recovered from the bottom of the pit. A clay-lined hearth, found near the center of the room at Level 8, measured 28 by 26 cm and was 12 cm deep (Figure 37). The hearth contained ashes, charcoal and rabbit bones. It was located 2.6 m from the north wall, 2.4 m from the east wall, and 2.4 m from the south wall.

Figure 37. Room 18, clay-lined hearth and metate.

Artifacts recovered on or near the floor included a large worked granite stone measuring 1.21 m long by 5 cm thick by 35 cm wide, ¾ grooved stone axes, tabular blades, bone awls, and part of a plainware bowl. Several grams of blue azurite, pulverized into fine powder, were found in two locations. Raw deposits of azurite and kaolin were also found.

Part of a human cranium was found in vandalized soil in Level 9. It was reburied in the same level.

Seven samples were taken from a stratigraphic column near the center of this room for microarchaeological analyses (see Chapter 8). Excavation hours = 904.

Room 19

Room 19 shares a common wall with Room 17 to the north and abuts Room 18 to the east (Figure 31). Wall measurements are: north wall 3.2 m, south wall 3.6 m, west wall 4.6 m and east wall 4.9 m. Large boulders or outcroppings were incorporated in the base of the east wall. Apparently the uneven bedrock surface was leveled with soil and then covered with clay. Vandals had destroyed the clay surface in some areas of the room. The south and west walls were constructed on the ground surface without use of footing trenches or stone foundations.

The doorway in the west wall opens on a plaza (see discussion in Chapter 2). The entryway is 67 cm wide at the top and 70 cm wide at the bottom. It is located 1.86 m from the north wall and 2.20 m from the south wall. The south side of the doorway was made of flat faced rocks laid 5 courses high. At the entryway were several flat slabs that might have functioned as steps.

The fire pit was centrally located in the room and was surrounded by rocks. It measured 34 cm north/south and 41 cm east/west, with a depth of 12 cm. It contained ashes and small chunks of charcoal. Soil samples were taken for analysis. Excavation hours = 487.

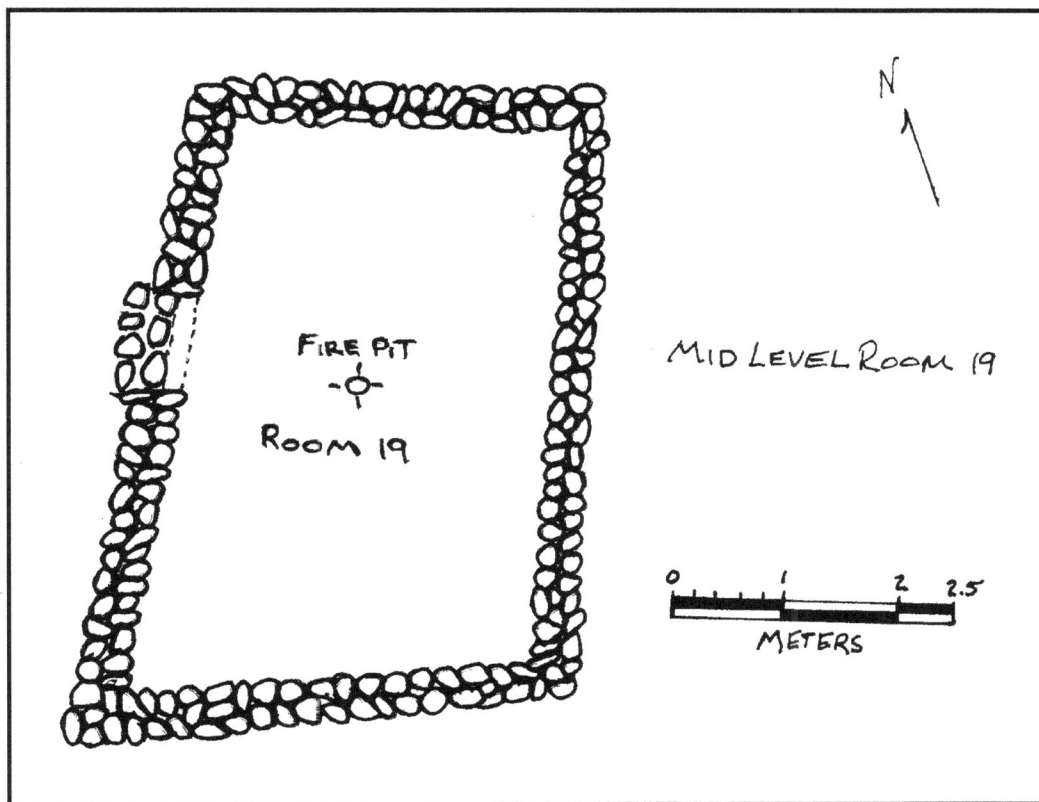

Figure 38. Plan of Room 19.

Room 22

Room 22 is rectangular and built as a separate unit at the southwest edge of the pueblo mound (Figure 29). The room provides an excellent view of the terrain to the south and southeast where the majority of agriculture took place. To the west there is a steep rocky slope that would make access to the room difficult. The room may have been used as a lookout post. The walls were crudely constructed and made of dry laid rock masonry. Bedrock outcroppings form the two corners to the west. Wall measurements are: northeast wall 4.3 m, northwest wall 4.4 m, southwest wall 4.9 m, and southeast wall 3.4 m. A doorway was located in the southeast corner leading to the corridor that runs along the mound. No prepared floor was found, and there was no evidence of habitation. A small number of artifacts were recovered. Excavation hours = 48.

Room 23

Room 23 lies southwest of the pueblo mound (Figure 29). The southwest wall incorporates two large bedrock granite boulders (Figure 39). The inside wall measurements are: northeast 4.7 m, southeast 3.4 m, northwest 4.4 m, and southwest 4.9 m. The doorway measured 83 cm at the bottom and 72 cm at the top, with a ramp 97 cm long. The doorway is located in the center of the northeast wall and opens on a corridor that runs along the mound.

Large unworked granite boulders located in the center of the room had to be removed prior to excavation. These boulders required two or three persons to move them. A fire pit, 78 cm in diameter and 42 cm deep, was located 30 cm from the northwest wall and 1.10 m from the northeast wall. Some blackened clay was located in vandalized soil near the center of the room, and this area was apparently another lined hearth. Soil samples were taken for analysis and are discussed in Chapter 10. A hard packed soil surface that contained clay and bedrock was exposed at a depth of 1.30 m and determined to be the floor. Excavation hours = 217.

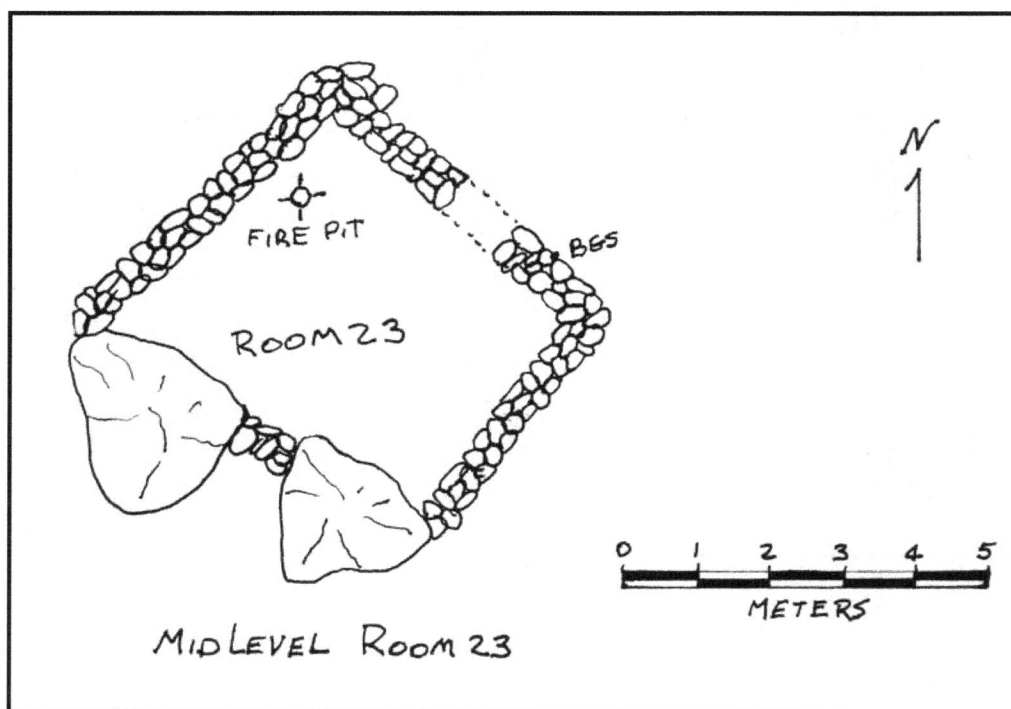

Figure 39. Plan of Room 23.

Room 27

This structure is marked as "Field House" on Figure 29. There was no evidence that this one-room structure was lived in. It appears the room was not completed, as what might have been the southeast wall differs drastically from other walls (Figure 40). The inside measurements of the room are approximately 3.05 meters by 4.03 meters. The three known walls were constructed of parallel lines of upright slabs on the interior and exterior, with mortar between the slabs. Small rocks and soil filled the space between the rows of upright slabs, forming a completed wall. The interior slabs ranged in height from 32 to 54 cm from the hard packed floor surface.

The structure is located close to an agricultural area, and may have been used as a ramada or field house. Grinding slicks on nearby granite boulders indicated the room might also have functioned as a food processing station. No features were found in the room, and there were only a limited number of artifacts. Excavation hours = 242.

Figure 40. Room 27, looking northwest.

Room 28/28a

This two-room structure appeared to have been destroyed by the inhabitants. It was later determined that the structure was too shallow to be considered a masonry room, and is shown in Figure 29 as Pit houses 1 and 2. The stone work was haphazardly done, using rocks of uneven shapes. Small upright slabs were used in parts of the walls. This careless construction resulted in walls that bowed inward or outward. A fire pit located between upright slabs contained deer bones and two bone beads. There were few other artifacts. The function of the structure could not be determined. Excavation hours = 258.

Room 38 was a separate structure built on a relatively level area southeast of the mound (Figures 29, 41, 42). The room is rectangular with interior dimensions measuring approximately 4 m by 3 m, with a depth of 55 to 65 cm below present ground surface.

The rubble-filled clay-lined rock walls were constructed of local material. The north and east walls incorporated large boulders. A number of rock slabs were used along the inner base. Smaller rocks were used as the height increased. The south wall was a mixture of large and small rocks. The west wall was the most crudely constructed, with rocks placed in a haphazard manner. Large openings between rocks were chinked with smaller rocks inserted as wedges and fillers. Wall height ranged from 85 to 112 cm from the floor surface. A doorway in the west wall measured 65 to 85 cm wide, with large boulders set on both sides.

A floor, defined by the presence of a biface mano, an antler flaker, a schist knife, two jasper scrapers and stacked sherds of a broken vessel, was found 55 to 65 cm below present ground surface. These artifacts were resting in loose fill. An unlined fire pit, measuring 38.1 cm by 42.8 cm and 10.2 cm deep, was a shallow irregular shape in the floor. It contained whitish colored ashes, small pieces of charcoal, and some burned rabbit bones. Soil samples were taken from the pit and are discussed in Chapter 10.

Skeletal remains of a woman and child were found 27 to 33 cm from present ground surface. Scratch marks on the bones indicate that an animal dug up the bones and scattered them on top of one another at varying angles. No funerary objects were found. The remains were reburied in the room. A cist was found near Room 38. This was probably used for storage. It measured 36 cm deep, 24 cm wide at the top and 15 cm wide at the bottom, with a rock slab in the bottom. Excavation hours = 339.

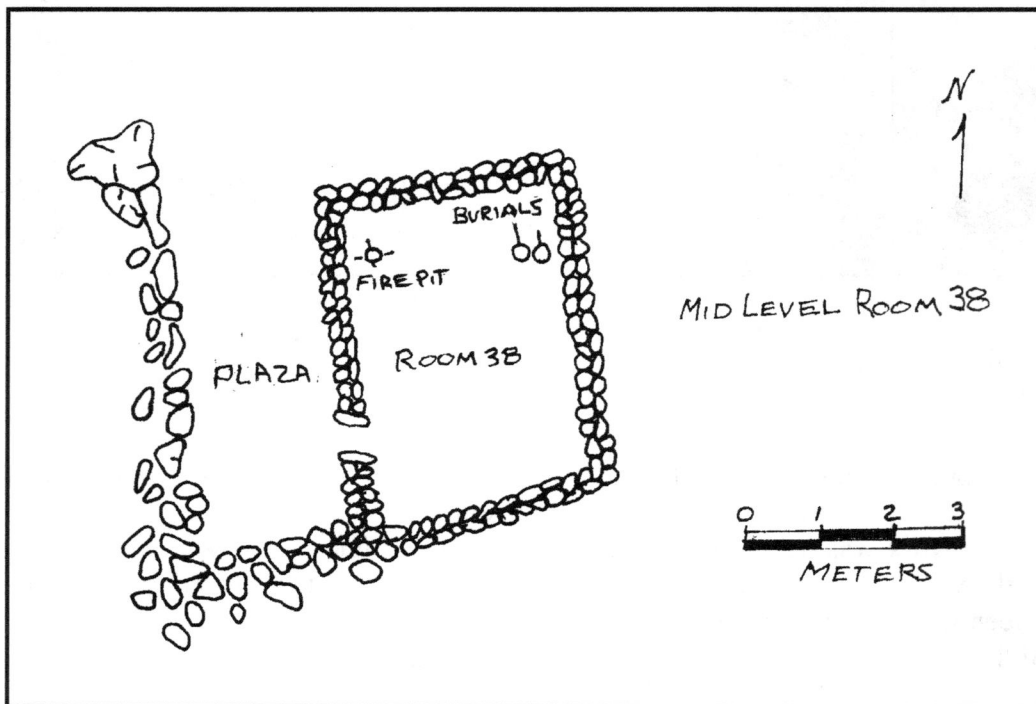

Figure 41. Plan of Room 38.

Figure 42. Room 38, view south.

A Note on Wall Abutments (A. L. Christenson)

In masonry or adobe architecture where structures have common walls the intersection of walls can be either by abutment or by bonding, with the former indicating a wall built later and the latter indicating contemporaneous construction. Minimally such an analysis can provide information on the construction sequence of the pueblo and in some cases can lead to inferences about the social units that lived there (Wilcox 1975). Because of the disconnectedness of the Coyote Ruin room groups, this method of analysis is less useful than it might be with a more contiguous construction.

No abutment analysis was carried out in the field, but examination of the photographs of the site taken during excavation provides a few bits of information. On the house mound, the only excavated room connected with another is Room 2 that at the north end had a wall abutting the southwest wall of Room 1 (Figure 30). Clearly the Room 1 wall was present before that Room 2 wall, but how much earlier cannot be determined from this analysis. The mid-level cluster to the east of the house mound had Room 19 with an abutting wall in the northeast corner and two bonded walls at the southwest and southeast corners (Figure 31). In the same cluster, Room 18 has a possible bonded wall in the northeast corner and a possible abutted wall in the southeast corner. To the northeast of the house mound, Room 14 has a possible bonded wall in the east corner. Of most interest is the south corner of Room 40, where the back wall of the room appears to abut with a side wall that continues into the mound (Figure 35). J. W. Simmons and the Yavapai Chapter excavators recognized that the house mound was artificially built up (see discussion in Chapter 14), but how this was done is unclear. One possibility would have been to build masonry cells that were then filled with dirt, rubble, or trash as did the contemporaneous Classic Period Hohokam (Doelle et al. 1995: 403). The only thing wrong with this idea is that a cell with an abutted wall on one end would seem to be an unstable choice for holding 2 m or more of fill! Another, seemingly less likely possibility is that there is another room behind the wall that was at some point filled in.

Walkway/Wall

A walkway 32 m long and 0.5 to 1.5 m wide, was leveled immediately downslope of a retaining wall constructed among the granite boulders near the top of the mound (Figure 30). It led from the north corner to the southeast corner of the mound, eliminating entry to Rooms 1, 1A, and 2 at the top of the mound. Steps in the southeast part of the wall led from the walkway to the top of the mound, terminating just north of Room 4. The walkway may also have been built to eliminate the possibility of rocks tumbling down on Rooms 17, 19, 20 and 40 below (Figure 29).

Water Control/Field Systems

As noted by J. W. Simmons when he first recorded the site (Chapter 2), the occupants of Coyote Ruin made use of a variety of constructed features to define gardens, to control runoff, to retain and replenish soil, and to slow erosion of agriculturally modified surfaces. The water control devices (WCD) included check dams, contour terraces, diversion walls, bordered gardens, diversion channels, and water catchments. These were not true irrigation systems, but were rainfall dependent systems that allowed for the efficient utilization of water runoff. What differentiates these systems from one another is the height of the rock walls and the configuration of the rock alignments (Figures 14-19, 43).

Check dams have low rock walls built across intermittent drainages. They slow the flow of water and help retain soil. They were placed where water runoff would irrigate the growing plots. The walls consisted of stacked stone masonry, using a variety of sizes of rocks found in the immediate area. Small windbreaks placed around the plants would have protected them as they grew.

Contour terraces are composed of curving alignments of boulders that are constructed across hillsides. Their primary function is to slow runoff, reduce erosion, and capture slope wash. Wall construction techniques vary. Chinking of larger wall stones with smaller cobbles is common, and some walls show gaps of low stones that may suggest doorways.

Garden plots perform three main functions. They retain water runoff, direct the flow of water, and increase absorption of the water by minimizing soil erosion on the slope. Consequently, these features can be constructed on much steeper slopes. Not only do the high rock walls impede movement of water and soil, they increase the amount of land suitable for crop production. Gravel mulched soil ranged from 30 to 46 cm deep.

The presence of grinding slicks in granite boulders near the plots suggest the processing of corn or grains. Charred remains of agave and corncobs were recovered nearby.

NOTE: A number of rock alignments found throughout the site were measured and some partially excavated but these could not be specifically identified as rooms or field system components. The artifacts recovered from these areas are included in the flaked stone and groundstone summary tables.

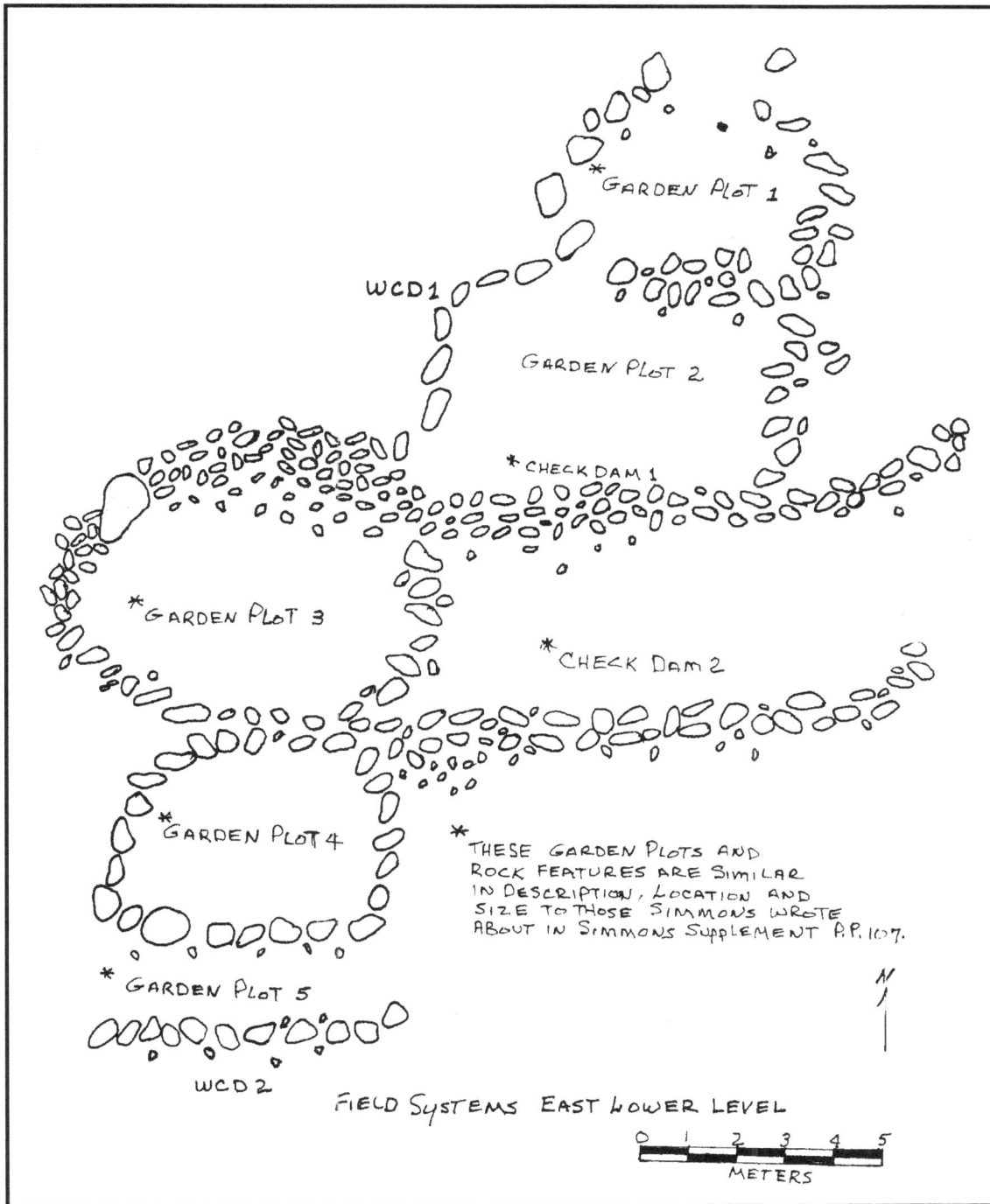

Figure 43. Plan of field systems just east of the lower level.

CHAPTER 4
PETROGLYPHS
Mary Spall

This chapter provides a general description of the ways in which the petroglyphs at Coyote Ruin were categorized and recorded, followed by a brief discussion of how they were created. No pictographs (painted designs) were found at the site.

Recording of the petroglyphs involved developing categories, and assigning each glyph element to a category. Terms reflect animal and human representations, abstract, and geometric designs. While there were glyphs that were ideal illustrations of each category, the majority were not heavily pecked, with attributes that might straddle category lines, making assignment difficult.

Table 3. Petroglyph images summary.

Amorphic pecking	16	Grids	6
Amorphic shapes	9	Grid rectilinear w/2 quadrupeds	
Animal-like figures	17	(1 with feet and horns) with	
Quadrupeds (other)	4	heavy pecking within each body	1
Horned	2	Human-like figures	20
Elongated Neck	1	biomorph with long arms	1
Feet and horns	2	with bow and arrow	1
Descending w/horns	1	dancers attached (rows)	2
Bipeds	2	descending	1
Tripeds		incomplete	10
Feet and horns	1	male	5
Long tail	1	Insect-like figures	2
Horned	1	Lines, angled	3
Elongated neck	2	Lines, parallel	11
Complex abstract	1	Rayed circle	1
Complex abstract with		Rayed circle enclosed	1
connected outlined circle	1	Rectilinear meanders	2
Connected circle	2	"S" curves with angles	3
Connected circle w/ appendages	1	Semicircles	3
Connected squares	1	Unidentified pecking	4
Curvilinear abstract	1	Unidentified shapes	4
Curvilinear meander	1	"U" shaped	1
Curved lines	3		
Footprints	3		
Geometric designs	4		

Twelve granite boulders with 122 elements were recorded (Table 3). Eight of the boulders have more than one panel. Images consisted of animal quadrupeds, tripeds and bipeds, human and human-like figures, dancers, human footprints, insects, geometric designs, grids, lines, rayed circles, abstract designs, and unidentified pecking and shapes. Representational depictions included animals (Figure 44), humans (Figure 45), human footprints, dancing people, mazes and even a bow and arrow. They may have been ritualistic, clan symbols, or merely doodles. Petroglyphs of people dancing have been interpreted as depictions of ritual activities; those at Coyote Ruin have no indication of the sex of the participants.

Figure 44. Petroglyph Panel A.

The dominant technique of creating these petroglyphs was controlled pecking using a hammerstone and a sharpened pecking stone. Pecked elements were either solid or stippled. Stipple pecked elements often do not result in removal of as much rock surface as do the more deeply pecked images. Desert varnish (patina) is removed in varying degrees according to the technique involved.

Figure 45. Petroglyph Panel B.

Moisture, sunlight and geologic formation contributed to the overall color and rate of the patination. All petroglyphs were in the open and exposed to these elements. Some of the figures face upward; most of them face east. Those facing upward and those located in exposed situations were more difficult to see and suffered more deterioration from weathering. Some were partially destroyed as a result of broken and spalling rock surfaces. It appeared that a single individual was the artist for several of the panels. It is rare that petroglyphs are found within a habitation site. At this site they are located within sight of Rooms 17 and 19, next to Room 23, and to the east and west of Room 38. It is also unusual not to have spirals and crosses, petroglyphs that are common at most petroglyph sites in the Prescott area. Neither of these elements was found at Coyote Ruin.

CHAPTER 5
CERAMICS

POTTERY VESSELS
Elizabeth S. Higgins

A collection of 45,856 pottery sherds from Coyote Ruin was analyzed by members of the Yavapai Chapter of the Arizona Archaeological Society under the direction of Elizabeth S. Higgins. The results were tallied separately for each of the 12 rooms excavated in the hope that a significant pattern might be seen in the numbers of sherds of various types which would help pinpoint one or more periods of occupation. The two surface collections, the test pits and the garden plots were tallied separately. No whole or restorable vessels were recovered. A summary of the wares found is given in Table 4. Pottery type counts by provenience are given in Appendix A.

Analytical Procedures

The identification of pottery types from Coyote Ruin was based largely on Colton's (1955, 1956, 1958) basic type descriptions, Prescott Gray Ware as defined at the Prescott Ceramic Conference held November 13-14, 1996, and by comparison with sherds in a ceramic type collection on loan to the Yavapai Chapter by the Museum of Northern Arizona. All sherds were examined on a fresh break with a 10X hand lens for temper and paste attributes. In addition, central Arizona plainware types (Prescott Gray Ware, Alameda Brown Ware, Wingfield Brown Ware, and Tizon Brown Ware) that were found in the rooms and larger than 3 cm on a side (size 3) were subject to a detailed attribute analysis. See discussion of the purpose of attribute analysis in Walsh and Christenson (2003: 55) and attribute analysis of the Coyote Ruin sherds by Andrew Christenson below.

Although use has been made of the ware concept in this report, as the analysis progressed, it became apparent that several types with different ware affiliations were closely related. For example, Prescott Gray (Prescott Gray Ware) and Verde Brown (Alameda Brown Ware) merge, and it was difficult to consistently separate the intergrade form into one type or the other. James (1974) noted this problem at Fitzmaurice Ruin as did Westfall and Jeter (1977: 379) at sites in Copper Basin (see Christenson's "Overview of Ceramic Studies in the Prescott Area", Walsh and Christenson 2003: 47-55). At sites excavated by the Yavapai Chapter since 1978 this problem has been noted, especially in later dated sites located in Prescott and to the east of Prescott. It was not noted in earlier dated sites located in the Williamson Valley area (author's personal observation).

The bulk of the analysis of the Coyote Ruin ceramics was done by four people: the author and members trained by the author and Peter Pilles, Jr., Coconino National Forest Archaeologist, in ceramics analysis. We decided to follow the criteria established by Walsh and Christenson (2003: 57) in their analysis of the ceramics of the Hassayampa Country Club sites:

Because of inconsistencies in type descriptions for Prescott Gray and Verde Brown pottery through the years, the authors decided in advance that the presence, texture, and abundance of specific tempering materials would be equated with specific ceramic types and that these attributes would be given more weight than others, such as the abundance and type of mica and surface treatment and color. We would then carry out a statistical analysis using all of the attributes as an independent evaluation of the success of our imposed typology. We further decided that Prescott Gray Ware sherds should have an abundance of (crushed) arkosic sand temper (decomposed granite consisting predominantly of quartz and feldspar) ranging in size from medium to course and either light or dark in color. We originally thought that an abundance of silver mica (muscovite) would aid in type identification, but modified our opinion when many of the sherds we examined had little or no mica but otherwise had the "correct" temper type for Prescott Gray Ware.

Based on conversations with Peter Pilles, Jr., Coconino National Forest Archaeologist, the analysts also decided a priori to distinguish Verde Brown, an Alameda Brown Ware type, from Prescott Gray on the basis of temper and surface characteristics. Thus, sherds identified as Verde Brown are tempered with a small to moderate amount of rounded or subangular arkosic sand, often with gold mica, and a smoother surface than sherds classified as Prescott Gray.

Initially we identified many sherds as a Prescott Gray/Verde Brown Intergrade when we did not feel comfortable assigning them to either classification. As our analysis progressed we tended to tally these difficult sherds as Prescott Gray since this type was predominant. About halfway through our analysis procedure we learned that many of the plainware sherds being excavated at Honanki in the Coconino National Forest were being classified as Prescott Gray. We arranged for our team of analysts to visit the Honanki analysts at their lab session on February 2, 2003, and took with us a sampling of sherds our team of analysts had identified as Prescott Gray and Verde Brown. We would have classified most of their "Prescott Gray" sherds as Verde Brown. They and Peter Pilles would have classified most of our "Verde Brown" sherds as Prescott Gray. On our return to Prescott we pulled out a random sampling from bags of previously identified Prescott Gray and Verde Brown sherds and looked at them again. In general we agreed with our original analysis, and to keep the results consistent we continued the analysis procedure as originally established.

Ware Descriptions

Prescott Gray Ware

Prescott Gray is the principal ceramic type indigenous to the Prescott region. Constructed by the paddle and anvil method, it has coarse crumbly paste with abundant clear arkosic sand and may have silver or (rarely) gold mica temper. Temper is more than 50% of the core. Sandy and micaceous varieties were tallied separately. Firing was generally done in a non-oxidizing atmosphere, producing the gray color typical of Prescott Gray Ware; however poorly controlled firing atmospheres could produce fire clouding and a wide range of colors on the vessel exterior including gray, reddish yellow, brown, reddish brown and orange. It was not uncommon for the vessel exteriors to be orange and the interior gray. About 61% of the sherds found at Coyote Ruin were of this type.

Table 4. Ceramic ware summary. T = trace.

Ware	Rooms		Surface		Test Pits		Garden Plots		Total	
	No.	%	No.	%	No.	%	No.	%	No.	%
Prescott Gray - Decorated	2,605	7.13	724	9.60	110	9.62	44	8.82	3,483	7.62
Prescott Gray - Undecorated	22,738	62.21	4,711	62.48	568	49.65	313	62.73	28,330	61.95
Alameda Brown	9,269	25.36	839	11.13	357	31.21	80	16.03	10,545	23.06
Wingfield Brown	1,513	4.14	1,117	14.81	99	8.65	55	11.02	2,784	6.09
S. F. Mtn. Gray	11	.03	1	T					12	.03
Tizon Brown	9	.02	1	T					10	.02
Mogollon Brown	24	.07	5	.07					29	.06
Tusayan White	266	.73	80	1.06	8	.70	2	.40	356	.78
Little Colo. White	67	.18	30	.40					97	.21
Tusayan Gray	5	.01	4	.05	1	.09	5	1.00	15	.03
Little Colo. Gray	1	T							1	T
Tsegi Orange	30	.08	13	.17					43	.09
San Juan Red			1	T					1	T
Hohokam Buff	10	.03	14	.19	1	.09			25	.05
Subtotal	36,548	99.99	7,540	99.96	1,144	100	499	100	45,731	99.99
Unclassified - Decorated									14	
Unclassified - Undecorated									111	
Total									45,856	

Prescott Black-on-gray is essentially Prescott Gray with the addition of a black (carbon) painted design. Over 7% of the sherds found at Coyote Ruin were of this type. Designs were found on the interior of bowls; jars were decorated on the interior or the exterior of the neck. Occasionally designs were found on the interior of jars as well, trailing down from the rim or in a crude all-over scroll design. Design motifs were generally geometric, often poorly planned and carelessly executed.

Other types of Prescott Gray Ware at Coyote Ruin included Prescott Red, Prescott Buff, Prescott Red-on-gray, White-on-gray, Polychrome, White-on-red, Red-on-buff; Aquarius Orange, and Aquarius Black-on-orange.

Alameda Brown Ware

The next most common type of pottery found at the site was Verde Brown (20%). Also constructed by the paddle and anvil method, it has fine to medium paste, brown to reddish-brown color, and 30 to 50% temper of medium-sized rounded arkosic sand, often with gold mica.

Sixteen other types of Alameda Brown Ware were identified and are listed in Table A1 and Table A2.

Wingfield Brown Ware

Phyllite-tempered Wingfield Plain comprised 5.8% of the sherds found.   Two other types of this ware, Wingfield Red and Wingfield Black-on-red, were also found. Since Colton (1941b: 46) originally defined Wingfield Plain it has been moved from ware to ware several times (Alameda Brown Ware, Pimeria Brown Ware, Phyllite Plain Ware.)   Because this phyllite-tempered brownware was apparently manufactured by several archaeological "cultures" over a large area of southern and central Arizona, for types containing at least 50% schist temper (including phyllite), regardless of other particles, the 1996 ceramic conference created a separate ware: Wingfield Brown Ware (Walsh and Christenson (2003: 54).

Other Plainwares

Twelve sherds of San Francisco Mountain Gray Ware and ten of Tizon Brown Ware were found at the Coyote Ruin.

Intrusives

Intrusive pottery from the northeast of Prescott included 356 sherds of Tusayan White Ware, 97 sherds of Little Colorado White Ware and lesser numbers of Tsegi Orange Ware, Mogollon Brown Ware, Tusayan Gray Ware, Little Colorado Gray Ware, and San Juan Red Ware. Twenty-five sherds of Hohokam Buff Ware were found.

Dating the Site

The technique of mean ceramic dating was originally developed by Stanley South (1972) for dating sites with historic ceramics. Steadman Upham (1978) was apparently the first Southwestern archaeologist to apply the technique, using it at Chavez Pass Ruin and other sites in the area. Lacking material that could be tree-ring dated, Yavapai Chapter has used the technique to date sites excavated by the chapter (see Cline and Cline 1983; Higgins 1997, 1999a, 2003; Johnson 1996, 1998).

Andrew L. Christenson, Yavapai Chapter Advisor and member, has further researched and developed the technique. In the introduction to his work "A Test of Mean Ceramic Dating Using Well-Dated Kayenta Anasazi Sites" (1994: 297) he states:

A common method of dating ceramic-period sites in the Southwest and elsewhere is to estimate the occupation date by examining the date range of the ceramic types present... A method is available, mean ceramic dating, that, given the same data plus ceramic type frequencies, provides absolute date estimates that are quite close to those obtained from independent absolute dating methods. The technique is demonstrated with a series of well-dated sites in the Kayenta Anasazi area of northeastern Arizona.

No materials were recovered from the Coyote Ruin that could be tree-ring dated, which would have provided the best dates. However, of the total of 36,548 sherds recovered from the rooms, 275 were tradeware of well-dated Anasazi or Hohokam types, or Elden Corrugated from the Northern Sinagua. The mean ceramic dating technique is described in Christenson (1994: 298-299; 1995: 110-111.) Tests of this method along with a sample calculation of a standard deviation and a further refinement of weighting the type dates inversely to the type range have also been discussed (Christenson 1994: 304-308).

Calculation of a mean ceramic date and standard deviation was done for each of nine rooms at Coyote Ruin based upon dates in Table 5. The further refinement of weighting the type dates was not done. Results of these calculations are shown in Table 6. (Rooms 27 and 28 at the base of the hill contained only one dated intrusive type: "Room" 41 contained none; therefore, these three rooms were not considered in our calculations.) A summary of the frequency of ceramic wares at Coyote Ruin is shown in Table 4 and may be used for comparison with eight other sites in the Prescott area shown in the Sundown site report (Higgins 1999a: 52-53, Table 7). Note that Wingfield Brown Ware types were previously included under Pimeria Brown Ware. This new ware was created at the Prescott Ceramic Conference in 1996 (Hays-Gilpin and Walsh-Anduze 1997). Table 5 shows all types found at the site for which dates were available and includes a graph of the range of dates.

Figure 46 is a map showing the rooms for which a mean ceramic date (MCD) was calculated. Room 2 is at the top of the hill, with Rooms 1-9, 1A and 12 clustered around but slightly below it. The MCD for Room 2 is 1136+/-55, the earliest of any of the rooms on the hill. Room 5, MCD 1175 +/- 117, is on a slope slightly below the cluster. Rooms 14 and 40 are "one-story" below the topmost rooms. MCD for Room 14 is 1145 +/- 89. MCD for Room 40 is 1193 +/- 81. Room 40 had been filled with trash and contained sherds from 16 of the 25 intrusive types found at the site. The ground- level doorway had been sealed prehistorically and had not been disturbed until our excavators opened the door (however, the room probably had a roof entrance as well). Adjoining Rooms 17, 18, and 19 are on approximately the same level as Rooms 14 and 40. MCDs for Rooms 17, 18 and 19 are 1184 +/- 73, 1172 +/- 92 and 1164 +/- 62 respectively. Continuing down the hill are Rooms 23, MCD 1151 +/- 80 and Room 38, MCD 1151+/- 120. Rooms 27 and 28 are at the base of the hill on the level of Old Coyote Ruin and contained a few sherds of Deadman's Gray which is not reliably dated (median date A.D. 975). These dates are mostly for trash thrown into the rooms after they were abandoned, although as noted below pothunting activities at the site have substantially mixed deposits.

Table 5. Dates for ceramic types.

Ceramic Type	Year 500 600 700 800 900 1000 1100 1200 1300 1400	Range of Dates (AD)	Median Dates (AD)	Sources
Wingfield Red		500-1300	900	1
Wingfield Plain		784-1385	1085	1
Prescott Gray		800-1400	1100	7
Prescott Black-on-Gray		800-1400	1100	7
*Santa Cruz Red-on-buff		850-950	900	9
Deadman's Gray		850-1100	975	1
*Wepo Black-on-white		850-1060	950	3
*Black Mesa Black-on-white		900-1160	1050**	3
*Sacaton Red-on-buff		950-1100	1025	9
Padre Black-on-white		957-1275	1116	2
Aquarius Orange		1000-1100	1050	2
Verde Brown		1000-1300	1150	2
*Medicine Black-on-red		1040-1170	1110**	3
*Citadel Polychrome		1040-1200	1120	3
*Tusayan Black-on-red		1045-1240	1120**	3
*Holbrook Black-on-white		1050-1150	1100	8
*Sosi Black-on-white		1050-1180	1125**	3
*Dogoszhi Black-on-white		1050-1190	1120	3
*Shato Black-on-white		1080-1130	1105	1
*Elden Corrugated		1085-1200	1143	1
*Walnut Black-on-white		1100-1285	1192**	4
*Tusayan Polychrome		1110-1320	1225**	3
*Flagstaff Black-on-white		1130-1230	1195**	3
*Tsegi Red-on-orange		1150-1300	1225	1
Tuzigoot Plain		1150-1400	1275	2
Tuzigoot Red		1150-1400	1275	2
*Leupp Black-on-white		1200-1285	1242**	5
**Verde Red		1200-1300	1275**	2
*Tusayan Black-on-white		1230-1330	1275**	3
*Wupatki Black-on-white		1230-1300	1275**	6
*Tsegi Orange		1240-1320	1280	3
*Tusayan Black-on-white (Kayenta Variety)		1260-1330	1295	5
Bidahochi Black-on-white		1320-1400	1360	2

* Types used to calculate MCD   ** Christenson Mean Date

Sources: 1) Breternitz 1966; 2) Colton 1955; 3) Christenson 1994; 4) Christenson 1995; 5) Christenson 1997a;
6) Christenson est.; 7) Hays-Gilpin and Walsh-Anduze 2001; 8) Douglass1990; 9) Wallace 1995.

Room	# of Sherds	# of Types	Mean Ceramic Date (A.D.)
2	6	5	1136 +/- 55
5	4	3	1175 +/- 117
14	33	10	1145 +/- 89
17	18	8	1184 +/- 73
18	43	16	1170 +/- 91
19	23	10	1164 +/- 62
23	5	3	1151 +/- 80
38	6	4	1151 +/- 120
40	137	16	1193 +/- 81
All	275	21	1178 +/- 84

Table 6. Mean ceramic dating results.

According to South (1977:443), the *interpreted occupancy period* represented by the ceramics may be determined by using the calculated mean ceramic date with the earliest date of manufacture of the latest ceramic type found. Based on this, the main part of Coyote Ruin was occupied around A.D. 1178 to 1320. Christenson has found that in his experience, sites with large standard deviations have a high probability of having been occupied over a long period of time or in separate occupancy periods (2008: personal communication.)

Two samples sent to Beta Analytic, Inc. for radiocarbon dating produced the following results:

corn cob from Room 40:   820 +/- 80 BP (95% cal range 1030-1290)
charcoal from Room 2:   550 +/- 160 BP (95% cal range 1295-1444)

The result on the corn cob corresponds well with our calculated MCD of A.D. 1193 for Room 40. The result on the charred material from Room 2 (which at 1136 had the earliest calculated MCD of the rooms on the hill) does not correspond (see Appendix G for complete laboratory reports).

Table 6 shows the distribution of intrusive sherds by levels in the three rooms with the largest number of sherds: Rooms 14, 18 and 40. Types of sherds tallied are shown across the top row and are in order by the median date of each type. In an undisturbed room you would expect to find the latest dated sherds at the top, the earliest at the floor level. However, all three rooms had been so disturbed that no such pattern appeared.

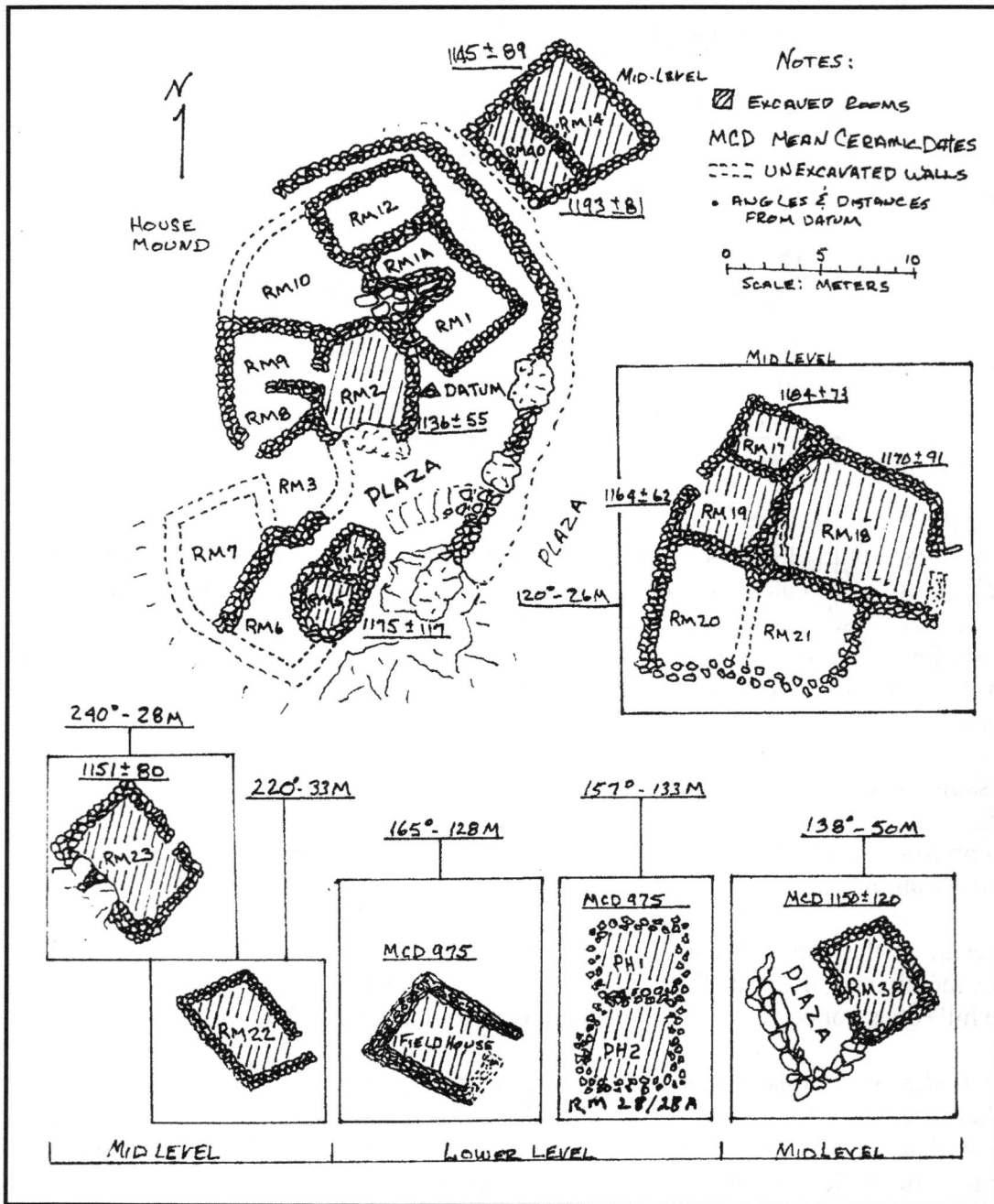

Figure 46. Excavated rooms with mean ceramic dates.
For mid-level and lower level rooms, angles and distances from datum given.

Rooms 14 and 18 had been disturbed by pothunters in recent times and Room 2 was excavated by J. W. Simmons. Room 40, which had no modern disturbance, contained sherds of every type used in the calculation of the MCD except four. Flagstaff Black-on-white, mid-range of the types of Tusayan White Ware, appeared in all but three of the levels. Why? Here is a possible explanation. An adult female and a 1-3 year old child were found buried beneath the lower of the two floors encountered. The lower floor was a hard packed and plastered surface with a clay-lined hearth. Metates, manos, abraders, hammerstones, and pottery anvils -- tools of everyday living -- rested on its surface, which was littered with fragments of sherds, animal bones, corn cobs, walnut and pinon nut shells. Was this room abandoned at the time the woman and child died and then used as a midden? Or was it lived in for a time until a second child (age 12-14) died and was laid to rest on that floor and covered with soil? A second "floor", 14 cm above the lower one, was loose soil containing charcoal and only a few broken pieces of pottery and lithics. The room, abandoned at this time, was then used as a midden. Fifteen centimeters above this second (upper) "floor" an adult male was buried, and even higher in the midden, an infant burial. Disturbance of the existing midden would have occurred when the two later burials were interred.

In this author's paper (Higgins 2000) on the designs found on Prescott Black-on-gray and Red-on-buff pottery at the Neural Site, it was suggested that the designs resembled those found on the Tusayan White Ware pottery brought or traded into the Neural Site and that the Prescott potters were emulating the designs they saw from northern Arizona in their own distinctive way. I suggest that the same may be true of the Prescott Black-on-gray pottery from Coyote Ruin. In Table 17 of the attribute analysis, four of the predominant Tusayan White Ware design styles are represented (Black Mesa, Dogoszhi, Sosi, and Flagstaff). Only the latest style, Tusayan, is missing. Possibly it had not been on the scene long enough for the Prescott potters to begin to try to use it as a design style. A reexamination of the 116 sherds by a single experienced analyst, as suggested by Christenson, might clarify the picture. This might give us a sequence of design styles through time that could be useful in dating a site. Figure 47 is a photograph of part of the Yavapai Chapter's exhibit "The Puzzle of Ancient Prescott: Pieces from Coyote Ruin" which was on display at the Smoki Museum. On the left are Prescott Black-on-gray sherds with uniquely Prescott designs. In the center are Prescott Black-on-gray, Prescott Red-on-buff and Prescott White-on-gray sherds whose designs appear to emulate those of the Tusayan White Ware and Little Colorado White Ware designs shown on sherds at the right.

Miscellaneous Clay Objects

Table A4 is an inventory of the miscellaneous clay objects found at Coyote Ruin and shows the distribution of these objects among the rooms. Of most interest was the number of ladle and scoop fragments found, as this number had seldom been seen at other sites excavated by Yavapai Chapter.

Three pieces of a large ladle handle of Tusayan White Ware were found in Levels 6 and 7 of Room 40 (Figure 48). One piece was undecorated and identified just as Tusayan White Ware. Two pieces were decorated and identified as Tusayan Black-on-white. Striped designs on both of these pieces were the same. One piece was the end of the handle which was flattened and decorated with a black-on-white striped design. Inside diameters of the three pieces ranged from 1.67 to 1.91 cm.

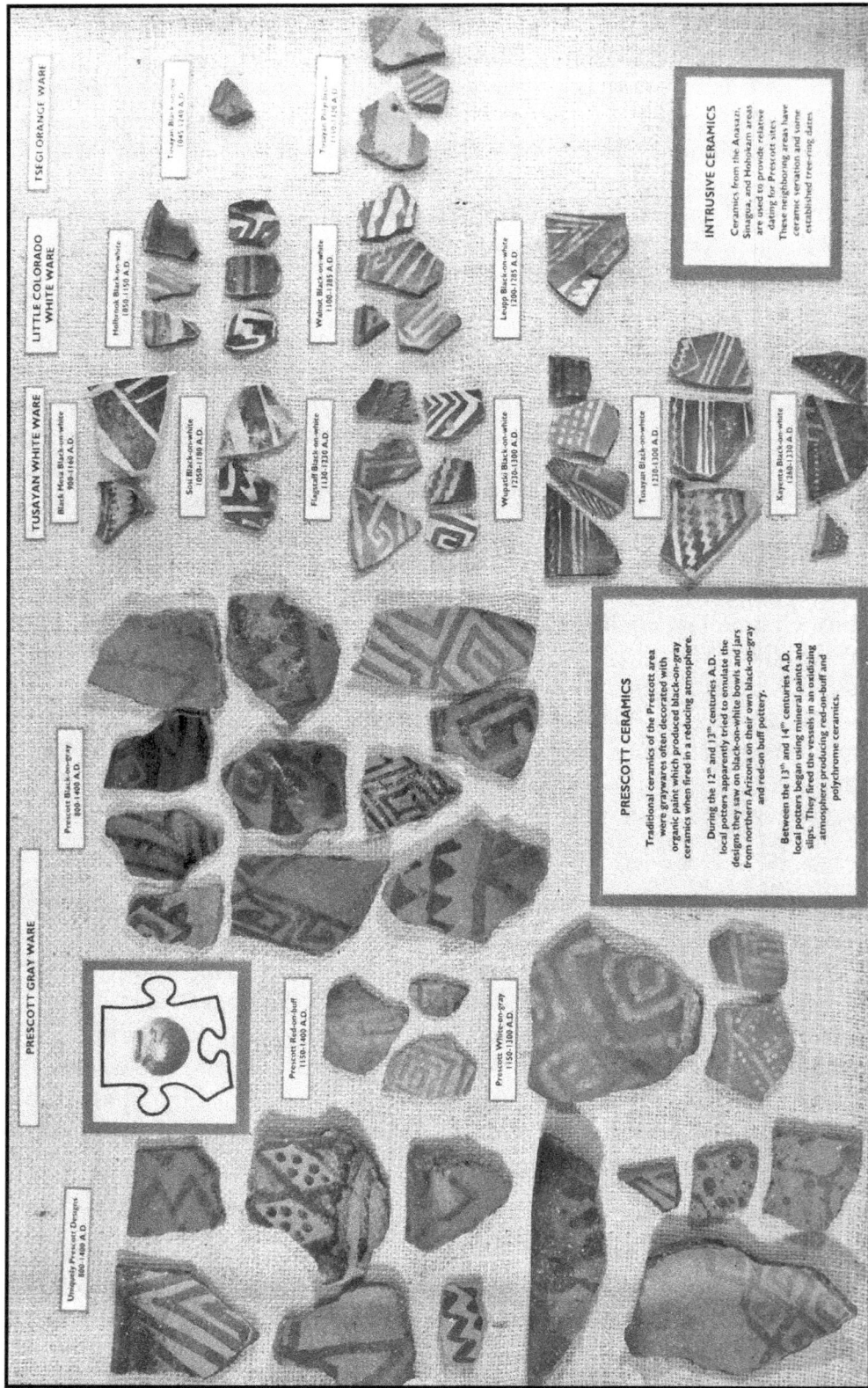

Figure 47. Designs on ceramics.

66

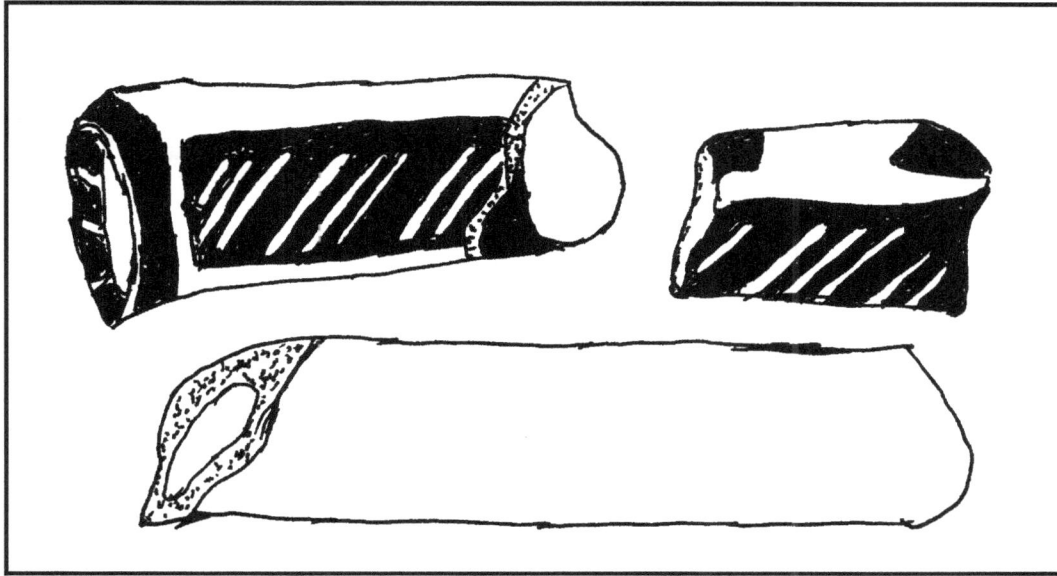

Figure 48. Three pieces of large Tusayan White Ware ladle from Room 40.
Combined length of the three pieces was approximately 29 cm. This was a large ladle!

Figure 49 shows an unusual Prescott Gray vessel fragment from Room 40. It was identified as a scoop because of a 7 mm high ridge separating the "handle" area from the main body of the scoop. However the shape of the fragment is more like a very thick-bottomed bowl. The curve of the 3.7 cm portion of the rim indicates that such a bowl would have had a 10 cm diameter. Most unusual is the variation in thickness ranging from 7 mm at the rim to 1.3 cm at the bottom.

Figure 49. Fragment of Prescott Gray scoop found in Room 40.

Fragments of two small, intrusive decorated jars were found in Room 40 in Level 7. One is Sunset White-on-red, the other Tusayan Black-on-white (Figure 50).

Figure 50. Fragments of jars from Room 40. Left is Sunset White-on-red; right is Tusayan Black-on-white. Drawings by Ginger Johnson.

Summary

Nearly 46,000 pottery sherds from Coyote Ruin were analyzed and identified by members of the Yavapai Chapter of the Arizona Archaeological Society. In addition a detailed attribute analysis was done on Prescott Gray Ware, Alameda Brown Ware, Wingfield Brown Ware and Tizon Brown Ware sherds (the central Arizona plainwares) found in the rooms.

The intergrade between Prescott Gray and Verde Brown continued to be a problem at Coyote Ruin. At sites excavated by Yavapai Chapter since 1978 this problem has been noted, especially in later dated sites located in Prescott and to the east of Prescott. It was not noted in earlier dated sites in the Williamson Valley area (author's personal observation).

No whole or restorable vessels were recovered. We were unable to determine the use of the various rooms based on the pottery assemblage.

Calculation of a mean ceramic date was done for each of nine excavated rooms and for all nine combined. These dates were calculated based on 275 intrusive sherds of well-dated Anasazi and Hohokam types, and of the Elden Corrugated type. The earliest of the rooms on the hill was Room 2 (MCD 1136). MCDs of rooms in the next tier down range from A.D. 1145 - 1184, except for Room 40 (MCD 1193) which had apparently been used as a midden until the site was abandoned. Two rooms at the base of the hill contained only a few intrusive sherds (not reliably dated) with MCD of 975.

C-14 dating of a corn cob from Room 40 corresponds well with the MCD for that room, but the C-14 date for charred material from Room 2 does not.

Among the miscellaneous clay objects, fragments of eight ladles and six scoops were of particular interest as very few artifacts of these types had been found at other sites excavated by the Yavapai Chapter. Most outstanding were three pieces of a large Tusayan Black-on-white ladle handle.

Basket impressions were observed, as was a cloth impression. One basket impression and the fabric impression are discussed below.

The pottery analysis and attribute analysis have given us a great amount of data and some new insights, but few firm conclusions. It is hoped that the information will add to the data base and be helpful in the future.

ATTRIBUTE ANALYSIS OF RIM SHERDS
Andrew L. Christenson

The purpose of attribute analysis is to examine variation within and between standard ceramic types (see discussion in Walsh and Christenson 2003). For plainware types, ware-level distinctions occur mostly in temper, and type-level distinctions tend to be made using surface treatment. Thus, simply using types to represent the variation in the pottery leaves considerable variation unexamined. The Coyote Ruin analysis is the largest of several attribute analyses done in the Prescott and Verde Valley areas of central Arizona and these data will eventually allow examination of spatial and temporal variation in central Arizona plainwares as well.

Variables

In addition to provenience information and sherd size, data recorded are ceramic ware and type, vessel form, rim diameter, rim shape, rim/sidewall curvature, temper type, texture and abundance, mica type and abundance, firing atmosphere (interior and exterior), surface modification (interior and exterior), and design style. Attribute states for the variables used will be discussed where appropriate. Through much of the analysis, attributes were recorded on all sherds, but only rim sherds will be included in the tables below to reduce the skewing effects of multiple sherds from the same vessel. I usually measure vessel thickness below the rim as part of my attribute analyses, although that was not done on these sherds.

Multiple analysts coded these data and although they worked closely together individual variation in interpretation is expected. Strong patterns are the ones that the heaviest interpretive weight should be placed upon. The author set up the attribute analysis, but did not analyze any of the sherds.

This discussion will use subsets of the data as appropriate. Because Room 40 had over four times as many sherds as any other room, it is the only room examined for many of the variables. The three most common types, Prescott Gray, Prescott Black-on-gray, and Verde Brown are generally the only types examined, although in a couple of tables, less common types are included for comparative purposes.

Vessel Form

All rooms have more bowls than jars, although Rooms 14, 18, and 38 show an excess of bowls compared to say, Room 40 (Table 7). Because the context of these different room samples includes both primary and secondary trash, interpretation of these differences is unclear. Looking at types, all except the decorated type have bowl/jar ratios around 2/1. The high frequency of bowls in Prescott Black-on-gray has been noted elsewhere and probably indicates a narrower range of functions for this type.

Table 7. Vessel form (bowls/jars) by type and room.

Type	R 14	R 17	R 18	R 23	R 27	R 28	R 29	R 38	R 40	R 41	Total	Ratio B/J
Prescott Gray	35/6	46/12	154/21	10/2	0/1	11/6	12/0	39/7	342/215		649/270	2.4
Prescott B/g	35/4	16/3	52/4	5/0	2/0	19/0	2/1	26/1	206/55		364/68	5.4
Verde Brown	33/3	39/4	3./6	2/2		2/1	1/0	6/1	222/109	1/0	336/126	2.7
Verde Red	7/1	1/1		1/0				3/0	16/16		28/18	1.6
Wingfield Plain	1/0	5/0	8/3			1/1			14/10		29/14	2.1
Total	111/14	87/20	245/34	18/4	2/1	33/8	15/1	74/9	800/405	1/0		
Ratio Bowls/Jars	7.9	4.3	7.2	4.5	-	4.1	-	8.2	2.0	-		

Temper

Because temper type is the critical defining variable for wares in this analysis, there will not be much variation within types. Temper abundance and texture are also closely tied to type definition. Tables 8 and 9 show data for the three most common types on these variables in Room 40 (Wingfield Plain is universally coarse and has abundant temper). As might be expected Verde Brown is medium or moderate on both measures while the Prescott types are coarse or high on both measures. Not quite as predictable is the fact that jars of all three types have more and finer temper than bowls. Because jars are much more likely to be cooking vessels subject to heat, this difference may relate to adaptation of the temper to meet certain physical demands.

Table 8. Room 40. Temper abundance by type and form. Percentages in parentheses.

Type	Low	Moderate	High	Total
Bowls				
Prescott Gray	10 (3)	100 (29)	232 (68)	342
Prescott B/g	3 (1)	74 (36)	129 (63)	206
Verde Brown	17 (8)	162 (74)	40 (18)	219
Jars				
Prescott Gray	7 (3)	51 (24)	157 (73)	215
Prescott B/g	1 (2)	12 (22)	42 (76)	55
Verde Brown	8 (7)	62 (57)	39 (36)	109

Table 9. Room 40. Temper texture by type and form. Percentages in parentheses.

Type	Fine	Medium	Coarse	Total
Bowls				
Prescott Gray	33 (10)	152 (44)	157 (46)	342
Prescott B/g	16 (8)	88 (43)	102 (50)	206
Verde Brown	32 (14)	185 (83)	5 (2)	222
Jars				
Prescott Gray	36 (17)	110 (51)	69 (32)	215
Prescott B/g	8 (15)	23 (42)	24 (44)	55
Verde Brown	28 (26)	79 (73)	2 (2)	109

Mica is one temper variable that does not currently serve as a type definition, although it has always been considered a characteristic of Prescott Gray Ware pottery (Colton and Hargrave 1937: 184). Comparison of Prescott Gray and Prescott Black-on-gray on this variable has been most enlightening. Table 10 provides tabulation of vessel form by type and mica for five rooms with the most sherds. Prescott Gray is more likely not to have mica by a ratio of 3 to 2, whereas Prescott Black-on-gray rarely lacks mica by a ratio of greater than 11 to 1. This variation between types is uniform for both bowls and jars. Previous attribute work has shown the predominance of mica in the decorated Prescott type and has led to the interpretation that Prescott Black-on-gray was not made with the same temper as the undecorated type (see review in Christenson 2005a). The petrographic analysis of Coyote Ruin sherds has confirmed that interpretation (see "Petrographic Analysis…" below). It is interesting that the first attribute analysis done on Prescott Gray Ware (then divided into Verde Gray and Verde Black-on-gray) showed no difference in the frequency of mica between the two types (Mueller and Schecter 1970: Table 22). Mueller and Schecter were the first to use sandy and micaceous varieties (as well as oxidized and reduced). This idea has had its ups and down since that time, but recent petrographic results indicate that the presence of mica, specifically large amounts of silver mica (muscovite) is indicative of something interesting going on with Prescott Gray Ware production. My preference is to analyze such variation through attribute (and petrographic) analysis rather than through creation of varieties.

The high quantity of mica in Prescott Black-on-gray could be the result of two alternatives with very different interpretations: a) it is the result of the makers using what they had locally to make pots, or b) it is the result of intentional inclusion of high-mica rock for functional or economic reasons. The makers of Prescott Black-on-gray are generally using a different granitic rock than that used in most of the Prescott Gray, which petrographic analysis indicates is made using residual clay or temper derived from Prescott Granodiorite or, less frequently, Dells Granite. The source of the granitic rock in Prescott Black-on-gray has not been located, so at the moment the idea that high mica content is simply a result of geology and geography cannot be ruled out. There are reasons to suspect, however, that a high mica rock was chosen, from a range of alternatives, to give it visual impact to the vessels (West 1992:35). Mica is known to increase strength/elacticity of pottery and possibly to improve transmission of heat (Cardew 1969:78; Carrillo 1997:131; Wallace 1989:39). This might be a functional issue with cooking pots, such as the micaceous bean pots produced in New Mexico (Anderson 1999; Carrillo 1997), but it is less likely to be one with the bowls that predominate in Prescott Black-on-gray.

Evidence so far suggests that Prescott Black-on-gray was mostly a local tradeware, but that it sometimes was traded outside the culture area. Attribute and petrographic analysis needs to be done on Prescott Gray Ware in nearby culture areas to see how it compares, visually or otherwise, to that present on Prescott Culture sites. No evidence has been encountered that temper or clay was obtained from a long distance by direct procurement or trade. Ethnographic data available (Arnold 1985: 50-52) indicates that the maximum distance to obtain such resources without water transportation is 6-9 km (4-6 mi.) which is a trivial distance on the scale that we are considering.

Table 10. Mica frequency by type, form, and room. Percentages in parentheses.

Type / Room	None	Low Silver	High Silver	Gold	Unkn.	Total
Bowls						
Prescott Gray						
18	117	22	14		1	
17	32	4	9			
14	18	9	7			
38	28	5	6			
40	180	63	79	8	2	
Total	375 (62)	103 (17)	115 (19)	8 (1)	3 (1)	604
Prescott B/g						
18	6	17	28		1	
17	1	3	10	1	1	
14	1	8	26			
38	7	12	6	1		
40	14	49	138	3	1	
Total	29 (9)	89 (27)	208 (62)	5 (1)	3 (1)	334
Jars						
Prescott Gray						
18	14	2	3		1	
17	7	2	3			
14	4		1	1		
38	6		1			
40	105	30	71	4	2	
Total	136 (53)	34 (13)	79 (31)	5 (2)	3 (1)	257
Prescott B/g						
18	1	1	1		1	
17		2	1			
14			4			
38			1			
40	5	14	35			
Total	6 (9)	17 (26)	42 (64)		1	66

Surface Treatment

Not much evidence of variation in surface treatment is present (Tables 11 and 12). Smoothing of surfaces is usually the only treatment, with polishing, smudging and wiping being rare. There appears to be no difference between interior and exterior surfaces except that smudging is more common on the interior.

Table 11. Room 40: interior surface treatment by type and form.

Type	None	Wiped	Smoothed	Polished	Smudged	Smudged & Polished	Total
Bowls							
Prescott Gray	4	11	270	23	21	11	340
Prescott B/g	1	6	193	5	1		206
Verde Brown	5	2	174	16	5	17	219
Jars							
Prescott Gray	3	18	172	5	14	2	214
Prescott B/g			54		1		55
Verde Brown	2	8	88	6	4	1	109

Table 12. Room 40: exterior surface treatment by type and form.

Type	None	Wiped	Smoothed	Polished	Smudged	Smudged & Polished	Total
Bowls							
Prescott Gray	3	11	284	26	11	4	339
Prescott B/g		7	191	5	3		206
Verde Brown	4	5	184	19	3	4	219
Jars							
Prescott Gray	2	16	185	8	2	1	214
Prescott B/g	1	2	52				55
Verde Brown	1	10	84	12	1		108

Rim Form

The shape of the rim is usually recorded in ceramic attribute analyses because it has been shown to vary through time and between types in other areas of the Southwest (Shepard 1956:245-247), although it has not been very interesting in the Prescott area so far. The Room 40 rim form data show a rather striking difference between Prescott Black-on-gray and the two most common plainwares (Table 13). Prescott Black-on-gray is dominated by rounded rims, while Verde Brown has many more flat rims. However, these same attributes were examined for the Room 18 sherds and all of the most common types had 50% or more rounded rims (table not shown). Thus, the significance of the Room 40 data is uncertain.

Table 13. Room 40: rim form by type and form. Percentages in parentheses.

Type	Flat	Round	Beveled	Tapered	Irregular/Multiple	Total
Bowls						
Prescott Gray	179 (52)	122 (36)	35 (10)	2 (1)	3 (1)	341
Prescott B/g	64 (31)	109 (53)	33 (16)			206
Verde Brown	150 (68)	48 (22)	21 (9)	3 (1)		222
Jars						
Prescott Gray	94 (44)	95 (44)	21 (10)	4 (2)		214
Prescott B/g	14 (26)	34 (63)	5 (9)	1 (2)		54
Verde Brown	63 (58)	33 (30)	11 (10)	2 (2)		109

Rim Curvature

As might be expected bowls and jars differ in terms of how the rims curve (Table 14). Bowls of all types have vertical rims 70-80% of the time, while jars have outcurved or recurved rims.

Table 14. Room 40: rim curvature by type and form. Percentages in parentheses.

Type	Outcurved	Incurved	Vertical	Recurved	Total
Bowls					
Prescott Gray	43 (13)	23 (7)	275 (81)	-	341
Prescott B/g	14 (7)	28 (14)	163 (80)	-	205
Verde Brown	35 (16)	23 (10)	163 (74)	-	221
Jars					
Prescott Gray	111 (52)	11 (5)	46 (21)	47 (22)	215
Prescott B/g	28 (51)	4 (7)	13 (24)	10 (18)	55
Verde Brown	55 (50)	5 (5)	39 (36)	10 (9)	109

Vessel Orifice Diameter

Diameter of vessels at the rim was estimated by fitting rim sherds with 6 or more cm of rim length to concentric circles. Table 15 provides this information for sherds from Room 40 grouped into 4 cm intervals. Although the mean diameters for all of the categories are not greatly different, the distribution of diameters is. In bowls, both Prescott Gray and Verde Brown have fairly wide ranges, while Prescott Black-on-gray occurs in a narrower range. Bowls are believed to have generally been for mixing and serving and the size of the bowl indicative of the amount mixed or the number of people served. The small bowls, say the ones under 10 cm, might have been used for small mixing activities, while the ones in the 40 cm range may have been for feeding large groups. Jars would have been for cooking and storage tasks, those with small orifice diameters for wet storage or carrying of liquids and those with large diameters for dry storage or cooking (see Smith 1985: Table 11.2 for summary of correlating vessel orifice with use behavior).

Table 15. Room 40: orifice diameters by type and form.

Type	Diameter (cm)									N	Mean (sd)
	6-8	10-12	14-16	18-20	22-24	26-28	30-32	34-36	38-40	42		
Bowls												
Prescott Gray	1	3	1	8	6	10	2	1	4		36	24.2 (8.1)
Prescott B/g		1		3	6	7	5	3	2	1	28	27.9 (7.0)
Verde Brown	1	2		4	2	4	1		2		16	23.2 (8.9)
Jars												
Prescott Gray		2	2	9	10	9	6	3	6	1	48	26.7 (7.9)
Prescott B/g					4	9	4	3	1		21	28.9 (4.3)
Verde Brown			4	10	12	4		1	1		32	22.4 (5.1)
Wingfield Plain		1	1	2	1	1	1				7	24.9 (6.2)

Firing

Eighty percent or more of surfaces on Prescott Gray Ware are reduced, whereas on Verde Brown it is around 50% (Table 16). At the Hassayampa Country Club, there was a marked difference between Prescott Gray and Prescott Black-on-gray in the frequency of oxidized surfaces, that was related to the need to keep the carbon painted designs on the decorated type from burning off (Walsh and Christenson 2003:65-66). In the Room 40 sherds at Coyote Ruin, there was little difference between the types for bowls, but the pattern shows up clearer for the jars. The presence of a few black-on-gray vessels that are oxidized all over indicates that there were conditions under which organic paint was not burned out in this firing atmosphere. Temperature, duration of firing, and clay porosity are all factors that affect the paint (Shepard 1956:34-35). Another possibility is that a pot was removed from the reducing fire when maximum temperature was reached and the quick cooling in air oxidized the surface without burning off the paint (Rye 1981:117-118).

Table 16. Room 40: firing by type and form. Percentages in parentheses.

Interior/ Exterior	Reduced/ Reduced	Oxidized/ Oxidized	Oxidized/ Reduced	Reduced/ Oxidized	% of Surfaces Reduced	Total
Bowls						
Prescott Gray	269 (79)	41 (12)	8 (2)	24 (7)	83	342
Prescott B/g	165 (80)	21 (10)	2 (1)	18 (9)	85	206
Verde Brown	111 (50)	89 (40)	5 (2)	16 (7)	55	221
Jars						
Prescott Gray	156 (73)	34 (16)	3 (1)	22 (10)	78	215
Prescott B/g	39 (71)	1 (2)	3 (5)	12 (22)	81	55
Verde Brown	46 (42)	52 (48)	3 (3)	8 (7)	47	109

Design Style

Designs on Prescott Black-on-gray can sometimes be matched to traditional styles found on Tusayan White Ware vessels. Decisions about similarities or differences between published designs and designs on sherds are much more judgmental than many of the other attributes. Such examination is best done by a single person familiar with the range of design variation. Table 17 provides a clue of the range of styles observed, but the data should not be used for comparative purposes.

Table 17. Room 40: Prescott Black-on-gray design style by vessel form.

Style	Bowl	Jar
Kana-a	1	
Black Mesa	11	1
Dogoszhi	1	
Sosi	16	3
Flagstaff	41	14
Chevron	33	10
dots/splatters	1	2
Indeterminate	94	22
Total	198	52

Conclusions

Perhaps the most important insight to come out of attribute analysis is the fact that although sherds are classified into the same ceramic type they do not share all their characteristics. Some of this variation within types may lead to understanding of interesting aspects of prehistoric behavior, although at the moment they may not be understandable. The clearest pattern to come out of this analysis is the very different vessel form, vessel size, and mica characteristics of Prescott Black-on-gray and Prescott Gray. The idea of high-mica Prescott Gray Ware being a nonutilitarian and trade ware has been suggested in the past (Gratz and Fiero 1974:9), but that idea has not been pursued in the 30 years since its suggestion. Recent attribute and petrographic analyses are beginning to indicate that the two types may in fact differ in use and production location. I would not use the term "nonutilitarian" to describe any of the Prescott pottery, as it all shows evidence of use in various production and mortuary activities. However, the idea that Prescott Black-on-gray, particularly high-mica bowls were produced for trade raises the possibility of a specialized tradeware production center or centers somewhere in the region. Until such centers are located, further development of these ideas must remain mostly speculative.

Acknowledgement. The late Ruth Barth accomplished the difficult task of inputting the attribute analysis data so they could be analyzed.

BASKETRY AND FABRIC IMPRESSIONS
Andrew L. Christenson and Robert Beck

Basket and textile impressions were observed on a number of sherds from the site. However, only one basket impressed sherd, one fabric impressed sherd, and one probable mat impressed clay piece were analyzed. The only information that we have on Prescott-area basketry and textiles comes from a few impressions in pottery (Beck 2005; Christenson 2005a:8.39, 8.44-45; in prep.; Higgins 1999b:129, Figure 53). The cultural comparisons made below are merely made to provide some reference to ethnographic basketry examples and should not be interpreted to imply prehistoric cultural connection.

One Prescott Gray bowl sherd from Level 1 of Test Pit #1 had a basket impression on the <u>interior</u> of the sherd. Bob Beck kindly examined this sherd:

> At first glance, the basket impression on the inside of this rim sherd appeared to resemble the split yucca leaf and coiled bunch construction of the historic baskets crafted by the people now known as the Tohono O'odham. However, on closer inspection and using a 10-power hand lens, it is noted that the impression on the sherd bears an eerily similar appearance and texture to historic Pima split bark and coiled bunch rod construction.
>
> The basket used for comparison purposes was a 1930 to 1940s Pima bowl with 6 rods per inch and 11 stitches per inch on each rod. Weft length per rod was 0.50 cm to 0.80 cm. Weft width was 0.20 cm. The basket impression on the sherd featured 6 rods per inch with 10 turns per rod. Weft width on the sherd sample is almost exactly the same at 0.19 cm to 0.21 cm. Weft length was 0.50 to 0.60 cm.
>
> The sherd shows wear and weft breakage on the host basket about 2.2 cm from the rim which perhaps suggests the basket used for the pot mold was an older, well-used utensil.
>
> Using baskets and pots with similar rim curvature, I have calculated the outside diameter of the prehistoric bowl at approximately 12.3 cm. Baskets used as comparison vessels in addition to the Pima bowl were a 1920 - 1930s Apache bowl and a 1930 - 1940s Tohono O'odham jar.
>
> The molding of a pot on the outside of a basket provides an interesting texture to the vessel interior, but this was also an easy way for an inexperienced potter to produce an acceptable vessel without having to build it up from coiling. Even experienced potters form the base of a large pot over an existing vessel used as a mold (e.g., Fontana et al. 1962: Figure 48-50). The rim is finished fairly well but the exterior of the vessel has a bump about 2 cm down from the rim where the basket had a similar bulge. The exterior is lightly wiped.

A sherd from a vessel of unknown form had a fabric impression on its interior (Room 40.6, B70). The sherd has fine, crushed phyllite and so is an unusual Wingfield Plain, which usually has very coarse temper. The vessel has a polished exterior. Although the warps and wefts cannot be distinguished the structure is plain weave with single warps/wefts (Teague 1998: Figure 3.6). The fiber material and yarn structure cannot be discerned. Both axes have yarn spacing around 11/10 cm. This diameter is similar to Hohokam and Casas Grandes textiles (Teague 1998: 50).

The third impression is on thick lump of clay, perhaps daub, from Level 6 of Room 40 (SPIT #1237). It shows a segment of twill plaited matting with two over two element intervals (a similar weaving pattern is used on a Choctaw carrying basket illustrated by James [1908: Figure 192]). Three strips that could be measured averaged 5.19 mm in width. The strips cross at an 84° angle. Bob Beck observed that this impression may be a Prescott Culture example of recycling where a piece of matting that had lost its usefulness in other activities was used to cover an area of roof or wall.

PETROGRAPHIC ANALYSIS OF SHERD, BEDROCK, AND CLAY SAMPLES
Andrew L. Christenson

Petrographic analysis is a method of examining sand- and sometimes silt-size particles in pottery or clay, to identify specific minerals and rocks with the goal of determining how the pottery was made and where it may or may not have been made. Absolute statements about such issues are usually not possible, but with knowledge of the local geology, statements of varying degrees of probability may be possible. Below is a discussion of several geological and archaeological petrographic samples obtained from or near Coyote Ruin and their significance in understanding ceramic technology.

The Sample

Table 18 provides information on the nine sherds selected for petrographic analysis. All the sherds were examined with a 10x binocular microscope and were recorded using a standardized attribute system for central Arizona brownwares. Three decorated (Prescott Black-on-gray) and four undecorated (Prescott Gray) Prescott Gray Ware sherds were chosen. One of the sherds considered to be Prescott Gray in this analysis was classified as Verde Brown/Prescott Gray in the sherd analysis. Two sherds had been called Verde Brown in the sherd analysis, but one turned out to be Fitzmaurice Brown (Sample 7), a recently defined gabbro tempered plainware (Christenson 2005b) and the other (Sample 8) could not be classified. Such differences between analysts is not unexpected, given the fairly subtle differences used to differentiate central Arizona brownware types.

Table 18. Sherd petrographic samples.

Sample	Room	Level	Form	Description - rim, temper, firing, surface treatment/design
Prescott Gray				
4	40	9	jar	medium texture, high abundance, no mica; reduced interior, oxidized exterior; exterior polished
5	40	5	possible scoop	round rim; coarse texture, high abundance, no mica; reduced firing
6	18	10	bowl	flat, vertical rim; medium texture, high abundance, no mica; oxidized firing;
9	18	unkn.	jar	fine texture, moderate abundance; oxidized firing; wiped interior; Gila shoulder
Prescott Black-on-gray				
1	40	unkn.	bowl	irregular, outcurved rim; medium texture, moderate abundance, abundant silver mica; smudge interior; linear design
2	18	10	jar?	medium texture, high abundance, minimal gold mica; reduced firing; splatter design
3	40	5	bowl	round, recurved rim; medium texture, high abundance, abundant silver mica; reduced firing; smudged, polished interior, polished exterior; linear design
Fitzmaurice Brown				
7	18	8	jar	round, vertical rim; medium texture, high abundance, dark mineral temper, no mica; oxidized firing; smudged interior and exterior
Unknown Brownware				
8	2	4	bowl	flat, outcurved rim; medium texture, high abundance, no mica; oxidized interior, reduced exterior

In addition to sherds, one bedrock sample and two fired clay samples were analyzed. The bedrock came from the granitic rock that outcrops at the site and the two clay samples came from an arroyo bank

1500 feet south of the site. Tom Weiss collected these samples and fired tiles for analysis. He felt that this was the likely clay for pottery manufacture at the site and so these samples were examined with that possibility in mind.

Methods

Samples were cut from sherds to approximately 30x20 mm with a lapidary saw. The sherds and bedrock pieces were submitted to Quality Thin Sections, Tucson, for impregnation with epoxy, staining for potassium and plagioclase feldspar, and thin-sectioning parallel to the vessel wall. The fired clay tiles were processed by the University of Utah College of Mines and Earth Sciences Sample Preparation and Thin Section Laboratory, Salt Lake City.

Thin sections were scanned at 40x with a petrographic microscope to make general observations. They were then point counted at 100x to get a count of about 200 sand-size grains. Point counting is done to provide an estimate of the frequency of minerals in a rock or inclusions in pottery. The point count technique used (Gazzi and Dickinson method) was developed for analysis of sedimentary rocks. Sand-size or larger (>0.065 mm) minerals were counted as the mineral, whether free or as part of a rock fragment. Minerals smaller than sand-size, but part of a rock fragment, were counted as the rock type (i.e., volcanic, igneous plutonic, etc.). Mineral or rock fragments smaller than 0.065 mm were considered matrix and not counted. Minerals and rocks that could not be identified were counted as unknown (alteration or poor staining of feldspars are the primary reasons inclusions could not be identified). A single linear sample of about 100 points was counted to obtain the relative frequency of voids, sand-size rock, and matrix (silt and clay).

A couple of the sherd samples could not be point counted because of poor feldspar staining, but could be examined qualitatively. The Fitzmaurice Brown sherd thin section was examined sufficiently to determine that it was gabbro tempered, but it was not point counted.

Results

Table 19 provides point counts for the samples that could be counted and qualitative information on the three samples that were not. In general most of the inclusions in the pottery were plagioclase feldspar and quartz.

Figure 51 provides a ternary plot of quartz, alkali feldspar and plagioclase for the point counted samples. Also included are mean plots of the composition of two nearby granites, Prescott Granodiorite and Dells Granite. This plot provides a quick visual method of seeing similarities and differences in the main constituents of the samples.

The bedrock at Coyote Ruin was originally called Prescott Granodiorite (Krieger 1965), but has been recently classified as Cherry Tonalite (DeWitt et al. 2008). Gabbro occurs nearby, and one sherd was examined that had gabbro inclusions, although there was no way to identify local vs. nonlocal gabbro.

The bedrock sample from the site that was analyzed is actually close to what is typical for Prescott Granodiorite, indicating that there is a mixture of granitic rocks in the area. The clay samples, the two Prescott Gray sherds (#5 and #9), and the unknown brownware sherd (#8) are in the range of what would be classified as tonalite. The clay is found along a wash that appears to be in the drainage that runs along the west side of the site. Tom Weiss, who found the deposits, felt that one sample was particularly good for making pots (#4[3]), while the other was less good (#4[4]). The test tiles that he made had abundant rock inclusions and it was necessary to pick out the larger pieces before crushing, thus the density of inclusions in these fired samples is somewhat less than in the clay as excavated from the bank. The clay samples had 41 and 24% rock. The mineralogically similar Prescott Gray sherd had 44% rock, while the similar unknown brownware had 33%.

Table 19. Point count data.

Type	Prescott Gray				Prescott B/g			Fitz. Brn.	Unkn. Brn.	Bed-rock	Clay Tile	
Sample No.	4	5	6	9	1	2	3	7	8	8	4(3)	4(4)
Minerals												
Quartz	+	87	+	94	137	82	150		63	66	82	70
Alk. Feldspar	+	6	+	1	5	92	19		7	30	4	7
Plagioclase	+	93	+	114	32	35	33	+	125	109	121	123
Unk. Feldspar (b)		23		6	4	23	12		21			6
Muscovite					44	1	12			3		1
Biotite					2	2				11		
Unk. Mica		5							1			
Pyribole		1	+		1			+	3		4	2
Epidote	+	4	+			2	1		21	6	12	7
Hematite					3	3	1		1		1	15
Opaque	1		+	10	5	5	1	+	2	1		
Unknown (a)		22		5	16	22	11		30	8	4	8
Rocks												
Volcanic												
Plutonic		1	3		1	2					1	
Metamorphic		7							9		4	4
Sherd								+			9?	
Unk.		11			11		3		13		1	6
Relative Frequency of Components												
Voids	13	9	9	9	5	5	10		13	-	4	2
Matrix	45	60	48	49	51	56	51		53	-	59	74
Rock	42	31	44	42	44	39	39		33	-	41	24

Note: a) large numbers in this row generally indicates poor staining of feldspars

The bedrock showing in the wash just downstream from sample 4(4) and immediately upstream from sample 4(3) is a peculiar folded rock that appears to be a migmatite with raft structure which results from the introduction of later igneous material into an earlier (parent) rock that has broken free as "rafts" within the later material (Thorpe and Brown 1985: 146, Figure 12.5a). In this case, the rafts appear to be granite. The newer material seems to be made up of bands of pink feldspar and quartz (?) and bands of darker mineral (epidote?) and quartz (?). Without cutting a thin section of the rock, identification of the specific minerals present is not possible. A migmatite is a mixed igneous/metamorphic rock and its presence near the clay samples may explain the occurrence of sutured quartz (evidence of metamorphism) in the nearby clay and in some of the Coyote Ruin ceramic thin sections.

The three Prescott Black-on-gray sherds are dramatically different from the Prescott Gray and the local granite and clay. Two of the decorated bowl sherds (1 and 3) appear to have been tempered with a mica schist while the third decorated sherd falls into the range of a typical granite. A pattern has been observed in a number of Prescott Gray ware thin sections from a range of sites that the decorated sherds, bowls specifically, have a mineralogy distinct from the undecorated sherds (Christenson 2005c, 2006a, b). The possible source of the high quartz, high muscovite rock in these sherds has not been determined. The two high mica, high quartz Prescott Black-on-gray sherds from Coyote Ruin are the first clear indication of use of schist in tempering Prescott pottery.

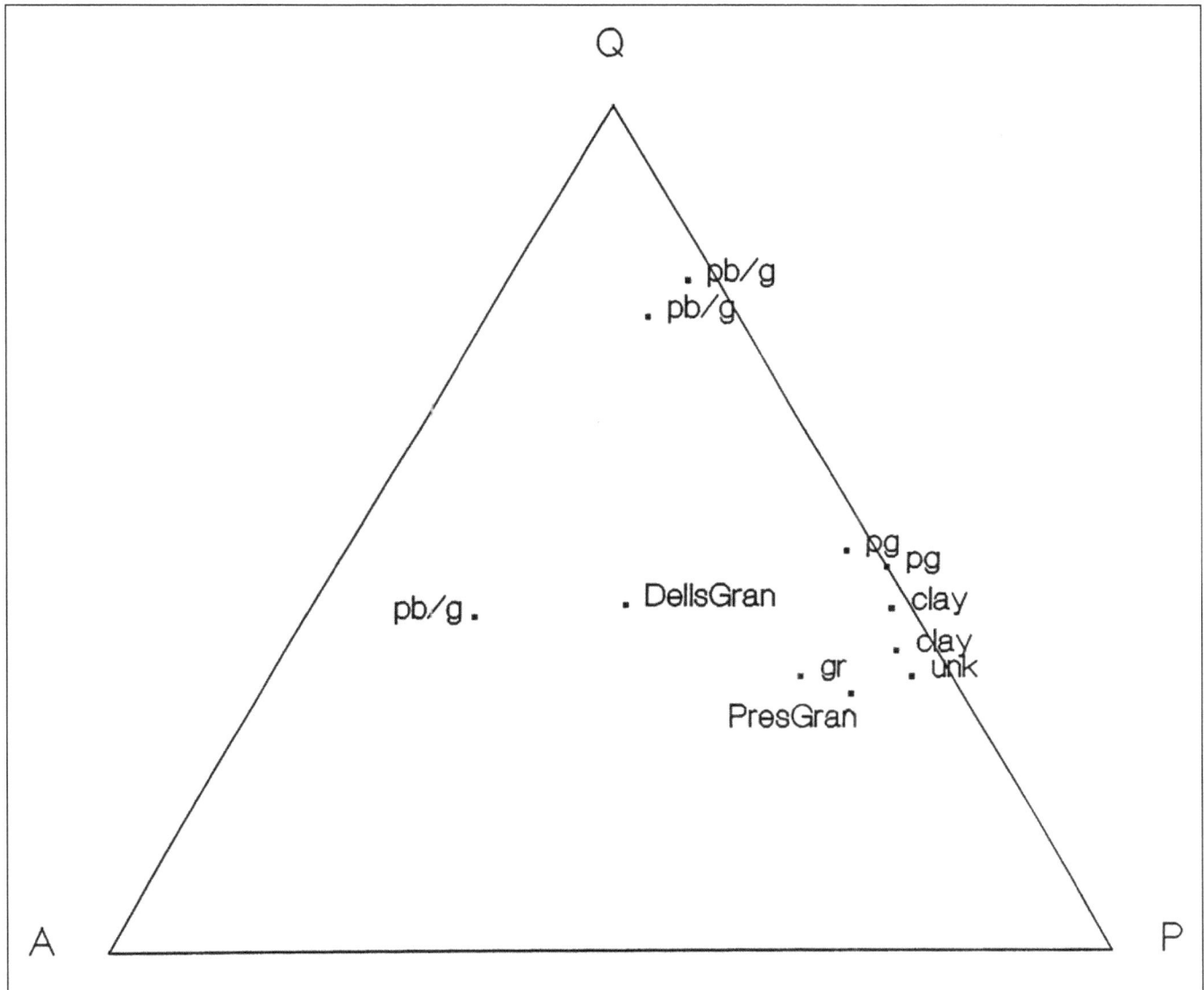

Figure 51. Ternary Diagram showing proportion of quartz (Q), alkali feldspar (A), and plagioclase (P) in 2 samples of clay, 1 sample of Dells Granite, 1 sample of Prescott Granodiorite, 1 sherd of unknown brown ware (unk), 3 sherds of Prescott Black-on-gray (pb/g), and 2 sherds of Prescott Gray (pg).

Conclusions

My previous petrographic work on Prescott Gray Ware has led me to suggest that its clays are nearly always non-alluvial, and its inclusions are either crushed and added granitic rock or are inclusions that would be expected in a residual clay (one derived from the disintegration of bedrock) (Christenson 2000:157, 160; 2003:147, 153). This conclusion was based upon the fact that Prescott Gray Ware almost never has basalt inclusions, whereas sand and clay samples collected in drainages always have abundant basalt. The clay samples collected near Coyote Ruin are the first not to have such inclusions and the similarity of these clay samples in mineralogy and inclusion density to some of the plainware sherds from the site provide our first evidence for the probable use of self-tempered alluvial clay to make Prescott Gray Ware. Previously collected sand and clay samples have generally been in middle or lower sections of drainages where contamination by basalt will always be present. It seems likely that clay samples higher up on drainages may be free from such contamination. The fact that the Coyote Ruin clay source comes from a mixed metamorphic/plutonic igneous rock is a geographic peculiarity and should not be used to argue that this is not Prescott Gray. That the inclusions in the pottery are different in ways only observable under high-powered microscopy should have no effect upon basic laboratory categorization, but it should give warning to those who want to use low-power microscopy to make conclusions about the nature of rock inclusions. Because the arroyo that the clay samples were obtained from is probably not 800 years old, we cannot say that the potters of Coyote Ruin obtained their clay from that specific spot, only that they appear to have obtained it from a clay source of similar geological origin.

The Prescott Black-on-gray result is a somewhat different issue, as it indicates use of a rock, mica schist, not associated with Prescott Gray Ware but with Hohokan Buff Ware and plainware (Gila variety). Recent work has indicated that decorated Prescott Gray Ware often has a distinctive high quartz, high muscovite rock, generally of plutonic igneous origin. Use of schist would be a logical way to obtain the high sparkle that seems to have been the goal on this type. That it was not used more often may simply relate to its relative rarity in the Prescott Region, although the high mica granite appears to be equally uncommon. At the moment this issue is one of high priority because this unique decorated pottery is what originally drew attention to Prescott as a distinctive culture area (Simmons 1931).

FIGURINES
Mary Spall

While found in many parts of the state, figurines were found in greatest concentration in two areas. The largest concentration was found at Snaketown, on the Gila River, and the other was found at Groom Creek, south of Prescott. Most of the Groom Creek figurines were excavated from burials and trash mounds in and around the dwellings, although some were found on the surface. What was their intended use? Children's toys, religious rites, and house blessings have all been suggested.

The temper or the mineral content and particle size of the material of which the article is made determines the place of origin of clay artifacts. Indications are that figurines were made and used primarily on the site. A total of 140 figurine/figurine fragments was found at Coyote Ruin. Table 20 summarizes the figurine/figurine fragments and their distribution. A complete inventory of the figurines is provided in Appendix B.

Table 20. Distribution of figurine/figurine fragments.

Item	Fragment	Animal	Human	Rod	Base	Total
Surface	6	6	6	11	0	29
Room 14	1	10	4	2	0	17
Room 17	0	1	0	0	0	1
Room 18	13	3	3	4	1	24
Room 19	3	5	1	1	0	10
Room 23	1	0	1	0	0	2
Room 38	0	1	0	2	0	3
Room 40	6	20	17	10	1	54
Total	30	46	32	30	2	140

Human forms were made of a cylinder of clay with one end flattened into a head and the other terminating either in a tapered point or an expanded base that allowed the figurine to stand. Heads were commonly snapped off at the neck (Figure 52). They were generally flat on top and flat or slightly concave in the rear. The clay was pinched into the shape of a nose or a pinch of clay was added to the center of the head to form a nose. Two heads found at Coyote Ruin have slit eyes, and one has a mouth. Four female torsos with breasts were also found. The other torso rods are extended, have no limbs, and no sex is indicated.

Various crude animal forms were represented and could only be assigned to the broad category of quadrupeds, owing partly to their fragmented condition, but mostly because of the lack of sufficient detail to assign them specific categories (Figure 53). Some of the quadrupeds have a molded perforation that extends entirely through the body, from chest through the hind end, indicating they were molded around a small twig. The hindquarters from other quadrupeds have a punctate indentation below their tail, presumably indicating an anus. Facial features present on the heads of a few of these animals are eyes, ears, noses, and slit or open mouths. The majority of the animals recovered had any number of appendages broken off, including legs, tails, ears, noses and heads. Others were broken in half across the midsection. Table 20 summarizes the figurine/figurine fragments and their distribution. A complete inventory of the figurines is provided in Appendix B.

Figure 52. Ceramic human figurine head fragments.

Figure 53. Ceramic animal figurines.

CHAPTER 6
LITHICS
Robert Beck

This chapter presents the classification and analyses of flaked stone (other than projectile points which are discussed in Chapter 7), and groundstone artifacts, and miscellaneous minerals and other stone artifacts recovered from the Coyote Ruin archaeological excavation by the Yavapai Chapter of the Arizona Archaeological Society in Prescott, Arizona.

The analyses were conducted by chapter members Bob Beck, Joanne Cline, Joanne Grossman, Betty Higgins and Ginger Johnson, with special assistance from Andrew L. Christenson. A number of attributes were recorded for each artifact including material, artifact class, artifact type, weight, dimension, and the presence or absence of cortex. Tables 21, 22, and 23 indicate where these artifacts were found. Stone pieces found to have no retouching, wear patterns, or other remarkable attributes were examined, weighed, and listed as debitage. These artifacts were returned to the site after recording, and are discussed at the end of this chapter in the debitage summary.

FLAKED STONE

A total of 214 flaked stone tools (other than projectile points) were examined (Table 21).

Cores

Cores are residual stones (either pebbles, cobbles or large flakes) from which flakes have been removed by percussion. The flakes are then retouched by hard or soft hammer percussion, or bone or antler tool pressure, to form projectile points, drills, knives and other artifacts. A core itself could be a preform that might be worked into a tool at a later time.

Twenty-two cores were recovered from the site. Fifteen were made of jasper, 4 were made of greenstone, and 1 each of diabase, chert, and obsidian.

Gravers

Gravers are usually short sharp flakes of harder crystalline stone that were probably used to perforate thin pieces of material such as deer hide, or make incisions into other materials such as ceramics, shell and argillite for decorative purposes. The broader base provides a holding place for the implement, which tapers dramatically into a sharp point.

Six gravers were found at Coyote Ruin, made of chalcedony, jasper, dacite, and obsidian. The dacite example had been retouched such that it could have been hafted.

Reamers

A reamer is a tool designed to enlarge a hole made by another tool or instrument. A reamer would be used in such materials as bone, shell, wood or ceramics, and is usually larger than the graver, with a bigger, wider flange as a contact point for the fingers, and a wide tapering body ending in a sharpened point.

Three obsidian reamers were found in different rooms. One had been heavily used, its flaking smoothed by abrasion or extensive contact. Its tip was extremely rounded, leading one to believe it could no longer serve its function, and had been discarded.

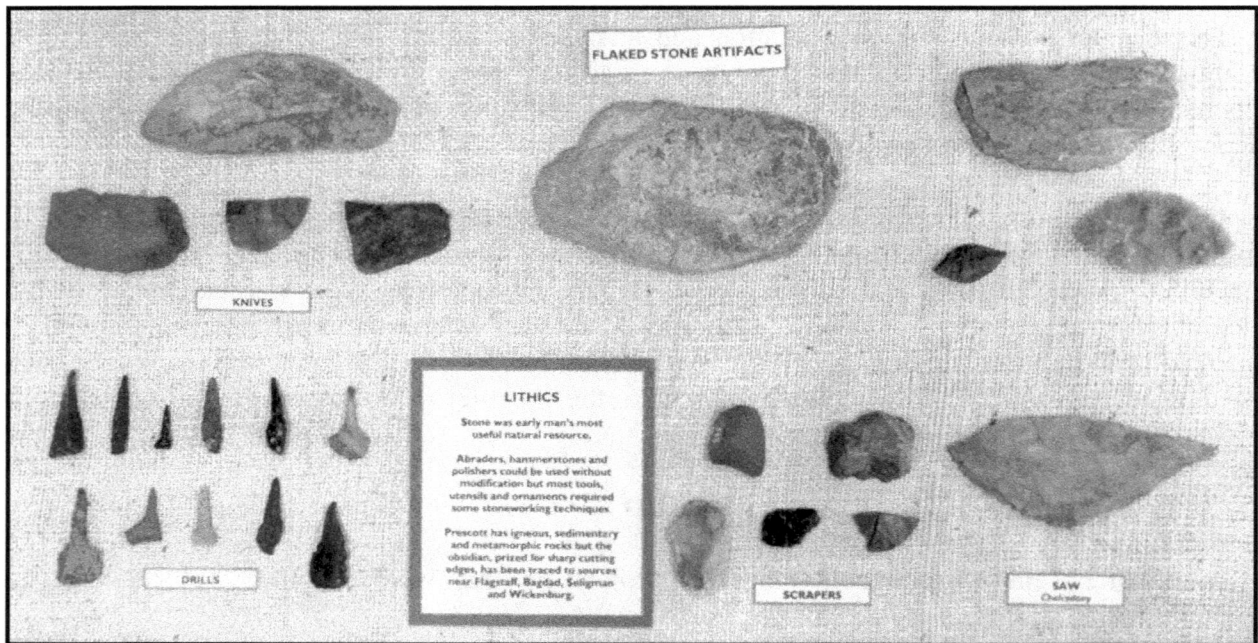

Figure 54. Representative chipped stone tools.

Drills

Generally, the same degree of intensive flaking that goes into projectile point manufacture extended to the making of flaked stone drills. The base or flange of most drills is wide, well shaped, and suitable for holding or hafting. The base tapers into a long shaft, often as thick as it is wide, for strength, ending in a point.

It has been suggested that drills with sharp points were used in creating holes in softer materials such as wood and ceramics, whereas drills with rounded points were used in the creation of holes in other stone such as argillite, or in the perforation of shell or bone.

The drills could be turned by hand using the base or flange, or with hafting that would allow the drill to be turned using the palms of the hand to rotate the shaft. Hafting would also allow the tool to be turned by a bow drill for drilling stones for beads, applying a relatively constant pressure.

Fifty-one drills of a wide assortment of sizes and materials were recovered, including 20 of jasper, 13 of chert, 11 of obsidian, 3 from greenstone, 2 from dacite, and 1 each of basalt and quartzite. In many other excavations in the Southwest, obsidian is the stone of choice for drills. However, the higher number of jasper drills at the Coyote Ruin may be accounted for by the availability of jasper at a quarry only a few miles northeast of the site.

Scrapers

Scrapers may be simply large, sharp flakes that were used with no further modification. Or such flakes may have been retouched to sharpen or shape them, often unifacially. There was no uniform shape, size, or material used in the manufacture of the Coyote Ruin scrapers. Scraping or smoothing wood, and removing fat, membranous tissues, and hair from animal skins would have been typical uses. Scrapers and knives may both have been multi-purpose tools, sometimes used interchangeably, depending on the task at hand.

Fifty-eight scrapers were recovered, 30 of jasper, 13 of obsidian, 8 of chert, 4 of greenstone, and 1 each of chalcedony, dacite, and slate. Again, perhaps because of the close proximity of jasper sources, jasper was the stone of choice, including many of the local Perkinsvillle variety. Two scrapers were notched in such a way as to suggest they may have been hafted.

Knives

Knives were made from flakes, or sometimes a bifacial core, retouched and shaped for a particular chore. Like many other flaked artifacts found at local sites, expedience was likely the inspiration for the manufacture of knives, although, of the 71 retained from this excavation, many have been retouched and flaked with an eye to artistry as well as proficiency.

A knife in its simplest form may be simply a flake, struck from a core with, perhaps, a single chore in mind. Studies have shown that the sharp edge of an unretouched flake, notably that of obsidian, can be as sharp, or sharper, than the finest steel scalpel. It has been noted that bifacial retouching of an edge reduces the actual sharpness of the blade, but gives the edge the ability to saw through muscle, tendon and vegetable products as well as cut or slice softer materials.

Fifteen varieties of stone were used in making the knives found at this site. Schist (phyllite) seemed to be the stone of choice for the 19 tabular knives whose size and shape suggest a use in harvesting agave, although one also retained traces of argillite on one surface. Generally smaller knives included 16 of jasper, 7 each of greenstone and chert, 5 of black obsidian, 1 of gray obsidian, 4 of slate, 3 of diabase, 2 each of chalcedony and basalt, and 1 each of dacite, diorite, shale, quartzite, and phyllite. One jasper knife was finished in the shape of a biconvex leaf and displayed a high degree of craftsmanship.

Hoes

Hoes were generally made from stone that occurred naturally in tabular pieces that were hammered and chipped into a shape that could be hand-held and utilized as a digging tool. The thicker edge would generally be held in the hand, and the thinner edge was chipped and ground to form the blade (or bit). Hoes are distinguished from tabular knives by the scratches and abrasions that are perpendicular to the bit, due to the constant entry and withdrawal from the soil.

Only two hoes were recovered from the site, both fine-grain basalt, and both show wear and polish on the blade. The larger hoe measured 14.6 by 11.5 by 1.1 cm, and weighed 353 grams. The other hoe was broken, and the remaining fragment measured 6.6 by 5.3 by 1.3 cm, and weighed just 56.8 grams.

Saw

One saw was recovered, manufactured from a flat sheet of chalcedony. It was remarkable in its similarity to modern day implements. Measuring 15.6 by 6.1 by 0.7 cm, the saw featured a serrated blade created by extremely selective chipping, and retained a sharpness that would readily cut through either wood or bone.

Table 21. Flaked stone artifact summary.

Provenience	Core	Drill	Graver	Hoe	Knife	Reamer	Saw	Scraper	Total
Room 1		1			2			3	6
Room 2		1			3			3	7
Room 4	1								1
Room 7		1							1
Room 11					1				1
Room 14	6	5	2	1	17		1	8	40
Room 17		4			3			2	9
Room 18	1	8	1		2	1		5	18
Room 19	6				8	1		2	17
Room 23	2				1			3	6
Room 38		2						5	7
Room 40	3	24	3	1	24	1		19	75
Test Pit	3								3
Surface		5			10			8	23
Total	22	51	6	2	71	3	1	58	214

GROUNDSTONE

A total of 212 groundstone items were examined (Table 22).

Hammerstones

It is this writer's contention that hammerstones belong in the groundstone category rather than flaked stone, although some hammerstones are exhausted cores that have been recycled. Hammerstones are generally expedient tools made from naturally found rocks, and fashioned by constant pounding in the breaking and shaping other artifacts. Flaking, chipping, and battering are generally limited to the edges and occur as the stone is utilized in the process of producing another artifact. A hammerstone is sometimes hafted but is most often a hand-held stone of hard material used to remove flakes from a core, or for other pounding functions, which result in the flaked, chipped and battered edges and surfaces of hammerstones. Occasionally the surface or edge of some other stone tool will be used as a hammerstone, such as a mano, or the poll or bit of a groundstone ax.

Seventy-six hammerstones were the dominant groundstone artifact recovered from Coyote Ruin. Of these, 46 were made of greenstone, most exhibiting two or more battered edges, and were examined and returned to the site; one had a cortex that included minute quartz crystal particles. The rest were made of quartzite (15), diabase (7), granite (3), fine-grain basalt (2), quartz (2), and dacite (1).

Three specimens showed evidence of being fire-scorched. One, of quartzite, weighing 1,134 grams, was battered only on one end. The other two, of greenstone, were battered in several areas. One of the granite hammerstones had pitted areas on two sides as well as being battered in several places; its function is unknown.

Manos

The term *mano* is taken from the Spanish word for hand. A mano is a stone that is held in the hand and used with an accompanying metate (grinding stone, netherstone) to mill or grind corn, beans and other materials for food use, or to grind minerals or softer rock types for use as paints or temper. Some manos show either prior use or a simultaneous use as a hammerstone, shaft straightener, pounder, or other tool, and sometimes show wear patterns at one or both ends and often on the sides. Many of the manos recovered from the Coyote Ruin were well used and well shaped. In addition, a number of broken manos were found in a variety of shapes and sizes. Many showed re-use, and it is easy to theorize that after being broken in use as a grinding tool they became the basic rock for any number of other uses, including pounder, nutting stone, abrader, or cooking stone.

A total of 49 complete manos was studied and recorded. Of those, 36 were basalt, 8 were granite, 4 sandstone, and 1 was quartzite. One of the basalt manos featured a heavy concentration of red material caught in the vesicles on one face. A comparison with ground argillite and hematite suggests that the red particles are argillite dust, and that argillite flakes were ground into jewelry blanks on the surface of the mano. In addition the mano had seen use as a hammerstone.

The smallest mano, made from sandstone, measured 6.0 by 5.2 by 2.8 cm, and weighed 110 grams. The largest mano, of basalt, weighed 3,089 grams.

One basalt mano measuring 10.4 by 5.5 by 8.6 cm, and weighing 594 grams, appeared to have served as a lapstone in addition to its duties in a metate.

Metates

The metate, along with its companion piece the mano, was probably one of the most utilized of all artifacts recovered from prehistoric Southwestern sites. The grinding of plants, seeds, and corn or maize into a meal, between two stones, mano and metate, was a daily function in the life of a prehistoric family and provided a basic foodstuff on days of shortage of other menu items such as animal proteins. Although there are several recognized types of metates found in the Southwest, only two, trough and basin, were recovered from this excavation at Coyote Ruin.

Figure 55. Representative groundstone tools.

Three complete trough metates and two fragments were recovered from the site. Two of the complete were made from vesicular basalt (see Figure 55), and one was made from sandstone. Weight ranged from around 9.9 to 11.3 kilograms (22+ to 25+ pounds). In a site as large as the Coyote Ruin it is unusual to find so few portable metates. Prior excavations and collecting may be part of the explanation for their scarcity (certainly, there are many metates reposing stolidly in the lawns and gardens of present-day Prescottonians). And a liberal use of grinding slicks by Coyote Ruin inhabitants may be a contributing factor: 36 grinding slicks on boulders (basin metates) and one bedrock mortar were recorded in various locations throughout the site (see Figure 29).

Additionally, what may be best described as a fragment of a small sandstone cup was found. It measured 4.3 by 2.3 by 2.4 cm, and weighted 41.0 grams. The depression was 1.3 cm deep.

Polishing Stones

A polishing stone is a smooth-surfaced, hard-textured rock used in polishing or smoothing some other object. The object being smoothed is altered by the harder surface of the polishing stone, creating a smoother and somewhat shinier surface. For instance a stone could be used to polish a clay pot before firing, closing minute surface orifices, making the surface smoother and less permeable.

Most of the polishing stones recovered from the site were water-polished pebbles put to use without any man-made changes. However, a few of the polishing stones showed deliberate modifications by the user. For example, several of the polishing stones made of sandstone were shaped to some degree by simply breaking the layered rock to a preferred size or shape.

Polishing stones were used on numerous artifacts, including axes, celts, wedges, jewelry and other stone items, as well as on wood, bone, and pottery. (Larger polishing stones used to smooth and compact clay and plaster floors and walls are discussed later under "Floor Polishers".)

Twenty-nine artifacts were identified as polishing stones. Although sandstone is used primarily for abrading purposes, 11 sandstone artifacts had fine-enough textures and smooth surfaces to be classified as polishers. Three presented unusual attributes. One was bifacial and partially burned; it weighed 45.8 grams. A second contained crystals of clear quartz embedded in the unpolished side of the stone that may have given it an aesthetic appeal for its owner. The third was intentionally grooved to serve a specific though unknown purpose.

Four other stone types were used as polishers. Nine were made from limestone, perhaps because of its texture or its ability to leave some of its "greasy" qualities on the surface of the item being polished. Four are unmodified fine-grained basalt pebbles. Four are granite, all exhibiting a high degree of use polish. One polishing stone made of slate, a softer stone than the others, showed a high degree of use on more than one surface.

Abraders

Many of the abrading stones found at Coyote Ruin were expedient tools selected for their abrasive qualities, and were seldom changed by the user to conform to any particular shape. To shape a tool or implement, abrading would begin with coarser stones, with the finer-grained stones being used in later stages to further shape the tool, or give a polish or sheen to its exterior or cutting surface. When working stone, pecking with a hammerstone would rough out the initial form of the desired product, followed by abrading to complete the shaping and surface finish.

Sixteen abraders were analyzed and recorded. Thirteen were sandstone of varying degrees of coarseness, the source of which is probably the Coconino Formation that lies to the east and northeast of the site. One of the sandstone abraders had hematite embedded in its surface. It is assumed that the hematite was ground and the powdered mineral collected for use as paint, be it on pottery, other items, or body paint. Of the remaining three abraders, two were basalt, and one was limestone.

Palettes

Palettes come in a variety of materials, shapes, degrees of workmanship and decoration. Substances of various colors (e.g. hematite, azurite, limonite, gypsum) could be ground and/or mixed on a palette's surface to make paint that could be used on ceramics, ceremonial objects, various other artifact types, and as body or facial embellishments.

Six palettes were recovered from Coyote Ruin. Three were made of sandstone, and one each of granite, greenstone, and limestone. None was decorated. Traces of hematite were found embedded in the mixing surfaces of two of the sandstone palettes (see Figure 55). One of the sandstone palettes measured 19 by 13 by 2.5 cm and weighed 896 grams. The greenstone palette measured 18.9 by 13.1 by 2.4 cm and weighed 1,344 grams.

Shaft Straighteners

This is a handstone with one or more grooves carved into its surface. The stone was heated, and a dampened length of cane *(Pragmites* sp.) was drawn through/across a groove in order to produce a straight arrowshaft. Arrowshaft straighteners not only allowed the straightening of a cane shaft, but smoothed the cane nodes/joints, and compressed any bulges in the cane wall, yielding a straight shaft of uniform diameter (Cosner 1951). Often the groove(s) aquire a high degree of polish and shine through long use.

A great majority of shaft straighteners found in the Southwest, and specifically in the Prescott area, were made from a vesicular basalt prevalent in the area. This is doubtless because basalt will tolerate repeated heatings and coolings without cracking, spalling, or disintegrating. Often a broken tool that had served another purpose, such as a mano, could/would be recycled into a shaft straightener. And indeed, of the five shaft straighteners recovered at Coyote Ruin, all were made of vesicular basalt, and of the five, three were reused mano fragment (see Figure 55).

Choppers

Choppers are usually made from cobbles of harder crystalline stones such as fine-grained basalt, quartzite, greenstone, or even granite, with a roughly percussion-flaked cutting edge. Without benefit of high-power magnification, it is impossible to ascertain whether a chopper was used as a food processor, or simply a cutting tool on non-food items (e.g. wood). Choppers often served a dual purpose, with the unflaked grip area serving as a hammerstone, as indicated by impact marks ("starring") in that area. And the flaked edge too sometimes served for precission pecking, when "sharpening" the grinding surface on a metate, or pecking grooves on tools such as axes, mauls, heavy two-handed manos, shaft straighteners, and pottery anvils. Such use eventually leads to a complete battering-down of the flaked areas, at which point the chopper has become, and would be identified as, a hammerstone.

Six choppers were recovered from the site. Five were made of greenstone, and one of quartzite. Neither had any remarkable characteristics.

Groundstone Axes

The groundstone ax was truly an all-purpose tool. It is thought that axes were used in a variety of tasks including chopping wood and cultivation. The poll, and the bit of a worn out ax, might be used as hammers in shaping mutates, or picks in mining. Hafting grooves on groundstone axes can go three-quarters around, completely around (full groove), and even spiral around the neck of the ax. Three-quarter grooved axes are typical of the Hohokam area. Full-grooved groundstone axes and chipped axes are typical of Anasazi areas. Spiral-grooved axes are a late prehistoric Rio Grande pueblo attribute. And double-bitted groundstone axes are typically associated with late prehistoric pueblo (including Salado) sites, and may have been made specifically as war clubs/axes.

Two basalt groundstone axes were found at the Coyote Ruin. One ax was three-quarter grooved and measured 14.5 by 5.9 by 6.2 cm. The other was fully grooved and measured 9.1 by 6.4 by 4.4 cm. Why more axes were not found is unknown.

Floor Polishers

Floor polishers or smoothers may be unmodified cobbles that, after extended use, exhibit one or more polished faces. Or cobbles might be minimally pecked to shape to make them easier to grip, or even their polishing surface(s). Size and weight of floor polishers tend, understandably, to be bigger and heavier than polishing stones used in pottery manufacture. As the name indicates, these tools are thought to have been used to polish or smooth clay or plaster after its application to floors and walls.

Five intact floor polishers were recovered, 2 of basalt, 2 of granite, and 1 of sandstone. A fragment of a sixth polisher, of basalt, was also found. Wear on one of the granite polishers suggests it may have also served as a hand-held abrader, or possibly as a netherstone; it weighed nearly six pounds (about 2.5 kilograms) and measured 14.4 by 11.4 by 10.8 cm.

Pottery Anvils

Pottery anvils are small stones pecked to a round outline, with two flat surfaces, and often a groove, pecked and ground into the edge to facilitate gripping. Stone anvils were used in the paddle-and-anvil method of shaping pottery, with the anvil held inside the wall of an unfired ceramic vessel while a wooden paddle was used to pat the clay into the proper thickness and smoothness.

Two anvils were found at the site. Both were made of granite and featured slightly convex surfaces on at least one face. One anvil had one highly polished surface, indicating a longer period of use, or duties other than, or in addition to, use as an anvil. Simmons found "pottery anvils" in one of the rooms north of Room 2; one may now be in the Arizona State Museum (see Appendix H).

Stone Balls

A great deal of conjecture accompanies the finding of stone balls in prehistoric sites. Sizes of the balls vary from one that might resemble a marble, to one with the dimensions of a small cannon ball. This alone suggests that the category of "stone balls" probably includes a number of unrelated artifact types. This is supported by ethnographic information for Southwestern tribes documenting that stone spheres of various sizes were used in games, as personal charms, and to imitate the sound of thunder when rolled across the floor of a kiva. Encased in rawhide, with a handle, they served as warclubs. Use as bola stones or slings stones are speculative. "Stone balls" can range from small, unmodified pebbles or concretions, to fist-sized cobbles or rocks that were pecked and ground to shape, to the occasional larger ball, or highly polished specimen.

Two stone balls were recovered at Coyote Ruin. Both were small and not highly finished. One is fine-grained basalt and measured 3.3 cm in diameter, with a weight of only 40.5 grams. The other is made of vesicular basalt/scoria, 4.3 cm in diameter, with a weight of 53.3 grams.

Pestles

Pestles were commonly used with mortars to grind wild seeds and nuts for foodstuffs. With or without a mortar, pestles could be employed to pulverize minerals for paint, and clay, stone and sherds for use in pottery making. Or any need that required crushing, grinding, or hammering. In some cases, a naturally elongate stone could be used without modification, or further shaped by pecking and abrading.

Six pestles or pestle-like tools were found at Coyote Ruin. Two were made of basalt. One was made of limestone, and showed use as both a mano and pestle. Three others were made of granite, one of which was bell-shaped.

Floor Supports

Floor supports are generally large rectangular slabs, made of locally available tabular stone. A semicircular or vee-shaped notch was generally chipped or hammered into one end to provide a secure seat for the wooden floor beam that was to be set into/atop it. Numerous floor beam supports have been recovered in other Prescott-area excavations, most notably at the Fitzmaurice Ruin.

Two floor supports were recovered from Coyote Ruin. One basalt support measured 23.5 by 11.7 by 10 cm, and weighed 9.5 pounds (4.3 kilograms). The second measured 24.3 by 12.2 by 11.0 cm, and weighed 12.3 pounds (5.6 kilograms).

Spindle Whorls

Thin discs, chipped and ground to a circular shape from sherds or tabular stones, centrally perforated, and sometimes with the upper and lower faces smoothed by grinding, are thought to have been the "flywheel" weights on the wooden spindles used in the spinning of cotton and agave thread. Conceivably they could have also been used on bow drills and fire-starters.

One slate spindle whorl fragment was recovered. It measured 5.2 by 2.7 by 0.36 cm, and was originally about 5.2 cm in diameter. The central perforation had been drilled biconically.

Unknown "Tool"

One large sandstone item was recovered and thought to be a lapstone or possibly a jar cover. The piece measured 28.5 by 18.5 by 6.6 cm, and had been chipped and pecked to shape.

Table 22. Groundstone artifact summary.

Item	Room 1	1a	2	5	6	7	8	12	14	17	18	19	20	23	27	28	40	Sur	n/p	Total
Abrader			4	1	1		1				1	1		1			4	1	1	16
Anvil																	2			2
Axe												2								2
Chopper					1					2							3			6
Floor Polish														1			3*	1		5
Floor Support											1						1			2
Hammerstone			4						7	7	4	14	1	2	1	2	24	5	5	76
Mano	2		5			1	1		2	1	4	2		6			25			49
Metate		1	1														3			5
Palette			1	1	2					1							1			6
Pestle			3			1								1					1	6
Polishing Stone	1					3			3	2	5	1					9	5		29
Shaft Straightener											1						4			5
Spindle Whorl																	1			1
Stone Ball											1						1			2
Total	3	1	18	2	4	5	1	1	12	13	19	18	1	11	1	2	81	12	7	212

Notes: *Fragment found in trash mound fill above Room 40

MINERALS, PIGMENTS, AND OTHER STONES

A total of 115 semiprecious gem and mineral items relating to ornamental use, charms or amulets, and pigments for body painting or decorating utensils or tools were examined (Table 23).

Pigments: Hematite, Azurite, Kaolin

Pigments, from crushing or abrading of certain minerals and stones, were probably used for body and facial ornamentation, for paint in pottery manufacture, and on ceremonial paraphernalia. Pigments found at the Coyote Ruin include red hematite (7 pieces), blue azurite (5), and white kaolin (1). Kaolin is quite soft and requires little preparation. The hematite and azurite would have to have been pulverized or ground to powder prior to mixing with water or a binder. Some of the azurite found was in the form of ground powder in Room 18.

Argillite Artifacts

Argillite is a reddish, soft, claylike stone available at a quarry located approximately 15 miles north of Coyote Ruin, and provided the raw material for many of the ornaments found at the site. It is probable that the argillite, either in raw pieces or as finished products, was an important export trade item for the local inhabitants.

Twenty-seven objects made from argillite were found: 11 pendants, 6 pendant blanks, 7 worked pieces, 2 fragments of a small bowl, and half of a smoking pipe or sucking tube. The pendants were worked into various geometric shapes and, for the most part, were carefully shaped and polished (Figure 56). One less well-made pendant showed signs of being burned.

The small bowl was expertly carved, but exhibited no decorations or incised marks. It measures 5.7 by 4.4 by 0.7 cm, and weighs 41.8 grams.

The most remarkable argillite artifact found was an intact half portion of what was either a two-piece smoking pipe, or a shaman's "sucking tube" (Figure 56). It measures 4.95 cm long and 1.80 by 1.80 cm, and weighs 13.1 grams. The piece was grooved in the center lengthwise and shows a high degree of polish and carefull workmanship. In use, a matching half would have been added and the two pieces would have been held together, perhaps by twine, sinew or pitch. It would have had the appearance of a hollow red stone cigar.

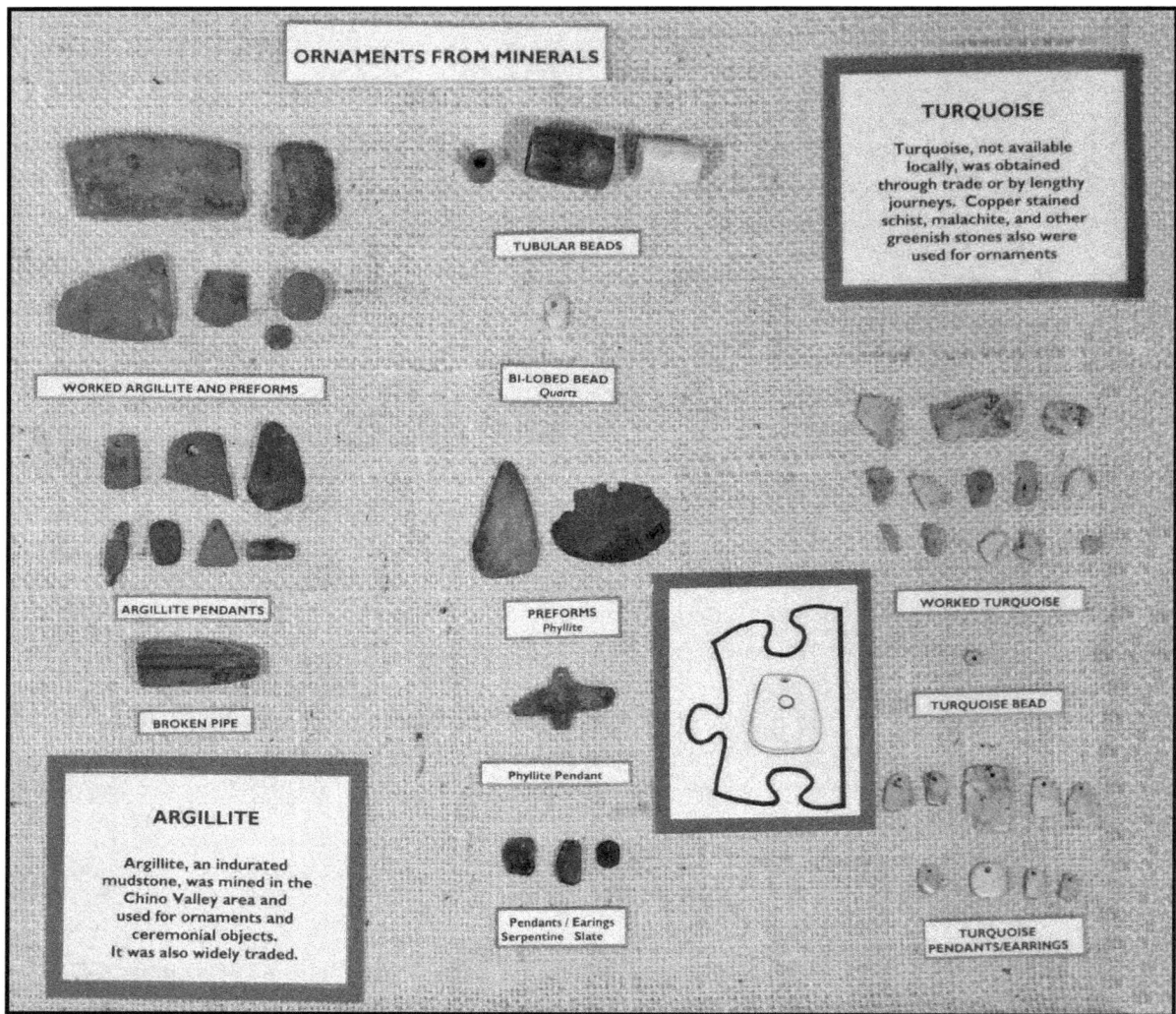

Figure 56. Stone ornaments.

Basalt Nodule

One fine-grained basalt nodule was recovered, shaped somewhat like a "Figure 8". It shows man-made polish and may have been a charm or amulet. It measures 7.7 by 4.8 by 3.0 cm.

Calcite Crystal

One calcite crystal was recovered at Coyote Ruin.

Cave Formation

One piece of a siliceous rock formation from a cave was found in Room 2.

Limestone Bead

One fairly large limestone bead was found, 2.43 cm in diameter. It is wedge-shaped in cross-section, measuring 1.55 cm thick on the wide side, and 0.40 cm thick on the narrow edge.

Marekanites

Three unworked marekanites (obsidian nodules/"Apache tears") were found.

Phyllite Pendants

Three pieces of phyllite were found, two pendants and a preform (Figure 56). Most remarkable was a bird-shaped pendant with drilled dots along the wings and tail. It measures 4.10 by 2.48 by 0.25 cm and weighs 0.6 grams. The other pendant was ovoid in shape, with a reamed hole for string or thong. It measures 4.73 by 3.15 by 0.023 cm.

Quartz Crystals

Five quartz crystals were found; all may have been personal items, carried by the owners as charms or objects of wonder. All are similar in appearance and size.

One bilobed quartz bead measures 1.50 by 0.57 by 0 .84 cm, and weighs 0.07 grams (Figure 56).

Schist Artifact

One piece of worked schist was recovered at Coyote Ruin.

Serpentine Artifacts

One pendant (Figure 56), and one unclassified ornament were recovered at Coyote Ruin.

Slate Artifacts

Eight artifacts of slate were recovered (Figure 56): 1 earring, 1 pendant, 1 polisher, 1 disk-like item, and 4 other ornament/amulet items. The polisher appeared to have been utilized for more than one chore. It measures 6.5 by 1.9 by 1.5 cm, and one end had been ground down, either by use or to alter its shape. The suspension hole in the solitary pendant was drilled from one side only.

Steatite Bead

One biconically-drilled, polished steatite bead was found, measuring 3.3 by 2.9 by 0.2 cm.

Turquoise

It appears that turquoise came into the Coyote Ruin as finished pieces rather than as raw material. There is no evidence at the site of the manufacture of jewelry from raw turquoise, although broken jewelry would almost certainly have been repaired or reworked. Colors of the recovered turquoise items ranged from a very deep blue to a dark green, suggesting origins at multiple sources. Some pieces included a lot of matrix, while others had very little.

Forty-seven artifacts were recovered: 14 pendants (drop or tab shaped), 2 earrings, 5 beads, 1 amulet, 23 worked (or reworked) fragments, 1 pendant or earring blank, and 1 bead blank (Figure 56). All pieces which had been drilled had biconical holes.

Table 23. Minerals, pigments, and other stone artifact summary.

Material	Surface	No Prov.	Rm 2	Rm 14	Rm 17	Rm 18	Rm 38	Rm 40
Argillite		25			1 pipe			1
Azurite	1					3	1	
Basalt		1						
Calcite Crystal		1						
Cave Formation			1					
Hematite		3						4
Kaolin		1						
Limestone						1		
Marekanites		3						
Phyllite						1		2
Quartz			1	3				2
Schist		1						
Serpentine	1							1
Slate		8						
Steatite		1						
Turquoise		47						

Debitage Summary

Debitage, or the flakes and shatter left from making or retouching flaked stone tools, made up the majority of lithic material recovered from the site. A total of 12, 394 flakes were recovered. Of these 30.6% (3,794) were jasper, 21.5% (2,676) were greenstone, 16.6% (2,002) were black obsidian, 11.7% (1,457) were diabase, 5.5% (687) were quartzite, 3.2% (399) were gray obsidian, and 2.8% (349) were chert. The remaining 8.1% included agate, andacite, banded iron, breccia, chalcedony, dacite, diorite, gabbro, gneiss, granite, phyllite, quartz, sandstone and schist. Over 27% of the debitage came from Room 18 (3,444) and 25% from Room 40 (3,160). The remainder was collected from the other rooms, test pits, and surface collections.

Andrew L. Christenson collected some volcanic rock samples from the Mingus Mountain area and submitted them along with a number of volcanic artifacts from the site for XRDF analysis. The results of that analysis are given in Appendix C.

SUMMARY

In conclusion, the types of lithic material recovered from the Coyote Ruin Site are consistent with the lithic material found at other sites in the Prescott Culture area. The proportions of specific lithic materials vary from site to site. In the case of Coyote Ruin, jasper was the predominant material, as it is in most sites. However, an unusual amount of greenstone artifacts was found. From site to site there are also variances in the type of tools. A relatively large number of manos (15 in two rooms) was found at the Neural Site. An unusual number of axes was found at Crest Ruin in the Matli Ranch complex. The Sundown Site had a high concentration of argillite artifacts. At the two Las Vegas Ranch sites 85 black obsidian nodules were recovered, and so the list goes. This possible evidence of specialization among the Prescott Culture sites, with possible trading among them, would be a good topic for further investigation.

CHAPTER 7
PROJECTILE POINTS
Andrew L. Christenson

This chapter includes discussion of completed projectile points and bifaces and fragments that could be broken or unfinished points. The focus is upon how these artifacts might have been used.

METHODS

Most bifaces and biface fragments from the excavation were examined. These artifacts were categorized as projectile points by size (in general, bifaces less than 40 mm in length are most likely to be projectile points), blade morphology (e.g., narrow, parallel-sided blades are more likely to be drills), wear (in general, projectile points will not have wear), or breakage. In regard to the latter, the tips of all of the specimens were examined for evidence of impact damage, which is the best evidence of use as projectile points. Experiments with projectile points show that impact damage of stemmed points is most common at the base or stem (Flenniken and Raymond 1986:607), but such damage is not unique to projectile use, whereas distinctive impact damage of the tip usually is. A rare type of impact damage called "spin-off fracture" was noted on two of the Room 18 points. This breakage occurs when a point snaps upon entering the prey and the fragment that is still attached to the shaft fractures as it hits the detached piece or bone (Huckell 1982:12; Nuzhnyi 1990:115).

The analysis below is primarily on the complete point or basal fragments where some measurements could be taken. Tip or blade fragments are tabulated, but not discussed. Items judged to be incomplete or broken during manufacture were tabulated, but are not included in the typological analysis.

A standardized projectile point analysis form was used. Measurements included length, width, thickness, weight, stem length, and neck width. Other information recorded included provenience, location of greatest width, blade outline, presence of serration, base shape, basal thinning (unifacial or bifacial), raw material, breakage, wear, evidence of reuse, and presence of cortex or original flake surfaces.

Measurements were made with a dial caliper. Breakage and wear was examined under a 10-30x binocular microscope. Unfortunately, the best photograph of the Coyote Ruin points that we have was taken when a sample of them was on display at the Smoki Museum. A somewhat fuzzy enlargement of this photo is shown in Figure 57. The rows have been numbered on the photo and if individual points are referred to they will be designated alphabetically from left to right.

TYPES

Although each biface is unique in some sense, there are size and morphological differences between groups of bifaces that suggest fairly well bounded categories. There is also evidence that constraints were operating to keep variation within some of these groups within a range.

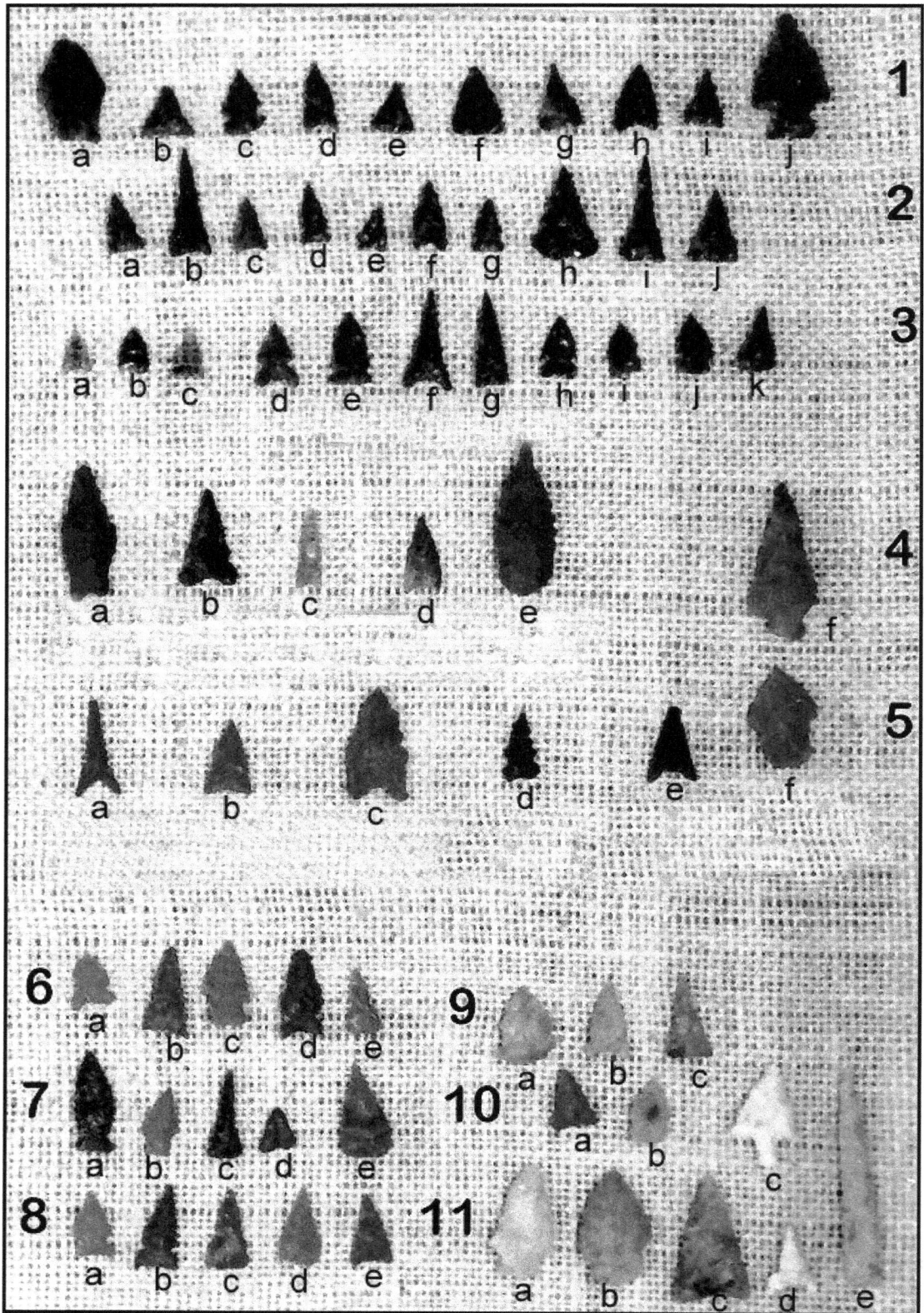

Figure 57. Selected points. 1a is 30 mm long. A few of these artifacts were classified as bifaces and were not included in the projectile point analysis.

Four basic categories were created - small triangular points presumed to be arrowpoints; small stemmed points presumed to be arrowpoints, large points that could be arrowpoints, and large points that are probably dartpoints. Arrowpoints were distinguished from atlatl dartpoints on the basis of size. Generally there is a break in weight at about 1 gram and in neck width at about 10 mm (Figure 58). Neck width is a good measure of the diameter of the shaft to which a point was hafted, as it is generally close to or slightly larger than the shaft (Thomas 1978). These are, of course not absolute barriers; one can have heavy arrowpoints or arrows with thick shafts, but aerodynamics and penetration requirements put fairly strong constraints on the size of arrowpoints (Christenson 1986a).

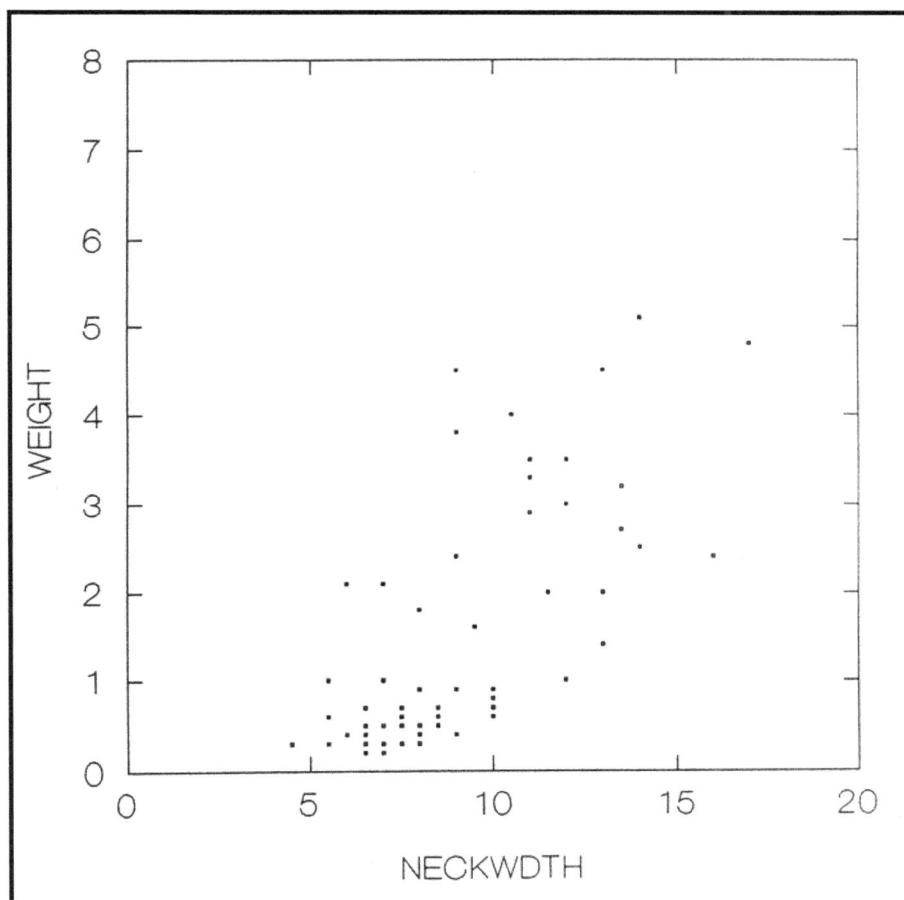

Figure 58. Plot of weight (grams) and neck width (millimeters) for complete points.

Tables 24-27 provide basic counts and measurements for all of the artifacts included in this analysis.

Small Triangular Arrowpoints

Unnotched

The most common point was an unnotched triangular point about 19 mm long, 12 mm wide and weighing 0.6 gram (Figure 57, includes many of the points in rows 1-3). Base shape is generally concave (52%) or straight (31%) with a few that are convex (8%). One example has a notched base. A little over one-half of these points are lightly to heavily serrated. Almost all of these points are obsidian (91%).

Table 24. Projectile point raw material by type. "BV" is black volcanic.

Type	Obsid.	Sub. BV	Fine BV	Chert	Chalced.	Jasper	Quartz	Quartzite	Unkn.	Total
1 Cottonwood Triangular	105	4	1	3	1	1	0	0	1	116
2 Pueblo Side Notched	38	1	1	3	0	0	0	0	1	44
3 Sm expanding stem	5	0	0	1	0	0	0	0	0	6
4 Sm. parallel/contracting Stem	2	0	1	0	0	0	0	0	0	3
5 Sm. leaf-shaped flake	2	0	0	0	0	0	0	0	0	2
6 Cohonina	0	0	0	1	0	0	0	0	0	1
7 Tularosa Corner Notched	0	0	3	1	1	0	0	0	0	5
8 Dolores Cluster	0	0	0	3	0	0	0	0	0	3
9 Indet. lg. arrowpoint	1	0	0	1	0	0	0	0	0	2
10 Pinto Cluster	2	2	0	1	0	0	0	0	0	5
11 Gypsum	0	0	1	0	0	0	0	1	0	2
12 Lg. Contracting stem/ unstemmed	0	0	2	2	0	1	0	0	0	5
13 Lg. triangular	6	0	0	1	0	0	0	0	0	7
14 Lg. Side notched	1	0	1	1	0	0	1	0	0	4
15 Lg. Expanding stem	2	0	0	3	2	0	0	0	0	7
16 Indet. Lg.	3	0	0	1	0	0	0	0	0	4
Total	167	7	10	22	4	2	1	1	2	216

Table 25. Point/biface fragments and unfinished points by provenience and raw material. "fbv" is fine black volcanic.

Part	Tip			Blade or Other			Unfinished		
Material Provenience	Obsid.	Chert	Other	Obsid.	Chert	Other	Obsid.	Chert	Other
Surface	2		chalced.			chal.; fbv; quartz	2		
2		2					2		
14	4	2	unkn.	3	1		6		chal.
18	12		fbv	5	2		13	1	
19	4	1		4			1	1	
23				1			1		
28	1			1					
34							1		
38				2			2		
40	8	1		2		chal.; jasper	19	2	fbv (2); unkn.
Total	31	6	3	18	3	5	47	4	4

Table 26. Point measurements by type.

Type	Length (mm)	Width (mm)	Thickness (mm)	Weight (g)	Neck Width (mm)	n (a)	Photo, Fig.
1 Cottonwood Triangular	19.0 +/- 4.5	12.2 +/- 2.1	3.1 +/- 0.8	0.57 +/- 0.25	-	88	1b, d-i; 2c, e; 3g; 6b; 8c-e; 9c
2 Pueblo Side Notched	18.3 +/- 3.5	11.3 +/- 1.8	3.0 +/- 0.7	0.50 +/- 0.21	7.8 +/- 1.3	32	2a, g; 3d, h; 6a; 8a-b; 9b; 10a
3 Sm. expanding stem	22.2 +/- 4.1	10.8 +/- 1.2	3.0 +/- 0.5	0.63 +/- 0.27	6.9 +/- 1.2	5	7b
4 Sm. Parallel/ contracting Stem	23.0	11.0 +/- 0.0	3.3 +/- 0.6	1.0	5.3 +/- 0.3	1	
5 Sm leaf-shaped flake	19.5 +/- 3.5	11.0 +/- 4.2	2.5 +/- 0.7	0.50 +/- 0.28	-	2	
6 Cohonina	59.0	11.0	4.0	2.9	-	1	11e
7 Tularosa Corner Notched	29.0 +/- 2.6	16.5 +/- 3.1	5.4 +/- 0.9	2.86 +/- 1.31	9.2 +/- 0.9	3	
8 Dolores Cluster	28.0	21.0 +/- 2.0	5.0 +/- 0.0	2.1	7.0 +/- 1.0	1	
10 Pinto Cluster	31.2 +/- 4.2	17.8 +/- 1.1	5.3 +/- 0.9	2.58 +/- 0.48	13.5 +/- 1.8	4	1a; 4a; 5c
11 Gypsum	33.0	17.5 +/- 0.7	5.5 +/- 0.7	3.40 +/- 0.57	10.5 +/- 2.1	1	
12 Lg. Contracting stem/ unstemmed	41.7 +/- 14.5	18.4 +/- 2.1	7.0 +/- 1.5	4.67 +/- 2.13	17.0	1	4e
13 Lg. triangular	28.8 +/- 5.1	14.6 +/- 3.4	4.8 +/- 0.6	1.67 +/- 0.68	-	6	11c
14 Lg. Side notched	23.7 +/- 2.5	17.0 +/- 0.0	4.2 +/- 0.6	1.47 +/- 0.50	12.0 +/- 0.7	2	
15 Lg. Expanding stem	30.8 +/- 2.7	19.1 +/- 2.3	6.3 +/- 1.5	3.41 +/- 1.24	12.4 +/- 1.3	6	1j; 5f; 11b

Note: (a) smallest number for which a value has been calculated for a type

Table 27. Point attributes by type. Percentages calculated for samples above 20.

Type	Serration (%)	Cortex (%)	Impact Fracture	Use Wear
1 Cottonwood Triangular	60/110 (55)	52/114 (46)	8	2
2 Pueblo Side Notched	26/41 (63)	18/44 (41)	4	2
3 Sm. expanding stem	3/6	4/6		
4 Sm. Parallel/contracting Stem	2/2	2/3		
5 Sm. leaf-shaped flake	1/1	2/2		
6 Cohonina	1/1	0/1		
7 Tularosa Corner Notched	4/5	1/5		
8 Dolores Cluster	1/3	0/3	1	
9 Indet. lg. arrowpoint	½	1/2		
10 Pinto Cluster	3/5	1/5	1	
11 Gypsum	2/2	1/2		
12 Lg. Contracting stem/unstemmed	4/4	0/5		
13 Lg. triangular	6/7	3/7	1	
14 Lg. Side notched	1/3	1/4		
15 Lg. Expanding stem	3/7	1/7		2
16 Indet. Lg.	½	0/4		

This category falls into the diverse type called Cottonwood Triangular (Justice 2002:261-67). Although some of them may be preforms for side-notched points, the bulk of them can be considered the day-to-day point used on arrows. Hafting would have been with mastic, sinew wrapping, or both. Examples of how the Southern Paiute hafted such points can be seen in Fowler and Matley (1979:Figure 52-53).

Notched

This category is similar to the above except that there are side notches and, in one case, a basal notch (Figure 57, 1c, 3d, 8a-b). These points are about 18 mm long and 11 mm wide and weigh 0.5 gram. Base shape is mostly concave (65%), with ears sometimes being present on the corner of the base (Figure 57, 3d). Serration is common on notched points (63%) and it tends to be heavier than on the unnotched triangular points. As with the unnotched, most of the notched points are of obsidian (87%). This group of points falls into the diverse category called Pueblo Side Notched (Justice 2002:289-302). If they were found farther to the west they would be called Desert Side Notched. A couple of these points (e.g., Figure 57, 3d) would now be called Buck Taylor Notched (Justice 2002: 313-314, Fig. 34.42-46), a type that I was not aware of at the time this analysis was done. Justice (2002: 314) suggested that the type was used by the Yavapai and Walapai and puts a ca. A.D. 1400 to 1800 date on the type. The presence of the type at Coyote Ruin indicates that the type goes back at least into the early 14th century.

These points would have been hafted to an arrow shaft using sinew. Examples of how the Southern Paiute hafted such points can be seen in Fowler and Matley (1979:Figure 52-53). The bulk of the triangular points, whether notched or not, were used as tips on arrows for hunting or warfare. One suggested pattern is that stone tipped arrows were used for larger game (deer, antelope), while smaller game would normally have been hunted with wood-tipped arrows (Ellis 1997:41-45). Another possible pattern is that thinner points were used for large game and the fatter points were to reduce breakage in the hunting of small game (Neusius and Phagan 1983). A third suggested pattern is that larger (wider) points were used on larger shafts for close shots and smaller (narrower) points for longer shots (Nelson 1986:173). Unfortunately our knowledge of the relationship of point form, weapon system, and hunting strategy is poor. The question of use of points in warfare will be discussed later.

The issue of whether some of these points are "toys" made for children or by children is not answerable. Just as small, crude pots probably represent the work of potters-in-training, so crude points could be in part the production of young knappers. At Head-Smashed-In Buffalo Jump in Alberta, toy points were defined by small size and poor manufacture (Dawe 1997).

The question of possible differences between the notched and unnotched points is also of interest. In a recent cross-cultural study of North American triangular arrowpoints, I was unable to find a clear difference in the use of notched and unnotched varieties (Christenson 1997c; see Ahler 1992:46-47). Notched points would provide secure hafting and reduce seizing interference during penetration, but many groups seem to have happily used both forms. The "Intersite Comparisons" section below notes that there may in fact be some cultural differences of this trait in Arizona.

Small Nontriangular Stemmed Points

A few smaller nontriangular points are present in the collection. They are in the same neck width and weight range as the triangular points, but have blade, stem or base shapes distinctive enough to be treated separately.

Expanding Stemmed (Figure 57, 7b)

Six points have stems 4 to 7 mm long that expand somewhat from the neck to the base and, except in one case, have a base width less than the shoulder width.

Three long (20+ mm), narrow (11 mm) points have distinct shoulders and narrow, parallel or contracting stems.

Leaf-shaped Flake Points

Two obsidian points have contracting stems with slightly concave bases. Both have original flake surfaces on both faces.

Large Probable Arrowpoints

There are several points, that although larger in width or weight than the previous points, have neck widths in the range that may represent arrowpoints. The neck width is a significant value because it is the largest diameter of the shaft or foreshaft that the point could be securely hafted to. On a sample of hafted arrowpoints and dart points in museums, Thomas found that the arrow foreshafts averaged 7.1 mm in diameter, while dart foreshafts were 10.0 mm (Thomas 1978:469). Point neck widths on the same sample of hafted points averaged about 3 mm wider than the foreshaft. In a study that expanded the sample of hafted dart points, Shott (1997) found a similar difference, although he concluded that shoulder width (basically the same as width in this analysis) was the best single measure to differentiate arrowpoints (14 mm) from dart points (23 mm). Any method of classifying dart or arrowpoints by one or more measures will always misclassify more dart points (15-23%) than arrowpoints (10%) (Schott 1997:Table 3), particularly because the number of hafted dart points to measure is minuscule. Perhaps this indicates that arrowpoints are subject to more stringent size constraints than dartpoints. Darts and arrows differ in aerodynamics and in how they kill prey and the general difference in size between these two projectile types is a result of these functional differences (Christenson 1986a, b, 1987).

Tularosa Corner Notched

Five points were independently classified together on the basis of their corner notched shape before examining the neck width (Figure 57, 4f). Tularosa is a new type defined by Justice (2002:216-226) on the basis of analysis of a large number of points across the Southwest. Interestingly, these points are suggested to date across the period when the atlatl was replaced by the bow and arrow (ca. 100 B.C. to A.D. 700-900; Justice 2002:217). This is not the place to consider how such a change could occur without major change in projectile point types. A more relevant issue is how such points got to the site (see below). Three of these points are fine-grained black volcanic, one is chalcedony, and one is brown chert.

Dolores Cluster

Three of the larger arrowpoints were barbed with either straight or expanding stems and appear to fall into the Dolores Cluster (Justice 2002:240-246) that includes Dolores Straight Stem and Dolores Expanding Stem (Figure 57, 10c). These points generally date to the Pueblo I period (A.D. 700-900) (Justice 2002:240), although they occur as late as A.D. 1000 on Black Mesa (Christenson 1987). All of these examples are of chert.

Cohonina

One point, although longer and heavier than the typical arrowpoint, is only 11 mm wide (Figure 57, 11e). This may be an unusually long Cohonina point (Justice 2002:270-272), although it is made of chert rather than the usual obsidian.

Indeterminate

Two points in this category are broken at the neck and cannot be further classified.

Large Probable Dartpoints

This category includes all points with neck width greater than 10.5 mm, as well as points greater than 18 mm wide, or greater than 1.1 gram in weight. Certainly it is not impossible that some of these were used to tip arrows, but there is a break in the size distribution of points that implies that these points are distinctive (Figure 58). Most of these points do not fall into named types.

Pinto Cluster

Four large points with characteristic bifurcated bases fit the narrow definition of the type fairly well (Justice 2002:138-142) (Figure 57, 1a, 4a, 5c, f). Formby (1986) included a wide range of shapes in his definition of Pinto and one of the points from Coyote Ruin has a broad, slightly contracting stem that is similar to one of his Pinto sub-types (1986: Figure 2g). This is a Middle Archaic type dating from ca. 6000-5000 B.C. until 3000 B.C. or after.

Gypsum

This type is a contracting stem point (Justice 2002:186-194). It dates to the Late Archaic from 2000-800 B.C. Both of the Coyote Ruin examples came from Room 40 with one being fine-grained black volcanic and one pink quartzite.

Contracting Stem/Unstemmed

Several points have either no shoulders or subtle shoulders, and are of a size more likely to be dart than arrowpoints. One biface (not illustrated) is perfectly symmetrical so that the base and tip can not be distinguished. This sometimes happens with heavily reworked Gypsum points (e.g., Justice 2002:Figure 24.18).

Large Triangular

Seven points are the right shape but outside the weight range of Cottonwood Triangular points (Figure 57, 11c).

Large Side-notched

All of these have neck widths in the 11.5 to 13 mm range. One of these is a light point with a large neck width and original flake surfaces on both faces which could simply be a large Pueblo Side Notched (Figure 57, 4b).

Large Expanding Stem

This category includes a variety of base and shoulder forms that do not clearly fit into any named type (Figure 57, 1j, 11b).

Indeterminate.

Three blade fragments have neck widths of 11 mm or more but are not further classifiable.

TECHNOLOGY

Claims have been made that chipped stone projectile point manufacture was predominantly done by specialists (Seeman 1985:16). This statement may be an example of the dangers of projecting ethnographic patterns into the past. Certainly, examination of the point collection from the Coyote Ruin does not give a strong impression of specialization.

Chipped stone analysts have recently been preoccupied with distinguishing biface technologies at one extreme from expedient tool technologies at the other. Many of the points at Coyote Ruin appear to fall into the category of "expedient" bifaces.

Whittaker (1987:2-3) provides an idea of the stages that arrowpoints would go through in manufacture -

- select material
- remove suitable flake (percussion)
- begin edge retouch and thinning (pressure, here, and all subsequent work)
- continue thinning and straighten edges
- thin base
- notch (if present)
- final trimming of edges (optional)

In many of the Coyote Ruin triangular points thin flakes were selected so that facial thinning was unnecessary and a large proportion of the points have original flake surfaces left on one or both faces (46% of unnotched points, 40% of notched points). Serration or notching of the edge was the finest retouch work done. In this category, edge treatments range from deep notching of the edge to fairly minor waviness that may or may not be intentional. Serration at the heavier end would most certainly create a more severe wound.

These edge-retouched, flake points were probably within the ability of minimally trained knappers. There are other points that clearly represent the work of more experienced knappers or at least greater effort spent in flaking. Whittaker (1987) found no clear evidence of specialized production of arrowpoints at

Grasshopper Pueblo, although there was a wide range of knapping skill, with the mediocre quality points taking 15 to 30 minutes or less to make and the exceptional quality ones taking an hour (p. 9).

It is unclear to what extent careful shaping of blade edges or base is necessary for proper functioning of the arrow. In general, the purpose of the tip of the arrow is to penetrate the skin of the animal and cause bleeding. For that reason, sharpness of the tip is critical to penetration (Raup 1976:283). Although some of the sharpest points seem to be minimally flaked examples, there is evidence that minimally retouched flake points do not penetrate as deep as bifacially retouched points (Odell and Cowan 1986:203). Most of the points from Coyote Ruin that have original flake surface remaining on the faces also have fairly regular bifacially retouched blade edges.

DATING

The use of projectile points to date Coyote Ruin would not make much sense because more accurate methods of dating are available for the site. The bulk of the projectile points fall into the late triangular categories that first appear about A.D. 900 (Cottonwood Triangular) or A.D. 1150 (Pueblo Side Notched) and were used up until metal became available (Justice 2002: 265, 298).

A number of the larger points found at the site were clearly of forms made in earlier periods. There are a number of possible explanations on how they could have gotten to the site, if we exclude the idea that they are later imitations (only one of the volcanic dart points had obvious patina). First, there may have been earlier occupation at the site. This might account for some of the earlier points that were surface finds. The bulk of the earlier points are in deposits dating to the thirteen century. These points were picked up, "used," and then discarded or lost in later deposits. It is not uncommon for Archaic points to be found in ceramic period sites and in fact the bulk of the excavated points of that period are found in such contexts. The attraction of ancient bifaces was certainly present in prehistoric cultures as well as our own. Use of such points as charms or simply curiosities is likely, though difficult to demonstrate.

INTRASITE DISTRIBUTION

Table 28 gives the count by type for projectile points on the surface and by room. Table 25 provides counts by provenience for the point fragments and uncompleted points. Small triangular arrowpoints comprise nearly 75% of the points at the site and make up 50% or more of the points in every room. Two of the rooms are rather peculiar in their point contents. Room 18 has the second largest number of points, although all but two of them are small triangular. Most extreme is Room 40 which has over a third of all the points on the site including at least one of each of the 16 categories identified (Table 29). These points are most abundant in Levels 4 through 6 although there does not appear to be any basic change in types between the lowest and highest levels. One must wonder why there would be such a concentration of points, including ones made well before the room was first occupied? This room had four of the five Tularosa Corner Notched, one Dolores Cluster, two of the five Pinto, both of the Gypsum, and nine of the 27 other large points. Large concentrations of points are usually in workshop areas or in burials (e.g., Whitttaker 1987). A novel but fairly ridiculous explanation of whole arrowpoints found in Hohokam middens is that they were poisoned and it was easier to discard than reuse them (Turney 1929:107). As discussed later, the types of poisons likely to be used in the Southwest probably did not have the toxicity that would require such careful handling.

In general, the bulk of the points in workshop debris should be broken, uncompleted, or finished but not used. In Whittaker's two workshop deposits at Grasshopper Pueblo, only 18 of 93 (19%) and 10 of 88 (11%) of the points were unbroken and completed (Whittaker 1987:Table 5) and none of them had impact fractures. The diversity of forms and raw materials in the Room 40 points suggests something other than workshop debris, although some of it certainly could be. This interpretation is also supported by the presence of impact fractures on five of the Cottonwood Triangular, two of the Pueblo Side Notched, and one large triangular point from the room deposit.

INTERSITE COMPARISON

Coyote Ruin has far more projectile points than any site excavated in Yavapai County other than Tuzigoot Ruin. Even the 23 rooms excavated by Barnett at Fitzmaurice Ruin only yielded 68 "arrowpoints" of which a number appear to be dart points (Barnett 1974:68, Figure 37). At late sites in the area, including Coyote, unnotched triangular points predominate over notched triangular about 5 to 2 (Table 30). The Neural Site is the only Prescott-area site that shows a predominance of notched over unnotched. This was also true of the Northern Sinagua Lizard Man Village, the Southern Sinagua Tuzigoot Ruin (exact count not available; Caywood and Spicer 1935:73-74) and at a couple of Hohokam collections that were examined. The only other culture area in Arizona that appears to have such a high percentage of unnotched points is the late PIII Kayenta Anasazi (Beals et al. 1945: 73, Plate 13b; Lindsay 1969:277, Fig. 38). The apparent focus in the Prescott Culture area upon unnotched arrowpoints is a pattern that has not been recognized before.

Ideas about the "meaning" of projectile point shape have varied from it being "a matter of individual taste or of convenience" (Rau 1876:8-9) to use "to aid hunters and warriors in crediting kills, and for marking social group affiliation" (Bryant 1982:27). Neither of these extremes is likely to have been true in the case of the Coyote Ruin points. There was a universal preference across much of North America for triangular points in the post-A.D. 1100 period (Christenson 1997b:132-134) probably indicating strong selective pressures for simple arrowpoints. There was variation in shape that may have had a geographic/ethnic correlation, but it is unlikely that this was intentionally done to mark groups or individuals, as that could more easily be done with things such as ribands (painted stripes). That having been said, Hoffman (1997) has made a fairly strong case for the use of multiple non-functional barbs on Hohokam arrowpoints to convey messages about ethnicity, wealth, etc. What he is suggesting is the creation of special arrows for display purposes. Considering the generally low contribution that large game made to the Hohokam diet, a contribution that declined through time (James 2003:76, Figure 4.1), the Hohokam had a fairly low need for stone tipped arrows unless for warfare (Hackbarth et al. 1993:573-574) or display as suggested by Hoffman. In contrast, the population of the Prescott area seems to have done a fair amount of large game hunting and may also have been involved in warfare. But in the Prescott area, there are few of the heavily barbed arrowpoints such as are found in the Phoenix Basin.

113

Table 28. Point types by provenience.

Type	Sur.	1	2	5	12	14	17	18	19	23	28	38	40	Total
1 Cottonwood Triangular	13	1	5	1	1	10	5	29	1	1	2	2	45	116
2 Pueblo Side Notched	4	1	2	0	0	8	2	13	1	0	0	0	13	44
3 Sm expanding stem	0	0	0	0	0	1	1	1	0	0	0	0	3	6
4 Sm. Parallel/contracting Stem	1	0	0	0	0	0	1	0	0	0	0	0	1	3
5 Sm leaf-shaped flake	0	0	0	0	0	1	0	0	0	0	0	0	1	2
6 Cohonina	0	0	0	0	0	0	0	0	0	0	0	0	1	1
7 Tularosa Corner Notched	0	0	0	0	0	1	0	0	0	0	0	0	4	5
8 Dolores Cluster	1	0	1	0	0	0	0	0	0	0	0	0	1	3
9 Indet. lg. arrowpoint	1	0	0	0	0	0	0	0	0	0	0	0	1	2
10 Pinto Cluster	0	0	0	0	0	1	0	1	0	0	0	1	2	5
11 Gypsum	0	0	0	0	0	0	0	0	0	0	0	0	2	2
12 Lg. Contracting stem/unstemmed	2	0	0	0	0	0	0	0	0	1	0	0	2	5
13 Lg. triangular	0	1	1	0	0	1	0	0	0	0	0	0	4	7
14 Lg. Side notched	2	0	0	0	0	1	0	0	0	0	0	0	1	4
15 Lg. Expanding stem	5	0	0	0	0	0	0	0	0	0	0	1	1	7
16 Indet. Lg.	2	0	0	1	0	0	0	0	0	0	0	0	1	4
Total	31	3	9	2	1	24	9	44	2	2	2	4	83	216

Table 29. Room 40, Point types by level.

Type	3	4	5	6	7	8	9	Indet.	Total
1 Cottonwood Triangular	3	7	13	4	2	2	2	12	45
2 Pueblo Side Notched	0	2	3	2	2	1	1	2	13
3 Sm expanding stem	1	1	0	1	0	0	0	0	3
4 Sm. Parallel or contracting Stem	0	0	1	0	0	0	0	0	1
5 Sm. leaf-shaped flake	0	1	0	0	0	0	0	0	1
6 Cohonina	1	0	0	0	0	0	0	0	1
7 Tularosa Corner Notched	0	0	0	1	1	2	0	0	4
8 Dolores Cluster	0	0	0	1	0	0	0	0	1
9 Indet. lg. arrowpoint	0	1	0	0	0	0	0	0	1
10 Pinto Cluster	0	0	1	0	1	0	0	0	2
11 Gypsum	0	1	0	0	1	0	0	0	2
12 Lg. Contracting stem/unstemmed	0	0	0	1	1	0	0	0	2
13 Lg. triangular	0	1	3	0	0	0	0	0	4
14 Lg. Side notched	0	0	1	0	0	0	0	0	1
15 Lg. Expanding stem	0	0	0	1	0	0	0	0	1
16 Indet. Lg.	0	0	1	0	0	0	0	0	1
Total	5	14	23	11	8	5	3	14	83

114

Table 30. Notching type of triangular arrowpoints at Arizona sites.

Culture/Area	Site/Area	Unnotched	Notched	% Unnotched	Reference
Prescott	**Coyote Ruin**	**116**	**44**	**73**	**this report**
	King's Ruin	48	4	92	Spicer 1936
"	Fitzmaurice Ruin	35	8	81	Barnett 1974
"	Neural Site	13	22	37	Christenson 1997a
"	Las Vegas Ranch E&W	24	2	92	Barnett 1978
"	Matli Ranch sites	39	10	80	Barnett 1970
	Yolo	4	1		Euler 1958
	Prescott Total	279	91	75	
Northern Sinagua	Lizard Man Village	38	58	40	Kamp & Whittaker 1999
Hohokam	Santa Cruz Flats	20	43	32	Montero 1993
"	P. Grande-Early Classic	27	41	40	Peterson 1994
"	P. Grande-Late Classic	15	26	37	"
	Hohokam Total	62	110	36	
Salado	Second Canyon	20	12	62	Franklin 1980
Walapai	NA 4377	17	13	57	Euler 1958

POINT DESIGN AND WARFARE

The question of projectile points and warfare is relevant to Coyote Ruin because it was occupied during a period when many of the sites in the area may have been organized into systems of intervisibility related to warfare. Coyote Ruin has been suggested to be the center of one of these small systems (Wilcox et al. 2001:119, 140) (see discussion in Chapter 14).

Of course, projectile points are merely the cutting edge of a complex machine, variation in which also relates to how arrows were used. Variation in bow types and the varieties of ways that arrows could be made have relevance to warfare (e.g., LeBlanc 1999:99-103), but the projectile point is the only part that is commonly preserved, so we have to make do with it.

Two related claims have been made about war points compared with hunting points. First, it is frequently said that barbed arrows were used for war and leaf-shaped/rounded shouldered ones for hunting (Jackson 1943:44), the idea being that it was advantageous for the point to remain in the wound for war but not for hunting (Catlin 1844:I, 33; James 1823:II, 11; Medicine Crow 1978:251; Wyeth 1851:212). Although this was apparently an ideal held by some Indian groups, examination of arrowpoints used in war indicates that they are the same as hunting points: shoulderless (Baker and Campbell 1959:52; Hanson 1975:29). As there does seem to have been a change in arrowpoint size and form with the arrival of metal (Pyszczyk 1999), it is possible that this cultural ideal related to a stone age past rather than to the metal-age present of the mid-nineteenth century. Most of the Coyote Ruin arrowpoints would have had basal edges sticking out beyond the binding only about 2 mm on each side, which probably would have had minimal resistance to removing the point from a wound.

A related version of this argument is that war arrows were brittle so that they broke on impact and that they were held on by gum and would be left behind when the arrow was pulled out (Apache; Brodhead 1973:90). A more complex version of this latter argument is that the sinew used to bind the point to the arrowshaft would be tied loosely or not be treated so that it would swell when bathed in blood and the point would remain when the shaft was removed (Belden 1870: 104; Catlin 1844: I, 33; James 1823: II, 11; Latta 1949:53). In rare cases, war arrows were wood tipped whereas large game hunting arrows were stone tipped (Jones 1945:163; Kroeber 1925:530).

It is almost universal for stone points to be used on both war arrows and hunting arrows primarily because stone tips cause deeper and more lethal wounds, and that the breakage of the stone point in the wound was advantageous (Ellis 1997:50-52). In general, keeping the point in the wound was advantageous whether the target was an animal or a human. Animals would not have tried to pull the arrow out, but running away through the underbrush could have had the same effect. Whether in war or hunting, if the shot did not kill the target immediately, then the bleeding and ultimately infection caused by the tip might do the job. In hunting this means that the injured game needed to be dispatched using more arrows or other weapons or tracked until found, while in warfare the victim would need to be similarly dispatched or if escaping, would have to deal with removal of point with the methods available (summarized in Stockel 1995). Poisons are often mentioned relating to arrow use, but there is question whether, for example, putting juice from a snake bitten deer liver would have had much effect (Ellis 1997:55-56). The North American Indians did not have access to such poisons as curare and strychnine and so there is reason to question the efficacy of poison in hunting, although it could have had long term detrimental effects to humans hit in warfare.

The upshot of the above information is that it is unclear that there is any universal morphological criteria for distinguishing points for war arrows from points for hunting arrows. That said, it may be possible in specific cultural-historical contexts to find such a correlation.

CHAPTER 8
MICROARCHAEOLOGY
Andrew L. Christenson

INTRODUCTION

Microarchaeology can be defined as the recovery and analysis of cultural remains smaller than that normally obtained during excavation. Recovery of botanical remains by flotation and pollen by acid extraction has a moderately long history in archaeology and is done fairly often. Recovery of artifacts such as sherds and chipped stone, and food remains such as bone by micro-screening has been done less extensively (Figure 59). Fladmark (1982) pioneered the study of microdebitage, which he defined as flaking residue less than 1 mm in maximum size. Recently, one-quarter inch (6.35 mm) was suggested as the upper end of microartifacts so as to not leave a gap between what a microanalyst would look at and what is caught in a ¼ inch screen (Sherwood 2001:328).

Figure 59. Microartifacts from Room 18. Head of Pin for Scale.
Top row - flake, flake, calcined bone; bottom row - burned bone, flake, sherd.

The most broad-spectrum microarchaeological analyses are those of Rosen (1986, 1989) on tell sites in the Near East, where she studied not only microartifacts and ecofacts, but also the microscopic components of the soil of which the tell consisted. In the Southwest, the only microarchaeology studies done prior to this at Coyote Ruin have been on two Hohokam house floors at La Ciudad de los Hornos (Chenault 1993, 2002), two kiva floors at Yellow Jacket (Chenault and Cater 1993), and at a pueblo in Bandelier National Monument (cited by Chenault 2002).

Previous archaeological microanalyses have been concerned with two issues - evidence for distinguishing primary refuse from secondary refuse, and use of primary refuse to study the spatial distribution of specific activities. For example, analysis of soil samples from the floor of two kivas indicated that knapping did not occur there (Chenault and Cater 1993). In two structures at the Hohokam site, a large number of samples were collected across the floor so that the distribution of microartifacts could be discerned. Remains were distributed nonrandomly and suggested that activities were concentrated in some areas of the room and that the structure of activities in the two rooms differed (Chenault 2002).

The study of microartifacts on prehistoric living surfaces is based upon several premises. Of critical importance is that no matter how cleanly a culture may be, small artifacts and ecofacts will have a high probability of being incorporated into the living surface at a site and the probability of being trampled into the surface or of falling into crevices increases with decreased size (DeBoer 1983:22-25). In terms of understanding the spatial distribution of activities as evidenced from artifacts, primary refuse (residue from activities that is discarded or lost in place), will provide direct evidence. Living surfaces such as house floors or patios are subject to a variety of processes that may remove refuse from its primary location. Scuffage of larger artifacts will move artifacts and debris from high traffic areas to those of low traffic. Cleaning processes such as raking or sweeping will remove artifacts and debris from its primary location and lead to deposition as secondary refuse. Middens and trash pits are examples of areas with high densities of artifacts that are no longer in their place of use (secondary refuse) and thus cannot inform us about the spatial distribution of activities (other than refuse disposal).

This study follows in the path of Rosen and Chenault, although it was not possible to take large quantities of samples nor to conduct detailed analyses of all of the remains found. It is a feasibility study to determine whether, and what kind of, micro-remains are present at one site and what might be learned from recovery of such remains.

METHODS

Samples were taken from four rooms and one exterior surface area with a high density of artifacts. In Room 18, seven samples were taken in a column in room fill both above and below the floors (S12 E22; Figure 60). One sample was taken from the upper floor in the northeast corner of the same room. Another was taken on the floor next to the hearth (F2, S10 E20). In Room 19 a sample was taken of mortar in the north wall. Finally, floor samples were taken from Room 38 and near a clay-lined feature on Floor 2 of Room 40.

Floor samples were taken in a 10 x 10 cm area to a depth of no more than a couple of cm. Column samples were taken in different levels and the thickness of the level sampled depended upon soil changes, but ranged from 1.5 to 6 cm.

Each sample was measured by volume and weighed. Samples were then water screened under moderate pressure through screens of 11, 2, 1, and 0.5 mm mesh. The screens were not agitated too much because I did not want to break up charcoal, although this meant that some silt and clay did remain on larger particles (Figure 59).

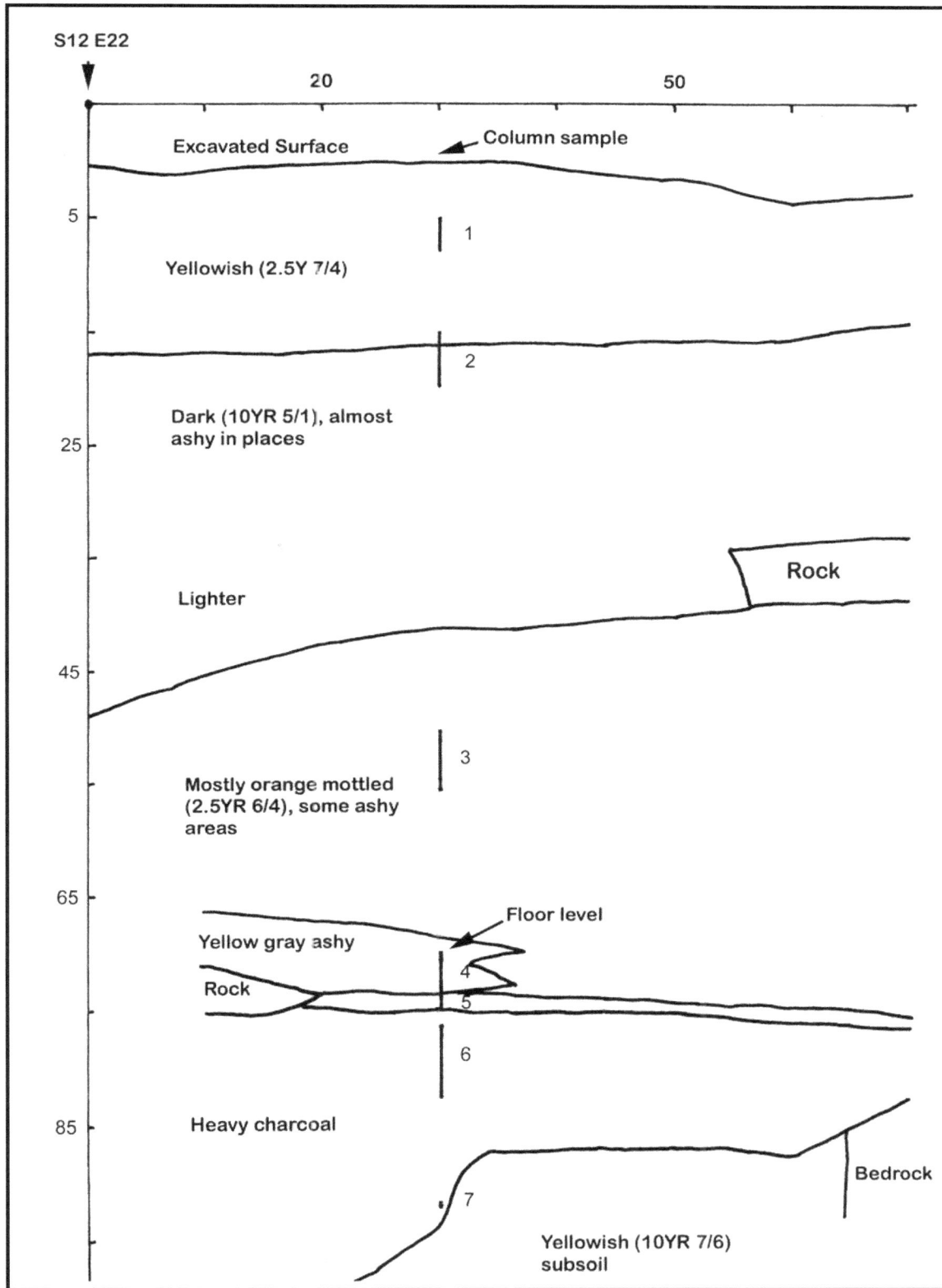

Figure 60. Stratigraphic Section of Room 18 showing location of numbered microarchaeology column samples. Vertical and horizontal numbers are centimeters.

119

The rock and other particles remaining in each screen were weighted after drying. The items in the 11mm screen were examined and tabulated, but are not included in the analysis discussed here. Seven sherds, two pieces of burned rock, and one piece of charcoal were the only definite cultural items found in this largest screen.

The contents of the 2 and 1 mm screens were examined under a binocular microscope in their entirety. Most work was done at 10x, but occasionally it was necessary to increase magnification to 30x. Bone, sherd, debitage, and unidentified items were separated out and placed into gelatin capsules. Charcoal was originally counted, but the quantity was so large that this method was not continued and only whole seeds and other possibly identifiable items were separated out. Phyllite was noted in samples, but counts were not always made. Only some of the 0.5 mm screen samples were analyzed. For most of these samples only a portion was examined and the artifacts counted, but not separated out.

Initially, all bone was lumped together in the counts, but later, separate counts were made for burned and calcined bone (not given in Table 31).

RESULTS

Table 31 provides counts by provenience for bone, sherds, debitage, and other items. Some comments about each category are provided.

Charcoal

Charcoal was present in all samples, even a little in the sterile soil at the bottom of the column sample, where it no doubt fell from above, during sample collection. (To preclude this in the future, samples in a column could be taken starting at the bottom, and proceeding upward.) Most appeared to be wood charcoal, but there were occasional seeds and corn kernels. Burned seeds were seen in the exterior surface sample but are presumed to be modern.

Bone (and Teeth)

Nearly 50% of the bone was unburned and most was fragmentary. The other half was either burned (black) or calcined (white). Some of the whole, unburned bones were certainly noncultural, i.e., from natural death of rodents in the deposit. However, the high fragmentation rate of the bone, suggests that most of it is cultural. There may be situations where carnivores break up bone in a similar manner (Johnson 1980), but that does not seem likely in this case. Fragmentation is probably from either making bone grease (M. Brown 1994:206; Vehik 1977:172) or pounding whole small animals for cooking (Haury 1976:119). The Pima pound up jackrabbit bones for the marrow, either pounding it fine enough so the bones can be eaten or simply spitting the bones out (Rea 1998:89-90). A similar process is described for the Kiliwa in Baja California (Michelsen 1967:76, 77) and the Zuni (Cushing 1920:599-600) both of whom pounded up roasted woodrats prior to eating.

Table 31. Microartifact raw data.

Provenience	Depth (cm)	Screen Size (mm)[a]	Bone	Sherd	Debitage (obsidian)	Other	Sample Weight (grams)
R 18 - Column Sample 1	4 to 8	2	3				332
		1	8	2	9(1)		
2	20 to 25	2	2	1			325
		1	18		4(1)		
3	55 to 60	2	8	3	1(1)		626
		1	23	1	14(5)		
4	69 to 73.5	2	5		2(0)		410
		1	11		10(1)		
5	73.5 to 75	2	15	1	4(2)		128
		1	22		16(1)	burned chert	
		0.5(.50)	26		11(5)	azurite	
6	77 to 83	2	45	4	13(7)	biface frag.; corn (2)	271
		1	77	4	26(11)		
		0.5(.18)	42		11(6)		
7	95	2					174
R 18 - upper floor, NE corner		2			1(0)		91
		1	3	+	6(1)	fossil (?)	
		0.5(.56)	1		4(1)		
R 18 F2, next to hearth		2			3(0)		177
		1	19		10(0)		
		0.5(.62)	20		4(1)		
R 19, wall mortar		2		1	1(0)		170
		1	3		8(1)		
		0.5	1				
R 38 floor		2		1	5(3)		699
		1	23		11(0)		
		0.5(.21)	10		5(1)		
R 40, Floor 2		2	2				375
		1	8		4(0)		
Exterior Area (surface)		2	6	16	15(5)	unworked obs.	799
		1(.51)	31	2	14(8)		
		0.5(.20)	15		8(7)	tin foil	

[a] number in parentheses indicates the portion of sample analyzed

Debitage

Debitage could sometimes be classified as to material (e.g., obsidian, chalcedony), but much of it was not clearly identifiable. The bulk of the non-obsidian appears to be chert or chalcedony. Only one formal chipped stone artifact was found, an obsidian biface fragment. The bulk of the flakes are assumed to be from either retouching of tool edges or removal of flakes from cores. The debitage is discussed more below.

Sherds

The rarity of sherds was surprising, given the quantity of sherds present at the site. The exterior sample was the only one to have many sherds - five in the 11 mm screen, 16 in the 2 mm screen, and two in the 1 mm screen. It is possible that the breaking down of sherds below a certain size into unidentifiable constituents may account for this result. Such a process was suggested to account for the lack of sherds in the 1-2 mm range at a site in Turkey (Ozbal 2000).

Phyllite Pieces

Pieces of phyllite were present in most samples. As this rock does not occur naturally on the site (phyllite is present at the mouth of Yeager Canyon), its presence in the site sediments is the result of some cultural activities, perhaps including use of phyllite tools (which are common on the surface of the site), manufacture of phyllite ornaments, or, perhaps, crushing of phyllite for temper in Wingfield pottery.

SUMMARY

Because size of samples varied between proveniences, total sample weight (excluding the 11mm + material) was used to standardize counts for comparison. Counts were standardized to 100 gram weights by taking the count, dividing by the total weight, and multiplying by 100.

Table 32 summarizes this density information for four contexts - a) the densest trash layers (73.5-75 cm and 77-83 cm of the column sample in Room 18); b) the floors (two in Room 18 and one in Rooms 38 and 40); c) the mortar sample from Room 19; and d) the sample from the surface of an exterior activity area. These data show some interesting patterns that may inform us about the location of activities, the nature of housekeeping, and trash disposal.

Comparison of the density of artifacts in the heavy trash, presumed to be secondary refuse because of its location and heavy concentration of ash and charcoal, and in the room floors, presumed to be primary refuse because of its location, shows some similarities as well as differences. First of all, the densities of trash in the two contexts are different, with the floors having densities from 1 to 30% that of the trash. This pattern is expected, since trash is by definition a concentration of waste products, whereas the waste imbedded in the floors is the result of an accidental process.

Of particular interest is the lack of bone over 2 mm long in the floor contexts, whereas 15 pieces were recovered from every 100 grams of the heavy trash samples. Bones dropped on floors are more likely to break and become imbedded into the floor as smaller pieces. Larger bones are less likely to be missed in the cleaning up of the room floor and, thus, will end up in secondary trash deposits or be left in corners

(Matthews et al. 1997:298). The trash deposits in Room 18 were of two types, the 73.5-75 cm level was ash, presumed to have come from cleaning out of interior hearths, as the high wind at the site would probably obviate the need to clean out exterior hearths. The 77-83 cm deposit was high in charcoal and its origin is less certain.

Table 32. Microartifact 100-gram-sample standardized counts.

Provenience Type	Screen Size (mm)	Bone		Debitage	
		#/100 g	%	#/100 g	%
Heavy Trash (Secondary Refuse)	2	15.0	0.13	4.6	0.13
	1	24.8	0.22	10.6	0.29
	0.5	71.5	0.64	20.8	0.58
Floor (Primary Refuse)	2	0.1	0.01	0.2	0.03
	1	4.2	0.33	3.1	0.44
	0.5	8.6	0.67	3.8	0.53
Wall Mortar	2	0	0	0.6	0.11
	1	1.8	0.75	4.7	0.89
	0.5	0.6	0.25	0	0
Exterior Area	2	0.8	0.05	1.9	0.18
	1	7.6	0.43	3.4	0.33
	0.5	9.3	0.53	5.0	0.49
				#	%
Maya Chert Dumps	5			5733	0.02
	1			39720	0.11
	<1			311317	0.87
Maya Floor	5			907	
	1			3984	
	<1			not counted	

The trash deposits have debitage densities of from 5 to 23 times greater than floor densities and proportions of the two largest categories differ, although both have over 50% in the smallest category. Hull (1987:773) argues that secondary refuse can be distinguished from primary refuse by the lack of microdebitage. Studies of modern Maya knappers show that when they work inside they are very careful to catch debitage on cloths, because the pieces are a major hazard to people, who mostly go bare-footed (Clark 1986:24; 1991a:66-67). Thus, Maya secondary chert-knapping refuse includes the complete range of debitage sizes and there is little difference in size between primary and secondary refuse (Clark 1986:Table 1). In the lower part of Table 32 is summary information for dump deposits of three Maya knappers. The count for the less-than-1-mm sample is an estimate. These data are not directly comparable with the Coyote Ruin microdebitage samples because screen sizes are different and the smallest size includes much smaller

123

flakes than counted in this study. However, they do clearly show that these secondary deposits are dominated by the smallest microdebitage, contradicting Hull's argument. Even with the use of cloths to catch knapping debris many of the smallest flakes do miss and end up on the working surface (Clark 1986:25). Table 32 also provides counts of two sizes of debitage found on and in an abandoned workshop floor (Clark 1991b:Table 5).

Cloth was certainly available to the occupants of Coyote Ruin, as was skin, but it is unclear if they were used to catch knapping debris. It seems likely to me that a lot of the hard hammer knapping at Coyote Ruin would have been done outdoors and that indoor knapping would be limited primarily to retouching of tool edges. The exterior sample from Coyote Ruin did not have any large debitage (i.e., 11 mm or over), although such artifacts were common in the area. The Maya do not take as much care with debris from retouching as they do from knapping, because the small size of flakes generated is not as likely to cause harm (Clark 1986:25; 1991a:68, 72).

The presence of artifacts in the wall mortar sample indicates that mortar was being procured from cultural deposits.

The sample from the exterior area is similar to the trash samples (Table 32). Such exterior areas are assumed to have been the location of much of the knapping activities and perhaps trash dumping. The somewhat attenuated frequency of the smallest debitage and bone may be the result of removal by the strong winds that frequent the area. Particles most likely to be moved by wind entrainment are in the 0.1 to 0.84 mm range (Waters 1992:186) and evidence has been found in archaeological sites in sand dunes of the removal of small debitage by wind or a combination of wind and water (Christenson 1993; Fladmark 1982:217). Of course, these artifacts and ecofacts are not destroyed, but merely moved from high density archaeological contexts to low density natural contexts.

CONCLUSIONS

This abbreviated analysis of several contexts at Coyote Ruin indicates that there is plenty of interpretive potential for microarchaeology at this and similar sites. The potential for the work is only limited by the time available to process and examine the samples.

One useful result that was obtained is additional confirmation that the levels defined as floors in rooms 18, 38, and 40 do indeed have microscopic differences that appear to distinguish them as floor. Although determining the floor level is less of a problem in rooms that have floor features such as hearths, it is not uncommon to have rooms where the floor level is indeterminate. Microarchaeology might provide a way of distinguishing floors from trash deposits in rooms, although more work needs to be done on this question. Artifact breakage has been used to determine the presence of intensive trampling on archaeological surfaces (Rosen 1986:105-106), and in theory it should be possible to go in the opposite direction and use the presence of small artifacts to define activity surfaces that might not be evident otherwise.

In terms of reconstructing activities, the microanalysis indicates several things. Not surprisingly, processing and consumption of small animals occurred in the rooms sampled. The unburned bone represents bone discarded on the floor during processing and consumption, while the burned bone may be from discard into the fire and perhaps dropage during cleaning of the hearth. The debitage recovered from the floors indicates that knapping did occur inside rooms. The character of this stoneworking is more difficult to determine. Pressure retouching of tool edges is an obvious thing to do around a fire with others on a winter night, and the presence of debitage in the ash layer in the column sample is a good clue that this occurred. To what extent percussion knapping occurred in the rooms is difficult to determine. Modern Maya do such flaking in their houses, although this would seem to be less likely to occur when other people are nearby.

The trash deposit in Room 18 does indicate something about activities in rooms as well. It is assumed that the ash came from clearing out interior hearths and that the artifacts in the ash are an indicator of activities that occurred around the hearth. Whether floors were swept as recorded ethnographically among the Pueblo Indians, and other settled populations (Murray 1980:Table 1), is less certain. The small number of flakes in the 2+ mm range may be indicative of such an activity.

CHAPTER 9
THE FROG IS THE PRINCE: COYOTE RUIN SHELL
Sharon F. Urban

INTRODUCTION

This hilltop site produced a total of 191 pieces of artifactual shell from 14 distinct locations. Contained within this total were 16 genera of which one was fresh water and the remainder of marine origin. Also noted were a few pieces for which a genus could not be determined, but shell bulk indicated that these were also marine shell. Four basic artifact categories were used: Raw Material, Worked Material, Personal Adornment, and Utilitarian. Details for the genera, sources, and artifact types, along with their provenience form the basis of this report.

GENERA AND OBTAINABILITY

Genera found at this site were surprisingly numerous considering the distance from the source (Table 33). With the help of Bequaert and Miller (1973), Keen (1984) and Morris (1966) most of the shell pieces were identifiable (Table 33).

Table 33. Shell by source and genus.

Source	Genus	Count
Freshwater	*Anodonta californiensis* Lea	5
Marine	*Cerithium* Bruguière	1
	Cerithidea albonodosa Gould	3
	Conus Linné	11
	Conus regularis Sowerby	1
	Cypraea Linné	1
	Dosinia ponderosa Gray	1
	Glycymeris Da Costa	79
	Haliotis rufescens Swainson	1
	Laevicardium elatum Sowerby	32
	Olivella dama Wood	42
	Pectin vogdesi Arnold	1
	Pteria Scopoli	1
	Pyrene Röding	2
	Spondylus princips Broderlip	1
	Turritella Lamarck	1
	unknown	8
Total	16	191

The freshwater species *Anodonta,* requires a free-flowing stream (Bequaert and Miller 1973:220-223). For this area, there is no mention of this genus having been found in the Verde River or any of the smaller streams near Prescott, but it had been noted from Oak Creek as a live specimen by Mr. E. H.

Hannibal (Bequaert and Miller 1973:222). More than likely this genus was abundant in most of the faster free-flowing streams of the time.

The marine genera live in both the Pacific Ocean and the Gulf of California. *Haliotis* is only found within the Pacific Ocean, but the *Laevicardium* genera may come from both the Gulf and the Pacific. *Haliotis, Spondylus,* and *Turritella* live at what is know as a moderately deep sea or between 80-200 feet (27-67 m) while all of the other genera are found within shallow (tidal to 30 feet – 0-10 m) or moderately shallow 30 to 80 feet (10-27 m) waters. For cultures that lived along the ocean these specimens would have been easily obtained by shallow wading or diving, and on occasion, a deep dive. Shells can also be obtained by beach combing, especially after a storm.

Richard Nelson (1991) in his *Hohokam Marine Shell Exchange and Artifacts* notes that early on Fewkes (1896) proclaimed that sea shells to the historic northern pueblos came via a trade route on an easterly trek from the Pacific. Others dealing with the trade routes of shell, Brand (1938), Colton (1941a), and Tower (1945), were beginning to look toward the south and the Hohokam people as a source of shell. As excavation projects took place on the western deserts, Fontana (1966), Hayden (1970), Rosenthal et al. (1978:191-207), and finally Howard (1993), have all indicated the tell tale signs of shell trade from the south, seemingly the accepted theory today. Granted there was more than one route from the south, but the majority of shell went from south to north.

Most recently Wilcox et al. (2000) once again bring up Fewkes' (1912: 207) mention of the"…well-worn Indian trail from the Colorado River, past Mount Hope, through Aztec [Juniper] Pass, down Walnut Creek, and across Williamson and Chino Valleys to the Verde….". Wilcox et al. (2000:122) continue "Like Fewkes, we infer that the Hardyville-Prescott route is an eastern extension of that Mohave Trail, which arguably brought Pacific shell eastward into the Chino and Verde valleys (Barnett 1974)." Further comments on this Pacific connection will be discussed in the conclusions.

ARTIFACT CATEGORIES

Gladwin et al. (1937) and Haury (1976) set up the framework used by most shell analysts, and herein. Raw Material (42 pieces) (Table 34) could be whole or broken pieces of shell however there is no evidence that any of the surfaces or edges have been cut, ground, drilled or abraded. In other words, there was no evidence of alteration by humans.

Worked Material (47) (Table 35) on the other hand does show some human modification in the form of cutting, grinding, drilling, grooving, or abrasion. These forms of alteration could take place on either a whole specimen or a fragment.

Personal Adornment (91) (Table 36) is usually the largest category, and was subdivided into Beads including barrel (5), disk (3), and whole shell (53); Bracelets (24) all fragments of *Glycymeris*; Pendants (6) that have been subdivided into geometric (1), frog (1), and whole shell (4). A few words about bracelets are in order. Gladwin, et al. (1937) and Haury (1976) established a typology for bracelets based on band width. The narrowest (2.5-4.0 mm in width thickness) was Type 1, the wider (4.0-6.0 mm) was Type 2, and the widest (6.0-10.0 mm) was Type 3.

Utilitarian (11) included awls (5), and tinklers (6) (Table 36). Coyote Ruin awls were all of *Glycymeris*, made from broken bracelet fragments, with one blunt end and one pointed end that had been ground to shape probably through use wear. Tinkers (always of *Conus*) could be an item of personal adornment, but in this study they are considered a musical instrument.

Table 34. Shell raw materials.

Provenience	Anodona	Cerithidea	Cerithium	Conus	Cypraea	Glycymeris	Laevicardium	Olivella	Pectin	Pteria	Pyrene	Turitella	unknown	Total
Surface							2							2
T.P. 1													1	1
TP2						1								1
R 14	1	1				1		1						4
R 18	1				1	1	3	2	1		1	1	1	12
R 19							1							1
R 23				1				1						2
R 38							1							1
R 40		2	1			3	3	7		1		1		18
Total	2	3	1	1	1	6	10	11	1	1	1	2	2	42

Table 35. Worked shell.

Provenience	Anodonta	Dosinia	Glycymeris	Haliotis	Laevicardium	unkn.	Total
R 1					2		2
R 1A					1		1
R 2					2		2
R 14			3		1		4
R 17			2		1		3
R 18	1		2		4	1	8
R 19		1			2	1	4
R 23					2	2	4
R 38			1				1
R 40	1		9	1	7		18
Total	2	1	17	1	22	4	47

129

Table 36. Shell personal adornment and utilitarian artifacts.

Type	Barrel Bead			Disk Bead	Whole Shell				Bracelet	Geometric	Frog Pendant	Whole shell Pendant	Awl	Tinkler	
Genus															
Provenience	*Conus*	*Olivella*	*Spondylus*	*unknown*	*Pyrene*	*Conus*	*Glycymeris*	*Olivella*	*Glycymeris*	*Anodonta*	*Glycymeris*	*Glycymeris*	*Glycymeris*	*Conus*	*Total*
Surface					1									1	2
R 1			1												1
R 2							1								1
R 5													1		1
R 14							4	5				1	1		11
R 17							1		2						3
R 18		1						8	1				1	1	12
R 19						1			2						3
R 23									1				1		2
R 38							1								1
R 40	2	2		2		1	15	15	18	1	1	3	1	4	65
Total	2	3	1	2	1	2	22	28	24	1	1	4	5	6	102

Figure 61. Shell artifacts. Approximately life size.

ARTIFACTS BY PROVENIENCE

Surface (4 specimens). Two pieces of worked *Laevicardium* were found. One whole shell bead of *Pyrene* was recovered with its extreme tip ground off, turning it into a bead. The last item was a longitudinal fragment of a *Conus* tinkler that has a drilled hole, rather than the more typical V-shaped slit, for suspension.

Test Pit 1 (1). One piece of unworked marine shell (flat with some radiating sculpture lines).

Test Pit 2 (1). One piece of unworked, burned, *Glycymeris* body, with exterior polish.

Room 1 (3). Two worked pieces of *Laevicardium.* One body piece had a burned section on the exterior, and two ground edges; the other was very thin, from the lateral margin. The third item was a disk bead of *Spondylus princeps* that was wedge shaped in cross-section, with a central conical suspension hole.

Room 1A (1). One burned lateral edge piece of *Laevicardium* with one cut edge.

Room 2 (3). Two lateral margin pieces of *Laevicardium* were found. One had cut edges; one had cut marks on the body of the valve. A coating on one piece suggests it may have been from, or near, a burial. The third item was a whole shell bead made from a juvenile *Glycymeris* valve; the beak had been ground to create a suspension hole, and there was grinding around the hole edge.

Room 5 (1). One awl was made of a reworked *Glycymeris* bracelet fragment (Type 1).

Room 14 (19). Nineteen artifacts were found in this room, making it the third largest producer of shell artifacts at the site. There were four pieces of raw material of four genera. The *Anodonta* was highly fragmented, the *Cerithidea* was heat fractured, the *Glycymeris* was nearly a whole valve with a part of the lateral margin broken away, and the *Olivella* was an unworked shell. There were four pieces of worked shell: three of *Glycymeris* and one of *Laevicardium.* Of the *Glycymeris,* one was burned with the distal edge ground and may have originally been a small pendant, another was squarish in shape with the distal margin ground, and the third piece was a lateral section of the valve with cut edges. The *Laevicardium* was a medial body segment from a large valve with three ground edges. Personal adornment was represented by beads, with four whole shell *Glycymeris*, and four of *Olivella*. Two of the *Glycymeris* and one of the *Olivella* beads were burned. One of the *Olivella* beads shows evidence of stringing wear at the canal end. There was one *Glycymeris* pendant of the juvenile form (but larger than the whole shell beads of this genus). Its beak had been ground off, creating a perforation for stringing, and the surrounding inner edge had also been ground down, and the high point on the domed vault had also been ground, resulting in a flat spot. The final piece was an awl of a reworked bracelet fragment (Type 2) with one end being pointed and the other more blunt; it was burned.

Room 17 (6). Three pieces of worked material were found, two ground inner valve margins of *Glycymeris,* and one body piece of *Laevicardium* with one cut edge. Three items of personal adornment were found, including one whole shell bead of *Glycymeris,* and two Type 1 *Glycymeris* bracelet band fragments.

Room 18 (32). This was the second highest shell-producing room with 32 items recovered. There were 12 raw material pieces represented by *Anodonta*, *Cyprea*, *Glycymeris*, *Laevicardium*, *Olivella*, *Pectin*, *Pyrene*, and unknown marine (Table 34). The *Olivella* shells and *Laevicardium* piece were burned; the *Cyprea* was a longitudinal body section; and the *Glycymeris* was a juvenile.

Eight pieces of worked material were present (Table 35). Most of these pieces were not remarkable. There was a juvenile *Glycymeris* with the beak perforated but the hole broken out – it could have been counted as a whole shell bead. One piece of *Laevicardium* was burned.

Olivella beads included one barrel, and eight whole shell beads (one of which was burned). One Type 2 bracelet fragment was recovered. The final two artifacts included one *Glycymeris* awl, and one *Conus* tinkler fragment; the tinkler was burned and had a drilled suspension hole.

Room 19 (8). Of note was a distal piece of *Dosinia* with grinding on the margin and flakes had been removed from the inner surface. One whole *Conus* shell bead was present. Two wide Type 3 bracelet fragments were unusual. Both included the beak and umbonal area of the valve with the umbonal area accentuated. There were no "arms" to either side and one had a perforated beak.

Room 23 (7). Raw material, worked material, a bracelet and one awl make up the collection recovered from this room. One medial band section of a *Glycymeris* bracelet was classified as Type1 due to its extreme thinness of band width. The awl was a very thin reworked fragment of a Type 1 bracelet with one end ground to a rounded outline.

Room 38 (3). Included are one piece of *Laevicardium* raw material, one worked piece of *Glycymeris*, and a whole shell bead of *Glycymeris*.

Room 40 (101). One could say that this room was the shell "treasure box" of the site, containing 101 pieces (Tables 34-36). Raw material (18) included *Cerithidea* (2 pieces), *Cerithium* (1), *Glycymeris* (3), *Laevicardium* (3), *Olivella* (7), *Pteria* (1), and *Turritella* (1). Of the seven *Olivella*, four were burned, one of which was a juvenile. One of the *Cerithdae* was burned, as was one of the pieces of *Glycymeris*. Another one of the *Glycymeris* shells was a juvenile, and another was most of a large valve.

Worked material included 18 pieces, with *Anodonta* (1), *Glycymeris* (9), *Haliotis* (1), and *Laevicardium* (7). Five of the *Glycymeris* pieces deserver further description. One was a whole shell bead that the perforation broken through. One was a juvenile shell with ground upper and lower edges. One large umbo had a perforated beak and where the arms would have been if it came from a bracelet, the piece had been smoothed. One nearly whole valve had the distal quarter broken off. And there was one burned piece.

Beads were numerous in this room, with four barrel beads, two each of *Conus* and *Olivella*. (To make this type of bead both the canal and spire ends were removed by grinding.) Two disk beads of an unknown marine genus were recovered; both were flat with large straight-sided central perforations. The whole shell beads win the jackpot for the most beads at the site, with 15 each of *Glycymeris* and *Olivella*, and one of *Conus*. Bracelet is another well-filled category with 18 specimens. All were of *Glycymeris* with four Type 1, eight Type 2, and six Type 3. The Type 1 bracelets were unremarkable. Type 2 had some distinctions in that three were burned (one actually cremated), one broke during manufacture, and one was carved with a running chevron pattern around the outer edge. The Type 3 bracelets included another of the large umbonal area type, and one specimen was burned. Five pendants were found. One fragment of *Anodonta* was cut and ground to a rectangular outline, with a biconical perforation at a corner. There are three whole shell *Glycymeris* pendants with one having a perforated beak with that hole enlarged and all of the inner margin ground to shape. One had a ground beak that was perforated, and the distal edge chipped to shape.

The final pendant is the most beautiful and striking piece of the entire shell assemblage: it is a frog carved out of a whole *Glycymeris* valve (Figure 61 and cover). All four legs were carefully delineated, even to the carving of toes. There were two round bas-relief eyes in the correct anatomical position, and the whole is beautifully polished!

Utilitarian pieces from this room include four *Conus* tinklers, and one typical *Glycymeris* bracelet band reworked into an awl. One of the tinklers is tinkler blank, in that the spire has been ground off but the lip is missing and there was no indication of a suspension groove (perhaps this too should have been classified as worked material). Two others had a deeply incised groove with a punched hole in the groove for suspension. And the fourth piece had a deep groove with no hole.

DISCUSSION

This Coyote Ruin shell assemblage is unique because of its location within the state, distance from the sources of the shells, variety of genera present, and quantity. Since only five pieces of *Anodonta* (the fresh water shell) were found, this indicates that the source for the marine shell was steady. Often sites out of the main stream of trading made good use of this fresh water shell, perhaps as a means of tiding one over as in "gee I need a shell pendant for the dance tonight and the trader has not come by lately" type of situation. This kind of scenario did not exist at Coyote Ruin. Just the fact that 14 genera were found, seems to indicate good trading connections, and almost to the point of special orders. Even Hohokam sites farther south, and supposedly on the shell trade main line, seldom contain this kind of variety.

Manufacturing does not seem to be a big thing at this site. Granted that there were many pieces of both raw and worked material, debris from the manufacturing process was not found. One bracelet was in the process of being made, and if a whole *Olivella* or juvenile *Glycymeris* shell was to be turned into a bead, a simple swipe across a sandstone slab would have produced a hole for stringing, with the resulting shell dust blowing away. Bracelet fragments reworked into awls or pendants are considered repair jobs and not manufacturing. The only "real" manufacturing might have been turning an *Anodonta* valve into a pendant, and apparently that did not happen often.

No one feature or room contained every genera and each artifact type, but Rooms 18 and 40 came very close. Room 40 contained by far the most shell genera and artifact categories, and the highest numbers in both.

A few pieces of shell contained a coating that has been thought to come from a burial context, where the decomposing body fluids settled upon the shell. Since the site had been previously dug, and pothunted, and the current excavation obtained shell from upper fill contexts, it is possible that some of this apparent burial shell did indeed originate from burials. If correct, this would be an indication that shell grave goods were among the types of goods placed with the deceased.

However, the burned pieces of shell need not be interpreted as indicating the presence of cremations at Coyote Ruin. One can imagine that broken pieces of shell might occasionally casually get tossed into fires and get burned, or perhaps a basket or pot full of hot ashes and embers got tossed on the midden and "cooked" any shell piece that was under the dumped load.

The large *Glycymeris* umbo pieces without the band (or only short sections thereof) were of particular interest. This type of big, heavy bracelet (Kelly 1978:119) was most indicative of the Classic Period of the Hohokam chronology and could mean some fast walking on the part of the shell traders! The occupants of Room 40 seem to have been enamored of this style!

CONCLUSIONS

Some of the shell specimens in Room 18 were from floor fill, but all other specimens came from room fill or surface contexts. As such, attempting to date any of the features on the basis of the shell assemblage would not be of much help. However, a few generalizations can be made with regard to Haury's (1976) observations on the dating of shell genera and artifact types in Hohokam sites. Many genera were associated with the Sedentary Period, and the larger, plain pieces with the Classic. Overall this site seems to fit here nicely, but I would not like to have this site dated purely on the shell content!

Regarding Wilcox and Samples (1992), and Wilcox et al. (2000), who strongly support Fewkes' shell route from the Pacific directly east to the general Prescott area, I beg to differ. From the Coyote Ruin collection the only specimen that was only found in the Pacific Ocean was the one piece of Red Abalone, *Haliotis rufescens*. True *Laevicardium elatum* can be found in the Pacific Ocean, but was also lived in the Gulf of California, along with all of the other marine genera from this assemblage. Historic shell trade may indeed have come from the Pacific Ocean as postulated by Fewkes (1912), but the collection at hand bespeaks a southern origin.

With the bulk of the shell artifacts coming from two rooms (18 and 40), one could suggest that these two rooms may have been the quarters of people of high status. Or, on the other hand, and for whatever reason, these two rooms may have been chosen for the shell dump!

The Sundown Site (Barth and Cline 1999), also in the Prescott area and occupied during a time frame similar to that of Coyote Ruin, had some similarities in shell content to that of Coyote Ruin. Species and artifact types comparable to those found at Coyote Ruin include bracelets, disk and barrel beads, many whole shell *Glycymeris* beads, *Columbella* (now *Pyrene)* beads, and large heavy *Glycymeris* valves. The Sundown Site also had a couple of pieces of *Haliotis*. Overall, these two sites are quite similar in their shell content.

CHAPTER 10
PLANT REMAINS FROM COYOTE RUIN, NA 6654
Scott M. Kwiatkowski

This report presents the results of the analysis of ten flotation and five wood charcoal samples collected from the Coyote Ruin, NA 6654 (a.k.a. Ken Austin's Emilienne Site, NA 3810, and NA 14549), a Prescott Culture hilltop habitation site located on a rocky butte that dates to the Chino phase (ca. A.D. 1100–1300) (Wilcox et al. 2001: Appendix 6.4). This study was undertaken to help understand the kinds of plants that were used for food, fuel, construction material, and other purposes at this prehistoric settlement.

ANALYTICAL METHODS

Flotation Analysis

Flotation analysis is a technique that uses water to separate light-weight biological material such as fruits, seeds, and charcoal in sediment samples from its heavier, inorganic matrix. While several methods are currently used to process flotation samples, the one employed during this study has been preferred by a number of Southwestern archaeobotanists over the years (e.g., Robert E. Gasser, Julia E. Hammett, Molly S. Toll, the author, others). Processing began by selecting several (n=3) of the samples for the intentional introduction of 100 charred poppy (*Papaver somniferum*) seeds (Wagner 1982). These seeds were added to evaluate the efficiency of the processing technique. Next, approximately one liter of sediment at a time was poured into a five-gallon (19 liter) bucket that had been filled approximately three-fourths full of water. The sample was stirred with a metal rod and decanted through 100 percent polyester chiffon; this fabric caught the "light flotation fraction." The bucket was refilled three-fourths full with water, stirred again, and the decanting process was repeated. The "heavy fraction," retained at the bottom of the bucket, was poured out onto window screen (ca. 1.4-millimeter mesh). This double-decanting procedure for each liter of soil was repeated until the entire sample had been processed. Both light and heavy fractions were rinsed with water following each decant; this removed much of the remaining fine, inorganic sediment. Both fractions were air-dried, the light fraction still in chiffon, and the heavy fraction on newspaper.

The dried light fractions were screened through 2.0-, 1.0-, 0.5-, and 0.25-millimeter mesh geological screens to group similar-sized particles together and facilitate microscopic examination. Because the flotation samples were typically very large, and proved time-consuming to analyze, their light fraction residues less than 0.25 millimeters, which typically do not contain identifiable charred plant material, were not examined.

Next, the contents of each screen was examined at 10–11X magnification using a reflected light binocular microscope. All nonwoody plant remains were identified using reference manuals (e.g., Benson 1969; Gould 1951; Kearney and Peebles 1960; Martin and Barkley 1961; Parker 1972; USDA Forest Service 1974), the Internet (e.g., <www.usgs.nau.edu> <www.npwrc.usgs.gov> <www.eiu.edu>), and by comparison to the author's modern seed reference collection. Common names follow Lehr (1978) whenever possible.

Identifiable remains in the flotation sample were either counted or their numbers were estimated. The quantities of selected taxa were estimated by sorting a portion of the material (e.g., one-ninth) and then multiplying the result as appropriate (e.g., by nine). The remainder of this screen was then inspected for the presence of other, less common material.

The total volume of each light fraction (excluding the unanalyzed material less than 0.25 millimeters) was measured using a graduated cylinder after the material had been analyzed. Then, the amount of charcoal present in the analyzed portion of the sample was estimated as a percentage of the total volume of the light fraction. Finally, the sample's heavy fraction was examined without a lens. As with the light fraction, the heavy fraction was sifted through one or more standard screen sizes (e.g., 2.0- and 1.0- millimeter mesh) to facilitate analysis by grouping together particles of similar size.

Due to time constraints, only seven of the 10 flotation samples were completely analyzed. Only the heavy flotation fractions of the other three samples were examined. The completely analyzed flotation samples were from Room 2, Room 14, Room 17, and Room 22, and the partially analyzed samples came from Room 5, Room 14, and Room 18.

At an open-air site like the Coyote Ruin, only carbonized (i.e., burned or charred) plant remains are typically considered to date to the prehistoric occupation of the site, unless reasons exist to believe otherwise (Keepax 1977; Minnis 1981). This topic will be discussed in more detail later in this report.

Non-Woody Plant Remain Identification Notes

Poorly preserved plant remains resembling a particular taxon received a tentative "cf." identification. Because these cf.-level identifications may be inaccurate, little significance should be attached to them. Plant remains classed as "Indeterminate" are even more poorly preserved than cf.-level identifications. The category "Miscellaneous" refers to plant parts that have little diagnostic value.

The criteria used in agave (*Agave* sp.) identifications generally follow Bohrer (1987:72–73). Fibers with trough-shaped cross sections are considered to be from agave plants, whether or not they exhibit white styloid crystals (Mauseth 1988:33–34) that are probably made of calcium oxalate (Franceschi and Horner 1980). Fibers with round cross sections and white styloid crystals are identified as cf. agave.

Because it is sometimes difficult to separate seeds in the Goose Foot Family (Chenopodiaceae) from pigweed (*Amaranthus* spp.) seeds (Bohrer 1987:99), the charred seed fragments of this type have typically been classed as "cheno-am," which includes these two taxa. However, since Bohrer (1987:Table 9.25) has described several morphological seed traits that help discriminate between goose foot (*Chenopodium* spp.) and pigweed, many of the whole seeds in this category have been identified more precisely. During this study, all charred cheno-am seeds identified to the species level are thought to be goose foot, i.e., none are believed to be pigweed seeds. The identified goose foot seeds were typically round in facet view, had no distinct rims, and possessed either smooth or micro-reticulate seed coats.

Wood Charcoal Analysis

Two types of wood charcoal samples were analyzed. The first consisted of five macrobotanical samples containing multiple pieces of relatively large, burned, woody material. Each piece of charcoal in this first type of sample was large enough to be readily visible to the naked eye. These samples came from Room 2, Room 17, and Room 40. The second type of sample consisted of the largest pieces of wood charcoal present in the flotation samples. Only pieces at least 2.0 millimeters in greatest dimension, i.e., those that were large enough to be able to manipulate and that retained sufficient morphological detail for identification, were considered for analysis. While the goal was to analyze up to 20 pieces of charcoal from each flotation sample, none of the samples yielded sufficient large charcoal to attain this goal. Wood charcoal was identified within flotation samples from Room 2, Room 14, Room 17, and Room 22.

Regardless of sample type, the individual pieces within it were analyzed by first breaking a small fragment of each specimen to expose a fresh cross section. Break edges were examined under a binocular reflected light microscope at 25X and identifications were made using identification keys and manuals (e.g., Adams 1994; Miksicek 1986; Minnis 1987) and by comparison to the author's collection of modern, carbonized reference material. Then, each piece of charcoal was counted. For the macrobotanical samples, morphologically-similar groups were weighed on a triple-beam balance to the nearest 0.05 gram. The wood charcoal present in the flotation samples was not analyzed because it typically weighed very little.

Because of the relatively low power used during the analysis, and also because wood structure can vary in response to a number of different factors, the wood charcoal identifications should best be viewed as preliminary (Bohrer 1986). Examples of variables that may influence wood appearance within the same species include idiosyncratic growth conditions, the age of the plant, and the position of the sample on the plant (e.g., root, trunk, branch). Because of these potential problems, wood charcoal from the Coyote Ruin was identified to relatively broad taxonomic groups.

Wood Charcoal Identification Notes

Gymnosperm wood charcoal with resin ducts was identified as pine type (*Pinus* type), even though Minnis (1987) has suggested that pinyon type (*Pinus edulis* type) charcoal can be separated from ponderosa pine type (*Pinus ponderosa* type) charcoal because the former has smaller-diameter resin ducts. The reason that these two types were not separated in this study is that virtually all of the charcoal that the author observed from the Coyote Ruin had relatively large resin ducts that were comparable to his ponderosa pine type reference material, yet staff at the Laboratory of Tree-Ring Research (LTRR) at the University of Arizona examined one of the samples containing this charcoal type and stated that, in their opinion, it was "probably pinyon" (letter Jeffrey S. Dean of LTRR to Mary Spall of the Arizona Archaeological Society, February 3, 2004). In light of this discrepancy, as well as the fact that other archaeobotanists who have worked in the area do not separate these two charcoal types (e.g., Cummings and Puseman 1995; Cummings *et al.* 2003; Huckell 2005), it seems most appropriate to use the larger morphological category of pine type wood charcoal at the Coyote Ruin.

RESULTS

Flotation Samples

The flotation analysis raw data from the seven completely analyzed samples is presented in Table D1, and the raw data from the analysis of three flotation sample heavy fractions is listed in Table D2. The carbonized non-woody plant remains identified in the flotation samples are summarized in Table 37, the uncarbonized non-woody plant remains is presented in Table 38, and the non-plant matter present in the flotation samples is summarized in Table 39.

Although three flotation samples had charred poppy seeds introduced into them, only one of these was completely analyzed. A sample taken from burned Room 14, taken 1.30 meters below ground surface (BGS), produced 91 of the original 100 charred poppy seeds introduced into it. This 91% recovery rate is comparable to the best flotation sample processing methods discussed by Wagner (1982).

137

When cf.-level identifications, indeterminate plant remains, miscellaneous plant parts, unknown plant remains, and the incompletely analyzed samples are omitted from consideration, 875 charred plant parts remain (Table 40). Four charred plant taxa were only recovered from the partially analyzed flotation samples: manzanita fruit fragments, monocot cf. common reed culm fragments, maize embryo fragments, and maize glumes. The relative abundance of these 875 charred plant remains is graphically depicted on Figure 62. Inspection of this figure indicates that the bulk (78.97%) of the identifiable non-woody charred plant assemblage consists of just two taxa, agave leaf parts and cheno-am seeds. Four other taxa were less well represented, but still each comprised more than 1% of the total: maize cob parts, purslane seeds, winged pigweed seeds, and maize kernel fragments.

Table 41 depicts the distribution of charred plant parts per liter, excluding cf.-level, indeterminate, and unknown plant remains, in the seven completely analyzed flotation samples. All rooms yielded charred cheno-am seeds. Room 2 had the most unusual assemblage in that it produced no agave, maize, or purslane remains, but it did contain the only occurrences of charred carpet weed and pepper grass seeds recovered from the site. The anomalous seed assemblage in Room 2 is likely due to sample-size issues, as only 1.0 liter of sediment was examined from it.

Table 37. Summary of the carbonized non-woody plant remains present in the flotation samples (N=5004).

Common Name	Scientific Name	Number and Type of Parts Present
Agave	*Agave* sp.	4 cf. Caudex Fragments; 391 Fibers; 789 cf. Fibers; 2 Fiber Bundles; 4 cf. Fiber Bundles;
Bear Grass	*Nolina* sp.	3 Leaf Frags.; 8 cf. Leaf Frags.
Blazing Star	*Mentzelia* sp.	5 Seeds; 1 Seed Frag.
Bottle Gourd	*Lagenaria* sp.	1 cf. Rind Frag.
Carpet Weed	*Mollugo* sp.	1 Seed Frag.
Cheno-am	Chenopodiaceae or *Amaranthus* sp.	2 Seeds; 240 Seed Frags.; 195 cf. Seed Frags.
Cholla/Prickly Pear	*Opuntia* sp.	2 Seed Frags.; 4 cf. Embryo Frags.
Drop Seed Type	*Sporobolus* Type	5 Grains; 1 Grain Frag.; 6 cf. Grains; 6 cf. Grain Frags.
Goose Foot	*Chenopodium* sp.	33 Seeds; 23 Seed Frags.
Grass Family	Poaceae	1 Culm Frag.; 8 Grain Frags.
Grass Family cf. Common Reed	Poaceae cf. *Phragmites* sp.	1 Culm Frag.
Hedgehog Cactus	*Echinocereus* sp.	1 Seed
Indeterminate	Indeterminate	20 Fruit/Seed Frags.; 6 Grain Frags.; 4 Nut/Seed Frags.; 24 Seed Coat Frags.; 347 Seed Frags.
Juniper	*Juniperus* sp.	2 Branchlet Frags.
Little Barley Grass	*Hordeum* sp.	4 cf. Grain Frags.
Lovegrass Type	*Eragrostis* Type	1 Grain
Maize	*Zea mays*	1 Cob Frag.; 1 Embryo Frag.; 1 cf. Embryo Frags.; 7 Cupules; 43 Cupule Frags.; 39 cf. Cupule Frags.; 1 Glume; 18 Glume Frags.; 23 cf. Glume Frags.; 13 Kernel Frags.; 21 cf. Kernel Frags.
Manzanita	*Arctostaphylos* sp.	1 Fruit Frag.; 1 cf. Fruit Frag.
Mesquite	*Prosopis* sp.	2 cf. Seed Frags.
Miscellaneous	Miscellaneous	37 D-Shaped Fibers; 217 Endosperm Frags.; 40 Flat Fibers; 92 Frags. with White Styloid Crystals; 2,099 Round Fibers; 6 Round Fiber Bundles; 6 Spiral Twists
Monocot	Monocotyledonae	8 Stem Frags.
Monocot cf. Common Reed	Monocotyledonae cf. *Phragmites* sp.	1 Blade Frag.; 3 Culm Frags.
Monocot cf. Grass Family	Monocotyledonae cf. Poaceae	6 Culm Frags.
Pepper Grass	*Lepidium* sp.	1 Seed
Poppy[1]	*Papaver somniferum*	91 Seeds
Purslane	*Portulaca* sp.	20 Seeds; 10 Seed Frags.
Salt Bush	*Atriplex* sp.	1 Fruiting Bractlet
Seep Weed	*Suaeda* sp.	1 cf. Seed Frag.
Tansy Mustard	*Descurainia* sp.	2 Seeds; 10 cf. Seed Frags.
Winged Pigweed	*Cycloloma atriplicifolium*	4 Seeds; 12 Seed Frags.; 10 cf. Seed Frags.
Unknown	Unknown	1 AZ U:9:24 (ASU) Unknown A; 1 Unknown Seed

Notes: Frag. - Fragment; [1]Intentionally introduced into flotation samples to monitor the flotation sample processing efficiency

Table 38. Summary of uncarbonized non-woody plant remains present in the flotation samples (N=2779+).

Common Name	Scientific Name	No. and Type of Parts Present
Angiosperm	Angiospermae	1 Anther; 1 Anther Aggregate
Barley Tribe	Hordeae	9 Florets
Blazing Star	*Mentzelia* sp.	87 Seeds; 69 Seed Frags.; 2 cf. Seed Frags.
Borage Family cf. Stick Seed	Boraginaceae cf. *Lappula* sp.	4 Seeds
Bristle Grass	*Setaria* sp.	1 Fertile Floret
Bromegrass Type	*Bromus* Type	11 Fertile Florets; 14 Grains; 2 Grain Frags.
Carpet Weed	*Mollugo* sp.	74 Seeds; 23 Seed Frags.
Cheno-am	Chenopodiaceae or *Amaranthus* sp.	1 Seed; 76 cf. Seeds; 126 Seed Frags.; 42 cf. Seed Frags.
Cholla	Cylindropuntia	1 Seed; 3 Seed Frags.; 3 cf. Seed Frags.
Cholla/Prickly Pear	*Opuntia* sp.	22 Seed Frags.
Creosote Bush	*Larrea tridentata*	2 cf. Leaf Frags.
Cryptantha	*Cryptantha* sp.	237 Seeds; 1 Seed Frag.; 1 cf. Seed 4 cf. Seed Frags.
Dicot	Dicotyledonae	4 Leaves; 3 Leaf Frags.
Drop Seed Type	*Sporobolus* Type	129 Grains; 1 Grain Frag.; 37 cf. Grain Frags.
Fiddle Neck	*Amsinckia* sp.	22 Fruits; 1 Fruit + Stem; 17 Seeds; 3 Seed Frags.; 1 cf. Seed Frag.
Globe Mallow	Sphaeralcea sp.	16 Seeds; 2 cf. Seed Frags.
Goose Foot	*Chenopodium* sp.	259 Seeds; 4 Seed Frags.
Grass Family	Poaceae	8 Culm Frags.; 98 Florets; 1 Floret Frag.; 4 cf. Floret Frags.; Numerous Glumes/Lemmas/Paleas; 3 Grains; 11 cf. Grain Frags.; 2 Rachis Joint Frags.; 5 Spikelets
Hackberry	*Celtis* sp.	1 Fruit Frag.
Heron Bill	*Erodium* sp.	21 Fruits; 56 Fruit Frags.; 10 cf. Fruit Frags.; 16 Seeds; 7 Seed Frags.; 5 cf. Seed Frags.; 9 Spiral Twists
Filaree	*Erodium cicutarium*	2 Fruits; 6 Fruit Frags.; 1 Seed
Indeterminate	Indeterminate	31 Fruit Frags.; 14 Fruit/Seed Frags.; 3 Inflorescences; 2 Inflorescence Frags.; 1 Seed Coat Frags.; 112 Seed Frags.
Horse Purslane	*Trianthema portulacastrum*	2 Seeds; 5 Seed Frags.; 1 cf. Seed Frag.
Lovegrass Type	*Eragrostis* Type	2 Florets; 182 Grains; 23 Grain Frags.; 6 cf. Grain Frags.
Mallow	*Malva* sp.	12 Seeds; 1 Seed Frag.
Miscellaneous	Miscellaneous	15 Spiral Twists
Monocot cf. Grass Family	Monocotyledonae cf. Poaceae	375 Blade Frags.; 10 Blade + Culm Frags.; 186 Culm Frags.
Mustard Family	Brassicaceae	1 cf. Fruit Frag.
Oats Tribe	Aveneae Tribe	14 Florets
Pigweed	*Amaranthus* sp.	13 Seeds; 9 Seed Frags.
Pine	*Pinus* sp.	1 cf. Cone Frag.
Nightshade Family	Solanaceae	1 Seed Frag.
Nightshade Family cf. Ground Cherry	Solanaceae cf. *Physalis* sp.	3 Seeds
Purslane	*Portulaca* sp.	62 Seeds; 20 Seed Frags.
Seep Weed	*Suaeda* sp.	1 Seed
Spurge	*Euphorbia* sp.	5 Seeds; 4 Seed Frags.
Sunflower Family	Asteraceae	20 Achenes; 12 Achene Frags;
Tansy Mustard	*Descurainia* sp.	13 Seeds; 13 cf. Seeds; 9 cf. Seed Frags.
Wild Buckwheat	Eriogonum sp.	1 cf. Fruit
Wild Rye	*Elymus* sp.	4 Florets
Vervain	*Verbena* sp.	1 Nutlet

Table 39. Non-Botanical material present in the flotation samples.

Material Type	Quantity
Abundant Material	
Insect Exoskeleton Fragments	Numerous
Insect-Sized Fecal Pellets	Numerous
Macrospores	Numerous
Rodent-Sized Fecal Pellets	Numerous
Less Abundant Material	
Faunal Bone Fragments (burned)	1,192
Faunal Bone Fragments (unburned)	1,103
Chipped Stone Microflakes	394
Macrospore Clusters	239
Small Fire-Altered Rocks	115
Faunal Bones (unburned)	64
Ceramic Sherds	63
Ceramic Sherdlets	54
Shell Fragments	35
Chipped Stone Flakes	33
Faunal Bones (burned)	18
Insect Cases	17
Insect Case Fragments	15
Red Resin Globules	7
Snail Shells	6
Turquoise Fragments	6
Ants	5
Burned Animal Epidermis	4
Insect Wings	4
Charred Insect-Sized Fecal Pellets	3
Charred Termite Pellets	3
Chipped Stone Shatter	3
Beetles	2
Charred Termite Pellet Aggregates	2
Charred Termite Pellet Fragments	2
Azurite Nodule	1
Burned Insect Exoskeleton Fragment	1
Charred Rodent-Sized Fecal Pellet	1
Insect Wing Fragment	1
Probable Broom Bristle	1
Shell Bead	1
Wasp	1

Table 40. Carbonized and uncarbonized plant remains in completely analyzed flotation samples, excluding "cf.," indeterminate, miscellaneous, and unknown.

	Taxon and Parts	N
Carbonized Plant Remains (N=875)	Agave Leaf Parts	393
	Cheno-am & Goose Foot Seeds & Seed Fragments	298
	Maize Cob Parts	66
	Purslane Seeds & Seed Fragments	38
	Winged Pigweed Seeds & Seed Fragments	16
	Maize Kernel Fragments	11
	Monocot Stem Fragments	8
	Grass Family Grain Fragments	8
	Monocot cf. Grass Family Culm Fragments	6
	Blazing Star Seeds & Seed Fragments	6
	Drop Seed Type Grains & Grain Fragments	6
	Bear Grass Leaf Fragments	3
	Tansy Mustard Seeds	2
	Juniper Branchlet Fragments	2
	All Monocot cf. Common Reed Blade & Culm Fragments	2
	Cholla/Prickly Pear Seed Fragments	2
	Carpet Weed Seed Fragment	1
	Grass Family Culm Fragment	1
	Pepper Grass Seed	1
	Grass Family cf. Common Reed Culm Fragment	1
	Wild Buckwheat Fruit	1
	Hedgehog Cactus Seed	1
	AZ U:9:24 (ASU) Unknown A	1
	Salt Bush Fruiting Bractlet	1
Uncarbonized Plant Remains, Excluding Glumes/Lemmas/Paleas (N=2,326)	Monocot cf. Grass Family Blade & Culm Fragments	543
	Cheno-am & Goose Foot Seeds & Seed Fragments	390
	Cryptantha Seeds 7 Seed Fragments	238
	Lovegrass Type Grains, Grain Fragments & Florets	207
	Blazing Star Seeds & Seed Fragments	156
	Drop Seed Type Grains & Grain Fragments	130
	Heron Bill & Stork Bill Fruits, Fruit Fragments, Seeds, & Seed Fragments	114
	Grass Family Grains, Grain Fragments, Florets, Floret Fragments & Spikelets	107
	Carpet Weed Seeds & Seed Fragments	97
	Purslane Seeds & Seed Fragments	81
	Fiddleneck Fruits, Fruit Fragments, Seeds & Seed Fragments	41
	Sunflower Family Achenes & Achene Fragments	32
	Bromegrass Type Grains, Grain Fragments & Florets	27
	Pigweed Seeds & Seed Fragments	22
	Cholla/Prickly Pear Seed Fragments	22
	Globemallow Seeds	16
	Oats Tribe Florets	14
	Mallow Seeds & Seed Fragments	13
	Tansy Mustard Seeds	13
	Grass Family Culm Fragments & Rachis Joint Fragments	10
	Surge Seeds & Seed Fragments	9
	Barley Tribe Florets	9
	Dicot Leaves & Leaf Fragments	7
	Horse Purslane Seeds & Seed Fragments	7
	Eel Grass Type Florets	4
	Cholla Seeds & Seed Fragments	4
	Borage Family cf. Stickseed Seeds	4
	Nightshade Family Seeds & Seed Fragments	4
	Angiosperm Anthers & Anther Aggregates	2
	Seep Weed Seed	1
	Bristle Grass Fertile Floret	1
	Vervain Nutlet	1

Table 41. Summary of charred plant part densities within the completely analyzed flotation samples.

Provenience	Room 2, 1.3-1.4 m	Room 14, 1.3 m	Room 17, 0.7 m	Room 17, Ash Pit	Room 17, 0.98 m	Room 17, 1.5 m	Room 22, 1.35–1.45m	TOTAL PPL
Sample Size (l)	1.00	1.60	2.20	1.35	3.45	6.00	4.30	
Taxon								
Agave Fibers	–	81.9	1.8	6.7	30.7	23.2	0.5	144.8
Cheno-am Seed Frags	34.0	88.1	5.0	3.0	3.8	6.0	0.2	140.1
Goose Foot Seeds	1.0	13.8	2.7	0.7	–	0.5	–	18.7
Maize Cupule Frags.	–	7.5	–	0.7	5.2	0.7	1.2	15.3
Maize Glume Frags.	–	10.0	–	0.7	–	0.2	–	10.9
Purslane Seeds	–	9.4	–	–	0.6	0.5	–	10.5
Purslane Seed Frags.	–	6.9	0.9	–	1.2	–	0.2	9.2
Goose Foot Seed Frags.	–	–	5.0	–	–	2.0	–	7.0
Maize Kernel Frags.	–	3.8	0.5	–	0.9	0.2	–	5.4
Grass Family Grain Frags.	–	5.0	–	–	–	–	–	5.0
Monocot Stem Frags.	–	5.0	–	–	–	–	–	5.0
Maize Cupules	–	3.8	–	–	0.3	–	–	4.1
Winged Pigweed Seeds	4.0	–	–	–	–	–	–	4.0
Monocot cf. Grass Family Culm Frags.	2.0	–	–	0.7	–	0.5	–	3.2
Blazing Star Seeds	–	1.9	0.5	–	–	0.2	–	2.6
Drop Seed Type Grains	–	0.6	–	1.5	–	0.3	–	2.4
Winged Pigweed Seed Frags.	–	–	–	–	–	2.0	–	2.0
Bear Grass Leaf Frags.	–	1.9	–	–	–	–	–	1.9
Cholla/Prickly Pear Seed Frags.	–	1.3	–	–	–	–	–	1.3
Carpet Weed Seed Frag.	1.0	–	–	–	–	–	–	1.0
Pepper Grass Seed	1.0	–	–	–	–	–	–	1.0
Blazing Star Seed Frag.	1.0	–	–	–	–	–	–	1.0
Agave Fiber Bundle	–	0.6	–	–	0.3	–	–	0.9
Juniper Branchlet Frag.	–	0.6	–	–	–	0.2	–	0.8
Maize Cob Frag.	–	–	–	0.7	–	–	–	0.7
Grass Family Culm Frag.	–	0.6	–	–	–	–	–	0.6
Grass Family cf. Common Reed Culm Frag.	–	0.6	–	–	–	–	–	0.6
Lovegrass Type Grain	–	0.6	–	–	–	–	–	0.6
Cheno-am Seed	–	–	–	–	–	–	0.5	0.5
Drop Seed Type Grain Frag.	–	–	0.5	–	–	–	–	0.5
Salt Bush Fruiting Bractlet	–	–	0.5	–	–	–	–	0.5
Monocot cf. Common Reed Culm Frag.	–	–	–	–	–	0.2	0.2	0.4
Hedgehog Cactus Seed	–	–	–	–	0.3	–	–	0.3
Tansy Mustard Seed	–	–	–	–	–	0.3	–	0.3
AZ U:9:24 (ASU) Unknown A	–	–	–	–	–	0.2	–	0.2

Note: Frag. - Fragment; Frags. – Fragments; PPL - Parts per liter

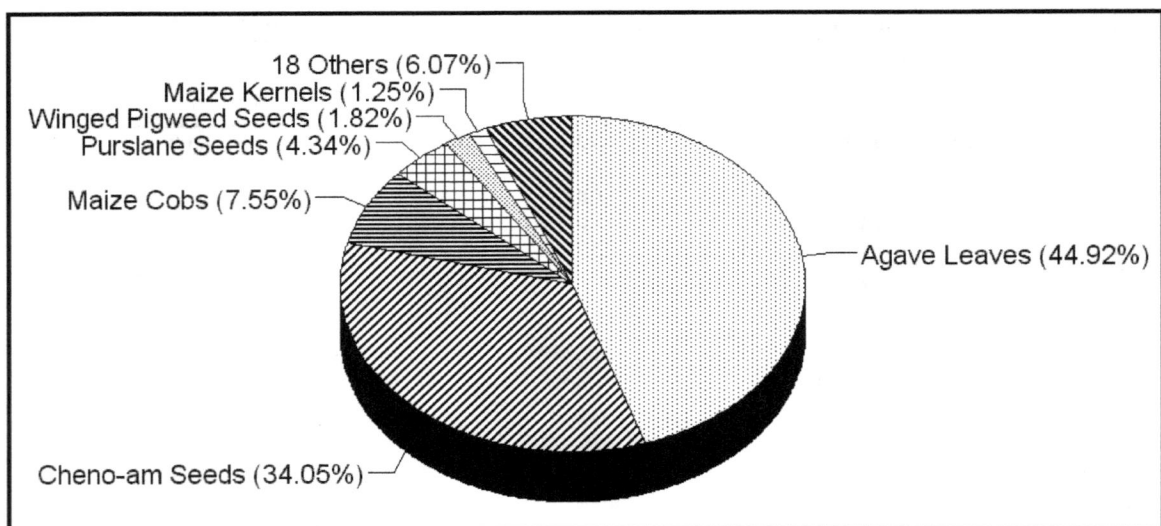

Figure 62. Relative abundance of charred plant remains in flotation samples.

Table 42. Presence of recent disturbance and prehistoric refuse indicators, per liter, in the samples.

Taxon	Room 2 1.3–1.4 m	Room 14 1.3 m	Room 17, 0.7 m	Room 17, Ash Pit	Room 17, 0.98 m	Room 17, 1.5 m	Room 22, 1.35–1.45 m
INDICATORS OF RECENT DISTURBANCE							
Insect-Sized Fecal Pellets	++	++	7	1	++	++	++
Insect Exoskeleton Frags.	++	++	6	4	6	++	++
Macrospores	374	668	13	200	366	331	980
Uncarbonized Plant Remains	++	73	4	3	20	167	207
Rodent-Sized Fecal Pellets	7	23	TR	6	++	17	TR
Unburned Bones & Frags.	11	91	3	4	13	20	2
Whole Insects	1	–	–	–	TR	1	1
INDICATORS OF PREHISTORIC REFUSE							
Charred Plant Remains	40	246	17	15	43	37	3
Burned Bones & Frags.	7	57	5	6	13	20	7
Ceramic Sherds	–	11	–	1	1	3	2
Chipped Stone	3	7	1	–	3	6	5
Fire-Altered Rocks	1	2	–	1	6	2	3

Notes: ++ - Abundant (> 50 parts per liter); TR - Trace (< 0.5 parts per liter).

The flotation samples typically contained abundant insect exoskeleton fragments and insect-sized fecal pellets (Table 42), indicating that substantial disturbance, or bioturbation, has occurred to the sediments at the Coyote Ruin since it was abandoned. Inspection of Table 42 finds that the upper two samples from Room 17 were relatively low in indicators of both recent disturbance and prehistoric refuse deposition, while the sample from Room 14 contained the most telltale signatures of prehistoric trash. Thus, it appears quite likely that refuse was dumped into at least one room at the Coyote Ruin after it had fallen into disuse during prehistoric times, but before the site was abandoned.

Wood Charcoal

A summary of the results of the analysis of the wood charcoal macrobotanical and flotation analyses is presented in Table 43.

Table 43. Relative abundance of wood charcoal types, by count and weight, in the flotation and macrobotanical samples.

Common Name	Scientific Name	Total No. in Flot. Samples	Total No. in Macro-botanical Samples	Total Weight in Grams (Macro-botanical Samples Only)	Average Weight per Piece in Grams (Macro-botanical Samples Only)
Cf. Palo Verde	Arboreal Legume cf. *Cercidium* sp.	–	69	198.60	2.88
Pine Type	*Pinus* Type	8	73	103.00	1.32
cf. Oak	cf. *Quercus* sp.	14	151	89.50	0.59
cf. Mountain Mahogany	cf. *Cercocarpus* sp.	3	34	25.25	0.74
cf. Mesquite	Arboreal Legume cf. *Prosopis* sp.	–	11	10.25	0.93
Unknown	Unknown	–	23	2.00	0.09
Cottonwood/Willow Type	*Populus/Salix* Type	–	2	<0.05	<0.05
Gymnosperm	Gymnosperm	1	–	–	–
Total		*26*	*363*	*428.60*	

Each of the five macrobotanical samples contained between 20 and 252 individually analyzed charcoal specimens, and each weighed between 2.0 and 315.4 grams (Table 44). In sum, 363 pieces of charcoal, weighing an aggregate total of 428.6 grams, were examined during the macrobotanical analysis (Table 44). All of the material listed on Table 44 was essentially entirely carbonized except for one incompletely burned piece from Room 2 that had a brown or "caramelized" appearance. Six known wood charcoal types, and one unknown type, were identified. The wood charcoal identified in the flotation samples was generally similar to that recovered in the macrobotanical samples; the primary difference was the lack of wood comparable to palo verde in the flotation samples. Inspection of Table 44 finds that the cf. palo verde wood consisted of the largest average pieces recovered, by weight. Charcoal pieces comparable to oak, by contrast, tended to be relatively small, weighing even less on average than the cf. mountain mahogany pieces.

Table 44. Wood charcoal identifications from macrobotanical samples.

Context	Weight	No.	Identification
Room 2			
N2, W6; 1.30 m BGS	66.25	20	Pine Type*
Grid N0, W10; Square N2, W4; 1.47 m	13.65	16	Pine Type
BGS	4.10	5	cf. Oak
	4.00	8	cf. Mountain Mahogany
Grid N0, W10; Square N4, W3; Level 4	21.20	35	Pine Type
	1.40	1	Pine Type (caramelized)
	0.60	1	cf. Mountain Mahogany
Room 17			
Feature 1; Grid S10, E10; Square S4, E18;	2.00	23	Unknown
0.85 m BGS; Southeast Corner and Along	<0.05	2	Cottonwood/Willow Type
Room 40			
Level 8, Floor	198.60	69	Arboreal Legume cf. Palo Verde
	85.40	146	cf. Oak
	20.65	25	cf. Mountain Mahogany
	9.25	9	Arboreal Legume cf. Mesquite Sap Wood
	1.00	2	Arboreal Legume cf. Mesquite Transitional
	0.50	1	Pine Type

Note: * - Submitted for dendrochronological analysis on December 23, 2003.

Table 45 depicts the distribution of wood charcoal types by room on the flotation samples. Two taxa, ponderosa pine type and cf. oak, were present in more than half the rooms sampled. One taxon, cf. mountain mahogany, was recovered from two rooms. The remaining taxa were each found in only one room.

Table 45. Presence of wood charcoal types, by room, in the flotation and macrobotanical samples.

Taxon	Room	Room 14	Room 17	Room 22	Room 40
Arboreal Legume cf. Palo	–	–	–	–	X
Pine Type	X	–	X	X	X
cf. Oak	X	X	X	–	X
cf. Mountain Mahogany	X	–	–	–	X
Arboreal Legume cf.	–	–	–	–	X
Unknown	–	–	X	–	–
Cottonwood/Willow Type	–	–	X	–	–
Gymnosperm	–	–	X	–	–

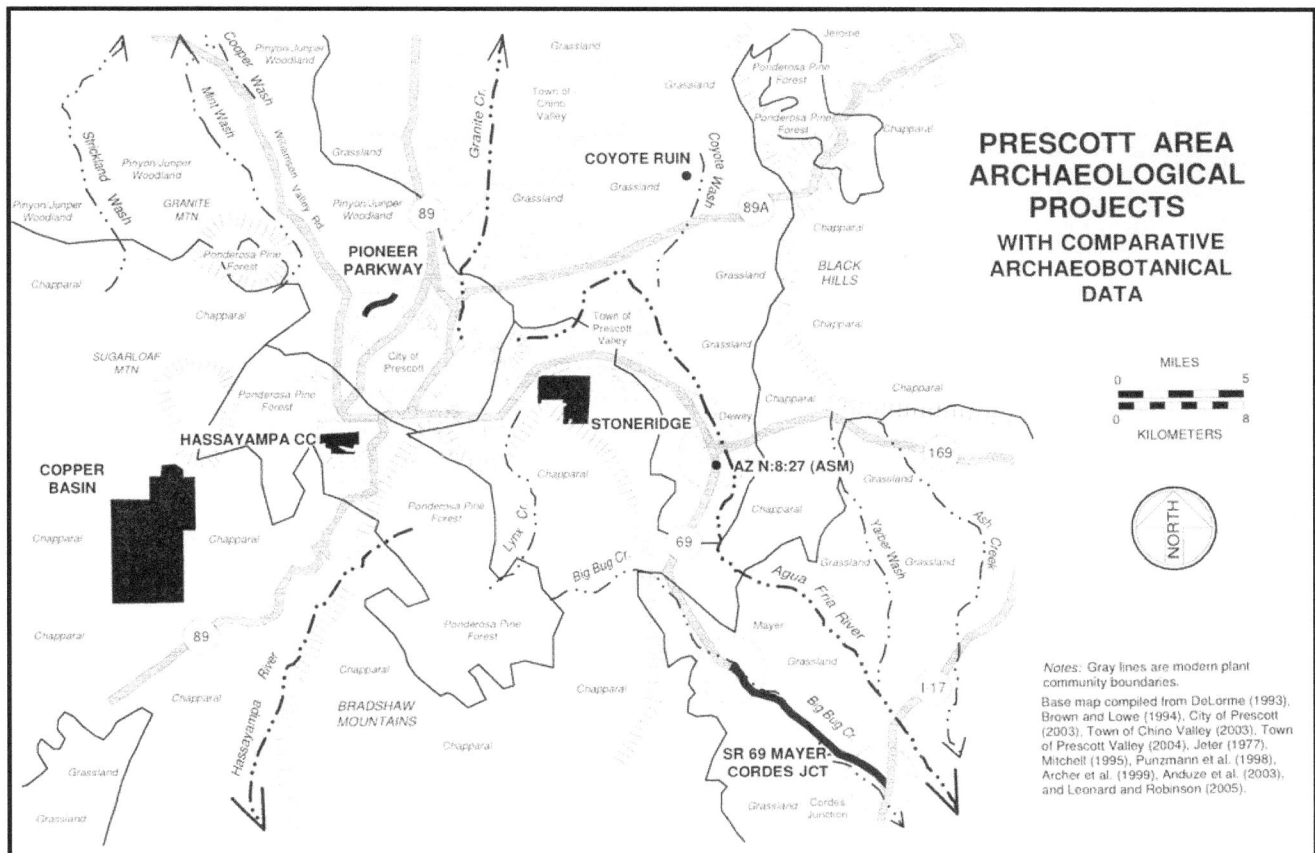

Figure 63. Prescott-area archaeological projects with comparative archaeobotanical data.

DISCUSSION

Two research questions are considered in this section: (1) How does the wood charcoal assemblage from the Coyote Ruin compare to other archaeological sites investigated in the Prescott area? (2) What types of plants appear to have been economically important at the Coyote Ruin?

Regional Comparisons: Wood Charcoal

Table 46 lists the wood charcoal types from 19 archaeological sites in the Prescott area that were identified during four large data recovery projects. The locations of these projects in relation to current landmarks and vegetative communities are depicted on Figure 63. Inspection of Table 46 indicates that the four most commonly recovered charcoal types have been: (1) oak; (2) juniper type; (3) pine type; and (4) mountain mahogany. Three of these four types were also recovered at the Coyote Ruin; the exception was juniper. The relative rarity of juniper type charcoal appears to be real rather than an artifact of sampling. Thus, the wood charcoal assemblage is most consistent with the exploitation of the Interior Chaparral Biome (oak, mountain mahogany) (Pase and Brown 1994b) and the Petran Montane Conifer Forest Biome (pine type, with relatively large resin ducts) (Pase and Brown 1994a) for fuel and structural material. In contrast, there was relatively little evidence that the Great Basin Conifer Woodland Biome (D. Brown 1994), or pinyon/juniper woodland, was being used for these purposes.

147

Table 46. Summaries of some prior wood charcoal studies in the Prescott Culture area.

Taxon	Pioneer Parkway (Holloway and Archer 1999)			Hassayampa County Club (Cummings et al. 2003)			StoneRidge (Huckell 2005)												SR69 (Cummings & Puseman 1995)	Total Presence
	N:7:173	N:7:195	N:7:196	N:6:20	N:7:155	N:7:156	N:7:228	N:7:241	N:7:247	N:7:255	N:7:260	N:7:262	N:7:263	N:7:265	N:7:267	N:7:283	N:7:284	N:7:286	N:8:27	
Phase[1]	C	C	C	C	C	C	F–P	U	P	P–C	U	P	U	P	C	P	Y	A–Y	C	
Oak (Quercus sp.) Wood	–	–	–	–	X	X	–	–	–	X	X	–	X	X	X	–	–	X	X	9X
Juniper Type (Juniperus Type)	–	–	–	–	X	–	–	–	X	X	–	X	X	–	X	X	–	X	–	8X
Pine Type (Pinus Type)	–	X	–	–	–	–	–	–	X	X	–	X	–	X	–	–	–	X	X	7X
Mountain Mahogany (Cercocarpus sp.)	–	–	–	X	X	–	–	–	–	X	X	–	–	–	–	–	X	X	–	6X
Cottonwood/Willow Type (Populus/Salix Type)	–	–	–	–	–	–	–	–	–	X	–	–	–	–	–	–	–	X	–	2X
Walnut (Juglans sp.)	–	–	–	–	–	–	–	–	–	–	–	–	X	–	–	–	–	X	–	2X
Rose Family (Rosaceae)	–	–	–	–	X	–	–	–	–	–	–	–	–	–	–	–	–	P	–	1P/1X
Ash (Fraxinus sp.)	–	–	–	–	–	–	–	–	–	–	X	–	–	–	–	–	–	–	–	1X
Cliffrose (Cowania sp.)	–	–	–	–	X	–	–	–	–	–	–	–	–	–	–	–	–	–	–	1X
Manzanita (Arctostaphylos sp.)	–	–	–	–	X	–	–	–	–	–	–	–	–	–	–	–	–	–	–	1X
Mesquite (Prosopis sp.)	–	X	–	–	–	–	–	–	–	–	–	–	–	–	–	–	–	–	–	1X
Pea Family (Fabaceae)	–	X	–	–	–	–	–	–	–	–	–	–	–	–	–	–	–	–	–	1X
Ponderosa Pine Type (Pinus ponderosa Type)	–	–	–	–	X	–	–	–	–	–	–	–	–	–	–	–	–	–	–	1X

Notes: P - Possibly Present; X – Present. [1]Date Codes: A - Archaic (pre-A.D. 1); F - Early Formative Period (ca. A.D. 1–800); P – Prescott Phase (ca. A.D. 800–1025); C - Chino Phase (ca. A.D. 1025–1310); Y - Protohistoric Yavapai, (ca. A.D. 1400–1850); U – Unknown.

Economically Important Plant Remains

The mere presence of charred plant remains in flotation samples does not necessarily indicate that they represent economically important plant remains (Minnis 1981). For example, naturally abundant members of the natural seed rain may become charred inadvertently within hearths or roasting pits. On the other hand, it is important to remember that only a minuscule amount of the soil at the site was examined for presence of charred plant remains. Furthermore, even if much more soil had been sampled, not all plants that would have been used prehistorically would be expected to produce evidence of their use within flotation samples (Munson et al. 1971). For example, plant remains such as maize that are typically processed by parching are expected to be much more common than fleshy plant foods, such as wild grapes, that are usually never exposed to flames during processing.

Three ways to evaluate which taxa present in the flotation samples were, in fact, economically important at any given site are: (1) to compare how similar the carbonized and uncarbonized plant assemblages appear to each other; (2) to determine whether the plant remains identified have known ethnobotanical use and would have been processed, used, and/or discarded in ways consistent with how they were found archaeologically; and (3) to ascertain how common the same plant taxa are in flotation samples analyzed from some nearby archaeological sites.

148

Comparison of the Carbonized and Uncarbonized Plant Assemblages

Applying the same procedures used earlier for the carbonized non-woody plant remains (i.e., omitting the cf.-level, indeterminate, miscellaneous, and unknown identifications) to the uncarbonized ones, marked discrepancies are evident (cf., Figures 62 and 64) (note that the uncarbonized data on Table 40 and Figure 64 omits the numerous Grass Family glumes/lemmas/paleas to avoid swamping the data). Maize and agave do not occur as uncarbonized plant remains. In contrast, cryptantha seeds, heron bill/filaree fruits/seeds, and fiddleneck fruits/seeds were not found carbonized. Monocot blades/culms, lovegrass grains, blazing star seeds, drop seed grains, and carpet weed seeds were much better represented by uncarbonized remains than charred ones. All of the heron bill fruits and seeds that could be identified to the species level were filaree, an introduced plant. These patterns appear most consistent with the belief that, like at most other open-air archaeological sites, the uncarbonized plant remains present in the flotation samples are essentially modern contaminants, while the burned matter represents material deposited during the prehistoric use of the Coyote Ruin.

Ethnographic Analogs

The best type of ethnographic analog for an archaeologist to use is the likely descendants of the archaeological culture being studied (Ascher 1968). In the Prescott area, this would be the Yavepe, or Northeastern Yavapai, who lived in the area during earliest historical times and who claim cultural affiliation to the Prescott Culture (although this ancestral connection is disputed by some archaeologists, most notably Euler 1958). However, while Edward Gifford's (1936) ethnography of the Northeastern Yavapai contains some ethnobotanical information, it is likely incomplete. Further, later attempts have also not been particularly successful in bridging the existing data gaps (Waddell 1986). In this case, it is thought best to supplement the incomplete Yavepe plant usage list with analogs from neighboring Southwestern Indian tribes. Accordingly, two plant usage tables have been constructed, one based on information in Gifford's (1936) ethnography (Table 47), and a second from Edward Castetter's (1935) study of uncultivated plant foods used by Southwestern Indians (Table 48).

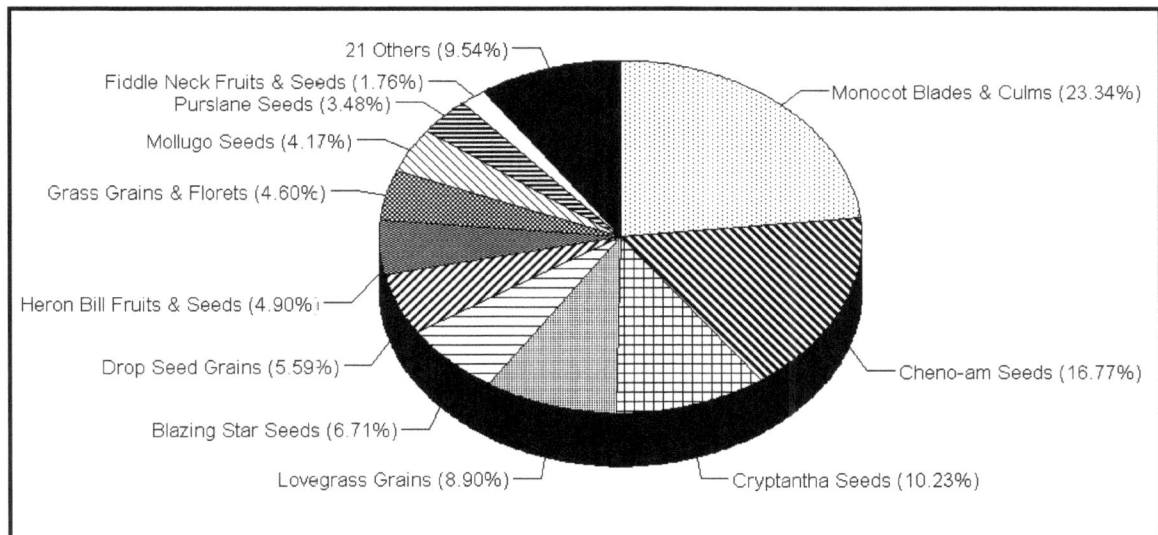

Figure 64. Relative abundance of uncharred plant remains in flotation samples.

- 21 Others (9.54%)
- Fiddle Neck Fruits & Seeds (1.76%)
- Purslane Seeds (3.48%)
- Mollugo Seeds (4.17%)
- Grass Grains & Florets (4.60%)
- Heron Bill Fruits & Seeds (4.90%)
- Drop Seed Grains (5.59%)
- Blazing Star Seeds (6.71%)
- Lovegrass Grains (8.90%)
- Monocot Blades & Culms (23.34%)
- Cheno-am Seeds (16.77%)
- Cryptantha Seeds (10.23%)

Inspection of Table 47 finds that the agave, cheno-am, and maize remains recovered from the Coyote Ruin are consistent with traditional Yavepe methods of preparation and use. Further, the drop seed, purslane, blazing star, and tansy mustard remains are consistent with how other Southwestern Indian groups have sometimes used these plants (Table 48). While bear grass, manzanita, hedgehog cactus, cholla/prickly pear, salt bush, and wild buckwheat were used by either the Yavepe or other Southwestern Indians, their traditional preparation/use methods would not normally be expected to leave the types of charred plant traces recovered from the Coyote Ruin (cf. Table 47-48). Some of these remains could have been burned accidentally, while others could represent food refuse intentionally disposed of within fires. A few remains, such as the monocot stems, the juniper branchlets, and the possible common reed culms, could represent tinder remnants.

Two charred plant remains recovered from the Coyote Ruin, a pepper grass seed and a carpet weed seed fragment, represent plant types that have not typically been used by Southwestern Indians for food or other economic purposes. It seems likely that these plant remains represent inadvertently burned components of the prehistoric seed rain. This idea seems supported by their low frequency of occurrence.

Table 47. Northeastern Yavapai uses of plants represented at Coyote Ruin, as recorded by E.W. Gifford (1936), with expected archaeological correlates. For foods marked with an asterisk (*), the ethnographically documented use is consistent with the presence of the types of charred plant remains found at the Coyote Ruin.

Plant Food	Preparation/Use Methods	Expected Archaeological Correlates
Agave (*Agave*) Hearts*	"Ripeness indicated by leaves tinged red and spread far out. . . To uproot plant, digging stick driven under it with cobble. Plant turned upside down, thick spiny leaves cut off with hunting or other knife of steel or iron. . .Leaf cut where exposed part joined white of unexposed base. . . With digging sticks, men and women dug pit 4 ft. deep for oven. Its diameter varied according to quantity of mescal to be cooked; maximum 10 or 12 feet. *Ceanothus greggii* branches used for kindling, piled both under and over fuel, Fuel was dead wood, mostly juniper and alligator bark juniper. Stones 8 or 10 in. in diameter piled over wood with small stones on top, forming mound. Same stones used many times. . . When fire burned out, stones worked to bottom of pit and cooled somewhat. Then mescal placed on them. Thick coating of grass laid on mescal, earth from pit spread over grass. Cooking usually started shortly after noon, lasted until dawn of 2d day thereafter. No fire built on top to expedite cooking. Each woman piled her mescal heads together in pit, having cut or poked holes in leaf stubs to indicate ownership. . .When removed from pit, mescal laid on grass spread for cleanliness over ground. Leaf stubs pulled off, heads peeled, scraps thrown in basket. Men provided stone slabs about 2 ft., 6 in. in diameter or length; on these women macerated mescal. Hard natural cobble with one side sharp or narrow used as hammer. First leaf stubs, then heads pounded to express juice. Brush swab of grass stems . . . used to transfer excess mescal juice from dish to slab, to be absorbed by drying mescal. . . Result, fibrous rectangular slab full of juice, about 3/4 in. thick, and 2 ft., 6 in. square. . . Slabs of pounded mescal laid to dry on litter. . . in sunny place. Slabs turned over after first day, but not again. Left to dry day and night for about 2 weeks, then stacked in piles" (pp. 259–260).	Large Roasting Pits; Hammer- stones; Large Flat Stone Slabs; Charred Agave Fibers
Agave (*Agave*) Leaves*	"Also dried mescal leaves for cordage" (p. 254).	Same as Above
Bear Grass (*Nolina*) Leaves	"Huts often had 3 layers of thatch. . . outer of ikanyur (bear grass), *Nolina microcarpa*, or of juniper bark" (p. 271).	None
Manzanita (*Arctostaphylos*) Berries	"Manzanita berries pounded on metate with muller used as hammerstone. Placed in tight basket, water added, stirred with stick. Decoction drunk from hand. Some persons, such as deer hunters, chewed berries, spat out hard parts" (p. 256).	Hand Stones or Manos; Grinding Slabs or Metates
Goose Foot (*Chenopodium*) Seeds*	"When seeds mature, tops plucked and placed in conical burden basket. Seeds extracted by spreading tops on flat surface and beating them with stick: seeds winnowed, parched with coals in basket, ground on metate, boiled, eaten" (p. 256)	Hand Stones or Manos; Grinding Slabs or Metates; Charred Cheno-am Seeds
Hedgehog Cactus (*Echinocereus*) Fruits	[as *Cereus engelmannii*] "In late June, ripe fruit eaten uncooked. Fruit knocked off with long sticks, handled with tongs. Spines removed with stick" (p. 256).	None
Pancake Pear (*Opuntia chlorotica*) Fruits	"Fruit exceptionally sweet, eaten raw after spines brushed off" (p. 257).	None
Opuntia erinacea Fruits	"Fruit eaten raw after spines brushed off" (p. 257).	None

Table 47 continued.

Plant Food	Preparation/Use Methods	Expected Archaeological Correlates
Maize (*Zea mays*)*	"Maize planted near stream's edge, not irrigated and usually not cultivated. . . Ground weeded first. After plants 1½ ft. high, people went S. Maize ripe when they returned. . .Seed saved for planting each year. Small circular areas prepared with digging stick of any kind of wood. Three or 4 seeds planted in each hole, grew up in bunches about 2 ft. apart. When plants about 18 in. tall, earth heaped about 6 in. high around them. . .This done to keep roots better covered. . . ripe maize dried in sun for ca. 1 month after husking. Grains removed from cob by hand, with thumb exerting principal pressure. . . Maize stored in burden baskets [in caves] covered with 1 or 2 in. of bear grass lashed on with soaproot *Yucca* leaves. Base of conical basket set in hole ca. 1 ft. deep, lined with grass; stones put around base to keep basket upright. Cave rats could not molest it. Ears of green maize boiled and eaten from cob, or roasted—husked or unhusked—in coals. Dry maize basket-parched, ground on metate, boiled in pot. Salted while boiling. . .Meal not used to thicken stew as was acorn meal. No other food cooked with maize-meal mush. No paper bread made" (pp. 262–263).	Manos and Metates; Wide-Mouthed Ceramic Vessels; Salt; Charred Maize Kernels and Cob Parts

Regional Comparisons

Table 49 summarizes the charred non-woody plant remains recovered during the analysis of flotation samples from 26 Prescott-area archaeological sites during five large data recovery projects (see Figure 63 for the project-area locations). Inspection of this table finds that the five most commonly recovered taxa during these studies have been (in decreasing order): (1) cheno-am seeds; (2) maize remains; (3) purslane seeds; (4) manzanita seeds; and (5) grass family grains. Examples of each of these taxa were also recovered from the Coyote Ruin. Interesting, the next three best represented taxa, juniper seeds, walnut fragments, and pinyon nuts, were not recovered from the Coyote Ruin during the present study. However, Simmons (Chapter 2) did report finding charred pinyon nuts on the floor of Room 2 during his 1920s excavations at the site. The relatively low representation of tree nuts at the Coyote Ruin is interesting, although the precise reason(s) for their absence are not clear at present.

Charred agave remains were more common at the Coyote Ruin compared to other all other sites used in the regional comparison database. The author suspects that the reason for this difference is more apparent than real in that other archaeobotanists may not be identifying small, charred fibers present within flotation samples as agave to the same extent. Agave was such an important food plant to virtually all Southwestern Indians during historic times (Castetter *et al.* 1938) that it is unlikely this food would have been neglected prehistorically within the Prescott area to the extent seemingly indicated on Table 49.

Table 48. Some Ethnographic uses of plants represented at Coyote Ruin, not recorded by Gifford (1936), but instead reported by Castetter (1935), with expected archaeological correlates. For foods marked with an asterisk (*), the ethnographically documented use is consistent with the presence of the types of charred plant remains found at the Coyote Ruin.

Plant Food	Preparation/Use Methods	Expected Archaeological Correlates
Drop Seed (*Sporobolus*) Grains*	". . .the Navajo make dumplings, rolls, and griddle-cakes from the ground seeds of *Sporobolus cryptandrus*, drop-seed grass, while among the Hopi the seeds of this species as well as of panic grass (*Panicum capillare*) are ground and mixed with corn mean for food" (p. 28).	Hand Stones or Manos; Grinding Slabs or Metates; Charred Drop Seed Grass Grains
Purslane (*Portulaca*) Seeds*	"The seeds of both species [*P. oleracea* and *P. retusa*] were at one time eaten as food by the Zuni and Navajo"(p. 43).	Hand Stones or Manos; Grinding Slabs or Metates; Charred Purslane Seeds
Salt Bush (*Atriplex*) Leaves, Stems, and Flower Heads	"*Atriplex nuttallii*, saltbush, is utilized by the Pima for food and flavoring purposes. The young stems and flower heads are boiled with wheat for the purpose of flavoring, the stems being cut in short lengths and sometimes used as a stuffing in cooking rabbits. Other species, especially *A. argenta* and *A. cornuta*, are used among the Pueblo Indians of the Rio Grande Valley by boiling alone or with various plant products and meats for flavoring. The young leaves of *A. argenta* are boiled and eaten as greens at Isleta. The fruits of the same species, *tweemutsi*, are eaten by the Acoma and Laguna as food as well as utilized for their salty flavor. These two pueblos also eat the young plans of *A. philonitra*, saltbush, *shita*, as greens, as do the Cochiti among whom the plant is known as *shikui*. By the Hopi the salty leaves are boiled and eaten with fat. This is the earliest of the six typical spring food-plants. Palmer records the use of six species of Atriplex as food by the Indians of Utah, Arizona, and California" (p. 18).	Wide-Mouthed Ceramic Vessels
Blazing Star (*Mentzelia*) Seeds*	"*Mentzelia albicaulis* Dougl. The Hopi parch and grind these seeds into a fine sweet meal and eat it in pinches" (p. 34).	Hand Stones or Manos; Grinding Slabs or Metates; Charred Blazing Star Seeds
Tansy Mustard (*Descurainia*) Seeds*	[listed as *Sophia pinnata* (Walt.) Britton] "The Seeds are parched and afterward ground to make meal, whereupon it is mixed with water by the Pima to form a pinole" (p. 52).	Hand Stones or Manos; Grinding Slabs or Metates; Charred Tansy Mustard Seeds
Wild Buckwheat (*Eriogonum*) Leaves	"Eriogonum corymbosum Benth. Among the Hopi the leaves are boiled, and with some of the water in which they are boiled they are rubbed on the mealing stone with corn and baked into a type of bread" (p. 29).	Manos and Metates

Date Code[1]: Taxon	Copper Basin (Gasser 1977) N:10:11 (ASU)	N:10:13 (ASU)	N:10:24 (ASU)	N:10:15 (ASU)	N:10:44 (ASU)	N:10:45 (ASU)	N:10:47 (ASU)	N:10:48 (ASU)	N:10:51 (ASU)	SR69 Cordes Junction–Mayer (Phillips 1998) N:12:14 (ASM)	N:12:22 (ASM)	N:12:24 (ASM)	N:12:25 (ASM)	N:12:44 (ASM)	N:12:57 (ASM)	Pioneer Parkway (Holloway & Archer 1999) N:7:173 (ASM)	N:7:195 (ASM)	N:7:196 (ASM)	Hassayampa CC (Cummings et al. 2003) N:6:20 (ASM)	N:7:155 (ASM)	N:7:156 (ASM)	StoneRidge (Huckell 2005) N:7:228 (ASM)	N:7:241 (ASM)	N:7:247 (ASM)	N:7:255 (ASM)	N:7:286 (ASM)	Total Presence
	C	P–C	P	P–C	P–C	P–C	P–C	P–C	C	A–P	F–P	F–P	A–P	P	F	C	C	C	C	C	C	F–P	?	P	P–C	A–Y	
Plants of Probable Economic Importance																											
Mesoamerican-Derived Cultivars																											
Maize (*Zea mays*)	X	–	X	–	X	X	X	–	–	X	X	X	X	–	X	–	X	–	X	X	–	X	X	X	X	X	18X
Huazontle (*Chenopodium berlandieri*) Seeds	–	–	–	–	–	–	–	–	–	–	–	–	–	–	–	–	–	–	–	–	–	X	–	X	X	X	4X
Beans (*Phaseolus* sp.)	–	–	–	–	X	–	X	–	–	–	–	–	–	–	–	–	–	–	–	X	–	–	–	–	–	–	3X
Squash/Pumpkin (*Cucurbita* sp.)	–	–	–	–	–	–	–	–	–	–	–	–	–	–	–	–	–	–	–	X	–	X	–	–	–	X	3X
Cotton (*Gossypium hirsutum*) Seeds	–	–	–	–	–	–	–	–	–	–	–	–	–	–	–	–	–	–	–	–	–	–	–	–	–	X	1X
Other Plants																											
Cheno-am (Chenopodiaceae and *Amaranthus* sp.) Greens/Seeds	X	X	–	X	X	X	X	X	X	X	X	X	X	X	X	–	–	–	X	X	X	X	X	X	X	X	22X
Purslane (*Portulaca* sp.) Seeds	–	X	–	–	–	X	X	–	–	X	X	X	X	–	X	–	–	–	X	X	–	X	X	–	–	X	13X
Manzanita (*Arctostaphylos* sp.) Berries	X	–	X	–	–	X	–	–	–	X	X	–	X	–	–	–	–	–	X	X	X	X	–	–	–	X	11X
Grass Family (Poaceae) Grains	–	–	–	–	–	–	–	–	–	–	X	X	X	–	–	–	–	–	X	X	–	X	–	X	–	X	8X
Juniper (*Juniperus* sp.) Berries	X	X	–	–	X	–	–	–	–	–	–	–	–	–	–	–	–	–	X	X	–	X	–	–	–	X	7X
Walnuts (*Juglans* sp.)	X	X	X	–	–	–	–	–	X	–	–	–	–	–	–	–	–	–	–	X	–	X	–	–	–	X	7X
Pinyon Pine (*Pinus edulis*) Nuts	–	–	–	–	X	X	–	–	–	–	X	X	X	–	–	–	–	–	–	X	–	–	–	–	–	–	6X
Little Barley Grass (*Hordeum* sp.) Grains	–	–	–	–	–	–	–	–	–	X	–	X	X	–	–	–	–	–	–	–	–	X	–	–	–	X	5X
Bear Grass (*Nolina* sp.) Leaves	–	–	–	–	–	–	–	–	–	–	–	–	–	–	–	–	–	–	–	–	–	–	X	X	X	X	4X
Blazing Star (*Mentzelia* sp.) Seeds	–	–	–	–	–	–	–	–	–	–	–	–	–	–	–	–	–	–	–	–	–	X	–	X	X	X	4X
Winged Pigweed (*Cycloloma* sp.) Seeds	–	–	–	–	–	–	–	–	–	–	–	–	–	–	–	–	–	–	–	–	–	X	–	X	X	X	4X
Grass Family (Poaceae) Culms	–	–	–	–	–	–	–	–	–	–	–	–	–	–	–	–	–	–	–	–	–	X	–	X	X	X	4X
Juniper (*Juniperus* sp.) Branchlets	–	–	–	–	–	–	–	–	–	–	X	X	X	–	–	–	–	–	–	–	–	–	–	–	–	X	4X
Prickly Pear Cactus (Platyopuntia) Fruits/Seeds	–	–	X	–	X	–	–	–	–	–	–	–	–	–	–	–	–	–	X	X	–	–	–	–	–	–	4X
Cholla/Prickly Pear (*Opuntia* sp.) Fruits/Seeds	–	–	–	–	–	–	–	–	–	–	X	–	X	–	–	–	–	–	–	–	–	X	–	–	–	–	3X
Elymoid Grass (*Bromus* sp. and *Elymus* sp.) Grains	–	–	–	–	–	–	–	–	–	–	–	–	–	–	–	–	–	–	–	–	–	X	–	–	X	X	3X
Drop Seed Grass (*Sporobolus* sp.) Type Grains	–	–	–	–	–	–	–	–	–	–	–	–	–	–	–	–	–	–	–	–	–	X	–	P	–	X	1P2X
Arboreal Legume (Fabaceae) Seeds	–	–	–	–	–	–	–	–	–	–	X	–	X	–	–	–	–	–	–	–	–	–	–	–	–	–	2X
Cholla (Cylindropuntia) Fruits/Seeds	–	–	–	–	–	–	–	–	–	–	–	–	–	–	–	–	–	X	–	X	–	–	–	–	–	–	2X
Rose Family (Rosaceae) Fruits	–	–	–	–	–	–	–	–	–	–	–	–	–	–	–	–	–	–	X	X	–	–	–	–	–	–	2X
Salt Bush (*Atriplex* sp.) Leaves/Flower Heads	–	–	–	–	–	–	–	–	–	–	–	–	–	–	–	–	–	–	X	X	–	–	–	–	–	–	2X
Sunflower Family (Asteraceae) Achenes	–	–	–	–	–	–	–	–	–	–	–	–	–	–	–	–	–	–	–	–	–	X	–	–	–	X	2X

Table 49. Summaries of some prior flotation studies in the Prescott Culture area, continued.

	Copper Basin (Gasser 1977)									SR69 Cordes Junction–Mayer (Phillips 1998)						Pioneer Parkway (Holloway & Archer)			Hassa-yampa CC (Cummings et al. 2003)			StoneRidge (Huckell 2005)					Total Presence
	N:10:11 (ASU)	N:10:13 (ASU)	N:10:24 (ASU)	N:10:15 (ASU)	N:10:44 (ASU)	N:10:45 (ASU)	N:10:47 (ASU)	N:10:48 (ASU)	N:10:51 (ASU)	N:12:14 (ASM)	N:12:22 (ASM)	N:12:24 (ASM)	N:12:25 (ASM)	N:12:44 (ASM)	N:12:57 (ASM)	N:7:173 (ASM)	N:7:195 (ASM)	N:7:196 (ASM)	N:6:20 (ASM)	N:7:155 (ASM)	N:7:156 (ASM)	N:7:228 (ASM)	N:7:241 (ASM)	N:7:247 (ASM)	N:7:255 (ASM)	N:7:286 (ASM)	
Date Code[1]: Taxon	C	P–C	P	P–C	P–C	P–C	P–C	P–C	C	A–P	F–P	F–P	A–P	P	F	C	C	C	C	C	C	F–P	?	P	P–C	A–Y	
Plants of Probable Economic Importance, Cont.																											
Other Plants, Continued																											
Tansy Mustard (*Descurainia* sp.)	–	–	–	–	–	–	–	–	–	–	–	–	–	–	–	–	–	–	–	–	–	X	–	–	–	X	2X
Oak (*Quercus* sp.) Acorns	–	–	–	–	–	–	–	–	–	–	–	–	–	–	–	X	–	–	–	–	–	P	–	P	–	P	3P/1X
Agave (*Agave* sp.) Hearts & Leaves	–	–	–	–	–	–	–	–	–	–	–	–	–	–	–	–	–	–	–	P	–	–	–	–	–	X	1P/1X
Wild Buckwheat (*Eriogonum* sp.)	–	–	–	–	–	–	–	–	–	–	–	–	–	–	–	X	–	–	–	–	–	–	–	–	P	–	1P/1X
Beeweed (*Cleome* sp.) Greens/Seeds	–	–	–	–	–	–	–	–	–	–	–	–	–	–	–	–	–	–	–	X	–	–	–	–	–	–	1X
Cactus Family (Cactaceae) Fruits	–	–	–	–	–	–	–	–	–	–	–	–	–	–	–	X	–	–	–	–	–	–	–	–	–	–	1X
Cattail (*Typha* sp.) Leaves/Pollen	–	–	–	–	–	–	–	–	–	–	–	–	–	–	–	–	–	–	–	X	–	–	–	–	–	–	1X
Globemallow (*Sphaeralcea* sp.)	–	–	–	–	–	–	–	–	–	–	–	–	–	–	–	–	–	–	–	–	–	–	–	–	X	–	1X
Ground Cherry/Tomatillo (*Physalis*	–	–	–	–	–	–	–	–	–	–	–	–	–	–	–	–	–	–	–	X	–	–	–	–	–	–	1X
Hackberry (*Celtis* sp.) Fruits	–	–	–	–	X	–	–	–	–	–	–	–	–	–	–	–	–	–	–	–	–	–	–	–	–	–	1X
Monocot Stem Frags.	–	–	–	–	–	–	–	–	–	–	–	–	–	–	–	–	–	–	X	–	–	–	–	–	–	–	1X
Panic Grass (*Panicum* sp.) Grains	–	–	–	–	–	–	–	–	–	–	–	–	–	–	–	–	–	–	–	–	–	X	–	–	–	–	1X
Ponderosa Pine (*Pinus ponderosa*)	–	–	–	–	–	–	–	–	–	–	–	–	–	–	–	–	–	–	–	X	–	–	–	–	–	–	1X
Wild Grape (*Vitis* sp.) Fruits	–	–	–	–	–	–	–	–	–	–	–	–	–	–	–	–	–	–	–	X	–	–	–	–	–	–	1X
cf. Agave (cf. *Agave* sp.) Flowering	–	–	–	–	–	–	–	–	–	–	–	–	–	–	–	–	–	–	–	–	–	–	–	–	P	–	1P
Plants of Questionable Economic Importance																											
Bug Seed (*Corispermum* sp.) Seeds	–	–	–	–	–	–	–	–	–	–	–	–	–	–	–	–	–	–	–	–	–	X	–	X	X	X	4X
Carpet Weed (*Mollugo* sp.) Seeds	–	X	–	–	X	X	–	–	–	–	–	–	–	–	–	–	–	–	–	–	–	–	X	–	–	–	4X
Borage Family (Boraginaceae) Fruits/Seeds	–	–	–	–	–	–	–	–	–	–	–	–	–	–	–	–	–	–	–	–	–	–	–	–	–	X	1X
cf. False Indigo (cf. *Amorpha* sp.) Seeds	–	–	–	–	–	–	–	–	–	–	–	–	–	–	–	–	–	–	–	–	–	–	–	–	–	X	1X
Hop Bush (*Dodonaea* sp.) Seeds	–	–	–	–	–	–	–	–	–	–	–	–	–	–	–	–	–	–	–	X	–	–	–	–	–	–	1X
Knotweed/Smartweed (*Polygonum* sp.) Seeds	–	–	–	–	–	–	–	–	–	–	–	–	–	–	–	–	–	–	–	X	–	–	–	–	–	–	1X
Lily Family (Liliaceae) Seeds	–	–	–	–	–	–	–	–	–	–	–	–	–	–	–	–	–	–	–	X	–	–	–	–	–	–	1X
Mint Family (Lamiaceae) Seeds	–	–	–	–	–	–	–	–	–	–	–	–	–	–	–	–	–	–	–	X	–	–	–	–	–	–	1X
Parsley Family (Apiaceae) Seeds	–	–	–	–	–	–	–	–	–	–	–	–	–	–	–	–	–	–	–	X	–	–	–	–	–	–	1X
Spiderling (*Boerhaavia*) Fruits	–	–	–	–	–	–	–	–	–	–	–	–	–	–	–	–	–	–	–	–	–	–	–	–	–	X	1X
Spurge (*Euphorbia* sp.) Seeds	–	–	–	–	–	–	–	–	–	–	–	–	–	–	–	–	–	–	–	–	–	–	–	–	–	X	1X

Notes: P – Taxa Possibly Present (but not necessarily the parts indicated); X – Taxa Present (but not necessarily the parts indicated). [1]Date Codes: A – Archaic (pre-A.D. 1); F - Early Formative Period (*ca.* A.D. 1–800); P – Prescott Phase (*ca.* A.D. 800–1025); C - Chino Phase (*ca.* A.D. 1025–1310); Y - Protohistoric Yavapai, (*ca.* A.D. 1400–1850); U - Unknown.

155

SUMMARY AND CONCLUSIONS

Ten flotation and five wood charcoal samples were analyzed from the Coyote Ruin. Due to time constraints, only the heavy fractions of three of the flotation samples were analyzed, while the remaining seven flotation samples were completely analyzed. A total of 19.9 liters of sediment was completely analyzed during the flotation analysis. Five thousand and four charred plant remains were recovered from the flotation samples. When uncertain and undiagnostic remains are omitted from consideration, 875 well-identified charred plant parts remain. Three hundred sixty-three pieces of wood charcoal, totaling 428.60 grams, were analyzed during the macrobotanical analysis. Additionally, 26 of the largest pieces of wood charcoal within the flotation samples were analyzed. One flotation sample had poppy seeds intentionally introduced into it to monitor the efficiency of the flotation processing technique. The resulting 91% recovery rate is at the high end of efficiency, compared to other processing methods.

Due to the relative abundance of artifacts and burned plant remains, it appears that Room 14 was filled with trash prehistorically. On the other hand, the upper levels of Room 17 were relatively free of both indicators of prehistoric refuse as well as modern contaminants.

A number of notable differences exist between the charred and uncharred plant assemblages. It therefore appears only the burned plant material recovered from this site dates to prehistoric times.

The non-woody charred plant assemblage was dominated by agave leaf fragments, especially fibers, and cheno-am seeds. Also relatively well represented were charred maize cob and kernel fragments, charred purslane seeds, and charred winged pigweed seeds. Less common were monocot stem fragments (which may include both grass and common reed culms), grass family grains, blazing star seeds, drop seed grains, bear grass leaf fragments, tansy mustard seeds, juniper branchlets, cholla/prickly pear seed fragments, a carpet weed seed fragment, a pepper grass seed, a wild buckwheat fruit, a hedgehog cactus seed, and a saltbush fruiting bractlet. Manzanita fruit remnants, maize glumes, and maize embryos were only recovered from within the heavy fractions of partially analyzed flotation samples.

Using ethnographic analogs from the Northeastern Yavapai and other Southwestern Indian groups, it was found that the traditional preparation methods of seven plants represented archaeologically are consistent with the types of remains recovered from the Coyote Ruin: (1) agave leaves and hearts; (2) cheno-am seeds; (3) maize cobs and kernels; (4) dropseed grains; (5) purslane seeds; (6) blazing star seeds; and (7) tansy mustard seeds. Representatives of six other plant types that were historically economically important were also present, although the plant parts recovered are not consistent with the ways they were traditionally processed and/or used: (1) bear grass; (2) manzanita; (3) hedgehog cactus; (4) cholla/prickly pear; (5) salt bush; and (6) wild buckwheat. Some of these latter plant parts may represent food refuse intentionally disposed of within fires. Two rare types of charred plant remains, a carpet weed seed fragment and a pepper grass seed, could represent inadvertently burned components of the prehistoric seed rain because the use of these plants is poorly documented in Southwestern Indian ethnobotanies. Several taxa, the monocot stems, the grass culms, the possible common reed culms, the bear grass leaf fragments, and the juniper branchlets, could represent tinder remnants.

The charred non-woody plant remains recovered from the Coyote Ruin were generally comparable to a database composed of flotation results from 26 other Prescott-area archaeological sites. The main difference was the relatively high presence of charred agave remains identified during the present study.

156

The author believes that this difference is more apparent than real in that he thinks it likely that charred agave fibers have not been consistently identified in many of the previous studies.

The wood charcoal assemblage at the Coyote Ruin was dominated by four taxa: cf. palo verde, pine type, cf. oak, and cf. mountain mahogany. Other identifiable types present were cf. mesquite and cottonwood/willow type. A regional comparative database of wood charcoal identifications from 19 Prescott-area archaeological sites finds these results to be generally comparable, except that cf. palo verde wood was relatively well represented, while juniper type wood was relatively rare. It is thought that the relative paucity of juniper type wood is real, and probably relates to the types of environments that were typically being exploited for fuel wood and for structural material. Based on the wood charcoal results, it appears that the interior chaparral and ponderosa pine forests were common wood sources for the residents of the Coyote Ruin, while pinyon/juniper woodlands were not.

CHAPTER 11
FAUNAL ANALYSIS
AND BONE AND ANTLER ARTIFACTS
Joanne S. Cline

* This chapter of the report is based almost entirely on faunal identification and notes completed by Joanne S. Cline, invaluable contributor to this publication and former publications on Prescott-area sites by Yavapai Chapter. At great loss to the Chapter and to all her loved ones, Joanne passed away in July of 2003. Joanne's notes are summarized by Beverley A. Everson.

INTRODUCTION

A total of 5551 un-worked bones, bone fragments, and teeth were excavated and collected from the Coyote Ruin and identified, mostly to species. Although usually broken and sometimes badly fragmented, the faunal remains were generally clean, hard, and well-preserved. The assemblage was dominated by mammals, including rabbits, rodents, deer, antelope, elk, canids (including domestic dog), cats, foxes, and a badger. Remains of a variety of birds, two types of snakes, and bony fish were also present. Table 50 provides a summary of all vertebrate fauna collected from the site. The unit faunal totals, with counts of burned, calcined, cut, or gnawed bones, are provided in Tables E1-E14. Vertebrate remains were found in the following units at the site: the Surface, Test Pits 1 and 2, and Rooms 2, 5, 14, 17, 18, 19, 23, 28, 29, 38, and 40. Microscopic bone is discussed in Chapter 8.

ANALYSIS METHODOLOGY

Excavation and collection methods varied at different locations at the site and included no control with surface collecting. The excavation and collection occurred in numbered levels, and also in trenches dug to various depths along room walls and in doorways (through any established levels), in the test pits and rooms. Rooms were situated on a hilltop and down the sides of the hill so none of the test pits or rooms or the levels within the pits and rooms were correlated in terms of depth or chronology.

All faunal remains, whether found on the surface, in situ during excavation of test pits and rooms, or in screening, were saved. Although a ¼-inch mesh was used in screening excavated materials, careful excavation and observation, as well as flotation of excavated material, resulted in the recovery of many smaller bones from the site. Unfortunately, most of these smaller bones were non-identifiable. This report discusses only specimens identifiable at least to genus, with the exception of fish that were identifiable only to Class.

Faunal remains were cleaned, repaired where possible, numbered and catalogued. Lab work and curation of the remains took place at the Yavapai Chapter of the Arizona Archeological Society Lab at Sharlot Hall Museum and in Prescott, Arizona. Bones were identified using comparative collections at Northern Arizona University and the Museum of Northern Arizona in Flagstaff, Arizona, and at the Arizona State Museum at the University of Arizona in Tucson, Arizona. Bones were also identified using vertebrate osteology references including Gilbert (1980), Gilbert et al. (1996), and Olsen (1964).

Table 50. Site Taxonomic Summary.

Class/ Order	Genus and Species	Burned/ Calcined	Cut	Gnawed	NISP/M NI
Mammalia/ Artiodactyla	*Cervus canadensis* (Elk)	0/1		1	9/5
	Odocoileus hemionus (Mule Deer)	148/27	4	5	488/52
	Antilocapra Americana (Pronghorn)	1/12	3	12	50/12
Mammalia/ Carnivora	*Canis latrans* (Coyote)				26/8
	Canis familiaris (Dog)				1/1
	Felis rufus (Bobcat)	5/1		1	29/29
	Felis concolor (Mountain Lion)				9/6
	Vulpes sp. (Fox)				2/2
	Taxidea taxus (American Badger)				1/1
Mammalia/ Lagomorpha	*Lepus californicus* (Black-tailed Jackrabbit)	125/6	5	65	838/118
	Sylvilagus audubonii (Desert Cottontail)	348/6	1	146	2357/185
Mammalia/ Rodentia	*Cynomys gunnisoni* (Gunnison's Prairie Dog)	90/1	1	69	961/196
	Eutamias dorsalis (Cliff Chipmunk)				5/3
	Microtus mexicanus (Mexican Vole)				77/10
	Neotoma albigula (White-throated Woodrat)	11		12	96/44
	Peromyscus sp. (Deer Mouse)				4/3
	Reithrodontomys megalotis (Western Harvest Mouse)				4/2
	Scuirus arizonensis (Arizona Gray Squirrel)	19/2	2	15	163/73
	Sigmodon arizonae (Arizona Cotton Rat)				9/4
	Spermophilus variegates (Rock Squirrel)	24		1	327/51
	Thonomys bottae (Botta's Pocket Gopher)			16	19/12
	Zapus princes (Western Jumping Mouse)				1/1
Aves/ Cuculiformes	*Geococcyx californianus* (Roadrunner)				3/3
Aves/ Columbiformes	*Zenaida macroura* (Mourning Dove)				2/2
Aves/ Falconiformes	*Buteo jamaicensis* (Red-tailed Hawk)				9/8
	Accipiter cooperii (Cooper's Hawk)				1/1
	Falco Sparverius (American Kestral)				1/1
	Circus cyaneus (Northern Harrier)				2/2
Aves/ Galliformes	*Callipepla californica* (California Quail)				2/2
	Callipepla gambelii (Gambel's Quail)				5/3
Aves/ Passeriformes	*Aphelocoma californica* (Western Scrub-jay)				1/1

Table 50. Site Taxonomic Summary.

Class/ Order	Genus and Species	Burned/ Calcined	Cut	Gnawed	NISP/M NI
	Corvus brachyrhynchos (American Crow)				1/1
	Pica hudsonii (Black-billed Magpie)				1/1
	Ara macao (Scarlet Macaw)				1/1
	Athene cuniclaria (Burrowing Owl)				1/1
	Tyto alba (Barn Owl)				1/1
Reptilia/ Squamata	*Crotalus atrox* (Western Diamondback Rattlesnake)				7/4
	Pituophis catenifer (Gopher Snake)				28/2
Osteichthyes	Bony fishes				6/4

Information recorded for each bone included a description of its completeness, its side (left or right) for paired bones, proximal or distal articulation or diaphysis, and whether it had been burned, calcined, cut, or gnawed. Bones of juveniles were distinguished from those of adults by the presence of unfused vs. fused epiphyses, and by bone size and texture.

Taxanomic abundances were determined by first counting the number of individual bone and teeth specimens (NISP) using the criteria described above. From the NISP, the minimum number of individuals (MNI) was calculated, based on the most abundant element for adults and juveniles per taxon for each. The MNI was calculated for individual levels in units (where levels were distinguished) and in trenches in the units, and then totaled for each unit.

Because of inconsistencies in excavation and collection methods at the Coyote Ruin and the resulting lack of firm provenience for some specimens, the MNI totals are problematic and should be treated as rough estimates of the number of individuals. MNI calculations were also skewed due to the fact that some of the vertebrate remains were found in trash deposits and because the site had been pot hunted and vandalized, further compromising the depositional history of some specimens.

THE VERTEBRATE FAUNAL ASSEMBLAGE

The following summary considers all of the mammal, bird and snake remains that were identified to genus, and bony fish. See Table 50 for scientific names of the animals discussed below.

Mammals – Mammalia

Most of the identified vertebrate remains were mammals. Desert Cottontail comprised 42% of the identified bone and teeth. Gunnison's Prairie Dog made up 17% of the total number of identified specimens, Black-tailed Jackrabbit 15%, Mule Deer 9%, and Rock Squirrel 6%. Arizona Gray Squirrel comprised 3% of the specimens, and White–throated Woodrat 2%. Mexican Vole and Pronghorn Antelope each comprised 1% of the specimens. The remainder of the identified mammals found at the site each made up less than 1% of the total individual specimens.

Birds – Aves

Fourteen different species of birds of various orders were found at the site. The birds as a whole represented about 1% of the total number of identified vertebrate specimens. Unexpected discoveries included the ulna of a Scarlet Macaw in Room 40, the premaxilla (upper beak) of a Black-billed Magpie in Room 18, and a humerus and femur of California Quail in Room 14. These are discussed further in the Environment section below.

Reptiles – Reptilia

Western Diamondback Rattlesnake and Gopher Snake comprised a small percentage of the identified vertebrate remains at the site, a total of about 1%.

Fish – Osteichthyes

Six specimens of bony fish were recovered from the site.

PRESCOTT AREA COMPARISONS

With the exception of a few small rodent species, the Coyote Ruin mammal assemblage matches those found in other local Prescott Culture sites, including Copper Basin, Fitzmaurice Ruin, Las Vegas Ranch Ruin - East, Las Vegas Ranch Ruin - West, Storm Site, Sundown Site and the Neural Site (Cline 1997; Cline and Cline 1983; Douglas and Whitman 1974; Hargrave 1974, 1978; Hevly 1978; Jeter 1977; and Rea 1978). Several taxa were found in all of the sites, including Desert Cottontail, Black-tailed Jackrabbit, and Mule Deer. Gunnison's Prairie Dog was found in all of the sites except for Copper Basin. Gophers were found at all of the sites except the Storm Site. Coyotes were found at all sites except the Las Vegas Ranch Ruin – West. And Pronghorn were found at all of the sites except for the Storm Site.

A few of the birds found at the Coyote Ruin were unusual, including American Kestral, Northern Harrier, Western Scrub Jay, American Crow, Burrowing Owl, and Barn Owl.

Western Diamondback Rattlesnake and Gopher Snake were found at other Prescott Culture sites, as were bony fish remains.

FAUNA AS FOOD

Specimens of several species, including Mule Deer, Antelope, Black-tailed Jackrabbit, Desert Cottontail, Gunnison's Prairie Dog, and the Arizona Gray Squirrel were burned and cut, suggesting that the animals had been processed as a food source. Cut and burned specimens were found primarily in Room 40. Other cut, or cut and burned, specimens from the same group of species were found in Test Pits 1 and 2, Room 17, and Room 18. Mammal bones identified only as indeterminate large, medium, and small (not included in the taxonomic totals for the site) were found cut, or cut and burned, on the Surface and in Rooms 2, 5, 14, 17, 18, and 23.

None of the bird, snake, or fish bone was burned, cut, or gnawed. This may be an indication that these were *not* food items, but it should be remembered that all of them could probably be dismembered/prepared for cooking or eating without the use of stone tools, and with minimal cooking that might not burn any bones. Also, snake remains in archaeological sites may represent individuals who died naturally in burrows, after a site was abandoned. Further comparisons with ethnographic food taboos (e.g. Rea 1981), and ceremonial use of birds and their feathers (e.g. McKusick 2001), might also shed further light on the likely *non-food* uses (or avoidance) of these species by the Coyote Ruin occupants. Most ethnographic groups in the Southwest strictly avoid snakes when possible (Rea 1981:72). Scarlet Macaws (either feathers or the whole bird) would almost certainly have been utilized in some (or several) ceremonial capacities (Hargrave 1970; McKusick 2001).

ENVIRONMENT

The Coyote Ruin assemblage generally represents taxa that are common in the Prescott area and in similar environments in the region (Hoffmeister 1986; Sibley 2003; Brennen and Holycross 2006), and does not indicate significant differences in the local environment during the occupation of the site. Seeming exceptions include a few birds which were, however, more likely trade items in the area, rather than indicators of a different local environment in prehistoric times. Scarlet Macaws are typically found in South and Central America, with rare occurrences as far north as the state of Veracruz, in southeastern Mexico (Peterson and Chalif 1973). The Scarlet Macaw at Coyote Ruin represents what was probably a live bird, coming into the area as a very valuable trade item, either ultimately from Mexico, but possibly from the Northern Sinagua area (Christenson, Chapter 14; Hargrave 1970). Black-billed Magpies occur today only in northeastern-most Arizona, with most of their range north and northwestward of Arizona, extending into Alaska (Sibley, 2003). This bird too could have been traded into the Prescott area, either as a live bird, or perhaps just a skin (the upper beak would likely be included as part of a bird skin prepared for trade). Finally, California Quail are currently found only in eastern Arizona; whether brought to the Coyote Ruin alive or dead is not possible to say.

The Collared Peccary (*Pecari tajacu*), present in the Prescott area now, is absent from the Coyote Ruin faunal assemblage, and from the assemblages of other Prescott Culture sites. Peccaries, along with Black Vultures *(Coragyps atratus)*, are neotropical species that have been expanding their permanent range northward in historic times, indicating that there is *some* environmental change happening in Arizona since at least the late 1800s. Although occasionally reported in the archaeological literature, no confirmed bones of these species have yet been found in prehistoric faunal assemblages in Arizona.

BONE AND ANTLER ARTIFACTS

As mentioned above, Joanne passed away in July 2003, leaving behind her extensive notes on the faunal collection of the Coyote Ruin Site, along with pages of statistics she had compiled. From these I have summarized the statistics and text she completed on bone and antler artifacts for this report. Question marks and "no entry" reflect where Joanne still had unresolved information. With respect, Ginger Johnson.

Seventy mammal bone and antler artifacts representing tools, items of personal adornment and one possible musical instrument were collected from nine of the excavated rooms. Table 51 summarizes this collection and shows the distribution of these artifacts. Thirty-eight artifacts (54%) were found in Room 40, a room that had not been previously excavated or vandalized. Fifteen artifacts (21%) were collected in Room 18, five (7%) from Room 17, four (6% from Room 14, three (4%) from Room 28, and Rooms 23, 29, and 38 yielded one artifact each at 1% per room.

Table 51. Bone and antler artifacts.

Room	Artifact	Element	Mammal	Measurement (cm)	Comments
2	Scraper	Rib frag.	Large mammal	10.2 x 1.95 x 0.9	Polish, use wear and scratches
	Punch	Radius	Jackrabbit	9.7 x 0.65 x 0.35	Use wear, appears to be scorched
14	Punch frag.	Radius frag.	Jackrabbit	5.11 x 0.56 x 0.31	Manufacture marks, use wear, polish
	Awl	Metacarpus	Mule Deer	6.72 x 0.72 x 0.45	Possible cuts, mfg. marks, sharply pointed
	Awl	Distal radius	*Canis sp.*	7.35 x 0.95 x 0.45	Use polish, scratched, gnawed, sharply pointed
	Awl tip	Radius	Jackrabbit	2.19 x 0.6 x 0.2	Use polish, burned, gnawed, sharply pointed
17	Punch frag.	Prox. Radius	Jackrabbit	5.87 x 0.7 x 0.5	Use polish, broken at hole
	Flaker?	Antler tine	Mule Deer	3.54 x 1.12 x 0.98	Cuts, weathered
	Scraper	Antler tine	Mule Deer	5.3 x 2.17 x 0.45	Gnawed, weathered, rounded end
	Flaker	Antler tine	Mule Deer	15.9 x 12.9 x 1.2	Gnawed (rodent), weathered
	Punch frag.	Radius	Jackrabbit	4.88 x 0.57 x 0.44	Scorched, use polish, tip missing, broken at hole
18	Awl	Long bone	Medium mammal	3.76 x 1.12 x 0.72	Burned, use polish
	Scraper frag.	Split metapodial	Artiodactyl	5.61 x 1.56 x 0.54	Use polish, scratched
	Punch frag.	Radius	Jackrabbit	4.4 x 0.61 x 0.37	Use polish, manufacture marks
	Flaker	Antler tine	Artiodactyl	3.24 x 0.73 x 0.7	Manufacture marks, nicks
	Awl frag.	Long bone	Small mammal	3.42 x 0.65 x 0.45	Use polish, abrasions
	Awl shaft	Long bone	Small mammal	2.45 x 0.34 x 0.32	Use polish, burned, abrasions
	Flaker	Antler tine	Artiodactyl	5.3 x 1.35 x 1.09	Use polish, cracked, cuts, gnawed
	Awl point	Long bone	Small mammal	1.67 x 0.89 x 0.24	Use polish
	Awl frag.	Long bone frag.	Artiodactyl	9.5 x 1.8 x 0.3	Polish on sharpened point
	Flute/Whistle	Long bone	Medium mammal	6.93 x 1.09 x 0.91, hole is 0.49 diameter	Manufacture marks, cuts, rootlet etching
	Flaker	Antler tine	Artiodactyl	2.02 x 0.89	Polish at tip
	Bead frag.	?	Medium mammal	2.57 x 1.68 x 0.22	Burned, abrasions may have had hole
	Awl frag.	Metacarpus	Mule Deer	4.96 x 0.56 x 0.42	Gnawed, point chipped
	Awl	Metatarsal	Mule Deer	15.5 x 2.05 x 1.75	Tip broken
	Awl	Distal tibia	*Canis sp.*	16.34 x 1.65 x 1.23	Polish, manufacture marks, tapered point
23	Awl frag.	Metapodial	Artiodactyl	2.6 x 0.81 x 0.72	Tapered point, manufacture marks, polish
28	Bead	Metapodial	*Canis sp.*	2.9 x 0.71 x 0.18	Burned, polish, manufacture marks, tapered
	Bead	2nd phalanx	Artiodactyl	1.92 x 1.0 x 0.15	Burned, cut, manufacture marks, tapered end
	Bead	2nd phalanx	Artiodactyl	2.91 x 1.6 x 2.0	Burned, tapered end, gnawed
29	Awl	Prox/diaph radius	*Canis sp.*	11.84 x 1.48 x 0.93	Manufacture marks, tapered, peeling cortex
30	Flaker	Antler tine	Artiodactyl	6.9 x 1.6	Tip flat on two sides
40	Flaker	Antler tip	Artiodactyl	1.1 x 0.8 x 0.7	Use wear, burned
	Flaker	Antler	Artiodactyl	6.6 x 1.2 x 0.8	Use wear, burned, scratched
	Punch	Radius, diaph.	Jackrabbit	7.31 x 0.6 x 0.38	Drilled hole, point missing, cut proximal end
	Flaker ?	Antler	Artiodactyl	14.2 x 2.7 x 0.4	Rounded tip, broken (2 pieces/glued), use polish, manufacturing marks
	Awl	Split radius	Mule Deer	19.0 x 1.64 x 0.68	Entire length tapered, use polish
	Awl frag.	Split long bone	Artiodactyl	6.2 x 1.5 x 0.35	Tip missing, use polish, tapered, mfg. marks

Table 51. Bone and antler artifacts.

Room	Artifact	Element	Mammal	Measurement (cm)	Comments
40	Awl frag.	Split long bone	Artiodactyl	3.55 x 0.9 x 0.55	Burned, use polish, long striations, mfg. mks
	Awl frag.	Split long bone	Artiodactyl	8.62 x 1.35 x 0.55	Use polish, both ends missing, long striations
	Awl frag.	Split long bone	Medium mammal	4.71 x 0.84 x 0.4	Use polish, broken, flat tapered point, manufacture marks
	Awl frag.	Split long bone	Artiodactyl	6.93 x 1.7 x 0.6	Use polish, long striations, mfg. marks
	Awl	Split metapodial	Artiodactyl	18.0 x 1.3 x 1.31	Tapered sharp point, mfg. marks, use polish, worn handhold
	Awl/punch?	Antler frag.	Artiodactyl	7.0 x 1.55 x 1.27	Use polish, blunted tip
	Awl/punch?	Antler frag.	Artiodactyl	6.9 x 1.96 x 1.4	Cuts, abrasions, no ends
	Awl point	Split long bone	Artiodactyl	5.84 x 0.65 x 0.48	Broken, sharply tapered point, burned
	Awl	Metacarpal	Artiodactyl	5.95 x 0.65 x 0.4	Sharp point, long striations
	Punch	Radius	Jackrabbit	4.95 x 0.61 x 0.4	Drill hole, mfg. marks, use polish, ends gone
	Awl point	Split long bone	Artiodactyl	4.36 x 0.84 x 0.36	Use polish, sharply tapered point, manufacture marks
	Awl handhold	Prox. radial, split	*Canis sp.*	7.2 x 1.58 x 0.4	Use polish, mfg. marks, tapered, no point
	Awl point	Split long bone	Artiodactyl	6.4 x 1.1 x 0.66	Use polish, mfg. marks, point angled, sharp
	Awl frag.	Split long bone	Artiodactyl	5.33 x 0.6 x 0.45	Sharply tapered point, rotational abrasions, mfg. marks, sharp broken end
	Awl frag.	Long bone frag.	Small mammal	2.6 x 0.41 x 0.16	Use polish, burned, mfg. marks
	Punch	Rt. Radius	Jackrabbit	9.95 x 0.55 x 0.32	Drilled hole, cut proximal end, mfg. marks, use polish, abrasions
	Punch frag.	Rt. Radius	Jackrabbit	6.82 x 0.58 x 0.41	Broken below drillhole, abrasions, mfg. marks, use polish
	Awl frag.	Long bone	*Canis sp.*	3.71 x 0.92 x 0.61	Burned, mfg. marks, use polish, abrasions
	Awl frag.	?	?	6.23 x 0.75 x 0.53	
	Punch frag.	Radius	Jackrabbit	7.35 x 0.61 x 0.33	Use polish, broken below hole
	Punch frag.	Radius	Jackrabbit	8.41 x 0.58 x 0.36	Slight polish, broken below hole, point missing, mfg. marks
	Punch frag.	Radius	Jackrabbit	8.15 x 0.55 x 0.4	Broken below hole, mfg. marks, polish
	Punch frag	Radius	Jackrabbit	4.6 x 0.6 x 0.3	Broken below hole, mfg. marks, use polish
	Flesher	Split long bone	Artiodactyl	18.4 x 2.59 x 1.17	Awl reshaped as flesher
	Cut piece	Metapodial, cut	Artiodactyl	7.65 x 2.6 x 0.48	Encircling cut at proximal end
	Awl	Prox./diaph. Radius	*Canis sp.*	13.12 x 1.3 x 0.41	Use polish, mfg. marks, tapered sharp point
	Awl	Ulna, no epiph.	Artiodactyl	9.42 x 3.94 x 2.2	Sharp point, mfg. marks, use polish
	Punch frag.	Radius	Jackrabbit	5.83 x 0.6 x 0.37	Broken below hole, mfg. marks, use polish
	Figurine?	Long bone	Artiodactyl	6.85 x 2.95 x 1.52	Carved deer hoof
	Punch frag.	Radius	Cottontail	4.51 x 0.61 x 0.33	Broken below hole, mfg. marks, use polish
	Punch frag.	Radius diaph.	Cottontail	4.89 x 0.56 x 0.26	Broken both ends, mfg. marks, burned, use polish
	Awl	?	Large mammal	7.0 x 0.9 x 0.4	Polish, mfg. marks

There is no sure way to calculate the number of animals represented in the artifact collection, as it is possible several artifacts could have been made from only a few animals. However, 21 (30%) were made from small mammal bones (up through the size of a jackrabbit), 11 (16%) were from medium-sized mammals (i.e. coyote or dog), and 37 (53%) were made from the larger animals (i.e. deer, elk, or antelope).

Typical of the Prescott Culture, awls (12) and awl fragments (20) dominated this collection. Other tools included 4 punches, 12 punch fragments, 9 flakers, 2 scrapers, 1 scraper fragment, and 1 flesher.

Artifacts of special note were a carved deer hoof that is probably bone (or possibly wood) (Figure 65), a figurine carved from a long bone of an unidentified artiodactyl from Room 40, a whistle or flute from Room 18, and 4 beads from Rooms 18 and 28. The carved hoof is quite similar to larger carved wooden wands found with the "Magician's Burial" near Flagstaff, which dates to around A.D. 1090-1125 (McGregor 1943). Based on the several types of wands found in that burial (topped with carved human hands, deer hooves, a serrated figure, and a seashell), and the richness of the other mortuary offerings, several Hopi men suggested that the individual was a very important person, and probably a member of a stick-swallowing society or fraternity. The carved hoof from Coyote Ruin is doubtless related in some way to these interpretations, but its small size suggests that, functionally, it is more likely the carved head of a man's hairpin.

The low number of specialized artifacts such as these may simply be a reflection of their rarity, or may have been skewed because of previous excavation and pilfering and the preferential collecting of unusual items. Or some combination of the two.

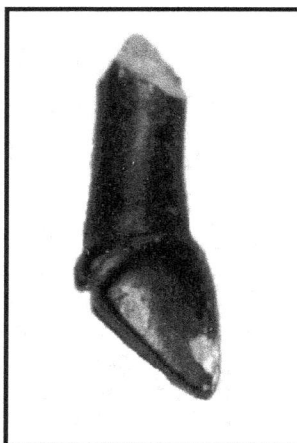

Figure 65. Carved deer hoof of bone or wood from Room 17.
Length 6.8 cm.

CHAPTER 12
HUMAN REMAINS
Mary Spall

A letter dated January 12, 1998, from Arizona State Museum Archaeologist Paul Fish to Mary Spall states in part, "I did visit the Emilienne Site (Coyote Ruin) at the invitation of the Yavapai-Prescott Indian Tribe and the Yavapai Chapter in the early 1990s. Vandalism had exposed human remains at a number of locations. The complexity of the site precluded recording in the ASM system at that time, and the abundance of human remains made collection impractical as well."

With this information, and the knowledge that J. W. Simmons excavated nine burials (see Appendix H), we anticipated we would encounter human remains during our work at the Coyote Ruin. Excavation in Room 2 revealed a human skull fragment and one human tooth. Excavation in Room 14 revealed a human skull fragment and two human teeth. Excavation in Room 17 revealed a human newborn. Excavation in Room 18 revealed a human tooth, one metatarsal, and 2 parietal fragments of a child.

In Room 38 remains of an adult and child were located 27-33 cm from the present ground surface. A meeting between YCAAS Archivist Elizabeth S. Higgins and Professor Charles F. Merbs, then with Arizona State University (ASU), at the YCAAS laboratory on September 21, 2000, resulted in the following information reconfirmed by Dr. Merbs in an e-mail dated June 6, 2007. "This is an unusual distribution of parts of two skeletons, an adult and a child. No teeth or adult vertebrae are included. The cranium of the child shows no evidence of anemia on the outer surface or on the roof of the orbits. Though the left parietal of the adult is very strong and solid, it had been broken postmortem. A coyote or other carnivore could have done this, but it was more likely caused by accidental or intentional trauma. The left femur of the adult shows a healed injury, more likely a soft tissue injury than a bone fracture. A complete fracture of the femoral shaft would have produced considerable distortion that is not seen here. A third trochanter is present on the femur, a condition sometimes associated with habitual running. The ends of the long bones are missing, probably gnawed away. This was more likely caused by carnivores like coyotes than by rodents."

Christy Turner, then Regents' Professor at ASU, also reported on human remains in Room 38, in a letter to Mary Spall, dated February 8, 2002: "My examination of the bones from NA6654 (Coyote Ruin) turned up no signs of human, carnivore, or rodent processing, chewing, or gnawing. No human bone was burned. Hence, there is no physical evidence of any untoward or deliberate damage by humans. All of the human bone damage was caused by natural processes. Only the left parietal of the adult female has perimortem breakage, and this could have occurred naturally also. In addition to the bones identified by Professor Merbs, I identified the following: Three-year old child. Right parietal; 14 rib fragments (one could possibly be rabbit); very mild porotic hyperostosis and cribra orbitalla."

"Adult female. Left parietal with perimortem breakage; the maxillary fragment has no torus (not unusual), shallow root sockets and medium grade of periodontal disease, hinting at a middle aged person, not a young adult; the clavicle has a possible perimortem break (uncertain); a distal femur fragment, a proximal rib fragment, the petrous portion of the temporal bone, a lower border of the mandibular horizontal ramus; of the many fragments Dr. Merbs reported as unidentifiable, I found that all seem to have postmortem breakage of vertebra, long bones, pelvis, sacrum, sternum, and mixed with these [was] one child's rib. There are no adult ribs."

"I also identified a rabbit-sized scapula fragment, six fragments of a deer sized animal; two burned non-human bone fragments, one with perimortem breakage; and another apparently non-human bone flake with perimortem breakage."

"I presume the pile of animal and human bones came from the most recent occupation as per your excavation notes. Context and very incomplete human inventory argue for the remains representing a secondary deposition antedating room abandonment. The selection of bones is curious. Whatever the story is about the selection, the remains show no sign of defleshing or any other considerate or inconsiderate activity."

In Room 40 two human skeletons were found under the lower floor and three were found in the trash fill above the second floor.

1. An infant with a plainware bowl covering it was found in level 5. Only about three-fourths of the bowl was found.
2. An adult male, age approximately 35-40 years, measuring 5' 9" in length, was found with his head resting on a rock slab. He was fully extended with his head to the south. The body had flat rocks placed on his knees and ankles. The base of the skull was broken which indicates he may have died from a fall or a severe blow to the back of the head. He was found about 29 cm above the lower floor and was covered with debris. Stone slabs surrounded his remains.
3. (F4) A subadult, approximately 12-14 years of age, was found in the southeast corner on the same level as the male, and was in a fetal position, with the head placed to the east.
4. (F3) An adult female, approximately 25-30 years of age, was found under the lower floor. She was in a fully extended position. She had an overly developed tibia and fibula on her left side, and the tibia and fibula on her right side were oddly shaped, indicating she had had an injury or perhaps arthritis for a long period of time. Her left arm lay across her chest. Her head was tilted forward with her chin resting on her chest. Flat rocks were placed on her ankles, knees and chest. A worked vesicular stone had been placed near her head.
5. A small child, 1-3 years old, was also found near the female, beneath the lower floor. Its head was placed to the south.

These remains were all left *in situ* (the infant was placed near the spot from which it was recovered). No other funerary objects were found. These remains are discussed further in the final chapter.

CHAPTER 13
HISTORIC ARTIFACTS
Judy Stoycheff

Because the Coyote Ruin had formerly been part of a ranch as well as a popular picnic spot for local residents, it is not surprising that seven areas generated historic artifacts during a surface survey of the site. Each area was separately analyzed and a total for all the areas was obtained.

The first area was labeled N 0 W 30 and N 30 E 0. The collections were made on October 4, 2000, November 2, 2000 and December 6, 2000, with the following results:

> Four .22 long caliber cartridges
> Five .30 caliber carbine cartridges
> One .45 ACP cartridge
> One fragment of a .30 caliber cartridge
> One unidentified fragment

The second area was labeled N 0 E 30. The collection date was not given:

> One 1985 penny
> Two .22 long caliber cartridges
> One 9 mm Luger cartridge
> One ACP pistol cartridge
> Four unidentified cartridge fragments

The third area was labeled Room 2. The collections were dated September 28, 2000, February 12, 2000, and April 1, 2000, with the following results:

> Two .22 short caliber cartridges
> One .22 Winchester magnum cartridge
> Seven .22 long caliber cartridges
> Three 9 mm Luger manufactured pistol cartridges
> Forty-five N1 carbine cartridges
> Four M1 Garand cartridges
> Twenty-seven 9 mm Luger pistol cartridges (one live bullet!)
> One battery core, approximately 1-3/4" long by ¼" diameter
> Four clear glass fragments of a stippled base bottle, indicating that the bottle was
> > manufactured after 1940 and was probably soda pop.
> Three clear glass fragments of a neck and top of a bottle that had a screw top
> > closure
> Three metal crown lids with "Bud" in red clearly visible, indicating that they
> > were Budweiser beer bottle caps
> One Coors beer can, opened with a church key, thus dating it from 1935 to 1962.
> Three fragments of thin, worked leather with very even stitch holes, indicating
> > that it was probably machine made. The largest piece was 3-1/4" long by
> > 1" wide. The other two were 2" by 2" and 2" by ½".

The fourth area was labeled Room 17. Material was collected on July 11, 2000:

One M1 rifle cartridge
One pull tab beer can (Old Milwaukee) manufactured after 1962

The fifth area was labeled Room 18. Collections were done on June 7, 1999, and March 17, 1999 to November 22, 1999, with the following results:

Three .22 long cartridges
Two unidentified pieces of metal
One beer can, unidentified, with church key opening
One Old Milwaukee beer can, with pull tab

The sixth area was labeled Room 19. Collections were made from September 17, 1999 to November 22, 1999, with the following results:

Two .30 M1 cartridges
Eight M1 or M16 rifle cartridges
One M1 carbine copper jacket, lead filled-bullet
One fragment M1 Garand bullet
One .22 long cartridge
Twelve fragments of lime-green glass, probably from a bottle
Five fragments of light green bottle glass with the letters OLS stenciled on one fragment
One fragment of a green bottle base, stippled, common after 1940

The seventh area was labeled Room 23. The collection dates were August 30, 2000 and during September, 2000.

Ten .22 long cartridges
Thirteen M1 carbine cartridges
One M1 carbine cartridge
One M1 carbine cartridge with lead bullet, copper-jacketed
One pull tab

SUMMARY

Beer cans
    Two with church key open cans
    Two with pull tab openings
    One actual tab
    Three Budweiser crown caps

Glass
    Four clear, stippled base fragments
    Three clear fragments with screw top
    One green base fragment, stippled
    Two fragments of lime-green glass
    Five fragments of light green glass with OLS stenciled

Metal
    1985 penny
    One battery core about 1" long

Leather
    Three fragments of thin, worked leather

Cartridges
    Twenty-seven .22 long caliber
    Two .22 short caliber
    Five .30 caliber, one fragment
    Two .45 ACP
    One live 9 mm bullet
    One Winchester magnum
    Sixty-eight M1 carbine
    Five M1 Garand
    Two .30 M1
    Three 9 mm Luger pistol
    One M1 copper-jacketed lead bullet
    One fragment M1 copper-jacketed lead bullet
    Six unidentified cartridge fragments

The cartridges were not examined specifically for manufacturer's marks for dating purposes, as they could have been recycled and used several times. Others, such as the Super X symbol have been on Western Cartridge bullets from 1902 to the present. The symbol Peters BV was used from 1898 to 1931. The symbol U on 22 longs represents Union Metallic Cartridge Co., and was used even after that company was purchased by Remington (1867 to 1962). The M1 rifle was used in WW II, Korea and the early part of the Vietnam War before being replaced by the M16. It was then retired and sold wholesale by the military to NRA members in 1963. Cartridge identifications were made using Goodman (1998).

CHAPTER 14
COYOTE PUEBLO IN CONTEXT -
SOME HYPOTHESES ON THE 13TH and 14th CENTURIES
IN THE PRESCOTT REGION
Andrew L. Christenson

The excavation of Coyote Ruin and the subsequent analysis of the remains found provide unique information about the history and way of life of one community in the Prescott Culture area. Of course, excavations are notorious for raising as many questions as are answered and the work at Coyote Ruin is no exception. Attempts to understand this one community are of course tied closely to contemporaneous communities, both within the culture that the pueblo was a part of as well as with neighboring cultures, however they might have been defined. It is useful to examine some of the questions that we have about the community and its neighbors and suggest where there are clear answers and where we can only suggest hypotheses for future examination.

We do not know the name that the occupants of the pueblo called their location. Of course they did not live in a ruin, so I will use the term Coyote Ruin, named after the Coyote Springs Ranch where it was located when first excavated, when speaking of the locality today as an archaeological site, and Coyote Pueblo when referring to the community when it was occupied.

Note: all of the years and dates in the remainder of the chapter are A.D. For example, 1183 is A.D. 1183.

WHEN WAS THE PUEBLO OCCUPIED?

The pottery identified from the site provides a better idea of its span of occupation than the couple of radiocarbon dates. The presence of such types at Sacaton Red-on-buff and Wepo Black-on-white means that Coyote Pueblo could have had occupation as early as the 900s. The latest well-dated pottery type present is Tusayan Black-on-white, Kayenta variety, which has a date range of about 1260 to 1330 (Christenson 1994: Table 1)[1], and could indicate occupation into the 14th century. The presence of Tizon Wiped also suggests the possibility of a post-1300 use of the site, although the dating of the early end of the type is not well known. Mean ceramic dates for the room fills are all in the 1100s (Table 6), which, allowing for the effect of time lag, indicates that mean of occupation for the site is around the end of the 12th and beginning of 13th centuries.

Radiocarbon dates are probability distributions, so that a given date can be represented by a curve (Figure 68), date ranges of varying probabilities, or a single number like a mean or midrange. One radiocarbon date from maize in Room 40 has a mean of 1183, but the highest probability range (63.5%) is 1154 to 1277 with a midrange of 1215. The second date from burned material in Room 2 gave a 95% probability range of 1295-1444, mean of 1372.

Simmons recognized an earlier occupation at the site and called it Old Coyote. This area with pit houses and burials is located in the southwest corner of the site (Figure 29). Considering that Prescott Black-on-gray was present in one of the Old Coyote graves, it is likely that there was some occupation in this area of the site after 1075-1100 or so, when the type becomes most common. However, the 12th century ceramic dates that predominate in the upper, supposedly later, part of the site suggest that much of New

Coyote was in fact contemporaneous for at least part of the Old Coyote occupation. Clearly, some of the middle level rooms were occupied and then used for trash dumping (e.g., Room 14, 18, and 40), and two of these trash deposits contained the latest decorated ceramic type at the site, Tusayan Black-on-white, Kayenta variety (1260-1330).

Over the years a phase sequence has been developed for the Prescott area and this is presented by Motsinger et al. (2000). This sequence will not be used here but this discussion of Coyote Ruin will focus mostly upon what is called the late Chino Phase and early Willow Creek Phase (13th and 14th centuries).

HOW MANY PEOPLE LIVED AT COYOTE PUEBLO?

Population estimation for a prehistoric society can be a complicated process, but with pueblo-dwelling groups in the Southwest, consistent numbers in the range of 1.5 to 2.0 people per room, irrespective of room function, have been suggested. 25 historic pueblos gave a mean of 1.66/room (Dohm 1990: Table 4). A value of 2.0 will be used here. Although there is evidence of late use of pit houses for habitation at some sites such as Willow Lake/Neural Site, it appears that such structures are most commonly associated with pre-1200 occupation. At sites where such structures might have been used post-1200, 5.0 people will be counted for each. Because all rooms at a pueblo are not actually occupied, population estimates based on all rooms will be high. A typical occupancy rate for pueblo rooms is around 75% of the dwelling units (Nelson et al. 1994: 116; Plog 1975: 98) and this number is used to adjust the estimates in Table 52.

Given the estimated 26 masonry rooms at Coyote Ruin, the maximum population estimate for the pueblo would be in the vicinity of 40 or so people. (2.0 people per room x 26 rooms x 75% occupancy rate = 39.) There was no evidence found that any of the pit houses at the site were occupied after 1200. Ken Austin (see site form in Appendix F) claimed that the house mound rooms were two stories tall, but the evidence for this is unclear, and only one-story occupation is assumed here.

In looking at a larger scale we can ask the question - How dense was the population in the Prescott area during the 13th century? Table 52 provides a list of all published sites in the Prescott area that have evidence of 13th century occupation, usually in the form of late Pueblo III trade pottery from the Kayenta Anasazi area, but also from radiocarbon dates. These sites are mostly in the Chino/ Lonesome Valley area, which is predominantly grassland with chaparral on some of the foothills, such as at Coyote Ruin. Survey in ponderosa forest to the south of Prescott has revealed Prescott Gray Ware sites, but trade items that might allow dating are scarce, so the presence of post-1200 occupation is indeterminate (McKie 2000) (Lynx Creek Ruin is one site in the sample from this biozone).

174

Table 52. Thirteenth century sites in the Prescott region. Data for Coyote Ruin are in bold.

Site	Dating	Basis of Dating	Size (rooms + pit houses)	Estimated Population (75% occupancy)	Source
		Large Sites			
Woolsey Ranch	?	architecture and size	80+	120+	Wilcox et al. 2001
Fitzmaurice	mostly 1200s	pottery	51	77	Barnett 1974
Argillite/Porter/ Windmill/Piedra Roja	into 1200-1300s	pottery	40[a]	60	Simmons 1937, Bartlett 1939, Walker 1983; Wilcox et al. 2008
Indian Peak	multi.	pottery	32	48	Wilcox et al. 2000
Coyote Ruin	**1100s-1300s**	**pottery; C14**	**26**	**39**	**this report**
King's Ruin	1200s	pottery; dendro	20	30[b]	Spicer 1935
		Small Sites			
Green Gulch, NA 4360	into 1200s	pottery	19	29	Wilcox et al. 2008
Humboldt/McMahon, NA 4365	1200s	pottery	18	27	"
Brady's Fort	into 1200s?	line of sight to Coyote	9	14	Simmons 1937
Rattlesnake	multi.	pottery	8	12	Barnett 1970
Yeager	into 1200s?	pottery	6	9	Simmons 1937
Neural/Willow Lake	1100s-1300s	pottery; C14	3+1	8	Grossman 1997
Las Vegas West	1200s	pottery	5	8	Barnett 1978
N:7:34	1200	C14	2+1	7	Horton & Logan 1993
Las Vegas East	1200s	pottery	4	6	Barnett 1978
Lynx Creek	mostly <1200?	C14	4	6	Horton 1994
Stoney Ridge	1200s	C14	3	5	Anduze et al. 2003
NA 26053	1100s-1200s	C14	0+1	4	Long et al. 2008
N:7:250, StoneRidge	1200s	C14	1	2	Leonard and Breternitz 2005
N:7:308	1200s	C14	1	2	Neily 2006
N:10:11, Copper Basin	1100s-1200s	pottery	1	2	Jeter 1977
YAV 74	900s-1500s	C14	1	2	Blan 2006
N:7:267, StoneRidge	1200s	C14	1	2	Leonard and Robinson 2005
N:7:279, StoneRidge	1200s	C14	[1]	seasonal	"
NA 1510	1100s-1200s	pottery	small	?	Wilcox et al. 2001
Sundown	mostly <1200	pottery	?	?	Higgins 1999a
N:7:286, StoneRidge	1200s	C14	?	seasonal?	Leonard and Robinson 2005
Cox/Stringfield, Upper Mint Wash	1200s	pottery	?	?	Simmons n.d. a
			Total	617+	

[a]Simmons (1937) estimated 12 to 14 rooms, Bartlett (1939) 30, Walker (1983) 75; an average of these numbers is used;
[b]this estimate is an upward revision of the one made in Christenson (2008b:12.14)

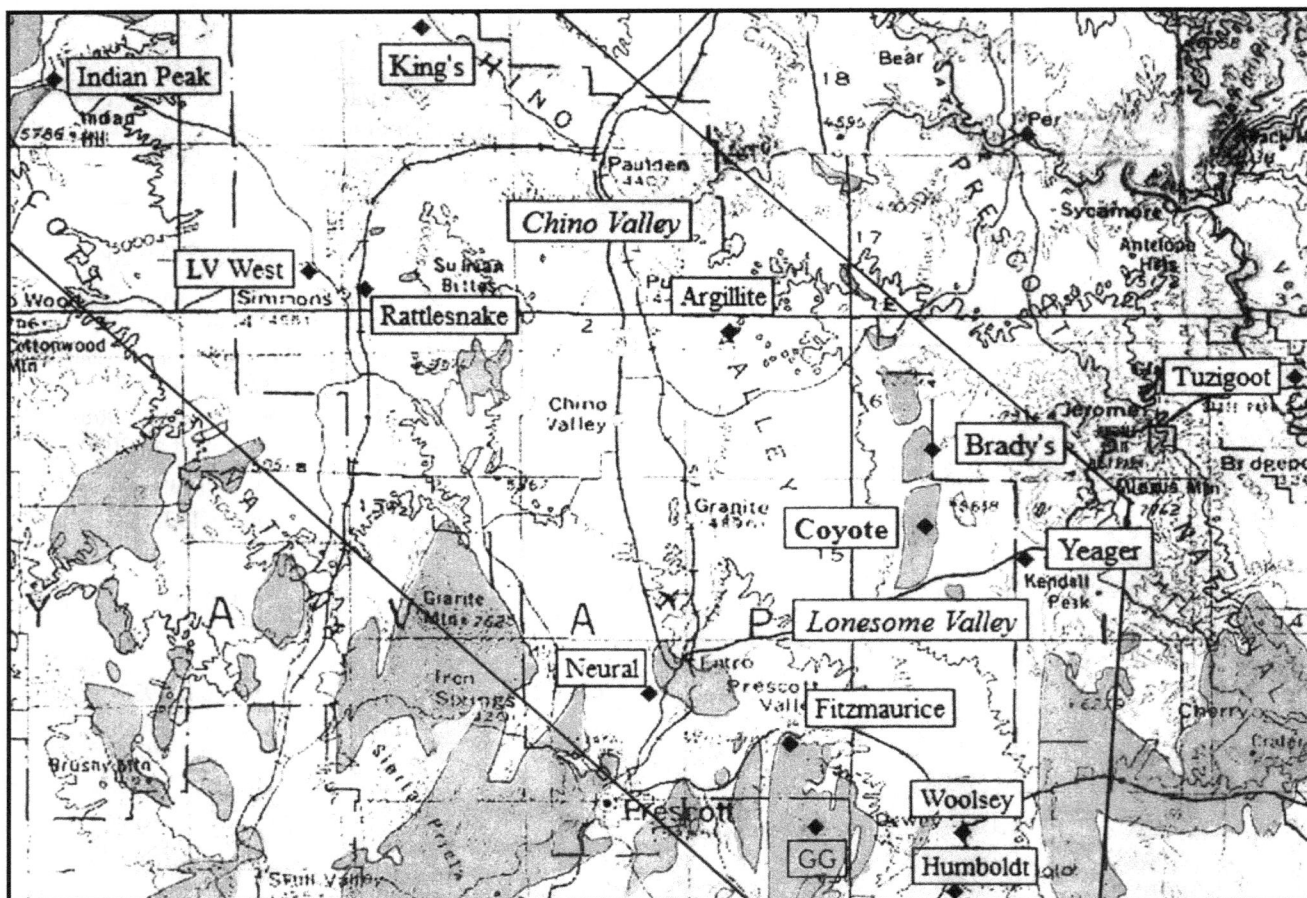

Figure 66. Thirteenth century sites of the central Prescott area likely to have had eight or more people. Shading indicates distribution of granitic bedrock. GG is Green Gulch site. Line (partly shown) indicates boundary of area used to calculate population density. Tuzigoot Ruin shown to indicate proximity of Verde Valley population center. Rectangles are townships that are usually 6 miles on a side.

Figure 66 shows the distribution of the largest of these sites, those that might have had a population of 8 or more people. A buffer of about 8 km (half the average distance between the largest sites) is shown as a line around the six largest sites (Indian Peak, King's, Argillite, Coyote, Fitzmaurice, and Woolsey) to provide an area to calculate population density (this area includes much of what North [2008: Figure 13.2] shows as 75-100% Prescott Gray Ware). Although the largest sites have probably been found for this area, there are no doubt smaller ones from this period for which we currently have no dating information (see Wilcox et al. 2001: Appendix 6.4). These estimates at least provide a baseline for some hypotheses.

One result of this population estimate is that there were not very many people in what is the Prescott Culture heartland. Taking say 600 people for an area of about 1000 sq. mi. gives a minuscule density of 0.6 people per square mile (0.23/sq. km) (Figure 66). This density is certainly an overestimate because we do not know the territory actually used by the settlements in question. The number is a fraction of the densities suggested for the same period in areas such as Mesa Verde (Varien et al. 1996: Figure 7.5) or Flagstaff (Colton 1949). In the Verde Valley, in an area half the size of the Prescott heartland being discussed here, there are 26 sites of 20 rooms or more for the 1150 to 1300 period (Pilles 1996: Table 5.1).

176

Given such a population a rough estimate of the maximum number of warriors (males, 15-45 years old) that could have been put in the field from these Prescott-area sites is about one-quarter of the total population (i.e., 150), although this is on the high side of the percentage of adult males that pre-state societies sent on war parties (Keeley 1996: Table 2.6).

Using the numbers above, if Coyote Pueblo had a resident population of 40 people then that might represent 8 families and only slightly more warriors.

At such a low population density, marriageable teenagers would have to look a long way to find suitable mates. The average mating distance (distance between birthplace of spouses) would be in the range of 40 km (MacDonald and Hewlett 1999: Figure 4), which means that we could expect some mates to come in from, or go out to, other groups as far away as the Flagstaff area, Perry Mesa, or the western Prescott Culture area. The closest dense population to Coyote Pueblo would have been in the Verde Valley (Tuzigoot Pueblo was only 24 km away as the crow flies) (Figure 66) and this is a likely source of marriage partners for villages in the eastern Prescott Culture area.

HOW DID THE COYOTE PUEBLO PEOPLE GET THEIR FOOD AND WATER?

As shown in Chapter 10, the people of Coyote Pueblo used a variety of plants, most importantly agave, a variety of seeds, but particularly chenopods and amaranths, and of course maize. Agave was a major source of fiber but also of carbohydrates obtained from roasting the heart. Agave is sometimes found on or near Prescott sites and it is possible that these plants represent "living archeological assemblages" (Hodgson and Slauson 1995: 138) remaining from prehistoric planting. Although the Hohokam actually cultivated large agave fields of a different species, no evidence of agave cultivation has been found in the Prescott region. Small seeds were no doubt a part of the diet and could, like agave, be anticipated to produce even in years when the corn crop was bad. Seed plants could have been cultivated, but would have also been present in corn fields as a useful (i.e., edible) "weed" and anywhere else there was some soil disturbance.

Maize was probably the most important source of food to the pueblo's inhabitants but the proportion in the diet is difficult to estimate. Based upon ethnographic data, Hard (1990) has proposed that mano length increases with agricultural dependence and so obtaining mean length from a site's groundstone assemblage can allow a general estimate of agricultural dependency. The mano length data for Coyote Ruin was not accessible as this analysis was being written up, but we did have a nearly equivalent measure - metate trough width - for the contemporaneous site of Fitzmaurice Ruin. There the average trough width was 19.8 cm (n = 54 metates; calculated from Barnett 1974: Table XIX). The average mano used in these metates would be slightly smaller, say 19 cm or so, which is well within Hard's (1990: Table 10.4) moderate to high (35-75%) agricultural dependence.

With an estimate of say 55% of the diet being corn, how much food would a population of 40 people have needed to live at the site year-round? Van West and Altschul (1994: 383) use a figure of 160 kg of maize per year to maintain an individual at 1500 to 1600 calories a day in an intensive maize economy, which would give about 90 kg needed per person per year.

Corn productivity can be estimated from research done by the University of Arizona Agricultural Experiment Station north of Prescott in the early 20th century. There, dry farming was done with a variety of Indian as well as hybrid maize types. Hopi yellow, blue and white varieties planted in at least 3 of the 4 years for which we have a planting results, produced an average of 800 pounds (364 kg)/acre (McOmie 1918: Table 47).[2] Thus, each acre would have fed about 4 people, and about 10 acres of corn would have been needed for the entire population. This number would have been significantly higher if "surplus" was grown for trading or storage for bad years, both of which are likely. Ideally, the Hopi stored up to a year's food in reserve and sometimes over two (Forde 1931: 393) and even with such a surplus there are stories of many Hopi or even the entire group forced to go elsewhere in bad years (Bancroft 1888: 265; Lockett 1933: 85-86). Crops such as beans and squash, not represented in the flotation samples but probably grown, would have required additional area.

Clearly, the garden plots located on the slopes of the Coyote Pueblo hill were only a minor part of the land needed to feed the population. Cobbly sand loam makes up the soil of the site. However, Lynx soils, which are the basic agricultural soils of the county, occur along Coyote Wash just over ½ mile southeast of the site and along Little Coyote Canyon 1¼ mile to the north (Wendt et al. 1976: Sheet 74), well within walking distance. Jeter (1977: 230-233) noted a strong association of major Prescott sites and Lynx soils. In these soils, the Coyote Pueblo people would have had the best luck with maize fields, not only because the soil is better, but because runoff water could have been used to supplement direct rainfall (Coyote Ruin is currently within the 16 to 18 inches/year rainfall contour).

In terms of animal protein in the diet, at Fitzmaurice Ruin, Barnett (1974: 49) estimated that deer represented about 70% of the meat, with antelope, rabbits, and prairie dog making up most of the remainder. Without doing any detailed calculations, Coyote Ruin seems to have less deer relative to antelope and rabbits, with wood rat, and prairie dog following (Table 50). However, the 9 elk bones from 5 individuals require alteration of the statement above. Coyote Pueblo was just beyond the distribution of elk today, which includes the Black Hills (Hoffmeister 1986: Map 5.125), but it is unclear to what extent this range has been restricted by modern hunting and ranching. Elk kills made very far from the pueblo would require substantial butchering at the kill location so the low number of bones could indicate that mostly meat was carried back home. With 3½ times the amount of meat of a mule deer, the elk would have provided more meat than all animals but deer.

The nearest permanent water to the pueblo, Coyote Springs, is over 3.5 miles east (Figure 2). It is unlikely that any of the drainages nearby had running water, except after storms, so the main way of obtaining water would be in catching and storing when it falls or by walking to the springs, which had evidence of prehistoric occupation (Simmons 1937), although Ranney (Chapter 1) does hold out the possibility that there was a small spring next to the site in the past.

Studies of water use in East Africa give a clue as to how much effort water procurement can take. For a 5-person household using 4 liters of water per person per day, one adult has to use about 45% of their caloric intake per day obtaining water from a source 3.5 miles away on a 4% slope (White et al. 1972: 107), which approximates the walk from Coyote Ruin to Coyote Springs. Clearly this is not a trivial cost, especially for a group that at times would have its hands full obtaining basic subsistence. One way that that water could have been caught and stored on site would be to have rooftops and other runoff locations drain into pots. This method would require large, wide-mouthed vessels to be placed around the village and would allow greater water storage during the rainy season, but it would not carry over into dry periods.

HOW WAS COYOTE PUEBLO ORGANIZED?

One thing that is more predominant in the 13th century than earlier is that the population is relatively concentrated in a few villages. If the numbers in Table 52 are anywhere close to reality, three-quarters of the population of the central Prescott Culture area was in a half-dozen villages. Smaller one-to-five family communities still existed in the region in the 13th century, although their relationship to the larger communities needs to be determined. We could expect pueblos to have field houses if farming areas were at a distance and various special activity sites such as hunting camps, pinyon camps, etc. Jeter (1977: Figure 43) provides a model of the types of specialized sites that would be expected to be used by residents of permanent base sites. Coyote Pueblo may have had Brady's Fort and Yeager as satellites and King's Pueblo had two nearby sites that might have been associated. Fitzmaurice Pueblo had lookouts nearby that had a better view across Lonesome Valley. Two of the sites excavated in the StoneRidge project had late dates that might indicate use as a field house or some other seasonal occupation from nearby Fitzmaurice Pueblo.

Population aggregation is a question that has received considerable attention in the Southwest and is most commonly explained by need for cooperation during uncertain environmental conditions or need for protection during warfare, but the question is complex (see discussion in Cordell et al. 1994: 109-111; Kohler 1989: 6-10). Although aggregation can solve certain problems, it can also create stresses. In some parts of the Southwest, aggregation led to development of ritual integrative mechanisms, formation of elites, and development of architecture such as kivas and plazas for large social groups. Except possibly for Woolsey Ranch, about which we know nothing except its large size, we would not expect too much along this line to have happened given the small scale of the aggregates represented in the Prescott area. Coyote Ruin did have one extra large room (Room 18 - 7.5x5.5m; 41 sq. m), which is at the very smallest end of the size range for Sinagua community rooms (Pilles 1996: 70), but no specific characteristics were identified during excavation that would indicate use as a special room. Burned soil was present in the lower strata of the room, covered by a floor, and then trash on top of that, so it may not have been in use at the late end of the occupation (Figure 60). A plaza was identified between the house mound rooms and the eastern mid-level room block that could have served as a small focal area for group activities (see Figure 31).

The burials at the site are peculiar. Six of the nine graves in Old Coyote found by J. W. Simmons were "anchored" (his term) with stones, either directly on the limbs or immediately over the body(ies) (Appendix I). One of these burials was in an abandoned pit house and another in a pit house that was just abandoned. An adult with a child was found in Room 38. In Room 40 an adult and child were found separately under the lower floor, and an adult, a subadult, and a child were found separately above the floor, placed in the room after it was abandoned. Both adults were "anchored." The older male was laid on some rocks and then had rocks put on knees and ankles and the grave was outlined in rocks. The younger adult female had rocks placed on her ankles, knees, and chest.

Simmons reported 3 or 4 of 41 burials at the Fitzmaurice Ruin cemetery "anchored" like this (Simmons n.d. b). No such burials occurred at the King's Ruin cemetery. At Tuzigoot, over 1/5th of the burials were called slab burials, where slabs of limestone were placed over the entire body (Caywood and Spicer 1935: 97-98), but this seems to differ from what was present at Coyote, where selected areas of the body were covered. There has not been much discussion of this phenomenon in the Southwest. Most adult burials in the Mimbres area are buried in rooms that were still in use and have subsurface cairns above them, perhaps to alert excavators of later burials to their presence, or perhaps to reinforce the floor when the body decays (Shafer 2003: 147). The Coyote Ruin burials seem different. The weighting down of a burial might also be an indication of necrophobia, fear of the dead, that is a long tradition in Europe (Taylor 2008) but it is unclear if this explanation has any relevance in this case.

Burial of children and infants in rooms, particularly ones that are still occupied, is not uncommon, while burial of adults in such a context is. At Tuzigoot, a contemporary to later pueblo in the Verde Valley, 168 of 271 individuals under 15 years of age were buried in room floors while 157 of 160 adult burials were in the cemetery outside the pueblo (Caywood and Spicer 1935: 95). The majority of burials found at both King's Ruin and Fitzmaurice Ruin were found in cemeteries outside the pueblo and this is a general pattern in Prescott Culture sites (Barnett 1981: 32). The three adult burials in rooms in the "New" part of Coyote Ruin, one in a floor and two in fill, are thus unusual.

In the Mimbres area, there is a shift from extramural to intramural burials after about A.D. 900 that is hypothesized to co-occur with a shift to more intensive irrigation agriculture and from basic extended family social organization to that of broader corporate groups (Shafer 2006). This shift is indicated by change from regular doorway entrance into habitations, to roof entrances, and from extramural burials to burial beneath the floors of occupied rooms and kivas. This cultural change is seen as indication of the rise of secret corporate ritual and restricted access to the dead who provided important ritual information (Shafer 2006: 180-181). Such an interpretation for Coyote Pueblo is tenuous given the lack of knowledge that we have of social organization or ritual activity at the site. The Room 40 adult burials were also unusual in that one had a fractured skull and the other severe arthritis and neither had burial goods (the woman had a basalt stone next to her head). The timing of the blocking of the doorway between Room 14 and Room 40 is unknown and could have happened either before or after the burials. Although there was ground level access between the rooms, either or both would have needed roof entries for anyone coming in from elsewhere on the site and the bodies buried in Room 40 would have been carried in down a ladder.

Comparing the three late sites for which we have ground plans, we can see how different Coyote Pueblo is from Fitzmaurice and King's (Figure 67). The latter two sites clearly have more formal layout, compared with Coyote's more "organic" structure, if that is the appropriate term. Of course it is unlikely that all of the Coyote rooms were occupied in the late use of the site, so it may not have been so spread out as indicated and the small house mound and surrounding slopes did not allow more formal arrangement of rooms as at Fitzmaurice. Fitzmaurice Pueblo had an interesting development history because the main pueblo was built in three units, although the temporal separation of the units is unknown (Barnett 1974: 41). Two large rooms south of the pueblo might be something more than regular habitation rooms (7x6.5 m and 8x5 m), although the excavator made no such interpretation (Caywood 1936: 94-96). The rooms located outside the main pueblo and separated from the main pueblo by a wall were interpreted as being occupied by late arrivals (Barnett 1974: 10), but again, the dating is unknown.

Wilcox et al. (2001: Appendix 6.4) list three main sites in line of sight and close proximity to Coyote Ruin: Aiken, which we call Brady's Fort; Stowell, which we call Yeager Canyon Ruin; and Nordwall. Simmons' thought that Brady's Fort was not a habitation site, but may have been built by inhabitants of small sites nearby (no details given; Simmons 1937: 18-19). He also thought that artificial building up of the upper rooms of Coyote Pueblo was done to see Brady's Fort. However, Brady's Fort is visible without any building up at Coyote Pueblo, so this explanation of the central part of the site's elevated nature seems unlikely.

Yeager Canyon Ruin is a walled, habitation site located at the mouth of the major canyon giving access to the Verde Valley. The only clue about dating the site is Simmons' statement that sherds of the "decadent" type were present, citing Gladwin, who used the term for the latest Hohokam period. Of interest is that Yeager has a line-of-sight view to the "lookouts" around Fitzmaurice Ruin (Barnett 1974: 5). Nordwall is a site of unknown affiliation and will not be further discussed here. Except for Simmons' note of small sites around Brady's Fort, no information is available that might indicate the density and size of other sites in the Coyote Ruin vicinity.

The location of these three intervisible sites near a major access route between Lonesome Valley and the Verde Valley is surely not a coincidence. As Simmons would have it, the Coyote Pueblo people were afraid of an enemy over the mountain to the east (1937: 68). To what extent fear was of people "over the mountain" or of neighbors in Lonesome Valley itself will be difficult to demonstrate, but a cycle of enmity-amity with neighbors is to be expected.

The Yeager Canyon route certainly had major traffic in both directions and Yeager Canyon site, which has a spring, Coyote Springs, and Coyote Pueblo would have been natural stops for travelers taking a break or having items to exchange. Of course there may occasionally have been parties coming over the mountain for less innocuous reasons and the built up central rooms of the site would have provided a fairly secure refuge as long as the hostile group was small and the hostilities short-lived (see discussion below).

The presence of a formal cemetery with multiple interments at King's Ruin hints at the existence of some sort of corporate social unit (Christenson 2008b: 12.14-12.15). Elaborate male burials in the Fitzmaurice and King's cemeteries are perhaps indicative of ritual specialists (Barnett 1974: 13; North 2008: 13.9). No such burials were found at Coyote, but as the site was heavily pothunted, we should not make too much of the absence of such evidence.

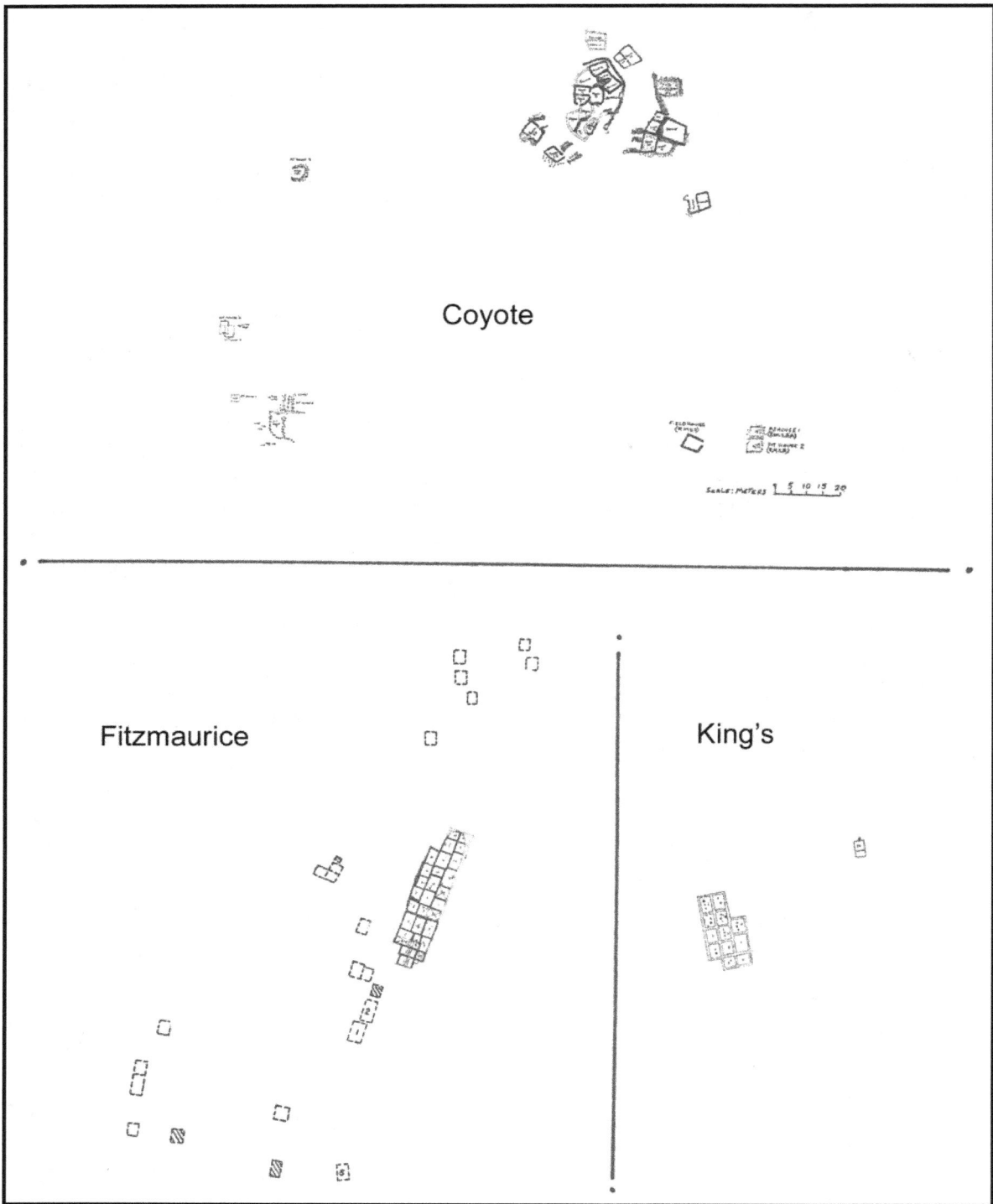

Figure 67. Comparison of layouts of Coyote Ruin, Fitzmaurice Ruin, and King's Ruin. Orientation (north at top) and scale is the same for all three sites (20 m scale shown in Coyote Ruin segment). Only habitation features shown. Far northern pit house at Coyote Ruin is not shown. Not all habitation features are likely to be contemporaneous.

HOW WAS PRESCOTT CULTURE CONNECTED TO SURROUNDING CULTURES?

The connections of the Prescott Culture with surrounding groups has not been studied in detail, so this section will simply consider some of the goods that may have gone out and those that may have come in.

First of all, we need to define what natural products or cultural goods were available for Prescott-area people to exchange with other groups. Argillite and jasper, found on the east side of Chino Valley, are present at virtually all sites and were either procured directly or obtained by local trade. The presence of one of the larger pueblos in the area at the argillite mines may indicate that there was local control of the mining and trade. Presley Wash and Partridge Creek obsidian sources are at the north edge of the culture area and, more importantly, materials from both sources have eroded out and are deposited along the terraces of Big Chino Wash and presumably down the Verde River. Perkinsville Jasper seems to be mostly an internal trade item, although obsidian, mostly Partridge Creek, does appear outside the culture area (Shackley 2005: 30).

It seems unlikely that the area was a significant exporter of maize, certainly not to the Verde Valley, but materials like processed agave hearts or fiber and perhaps other specialized plant products could be transported significant distances. Large game was probably more common here than in Hohokam or Anasazi country, so meat and other animal products might have been a valuable commodity for exchange.

Exported cultural products include, of course, Prescott Gray Ware, both decorated and undecorated, which has been found over a fairly large area (Small 2010). Although an argument has been made that Del Rio argillite was mostly traded unworked, evidence at the quarries indicates that working of the material was happening at the site nearby (Bartlett 1939: 77), so trade in both raw material and worked ornaments should be expected.

The one burial excavated at the site near the argillite quarry had both turquoise and shell ornaments (Simmons 1937: 82) and another found nearby had copper bells (Bostwick and Young 2000). Argillite could have been traded for all of these materials. Evidence such as the mano and knife with argillite residue found at Coyote Ruin (Chapter 6) and the partly worked argillite found at most Prescott sites indicate that at least some of the material was obtained raw or in blank form and was worked on site. Such an argument was made for the argillite found at Northern Sinagua sites (Kamp and Whittaker 1999: 133). Del Rio argillite has been sourced to a number of Sinagua and Hohokam sites (Elson and Gundersen 1992; Howell 1940; Madsen 1999).

The origin of Prescott Culture is obscure, but Prescott Gray Ware was being made before 900 (Christenson 2005a: Table 8.38). Colonial period Hokoham habitation sites (Henderson site; Antler House) were present on the Agua Fria at this time. Prescott Gray Ware is not common on these sites (Rodgers and Weaver 1990: 18; Weed and Ward 1970: 10), although there is reference to one site having contemporaneous Hohokam and Prescott pit houses (Weaver 1996, cited by Motsinger et al. 2000: 6).

Hohokam Buff Ware is found on Prescott-area sites of the pre-1100 period indicating connections to the south and such connections are also indicated in the later period by the use of the Gila shoulder on some jars and manufacture of a local red-on-buff pottery (but with designs that seem to have originated with the Kayenta Anasazi [Higgins 2000]). The copper bells in the area also probably came from that direction as did much of the shell. Some Prescott Gray Ware and a little Perkinsville Jasper (Christenson 2007a [1 flake],

2012a [3 flakes]) made its way to the south and a Prescott Culture colony has even been suggested for the lower Agua Fria River (Duering 1969).

The northernmost connection in the late period was with the Kayenta Anasazi, the source of Tusayan White Ware, Tsegi Orange Ware, and occasional Tusayan Gray Ware (prior to 1100, San Juan Red Ware from southeastern Utah was a common tradeware). It is unclear what was traveling in the opposite direction. Bartlett (1939: 76) says that the red ornaments found in northeastern Arizona (i.e., Kayenta Anasazi) is a different shade of red than the Del Rio material, but no sourcing has been done of this material which at one site is represented by necklaces with nearly 90,000 drilled beads (Crotty 1983: 33). Simmons thought that "Tusayan" people (i.e., Anasazi from the Four Corners/Hopi country) were coming into the area and sometimes burying their dead. While this is certainly not impossible, it is more likely that most of the pottery from that area was used by and buried with local residents.

Contact with the Hopi Mesa/Hopi Buttes areas is indicated by the presence of Little Colorado White Ware and Hopi Buttes variety of Tusayan White Ware. One 12th century female burial from Oraibi Wash had a Prescott Black-on gray bowl (Weed 1970: Figure 6c).

The Northern Sinagua are represented by occasional pottery, but the primary material coming from that area is obsidian from sources west of Flagstaff (Christenson 2009, 2010). The presence of substantial amounts of Prescott pottery in the Wupatki area suggested to H. S. Colton the possibility of a resident Prescott population (see Lambert 1998) but it could also indicate movement of unknown goods carried in the jars. The one macaw bone at Coyote Ruin, the second identified in the Prescott area (the other was found at Fitzmaurice Ruin), is from Room 40 and could also be an item that came from the Northern Sinagua, which was one hot-spot of macaw raising in the Southwest (Hargrave 1970: Figure 15, 36-42).

The necessity of marriage links over wide distance has already been mentioned and no doubt some of these links were "over the mountain." Evidence of links to the east is substantial. The Verde Valley was probably the "middle man" on pottery moving from the Kayenta, Hopi Mesa, and Little Colorado Anasazi areas, although there may have been occasions when Prescott Culture people traveled directly to those areas. It also seems likely that not just pottery, but also potters moved over the Black Hills. It has been suggested that some Prescott Black-on-gray was made in the Verde Valley (Christenson 1999; see also Caywood and Spicer 1935: 62) as well as an imitation of the type called Tuzigoot Black-on-grey [sic] (Caywood and Spicer 1935: 62). Verde Brown was being made in the Prescott area, certainly at the Neural Site (Christenson 2000) and possibly at Coyote Pueblo, given the abundance of the type there.

Argillite from Del Rio is present at Tuzigoot, in contexts indicating operation of the quarry into the 14th century (see below). The fish bones found at the site (no species identification) could have come from the Verde Valley. Many of the goods moving across the Black Hills may have been items not preserved in the archaeological record. Verde Valley Sinagua farmers may have produced varieties of maize or other crops not produced in the Prescott area. Although cotton has been found at one Prescott-area site (N:7:286; Huckell 2005: 11.69-11.71), it was no doubt produced in much greater abundance in the Verde Valley.

Wilcox et al. (2000: 124-127) have hypothesized an active east-west trade route passing through the Walnut Creek area and extending to the Verde Valley and points north and east. Material such as turquoise, which is abundant, particularly in Williamson Valley sites (Johnson 1995: 24; Macnider et al. 1989: 89), and shell, may have passed along this route. Contrary to what is often assumed, it appears that shell beads in the Southwest are mostly from the Gulf of California and that Gulf shell may have moved to southern California from the Southwest, rather than vice versa (Gamble and King 2011: 175). No chemical sourcing of turquoise has been done on Prescott sites, but visual matching of hundreds of pieces at Las Vegas Ranch Ruin West found most to be similar to the Los Cerrillos, New Mexico source (Barnett 1978: 79).

Prescott Culture sites extend considerably to the west and northwest as elegantly shown early on by the Gladwins (1930: Map). The distribution is confirmed by recent studies that find "pure" Prescott sites, at least ceramically, occurring in the upper Burro Creek area (Christenson 2008a) and "Western Prescott" extending to Kingman and the Colorado River (Simonis 2000). To what extent any of this occupation was post-1200 is unknown. However, Prescott Gray Ware is present at one site in southern Nevada in levels radiocarbon dated in the 13th (1 date) and 14th (3 dates) centuries (Seymour 1997: Tables 8 and 10).

HOW IMPORTANT WAS CONFLICT TO THE PEOPLE OF COYOTE PUEBLO?

Following in the footsteps of his mentor J. W. Fewkes, J. W. Simmons, who first documented Coyote Ruin, was a strong believer that warfare was a determinant of site placement and configuration. He felt that the central rooms of the site were built up to improve the view to the north (towards Brady's Fort) and improve defensibility of the site when under attack (Simmons 1937:68). Simmons also thought that the pueblo was camouflaged in a way by being located amongst the granite rocks, but at least from some perspectives, its location at the top of the hill would have stood out as an eye-catching place even to people who did not know the area (see Figure 5; cf. Wilcox et al. 2008:16.14). The built-upness of the main part of the site was also noted by Mary Spall and her team, who could not find any bedrock when excavating in the area east of the house mound.

In 1977, Austin (2000) and later Wilcox et al. (2001) continued this interpretive tradition with a model of line-of-sight defensive systems throughout central Arizona. However, these systems could have only worked for defense in prehistory if they were manned and if significant information could be transferred between them. Needless to say such a system would also require lots of practice. Sending a message, say, from the far southeast village in the area we are discussing, Woolsey Ranch, to the far northwestern village, King's Pueblo, would have been a major undertaking, involving many people. Both sites are in river valleys and a message would have to have been sent uphill and then along a chain of high points until it reached the end.

It seems likely that messages sent by smoke were generally simple, something like "alarm," "attention" (followed by another signal), or "we are here" (Mallery 1881: 537-539). More complex messages could be sent using varying smoke colors, varying numbers of fires, or blankets to break up the smoke column(s) (William Hardy, cited by Wilcox et al. 2001:120; Mallery 1881:536-537), but such elaborate messaging systems require a variety of natural and cultural factors to be working together and probably have low reliability. It is likely that most complex messages were sent by runner. The 35 miles between King's Pueblo and Woolsey Ranch could have been crossed in 5-6 hours or less given the 4-9 mph speeds recorded for Indian runners historically (Nabokov 1981:17-18, 21-23).

Certainly local use of signaling would be an effective way of calling together people if there were problems. Away from the pueblo someone could send a prearranged signal "Go to the pueblo immediately" or at the pueblo one could send a signal "Come immediately." Hilltops would not be critical in such situations and when seeing is good in places like Lonesome and Chino valleys, simple signals could be effective for considerable distances.

Conflict was certainly an important issue in the broader Southwest in the time period that we are considering (see LeBlanc 1999). Ethnographic evidence from the western U. S. indicates that over 80% of the tribes either raided someone else, or were raided themselves more than once a year (Keeley 1996:33). There are clues of conflict in the Prescott region in addition to the line-of-site system (see also Wilcox et al. 2000:127-130). For example, many of the rooms in the main pueblo at Fitzmaurice Ruin had evidence of burning and the excavator felt that grinding tools were broken to make them unusable, and thrown into the rooms (Barnett 1975: 19). Remnants of a defensive wall are also visible at the site (Caywood 1936: 91). Five rooms external to the main pueblo were burned and four had significant complete artifacts (grinding tools, pots, etc.) on the floor and no apparent salvaging of their contents (Barnett 1975:3; Baty n.d.). Such burning can occur through raiding and occasional small fires, but may also be the result of the inhabitants torching a site prior to permanent abandonment. The presence of complete room assemblages is a good indicator of permanent abandonment (Reid 1973, cited by Montgomery 1993: 158), whether planned or forced. Intentional breakage of artifacts, especially something like grinding tools, is a good clue that permanent abandonment was planned and not rushed. The only closely datable item in these rooms was a Flagstaff Black-on-white jar in Barnett's "Lower Room," a type that dates about 1130 to 1230. However, whole charred beams were recovered and saved from one of these rooms, so finer dating may be possible in the future for this abandonment event.

At Coyote Ruin, Room 2 burned once, was reused, and burned again, perhaps near the end of use of the site as indicated by the 14th century radiocarbon date from the deep fill/wall trench of the room. Rooms 14 and 17 also had evidence of burning.

At the Neural Site there was good evidence of burning in Room 2 and less so in Room 1 (Grossman 1997:14). Pit house 1 across the road at the same site was burned with a floor assemblage left in place (Mitchell and Motsinger 2010:19). The presence of Tusayan Black-on-white and several radiocarbon dates with high probabilities in the 1300s in both parts of the site suggest a post-1300 use and burning of structures at the site. Pit house 2 was apparently intentionally burned too, but had few artifacts on the floor (p. 23). No date is given for this feature.

House burning has received considerable attention in the Southwest and elsewhere in the Neolithic world, meaning pre-state agricultural groups living in small- to medium-size villages. A wide range of reasons can be found in the ethnographic record for house burning, from accidental (sparks from a cooking fire) to a range of intentional behaviors - the death of the owner or at least a resident,[3] a raiding party, village abandonment with no intent to return, or to "show social and material continuity" of society (see LeBlanc 1999:74-83; Stevanović 1997). Outside of doing a forensic study as Stevanović did in Serbia, it may be difficult to distinguish these different causes archaeologically (but see Lally and Vonarx 2011).

There is a strong relationship between exchange of marriage partners and goods, and violent conflict (Keeley 1996:123, 126). Such conflict might initially be restricted to a raid being made to kill a particular person or right another wrong, but could expand to an attempt of total annihilation. Also, hard times from environmental change is another common spur to violence (Keeley 1996: 140). The mostly dry farmers of the Prescott area would have suffered when rainfall declined and initiation of raids against neighbors is one possible reaction to the circumstances. Given the small size of raiding parties that most of the Prescott-area pueblos could field, such raiding would have most likely been intracultural, rather than against the well-watered Verde Valley, who could have retaliated massively.

The hints of conflict given by burned rooms and seemingly fortified sites, has not been substantiated by the burial record. The two largest cemeteries excavated in the area, at Fitzmaurice and King's, did not seem to have any examples of a person who died by violence. The excavator, J. W. Simmons, though not formally trained, was quite observant and would have noted obvious things like points in the ribcage or trauma to the skull. At King's Ruin, he had the help of a physical anthropologist who would have seen more subtle indicators of violence. The male burial in Room 40 at Coyote Ruin seems to be the only possible example of violent death in the post-1200 period. It is not uncommon in non-state societies to have from 5 to over 20% of the population, mostly males, die in warfare (Keeley 1996: Table 6.2).

WHAT WAS THE "PRESCOTT CULTURE" ?

Put briefly, traditions are ideas, beliefs, and ways of behaving that are passed down generation through generation for a significant period of time. Cultural anthropologists generally work with living people who tell them what culture they are (i.e., their identity) and the anthropologists then look at ideas, beliefs, ways of behaving and see how common they are within the culture and how they compare with other cultures. Archaeologists do not have that course of action available, and must deal with the material results of behavior, from which they see patterns that allow "creation" of archaeological cultures. Traditions have a beginning at one place and time but can spread through a large area occupied by many different cultures, each carrying on an adaptation of the original (e.g., corn agriculture). Some traditions originate and may be carried on by a family or small social unit and are never taken up by people elsewhere (e.g., a particular way a family of potters finishes a rim). A culture is a group of people that share a significant number of traditions (compare Willey and Phillips 1958: 37), with "significant" being an open-ended assessment. Long-term ties to a particular place can also be an important or even a defining characteristic of a culture, although migration has been shown to be a significant factor in the prehistoric Southwest, and so cultural continuity can outlast spatial continuity.

Historical Definition

Distinctive black-on-gray pottery in the Prescott area was known at least as early as the 1920s and was initially suggested as defining a district (Turney 1929: 155) and then a culture (Gladwin and Gladwin 1934: 15; Simmons 1931). Later culture traits other than pottery were added to the definition (Colton 1939: 30-32), although pottery and geographic location have always been the primary criteria. Simmons (n.d. b) protested the use of "Prescott" for a culture that he felt was centered to the north in the Chino-Williamson Basin. He suggested "Yavapai Culture," after the county, as a more appropriate term, but he was fighting a loosing battle.

Prescott Traditions

It is useful for this discussion to list a few material culture patterns on sites in the Prescott area that might be considered traditions. They include ceramic, lithic, and architectural traits. Patterns that are restricted to the late period only (1100-1300+) are so indicated:

- use of pottery made from residual clay with coarse, abundant granitic inclusions;
- non-symmetrical black-on-gray designs on vessels made from high mica clay (late);
- use of pottery figurines;
- use of unnotched, obsidian triangular arrowpoints;
- expedient, stream cobble-based chipped stone technology;
- use of notched floor support stones as intramural architectural elements;
- hilltop masonry structures with views of other such sites (late?); and
- lack of specialized religious structures (late).

Pottery. The basic "rules" of pottery manufacture/acquisition for most Prescott Culture communities, based upon the archaeological patterns seen so far are:

- select only clay close to the bedrock source;
- avoid volcanic clay;
- remove/reduce enough of the rock to get a texture of about 60% clay to 40% coarse rock;
- do not tightly control the firing; and
- produce only plain, unslipped pottery; trade for decorated pottery.

One thing that petrographic analysis has indicated is that most of the Prescott Gray Ware is made from residual, rather than alluvial, clays (Christenson 2000), where residual is considered to include clays immediately below a rock outcrop as well as clays in drainages running through or below outcrops that have not picked up significant minerals from other rock formations. Although the general characteristics of this pottery making was very much geologically determined, and similar to peoples over much of central Arizona, giving rise to Wood's (1987: 9) suggestion of the Central Arizona Plainware Tradition, the particular way of using the granitic clay, of avoiding alluvial clay, and of not being too concerned about the firing atmosphere are <u>local cultural choices that were made and adhered to for several hundred years.</u> This pottery-making technology was passed down through a significant period and so was a <u>tradition</u> that was shared by a large proportion of the potting community.

Table 53 provides sherd counts for eight sites, arranged in geographic order from northwest to southeast, that have good evidence of being occupied in the 13th century. Unfortunately, no complete sherd counts are available for King's Ruin, but black-on-gray and black-on-brown (both now classified as Prescott Black-on-gray) were abundant at the site (Spicer 1936: 33-34). With the exception of the nearly identical Las Vegas Ranch sites, there is a wide variation in the frequency of the major ceramic wares on these sites. This could be taken as indicative of some cultural difference between the sites, but other hypotheses need to be considered.

I suggest that there are multiple factors affecting these ceramic differences. A critical question to answer is which of these wares was manufactured on these sites. Ethnographic information indicates that although subsistence agriculturalists will often go 3-5 km to their fields, they prefer to stay under 1 km for procurement of clay and temper (Arnold 1985: Table 2.7). Of course, there are situations reported ethnographically of people going a long way for clay, but the general pattern of procuring very close to home allows us to create some hypotheses about distinguishing trade from locally-produced pottery. Taking Fitzmaurice Ruin as an example, we know that granodiorite, phyllite, and gabbro bedrock are all present within a kilometer or so of the site, and drainages coming out of the gabbro converge directly below the site. So with this site it is appropriate to hypothesize that most of the Prescott Gray Ware (granite/granodiorite-derived clay), Fitzmaurice Series (gabbro-derived clay),[4] and Wingfield Brown Ware (phyllite-derived clay) could have been locally made. In contrast, a few miles up Lynx Creek, Lynx Creek Ruin has significant Fitzmaurice Series sherds (described by Horton 1994: 44-45 as Prescott Gray, Black Mineral), but it is not near gabbro outcrops, so it makes sense to suggest that at this site this type was not locally made. Continuing the argument, both the Neural Site and Coyote Ruin are on or near granite/granodiorite (Figure 66) and a long way from phyllite, so it is reasonable to suggest that the granite-derived types are mostly locally made and the phyllite-derived pottery is a tradeware.

As noted, at Fitzmaurice Ruin, which is the second type site for Prescott Culture along with King's Ruin, Prescott Gray Ware and Wingfield Brown Ware could have been locally produced, but the village was at the end of a long local tradition of using gabbro-derived clay for the largest portion of its pottery. This pottery was originally confused with Tuzigoot Brown and Red, types produced in the Verde Valley, but it is in fact a local tradition operating parallel to that of Prescott Gray Ware and Wingfield Brown Ware. There is nothing inherently unlikely that the same potters could participate in all three ceramic traditions. As we go farther down the Agua Fria drainage east and south, potters near the drainage would have had less access to granitic clays but more to phyllite-derived clay. Does this mean they could not have been part of Prescott Culture? Of course not. But we are faced with the need for some other diagnostic criteria to determine cultural relationships. Lack of excavation of later sites in this area means that we have little to go on at the moment.[5]

Pottery function adds another dimension to the puzzle. Wingfield Brown Ware is interesting because the platy phyllite inclusions gave it great strength and allowed thinner walls (Van Keuren et al. 1997: 166-167). Although Prescott Culture potters were able to do a variety of things with their thick, coarse-tempered pottery, there were uses where Wingfield had advantages and it was imported into the easternmost Prescott sites (Christenson in prep.). Fitzmaurice is the only site in Table 53 where Wingfield could have been made.

Several patterns are suggested in Table 53. First, there is a west-east decline in the frequency of Prescott Black-on-gray; second, there is a corresponding increase in the frequency of Wingfield Brown Ware; and third, Coyote Ruin has an inordinate amount of Alameda Brown Ware, mostly Verde Brown.

Petrographic work has also indicated that most Prescott Black-on-gray could not have been made using the local Prescott Granodiorite or Dells Granite (Christenson 2006a, b). Where this type was made is not known, but the northwest to southeast gradient in frequency of the type shown in Table 53, if it is a fall-off curve related to distance to the source, indicates that the Las Vegas Ranch sites are closer to the source, and Fitzmaurice Ruin farther away. Although not shown in this table, there is also a temporal gradient, with painted grayware being rare until the late 11th century and increasing in frequency significantly by the 1200s (Christenson 2005a: Table 8.33).

As noted above, the geographic distribution of black-on-gray pottery initially suggested the existence of a distinct culture in the Prescott region. Although we do not currently know the production area of most of this pottery, it still does delineate a spatial and temporal group of pueblos in the Chino/Lonesome Valley area and beyond that shared in the use of, if not always the production of, this decorated type (Table 53; North 2008: Figure 13.3). Prescott designs have been attributed to "failure of the imagination" (Spicer 1936: 37-39) or poor execution (Harper 1998: 93), but it seems better to see their designs as being done with an unusual aesthetic (Christenson 2007b) that, unlike their Anasazi or Hohokam neighbors, put fairly low value on design symmetry and consistency (Harper 1998: 98). Notably, decoration usually occurs on vessels that had high visual impact from being made with high silver mica (muscovite) clay (see Chapter 5, Attribute Analysis).

Note also that there can be problems in some areas of distinguishing Prescott Gray and Verde Brown (Frampton 1978: 62; James 1974: 112-113), Tizon Brown Ware (Euler and Dobyns 1962: 79; Linford 1979: 192), Gila Plain (Euler 1978: 22), and earlier in time, Deadmans Gray (Purcell 2010; Simonis 2000: 200). Part of this similarity is from the widespread use of granite-derived clay which represents the idea of a Central Arizona Plainware Tradition but part comes from the variation in clay processing and firing that will always occur in a given pottery tradition. It may also be that the movement of potters (female?) may lead to such mixing of traditions (Simonis 2000: 200), but we really do not have enough understanding of the effect of outside potters upon a local plainware tradition.

The most common classification difficulty in the central Prescott Culture area is with Verde Brown. A common classification strategy taken, as was done at Coyote Ruin, has been to place the questionable sherds with Prescott Gray unless there are specific attributes that tend toward Verde Brown (James 1974: 112-113; Westfall and Jeter 1977: 379). Attribute analysis and petrographic analysis are approaches to begin to address the question of whether similarities and differences in an assemblage or region are between plainwares of local origin or involve trade/exchange.

Site Ware/Type	King's[a]	Las Vegas West	Las Vegas East	Neural	Stoney Ridge	Coyote	Lynx Creek	Fitzmaurice[b]
Prescott B/g		861 (31)	2651 (28)	4746 (14)	38 (12)	**3159 (7)**	38 (6)	59 (4)
Other PGW		1863(66)	6587 (69)	27235 (81)	262 (80)	**28654 (62)**	268 (46)	340 (25)
Alameda BW		14	135	819 (2)		**10545 (23)**	20 (3)	22 (2)
Fitzmaurice Series						17	128 (22)	681 (50)
Wingfield BW		2	3	828 (2.5)	22 (7)	**2784 (6)**	131 (22)	259 (19)
Tusayan WW		28	90	71		**356**		
Other		40	98	35	7	**341**		17
Total		2808	9564	33734	329	**45856**	585	1356
Latest Type	Tusayan B/w Kayenta var.	Tusayan B/w Kayenta var.	Tusayan B/w Kayenta var.	Tusayan B/w Kayenta var.; Jeddito YW	Holbrook A B/w	**Tusayan B/w Kayenta var.**	no datable trade-ware	Tusayan B/w Kayenta var.
Mean Ceramic Date[c]		1243	1254	1253		**1178 (multi-component)**		1232
Radiocarbon Date Mean / Midrange				1249; 1256	1265 (old cal.)	**1183**	1264	
Tree-Ring Date	1204							
Distance to nearest Granite (km)	11	6	5	1	on site	**on site**	1	1
Likely Pottery Wares Produced at or near Site	none?	none?	none?	PGW; ABW	PGW	**PGW; ABW; FS?**	PGW	FS; PGW; WBW?
Analyst	Spicer	Frampton	Frampton	Higgins et al.	Christenson & Walsh	**Higgins et al.**	Horton	Christenson/ YCAAS

Abbreviations: ABW - Alameda Brown Ware (i.e., Verde Brown); FS - Fitzmaurice Series; PGW - Prescott Gray Ware; WBW - Wingfield Brown Ware

[a]no overall counts available for the site

[b]sherd counts from excavation of two lower rooms by Johnston College in 1977; only sherds greater than 2 cm^2 counted

[c]from Christenson 1997a except Coyote Ruin data from this volume, which does not use weighting

As has been noted, we run into problems when we attempt to use Prescott Gray Ware as a universal indicator of "Prescott Culture." For example, King's Ruin, the "type site" for Prescott Culture in its late phase is miles from granitic rock (Figure 66) and Prescott Gray Ware as traditionally made could not have been made at the site, yet virtually 100% of the pottery at the site was Prescott Gray Ware. The two Prescott Black-on-gray vessels thin-sectioned from the site were made with granitic derived clays from somewhere else (Christenson 2003). This is a minuscule sample, so at the moment we can only hypothesize that either the pottery at the site was traded in or that alluvial clay from nearby Big Chino Wash was used. The same holds for the Las Vegas Ranch sites, Argillite Pueblo, the Perkinsville Site (NA 9426), and sites in upper Burro Creek. The Perkinsville Site is an interesting case because although it is outside the Prescott heartland and a distance from granitic bedrock, the ceramics appear to be mostly Prescott Gray with some quantity of Verde Brown (Fish and Whiffen 1967) (these identifications need to be confirmed!), as was true with Coyote Ruin.

Figurines. The issue of figurines in Prescott Culture is complex and can only be briefly reviewed. J. W. Simmons thought that there was a distinct effigy "culture" in the Groom Creek area and this idea was recently revived (Motsinger 2000). Figurines are present at most sites in the Prescott area as well as at Sinagua and Hohokam sites, but not generally Anasazi. Explanations of figurines run from toys, to involvement in women's fertility/healing activities, to formal ceremonial use based upon arrangements found at some Hohokam sites. Using the papillary line width of fingerprints on some figurines, Kamp et al. (1999) argued that figurines at the Northern Sinagua Lizard Man site were made by children. Following their methodology, I found some support for the idea that the figurines with measurable fingerprints at StoneRidge sites were made by teenagers or young adults (Christenson 2005a: 8.38), but I now think that there are uncertainties with the equations used to relate line width and age (Christenson 2008c), and so hesitate to make any firm statements at the moment. Prescott figurines are usually broken, as is true in Neolithic societies elsewhere in the world, and a school of research on figurines in Europe sees great ideological significance in their forms, breakage, and deposition (Bailey 2005; Chapman and Gaydarska 2007). There is clearly much more to be learned from these artifacts in central Arizona.

Stone Technology and Architecture. Even more so than the use of granite-derived clay, the use of stream cobbles in the flaked stone technology is a geological issue. Stream cobbles coming down Granite Creek, Lynx Creek, Coyote Wash, and other drainages were the principle source of knappable stone. Even obsidian from the Partridge Creek and Presley Wash sources was most easily available as cobbles in the Big Chino drainage although there is evidence that, at least for late arrowpoints, there was a preference for Flagstaff-area sources over the local obsidian (Christenson 2010). Bedrock chipped stone sources are more limited, the one distinct source being Jasper Hill, the source of what is called Perkinsville Jasper.

The prevalence of unnotched points on Prescott sites noted in Chapter 7 is curious and this pattern needs to be examined with a wider range of sites. Behaviors such as the use of notched support stones, hilltop line-of-sight structures, and the lack of specialized religious structures are traits common to a large area of central Arizona and so are traditions carried on by other "cultures" as well. Use of notched support stones is an example of a widespread Southwestern tradition (Schroeder 1953) that may have originated in the Hohokam area and was spread by migrant populations or by copying.

Internal Connections

What is the evidence that these communities of the Chino-Lonesome Valley area were connected other than by a shared pottery tradition?

The line-of-sight connection of hilltop sites would be definite evidence of a connection between sites, presuming that communication was actually happening between them. Of course there are other reasons for placing sites on elevations and it will be difficult to determine which of several possible functions a hilltop site was intended to fulfill (Wilcox et al. 2000: 130). Early warning in relation to warfare is only one possible reason for signaling between communities. Although no communal ceremonial structure have been found on late period sites (some ballcourts may have been present earlier on that would have served such a function), it is likely that various social and religious gatherings occurred. External trade connections discussed above could have been done on a one-on-one basis, but meetings of larger groups for trade of locally produced and exotic goods are also likely.

Argillite was a major local material that was obtained directly or internally traded and sent elsewhere. To what extent this material was used locally to indicate membership in large-scale or small-scale sodalities is unknown. Much of what we need to know about this material must come from Argillite Pueblo and associated sites that apparently controlled the quarry, so at the moment the role of argillite in connecting the Prescott area, if any, must remain speculative.

Continuity

Evidence of cultural continuity in the region is fairly strong (see also Leonard 2005: 15.21). As noted above, the local pottery tradition at Fitzmaurice Ruin, for example, began hundreds of years earlier, ca. 800 (Christenson 2005a). It is hypothesized that at some point dispersed year-round settlement in the Lynx Creek/Clipper Wash area was abandoned and the population aggregated into a pueblo which we call Fitzmaurice.

Continuity at King's Ruin, perhaps having a population size similar to Coyote Ruin, is very clear. Two pit structures, one overlain by the pueblo, indicate occupation at the site in the 11th and 12th centuries (Spicer 1936: 16-21). The large cemetery of the site, with some burials having multiple internments placed over time in the same pit, also suggests that social groups, perhaps lineages, considered the location a significant place (Christenson 2008b: 12.14 to 12.15).

Based upon ceramics and a radiocarbon date, Coyote Pueblo clearly had occupation from perhaps the 900s until the 1300s. Its location near a main route over the mountain probably meant that it was an important place not only to the inhabitants, but also to travelers passing by on a regular basis.

WHEN DID PRESCOTT CULTURE END?

Little paleoenvironmental reconstruction has occurred in the Prescott area. Detailed reconstruction of the lower Verde River stream flow has been done, however, and presuming that this information reflects conditions near the headwaters we may be able to get some clues about climatic conditions in the Prescott area in the 13th century. Prior to the later 14th century there is little evidence of periods of drought longer than 3 years (Jeter 1977: 269; Van West and Altschul 1997: 373). That being said, the period 1286-1288 had a significant drought, which would have been particularly a problem in the Chino-Lonesome Valley area where irrigation agriculture was absent or limited.[6] In the Tonto Basin, 1286 and 1288 were the third and tenth driest years on record from A.D. 740 to1380 (Rose 1994: 358). As noted above, the Coyote Pueblo people relied on rainfall agriculture, so droughts would directly impact their ability to live. Probable marriage and exchange ties with people in the Verde Valley, who relied primarily on irrigation, may have provided a safety mechanism for either short-term movement in bad years, or permanent migration.

The presence of post-1300 radiocarbon dates from Prescott Culture sites indicates that occupation of the area continued in some form or another. Because of the nature of radiocarbon dating, only coarse-scale ideas about this topic can be gained.

Table 54 provides a list of post-1300 sites in the region with their corrected radiocarbon dates. Figure 68 shows probability curves of the 14th century dates in the region along with the 13th century dates for comparison (some of the dates in the table cannot be included because the original radiocarbon date was not given in the published report). The radiocarbon curve wiggles substantially in the late prehistoric period so there are two high probability peaks for all dates at about 500 to 700 radiocarbon years bp.

Clearly there were people using the area in the 1300s sufficiently to leave burned material. The Neural/Willow Lake Site has pretty good evidence of use from the 12th into the 14th centuries both in pueblo rooms and in a pit house (Grossman 1997: Figure 46; Mitchell and Motsinger 2010: 71). The two Neural Site dates for which we have sufficient information have peaks at around 1290 and 1375. One Jeddito Yellow Ware sherd, that was probably not exchanged from the Hopi Mesas until after 1325 (Benitez 1999), was also found at that site. N:7:155 has a similar late date from the floor of a pit house.

N:7:286, a long-lived site in the StoneRidge project area, has a date with a peak in late 1200s and at 1375. YAV 74 has a date with the same peaks. The latter site also has 10 Tizon Brown Ware sherds, although it is possible that these sherds are associated with the occupation represented by the 16th century radiocarbon date from the site.

Later dates include two from a roasting pit at the Campground Site in Granite Basin with peaks at 1330 and 1400 to 1420. The artifacts on the site date to an earlier period, so these dates come from activities by some unknown later group. Coyote Ruin has a date from Room 2, the main room on the house mound with peaks about the same as the Campground site. A few Tizon Wiped sherds were also present, one on the surface and four in the Room 40 fill. There is evidence that in the historic period this pottery was associated with Yavapai and other Pai groups (Christenson 2005e) so its presentce at the site could indicate contact with ancestral Pai by the prehistoric occupants of the site.

The latest radiocarbon date in this group has a major peak about 1425 and a smaller one about 1340 and comes from YAV 22, a site where a possible Pai (i.e., Yavapai or their Arizona relatives) structure was placed within an earlier Prescott Culture room. This is the best evidence that any of these 14th-early 15th century radiocarbon dates represent an ancestral Pai presence in the region.

Table 54. Post-A. D. 1300 Prescott-area radiocarbon dates. In order by calibrated mean or midrange. Coyote Ruin date in bold. See Figure 68 for probability distributions.

Site	Provenience	Raw Radiocarbon Determination (B.P.)	Calibrated 95% Interval (A.D.)[a]	Mean/ Midrange (A.D.)[c]	Source
Neural	R1 or R2, masonry room	?	1210-1410 (old cal.)	1310	Grossman 1997
YAV 74	F1, rock structure	690 +/- 70	1215-1410	1312	Blan 2006
N:7:286	F205, pit	680 +/- 70	1220-1410	1319	Leonard and Robinson 2005
Neural	R1, masonry room	660 +/- 50	1270-1402	1334	Grossman 1997
Neural	Extramural	650 +/- 50	1275-1404	1338	"
Hassayampa, N:7:155	F2, pit structure	?	1275-1410 (old cal.)	1342	Anduze et al. 2003
N:7:16, Willow Lake	F1, pit house	?	1270-1440 (old cal.)	1355	Mitchell and Motsinger 2010
Campground Site	F4, roasting pit	580 +/- 50	1295-1426	1359	Logan and Horton 1994
Coyote Ruin	**R2, masonry room**	**550 +/- 60**	**1295-1444**	**1372**	**this report**
Campground Site	F4, roasting pit	530 +/- 50	1302-1448	1385	Logan and Horton 1994
YAV 22	F1, rock structure	510 +/- 70	1290-1512[b]	1405	Blan 2006
YAV 74	F1, rock structure	360 +/- 40	1450-1635	1543	Blan 2006
Neural	R2, masonry room (corn)	?	1420-1690 (old cal.)	1555	Grossman 1997
NA 18451	excavation unit	210 +/- 110	1485-1954	-	Dosh 1987
YAV 74	Checkdam	150 +/- 50[d]	1665-1952	-	Blan 2006

[a] IntCal 09 calibration database using OxCal 4.1.7; "old cal." indicates 95% calibration range done previously for which radiocarbon date and standard deviation were not given in report;
[b] 94% confidence interval - a 1% increase in confidence greatly increases the late end of the range of this date;
[c] mean calculated by OxCal 4.1.7; midrange used for dates with no raw radiocarbon date information; the post-1600 radiocarbon curve is fairly flat and so does not give a narrow range;
[d] probably modern contamination

These dates indicate occupation by Prescott Culture past 1300 at the Neural/Willow Lake Site, at N:7:286 in StoneRidge, and at YAV 74 on the Yavapai Reservation. A black-on-yellow sherd reported by Simmons at the Porter Ranch Ruin (a.k.a. Argillite Pueblo/Windmill Site) also indicates a post-1325 date. The late dates at the Campground Site and at Coyote Ruin are not as clear in their likely origin, although the Tusayan Black-on-white at Coyote Ruin could represent early 14th century occupation. As indicated above, the YAV 22 date could in fact be from an ancestral Pai occupation of a Prescott Culture site.

Under any circumstances, dating abandonment of a site or area is a difficult task. Useful dating methods like mean ceramic dating can provide accurate guides to the central occupation span of a site, but are less useful in determining initial or ending occupation dates. Even with tree-ring dating, not currently very useful in central Arizona, inferences about abandonment have to be couched in terms of how long people would live at a site without cutting new wood to repair roofs (Ahlstrom 1985: 651-653). A seeming equivalent technique that can date individual events, radiocarbon dating, has such a large error term that dated events are not much narrower than a century or so (see Figure 68). A technique of perhaps greater usefulness is to look at the ranges of individual pottery types, particularly the latest types in an area. Pottery types, however, have their own problems. The well-dated pottery types in the Prescott area were made far away in a different culture and so are indirect dates. We can use tree-ring dating to estimate the span of production/use/discard for these types in their source area, but these dates may need to be adjusted outside the core area because of time lag in being traded and in being discarded at the arrival point. The issue of time lag is discussed in Note 1 and one estimate suggests that this factor might shift a trade type date span two or three decades later.

An argument has been made of abandonment of the Prescott area about 1275 (Wilcox et al. 2008: 16.8) using the earliest date for the latest type (Tuwiuka Black-on-orange, a type that only has been recorded at Argillite Pueblo). However, it is extremely unlikely that the latest types came only into the area early in their production and in fact I would argue that the principle late type, Tusayan Black-on-white, Kayenta variety, may have been arriving into the area in the middle or even late period of its production. The type has an estimated date range in the area of production of 1260-1330 (Christenson 1994: Table 2). If, for the sake of argument, we say that the type was "ready for shipment" at the early end of its production and allow say a decade to actually first show up in the Prescott area and then maybe a decade to get broken, or used as a funerary offering, then we are already at 1280 or so for the first Tusayan pot to enter the Prescott-area archaeological record. This gives the earliest possible date the area could have been abandoned.

But if there were people in the area later in the type's production span, then the type could have easily been deposited archaeologically after 1280. Looking at another late ceramic category, Jeddito Yellow Ware, that probably did not begin coming into central Arizona until after 1325 (Benitez 1999), we find few sherds in the Prescott area. They are, however, present in abundance at Verde Valley Sinagua sites. Their infrequency in the Prescott region may be an indication that the area was not occupied or at least not receiving much tradeware after Jeddito Yellow Ware began coming into the Verde Valley which Benitez (1999: 41-42) estimates at 1325-1350 for this pottery at Tuzigoot. There, Prescott Black-on-gray seems to have been present when Jeddito Black-on-yellow and other later decorated types took the place of previously popular tradewares (Caywood and Spicer 1935: 63).

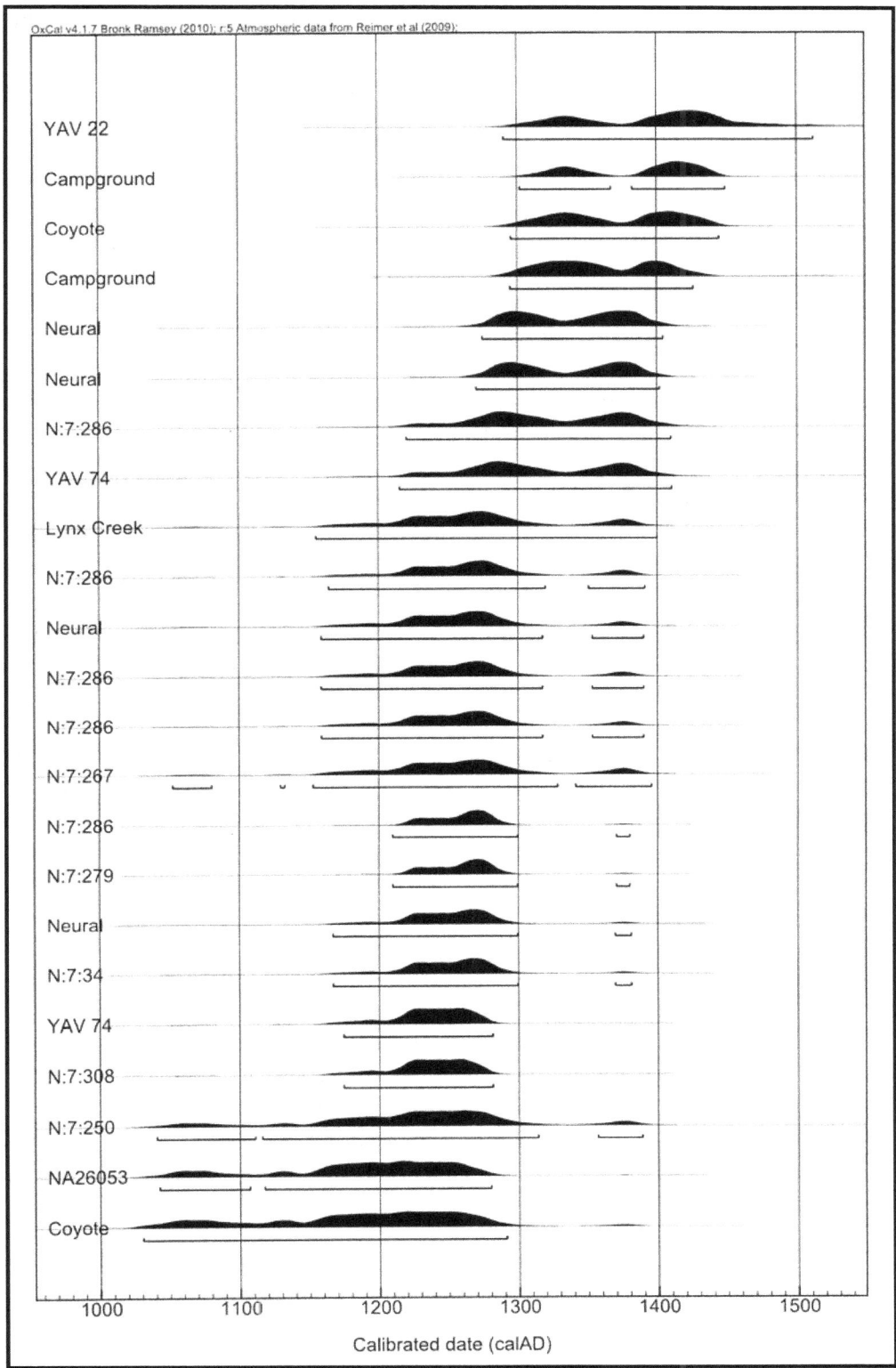

Figure 68. Probability curves for Prescott-area radiocarbon dates in the 13th and 14th centuries. Brackets indicate 95 percentile ranges. Three late dates from Table 54 not included because the raw radiocarbon date was not published. IntCal 09 calibration using OxCal 4.1.7.

There is evidence that some of this grayware may have been produced in the Verde Valley (Christenson 1999: 96), although it could not have been manufactured at Tuzigoot or Perkins Pueblo because of the unavailability of granite-derived clay (Christenson 2012b). Perkins Pueblo also has evidence of deposition of Prescott Black-on-gray and Jeddito in the same deposits (Alger 1968).

A non-ceramic related argument about late occupation, or at least use, of the Prescott area is the suggested dating of the Del Rio argillite source from 900 to 1400 (Bartlett 1939: 78). The late end of the range is presumably based upon the presence of Del Rio material at Tuzigoot, which is supported by chemical characterization (Elson and Gundersen 1992: 455). "Pipestone" and red beads do occur in burials at the site that also had Jeddito Yellow Ware (Anderson 1992: Appendix A), so unless we are dealing with heirloom jewelry, the quarries were still being worked well after 1325.

Of course, areas are never totally abandoned, but can remain as limited hunting or gathering areas and in some cases seasonal agricultural areas, by the same people who resided in the area previously. The distance that corn can be distributed efficiently is in the range of 50 km, which means that if, for example, Verde Valley populations had wanted to farm the abandoned Coyote Pueblo area or even the Fitzmaurice Pueblo area and carry the produce back to the valley at harvest time, it would have been economically feasible (Lightfoot 1979: Table 8). Even when a population ceases to reside in an area, ties to cultural and natural features would remain and visitation might be expected as long as memory of the places survived. As noted above there were strong ties to some locations, as best indicated by the King's Ruin burial ground.

To briefly summarize the interpretation of the data now available, the Prescott area seems to have been occupied at sites such as Neural/Willow Lake and possibly Coyote Pueblo into the 1300s by people who were producing Prescott Gray Ware and local versions of Verde Brown. At some point in the 1300s this occupation, whether year-round or seasonal, ceased or at least became archaeologically much less visible. Perhaps around the same time a group using brush shelters, side-notched arrowpoints, and Tizon Brown Ware, presumably the ancestral Pai, become archaeologically visible. The relationship of this archaeological culture and the overlapping or following protohistoric/ethnographic culture will be briefly discussed.

The Yavapai are long-term residents of the same area as occupied by the Prescott Culture. The Yavapai emergence story is in the Verde Valley, which would indicate a long history in the region (Gifford 1933:349, 353, 404). One interpretation of the linguistic evidence suggests splitting of Upland Yuman (Arizona Pai) and River Yuman less than 1000 years ago (Laylander 2006). The 14th century dates discussed above for Prescott Culture sites and the possible Pai related artifacts beginning to show up about the same time make temporal overlapping of ancestral Pai and the end of Prescott Culture likely (see Pilles and McKie 1998). Some Yavapai consider themselves directly related to the Prescott Culture (Kwiatkowski 2004).

The placement of a circular structure inside of a Prescott Culture masonry room at YAV 22 (N:7:81) is interesting particularly because the site has a Tizon Wiped sherd and a radiocarbon date in the 1300s or 1400s. Placement of a house directly on top of a previous house is one way of showing direct social continuity (Stevanović 1997: 387-388; Tringham 2000), but it can also be a simple case of expedient reuse of a location. The post-1400 radiocarbon dates from YAV 74 and NA18451 seem likely to have come from ancestral Pai use of these sites.

The idea that the Yavapai are descendants of Prescott Culture people who abandoned the sedentary agricultural way of life and reverted to a more mobile hunter-gatherer-horticultural life style (Kwiatkowski 2004; Schroeder 1975: 54; Simonis 2000: 201) has implications. Upham (1994) has made an argument for such flexibility of prehistoric Southwestern groups, but a transition from higher-density agriculturalists to low-density hunters and gatherers would require a large death rate or major population movement; in other words, only a small portion of the population could actually live that way. Estimate of Yavapai population at the time of contact (prior to introduction of disease) is maybe 3,000 (Braatz 2003: 68), which given a territory of say 22,000 sq. mi (using Khera and Mariella 1983: Figure 1) would be about 0.14 people/sq. mi.[7] Note that this number is one-quarter the rough density estimate made above for the central Prescott Culture in the 13th century (.60/sq. mi.), meaning that some portion of the population could have supported themselves using resources such as pinyon nuts, agave, and various seeds that they already knew as well as some agriculture, but the whole population could not have been so supported (see Jeter 1977: 254). A significant portion of the population would have either died or, more likely, moved somewhere else.

WHERE TO NEXT?

As is true with any archaeological excavation, the work at Coyote Ruin answered some questions, but raised many more. A number of tentative interpretations/hypotheses have been provided in this chapter, all of which require either additional field work or examination of extant data from new perspectives.

Ceramics play a large part in understanding Prescott Culture/Tradition because for better or worse they play a critical role in its definition. We have noted above the issue of geology in determining which ceramic wares can be locally made. On the one hand, the residents of the middle Agua Fria could not have made Prescott Gray Ware without extra effort and they chose to make primarily phyllite-tempered pottery. On the other hand, the residents of upper Burro Creek, located on volcanic rock, also could not have made Prescott Gray Ware but they chose to import it from elsewhere. Such patterns may be telling us something about how strongly tied to particular ways of making pottery a group was but we need more details on brownware production to convert these archaeological clues into more substantial explanations about what was happening in the past.

In regard to understanding the middle Agua Fria River and its connection to the Prescott core area, the Woolsey Ranch Site becomes fairly critical because of its size and location at the edge of high Prescott Gray Ware use. A small representative sample of pottery and other artifacts from the site might allow dating of the site and at least provide an idea about cultural connections.

The key diagnostic of late Prescott Culture, Prescott Black-on-gray, was clearly not made at most sites where it is common and the likely source area is not currently known (Christenson 2006b). Regardless, its presence at sites is good evidence of connections within the culture area but its method of movement and "meaning," if any, is unknown. On a larger scale, pottery and other items were clearly moving into and out of the culture area but so were people. Coyote Pueblo, being the closest Prescott Culture site to the Verde Valley is particularly relevant in this regard. How does the presence of a potter trained in another tradition affect the pottery of a community? Coyote has a high frequency of Verde Brown or Verde Brown-like pottery. Could this be the result of presence of a potter trained in the Verde Valley ceramic tradition or could it occur from simple visits being made between potter communities? The hypothesized manufacture of Prescott Black-on-gray or an imitation in the Verde Valley raises a similar question. It may seem inappropriate to recommend more work in the Verde Valley to understand the Prescott Culture, but the two areas had connections, and the Valley is one likely destination when Prescott Culture "abandoned ship."

The contemporaneous use of both pit houses and masonry rooms seems to occur on some late Prescott sites and the question arises of whether this represents a seasonal, functional, or ethnic difference.

The role of argillite in Prescott Culture intra- and extracultural connections has never really been examined. This material traveled significant distances north and east but if there was major movement of shell and turquoise from the west we should expect argillite to have traveled that way as well. Trade in raw materials vs. manufactured items has a major effect on the level of specialization present at the source area. Anybody can dig out the raw material and break it down into tradable sizes and it does not take too much skill to work the material into pendants, inlay, or other items, but manufacture of the tiny beads made of the material is an order of magnitude greater. At a site near Kayenta nearly 90,000 small beads from two burials, mostly red argillite that has not been sourced, would have required an estimated 5+ full-time person years to drill (Crotty 1983: 33). As we have almost no information about the archaeology of the quarry or the nearby pueblo sites, we do not know whether such intensive manufacturing was occurring there. One female burial from the Willow Creek Ruin (a.k.a. Neural Site), however, had about 7700 small mostly argillite beads, unsourced (Mitchell and Motsinger 2010: 32), suggesting that manufacture of tiny beads was occurring in the region.

The roll of warfare in the region has been a research topic since the late 1960s. As far as I know all of this work has involved the examination of hilltop sites and their intervisibility. No site has been specifically excavated with an aim of researching warfare. Burning of structures is often seen as a possible result of warfare, although there are other possible interpretations (see discussion above). As noted earlier, Fitzmaurice Ruin is one location where evidence of burning was found and the best interpretation ties this burning with the abandonment of the site, although not definitely with warfare. There remain unexcavated rooms away from the main pueblo that may have the potential to determine the cause of burning using forensic methods.

Finally, the "abandonment" of the area by Prescott Culture and "arrival" in the area of ancestors of the Yavapai are complex questions. The end date for the Prescott Culture has been placed as early as 1200 (Euler 1982: 60), but 1300 is a more common rounded ending date. The work at the Neural Site raised the possibility of continuation of use of the area perhaps into the 1400s (Grossman 2000). Additional radiocarbon dates as well as reexamination of ceramic dates discussed in this chapter provides support for continued use of the area in some form by manufacturers of Prescott Gray Ware into the 1300s. The idea that the latest Prescott Gray Ware was made in the Verde Valley (Macnider et al. 1989: 88) is intriguing and, if true, would shift some questions about the end of the Prescott Culture to that area.

Another effect of shifting the end date of the Prescott Culture somewhat later is that it increases the likelihood of temporal overlap of the latest Prescott Culture sites in the Prescott area and the earliest recognizable Pai sites. Whether this period represents culture replacement or merely culture change will be a challenge to pull apart archaeologically because of the aforementioned difficulty of studying the end of occupation in an area as well as the difficulty of archaeologically defining Pai. Again we have a question that in part concerns issues of the archaeology of the Verde Valley.

Mary Spall was often frustrated by the ambiguity of archaeological data and the difficulty of answering what seemed to be fairly straight-forward questions. She experienced the same frustrations that all archaeologists do. The excavation at Coyote Ruin did answer questions about the prehistoric occupation of the site but also raised many questions about the role of Coyote Pueblo in the region and the nature of Prescott Culture itself. This constant movement from question to answer to new question can be frustrating, but also gives the field its excitement - a constantly changing range of interesting questions.

Acknowledgments

Kelley Hays-Gilpin and E. Charles Adams provided advice on the dating of Jeddito Yellow Ware. Comments by Scott Kwiatkowski helped clarify some of the arguments in the chapter and he also arranged for permission from the Yavapai-Prescott Indian Tribe to include some data from excavations on their land in the chapter. Jim Christopher and Ginger Johnson provided comments and encouragement.

Notes

[1] A Note on the dating of Tusayan Black-on-white. This type is very distinctive and easily identified, but is ill-dated at its later end because of the abandonment of <u>part</u> of the area where it was manufactured by the end of the 13th century. An end date of 1300 is often used (e.g., Breternitz 1966: 78; Burgh 1959: 201). This is also an often cited beginning date for Jeddito Yellow Ware, although there is now evidence that yellowware was not likely to have begun circulating into central Arizona until after 1325 (Benitez 1999) and maybe as late as 1340—1350 (Adams 2002: 190-191). The Awatovi ceramic profiles (Burgh 1959) indicate overlap of the two types. Ambler suggests an end date of 1290 for Kayenta variety, with perhaps a decade or two later in the Hopi area (Ambler 1983: 53). My tentative estimate for the end of Tusayan Black-on-white is 1320 and the Kayenta variety, 1330 (Christenson 1994: Table 2), based upon the argument that ceramic types, although archaeological constructs, are measuring prehistoric design change that generally shows a gradual rise, peak, and gradual fall in relative frequency (Ambler 1983; Christenson 1994). Of course, in situations where a production area is abandoned (e.g., the Kayenta area ca. 1290-1300) the curve will actually be truncated, but if production continues elsewhere (e.g., the Hopi country), then the late end of the curve may show a monotonic decrease similar to that of other types.

A fly in the ointment when one is using tradewares to date sites is the potential for time lag. Kojo (1991: 371-372) estimates a lag of 20 to 30 years between production of Wepo and Black Mesa Black-on-white in the northern Black Mesa area and their and appearance in Flagstaff area sites, but found no lag in graywares. Claims by Upham (1988: 257) of lags of 125 years in tradewares at Nuvakwewtaga (Chavez Pass) are highly unlikely. A lag such as the one found by Kojo is not particularly a problem in the time period that he was looking at, but for the 13th to 14th century period considered here, a decade or two delay is of great importance in interpreting the abandonment of an area.

[2] Compare with the 672 pounds/acre at Hopi in 1893 (Stephen 1936: 954-955). The figure of one hectare (2 acres) needed per person used by Jeter (1977: 163) is much too high, although there are many assumptions and unknowns in doing such calculations (see Mabry 2005: 130-135).

[3] In regard to the "death of the owner" explanation, one of the lower rooms at Fitzmaurice had a partial skeleton of a teenage female that because of missing bones, Barnett (1975:5) suggested represented cannibalism. But the presence of matting under and over the upper body suggests an intentional burial, in a room that was apparently burned afterward, and the burial disturbed after that, contrary to Barnett's (1975:19) interpretation.

[4] The original analysis of Fitzmaurice Ruin ceramics recognized that the most common pottery was a locally-made brownware, which was called Tuzigoot Plain because of similarities to that type (James 1974: 107). At Lynx Creek Ruin, the type was called Prescott Gray, Black Mineral (Horton 1994: 44-45). Work on pottery from the nearby StoneRidge project found that this local

type was sufficiently different from both Prescott Gray and Tuzigoot Plain to place in a new category, Fitzmaurice Series, unattached to any ware (Christenson 2005b). Only a few Fitzmaurice Series sherds were recorded at Coyote Ruin, but the definition of the type did not occur until the analysis was well-advanced and so any of these sherds present in the early analysis would have been categorized as something else (the one Verde Brown sherd selected for petrographic analysis was actually Fitzmaurice Brown). Gabbro bedrock does occur one-quarter mile west of the site (Krieger 1965: Plate I), so it is possible that this series was produced here.

[5] Archaeologists of the SR 69 widening project called a hearth at one of their sites "Prescott Culture," although it has only a 13th century radiocarbon date with no associated artifacts (Punzmann et al. 1998: 174).

[6] A canal was found at the Henderson Site (Hohokam) (Weed and Ward 1970: 7) and Rogers (1928:23) mentions "acequias" on the Agua Fria in Lonesome Valley but no further information is given. Fewkes (1912:206, 214) saw irrigation ditches in the Walnut Creek area.

[7] Data in Martin (1973) give a similar density for the Hualapai/Havasupai. Kroeber (1939:Table 8) came up with a density for the Pai (i.e. Upland Yumans) less than half that, but was using a count for a population decimated by disease.

APPENDIX A – Ceramic Data
Table A1. Pottery type counts by room.

Rooms / Type	2	5	14	17	18	19	23	27	28	38	40	41	Total	%
Prescott Gray Ware														
Prescott Gray Sandy	452	270	1,439	712	2,724	2,402	312	88	339	799	4,715	19	14,321	39.18
Prescott Gray Micaceous	429	95	921	386	956	828	129	31	105	30	4,059	3	8,272	22.63
Prescott Black-on-gray Sandy	14	7	65	22	85	72	6	4	14	29	141	1	460	1.26
Prescott Black-on-gray Micaceous	49	22	255	111	275	256	50	2	11	60	769	2	1,862	5.10
Prescott Red-on-gray Sandy			6	1	15	11			1		9		43	.12
Prescott Red-on-gray Micaceous	2	1	2	5	11	8			1	1	13		44	.12
Prescott White-on-gray Sandy	1		1	1		3					7		13	.04
Prescott White-on-gray Micaceous					1								1	T
Prescott Polychrome Micaceous		1		2							3		6	.02
Prescott Red Sandy	1		15	4	16	13	4	3	1	4	45		106	.29
Prescott Red Micaceous			1	1	2	2			2		10		18	.05
Prescott White-on-red Sandy			1	1	2	1	1				7		13	.04
Prescott White-on-red Micaceous											1		1	T
Prescott Buff Sandy					5						14		19	05
Prescott Buff Micaceous											6		6	.02
Prescott Red-on-buff Sandy			1		3		2			3	1		10	.03
Prescott Red-on-buff Micaceous					3								3	.01
Aquarius Orange Sandy									1				1	T
Prescott Gray/Verde Brown Intergrade Sandy						32		14	21	45			112	.31
Prescott Gray/Verde Brown Intergrade Micaceous					30	2							32	.09
Total	948	396	2,757	1,246	4,128	3,630	504	142	496	1,271	9,800	25	25,343	69.36
Alameda Brown Ware														
Verde Brown	227	182	1,031	759	668	488	150	10	71	117	4,401	2	8,156	22.32
Verde Black-on-brown						1					15		16	.04
Verde Red	49	12	210	38	65	95	12		2	9	233		725	1.98
Verde Red-on-brown				1		2					10		13	.04
Verde Red-on-buff					1		1				4		6	.02
Verde White-on-brown				2							29		31	.08
Verde White-on-red	1		11	2	1						44		59	.16
Tuzigoot Plain	3	23	14	6	19	9	2			1	69		146	.40
Tuzigoot Red	3	1	9	5	12	9	1			1	30		71	.19
Tuzigoot White-on-red	1		1		1	1	1				2		7	.02
Tuzigoot White-on-plain					2						1		3	.01
Tonto Red			1		2	1							4	.01
Angell Brown					3	1							4	.01
Angell Red											1		1	T
Sunset Plain	3					1					2		6	.02
Sunset Red					2						3		5	.01
Fitzmaurice Series														
Fitzmaurice Brown			7		4	2	3						16	.04
Total	287	218	1,334	813	780	610	170	10	73	128	4,844	2	9,269	25.35

Table A1. Pottery type counts by room, continued.

Rooms / Type	2	5	14	17	18	19	23	27	28	38	40	41	Total	%
Wingfield Brown Ware														
Wingfield Plain	60	55	117	100	384	225	23	15	38	62	342	3	1,424	3.90
Wingfield Black-on-brown	1				18	3					4		26	.07
Wingfield Red	2	1	10	2	7	12	4			3	22		63	.17
Total	63	56	127	102	409	240	27	15	38	65	368	3	1,513	4.14
San Fran. Mtn. Gray Ware														
Deadmans Gray		1	1			2		2	1	3			10	.03
Untyped		1											1	T
Total		2	1			2		2	1	3			11	.03
Tizon Brown Ware														
Sandy Brown	1								3				4	.01
Aquarius Brown				1									1	T
Tizon Wiped											4		4	.01
Total	1			1					3		4		9	.02
Mogollon Brown Ware														
Elden Corrugated	1		2		1	3	3			2	12		24	.07
Tusayan White Ware														
Wepo Black-on-white										1	2		3	.01
Black Mesa Black-on-white	1	1	5	2	2	2	1				8		22	.06
Shato Black-on-white											1		1	T
Sosi Black-on-White	1		3	3	3						9		19	.05
Dogoszhi Black-on-white			1		4	2				1	10		18	.05
Flagstaff Black-on-white	2		8		8	5					21		44	.12
Wupatki Black-on-white				1	1	3					9		14	.04
Tusayan Black-on-white		2	5	2	6	1	1				36		53	.15
Tusayan Black-on-white (Kayenta var.)					1					2	5		8	.02
Bidahochi Black-on-white						1							1	T
Untyped	2	1	10	1	16	13	5	1	6	8	20		83	.23
Total	6	4	32	9	41	27	7	1	6	12	121		266	.73
Little CO White Ware														
Holbrook Black-on-white A		1	2		1						3		7	.02
Holbrook Black-on-white B			1			3					2		6	.02
Padre Black-on-white					1	3					7		11	.03
Walnut Black-on-white			3	1	3	2					7		16	.04
Leupp Black-on-white					1						6		7	.02
Untyped			5	1	2	3			2		7		20	05
Total		1	11	2	8	11			2		32		67	.08
Tusayan Gray Ware														
Untyped	1		1		1			1	1				5	.01
Little CO Gray Ware														
Untyped											1		1	T
Tsegi Orange Ware														
Medicine Black-on-red	1												1	T
Tusayan Black-on-red				1	3						2		6	.02
Citadel Polychrome				1									1	T
Tsegi Orange					1								1	T
Tsego Red-on-orange					1								1	T
Tusayan Polychrome				7	4	1					3		15	.04
Untyped				1	1	2					1		5	.01
Total	1			10	10	3					6		30	.08
Hohokam Types														
Santa Cruz Red-on-buff			1		2						1		4	.01
Sacaton Red-on-buff			2		1	1							4	.01
Gila Red			1										1	T
Untyped buffware					1								1	T
Total			4		3	2					1		10	.03
Grand Total	1,308	677	4,269	2,183	5,381	4,528	711	170	620	1,482	15,189	30	36,548	100

Table A2. Pottery type counts on surface, in test pits, and in garden plots.

	Surface	Test Pits					Garden Plots					Total
	Total	1	2	3	R34	Total	29	32	33	37	Total	
Prescott Gray Ware												
Prescott Gray Sandy	3,675	88	178	107	2	375	166	34	9	1	210	4,260
Prescott Gray Micaceous	959	84	54	55		193	51	2	33	15	101	1,253
Prescott Black-on-gray Sandy	367	5	2	2		9	5	12			17	393
Prescott Black-on-gray Micaceous	324	36	32	27		95	18	4	2	1	25	444
Prescott Red-on-gray Sandy	1	2	1			3	2				2	6
Prescott Red-on-gray Micaceous	1											1
Prescott Polychrome Sandy	1											1
Prescott Polychrome Micaceous		1				1						1
Prescott Red Sandy	11		1	1		2						13
Prescott Red Micaceous	2											2
Prescott Fugitive Red Sandy	2											2
Prescott White-on-red Micaceous	2											2
Prescott Red-on-buff Sandy	11											11
Aquarius Orange Sandy	7						1				1	8
Aquarius Orange Micaceous	2											2
Aquarius Black-on-orange Sandy	1											1
Aquarius Black-on-orange Micaceous	1											1
Prescott Gray/Verde brown Intergrade Sandy	68						1				1	69
Total	5,435	216	268	192	2	678	244	52	44	17	357	6,470
Alameda Brown Ware												
Verde Brown	775	192	104	33	7	336	11	13	33	12	69	1,180
Verde Red	46	8	7			15	3	1			4	65
Verde Red-on-brown	1								4		4	5
Verde White-on-red									1		1	1
Tuzigoot Plain	10	2	2	1		5						15
Tuzigoot Red	4											4
Sunset Plain	3						2				2	5
Fitzmaurice Series												
Fitzmaurice Brown			1			1						1
Total	839	202	114	34	7	357	16	14	38	12	80	1,276
Wingfield Brown Ware												
Wingfield Plain	1,087	29	51	6		86	25	18	8	4	55	1,228
Wingfield Red	30	3	5	5		13						43
Total	1,117	32	56	11		99	25	18	8	4	55	1,271

Table A2. Pottery type counts on surface, in test pits, and in garden plots, continued.

	Surface	Test Pits					Garden Plots					Total
	Total	1	2	3	R34	Total	29	32	33	37	Total	
San Francisco Mountain Gray Ware												
Deadmans Gray	1											1
Tizon Brown Ware												
Tizon Wiped	1											1
Mogollon Brown Ware												
Elden Corrugated	5											5
Tusayan White Ware												9
Flagstaff Black-on-white	7		2			2						3
Wupatki Black-on-white	2		1			1						8
Tusayan Black-on-white	6	2				2						2
Tusayan Black-on-white (Kayenta var.)	2											
Untyped	63	1	1	1		3	1	1			2	68
Total	80	3	4	1		8	1	1			2	90
Little CO White Ware												
Holbrook Black-on-white A	7											7
Padre Black-on-white	1											1
Walnut Black-on-white	2											2
Leupp Black-on-white	1											1
Untyped	19											19
Total	30											30
Tusayan Gray Ware												
Untyped	4	1				1	5				5	10
Tsegi Orange Ware												
Medicine Black-on-red	1											1
Tusayan Black-on-red	2											2
Tusayan Black-on-red Dogoszhi style	1											1
Citadel Polychrome	2											2
Tusayan Polychrome	1											1
Untyped	6											6
Total	13											13
San Juan Red Ware												
Deadman's Black-on-red	1											1
Hohokam Buff Ware												
Sacaton Red-on-buff			1			1						1
Untyped	14											14
Total	14		1			1						15
Grand Total	7,540	454	442	239	9	1,144	291	85	90	33	499	9,183

Table A3.   Intrusive pottery type counts in Rooms 14, 18, and 40 by level.

Type	Santa Cruz R/buff	Wepo B/white	Sacaton R/buff	Black Mesa B/w	Holbrook B/w	Shato B/white	Dogoshi B/w	Tusayan B/red	Sosi B/white	Elden Corr.	Walnut B/white	Flagstaff B/white	Tsegi Orange	Tsegi R/orange	Tusayan Poly.	Leupp B/white	Wupatki B/w	Tusayan B/w	Tusayan B/w, Kay. Var.
M.D.	900	950	1025	1050	1100	1105	1120	1120	1125	1143	1192	1195	1205	1225	1225	1247	1275	1275	1295
R 14																			
1			1	1	1		1		1	1		2						1	
2				2	1							1						1	
?	1		1		1					1	3	5						3	
R 18																			
1													1					1	
2			1				1		1			1							1
3										1							1	2	
4											1				4		1		
5	2											1							
6					1														
7															1			1	
8																		1	
9															9				
10				1							1	1							
?			1				4	1	1		1	5			2			1	
R 40																			
1				1															
2		2										1							
3										1		1						1	1
4			1		2		1	1			2	4				1	1	10	3
5	1			3			2		5	1	3	3				2	1	10	
6				2	1		2	1	2	3		5			2		5	6	
7			1		2		3		1	2		3				1	3	2	1
8				1						4	1								
9							1				1								
10												3							
?							1			2		1							1

? – level unknown

M.D. – Median Date

207

Table A4. Miscellaneous ceramic objects.

Artifact Type	Ceramic Type	R 2	R 5	R 14	R 17	R 18	R 19	R 23	R 27	R 40	Total
Small Jar fragment	Prescott Gray			1	1						2
	Sunset W/r									1	1
	Tusayan B/w									1	1
Miniature Jar fragment	Prescott Gray									1	1
Small Bowl	Prescott Gray				1						1
	Verde Brown	1									1
Miniature Bowl	Prescott Gray			3						6	9
	Prescott R/g				1						1
Miniature Dish	Verde Brown									1	1
Ladle fragment	Prescott Gray									2	2
Ladle handle	Prescott Gray			1		1				3	5
	Tusayan B/w									1	1
	Verde W/r									1	1
	Verde Brown									2	2
Miniature Ladle	Prescott Gray									1	1
Vessel handle	Prescott Gray		1			4				4	9
	Verde Brown			1						4	5
	Tsegi Orange						1				1
	Tusayan WW									1	1
	Verde Red								1		1
	Prescott W/g									1	1
	Verde W/r									1	1
Scoop fragment	Prescott Gray	1						1		2	4
	Verde Brown	1								1	2
Jar lid	Prescott Gray					1				2	3
Unperforated disk	Prescott Gray			2						1	3
	Prescott B/g			1						3	4
	Verde Red									1	1
	Verde Brown					2					2
Partly drilled disk	Prescott Gray			1			1			1	3
	Prescott B/g									1	1
Spindle whorl - disk fragment	Prescott Gray						1			1	2
	Verde Red		1								1
	Wingfield Pl.					1					1
	Verde Brown									1	1
Pendant blank	Tusayan B/w									1	1
Pendant, drilled, unfinished	Prescott Gray									1	1
Worked rim sherd	Prescott Gray									1	1
Spindle whorl, molded	Prescott Gray			1		1	1			7	10
Bead, molded	Prescott Gray				1					1	2
Gaming piece, conical	Prescott Gray									1	1
Clay ball	Prescott Gray									3	3
Knobs molded on outside of vessel	Prescott Gray									2	2
Knobs pushed out from inside of vessel	Sunset Brown									1	1
Total		3	2	11	4	10	4	1	1	63	99

APPENDIX B
Figurine Data

Table B1. Summary of figurines.
U = unknown fragment.

Spit No	Type	Description
2	Human, head	Concave, pinched nose
6	Rod	Tapered end
3	Rod	End broken
15	Animal, quadruped	Body, head and tail missing
18	Animal, quadruped	Body, performation through body
19	Rod	Ends broken
19A	U	Appendage
21	Human, head	Concave, pinched nose
23	U	Appendage
24	Animal, quadruped	Head, ears, nose broken
25	U	Appendage
32	Rod	Ends broken
33	Rod	Ends broken
34	Human, head	Unfinished
35	U	Appendage
36	Rod	Ends broken
52	Rod	Ends broken
59	Rod	Ends broken
411	Animal, quadruped	Body, one leg
412	Human, head	Unfinished
413	Rod	Tapered ends
414	Animal, quadruped	Head, nose broken
439	Human, female	Torso with breasts
492	Rod	Ends broken
495	U	Appendage
916	Human, head with neck	Head concave in rear, no face
981	Animal, quadruped	Hind end, back legs, tail
1070	U	Appendage
1072	Rod	Ends broken
Total 29	6 Unknown 6 Animal	6 Human 11 Rod

Spit No.	Type	Description
ROOM 14		
267	Animal, quadruped	Head, eyes, mouth, pointed nose
283	Human	Unfinished
287	Animal, quadruped	Head, ears, nose
294	U	Appendage
300	Human, complete	Base, torso, concave head, pinched nose
301	Animal, dog	Legs missing
305	Animal, quadruped	Head, ears, nose
307	Rod	Ends broken
347	Animal, quadruped	Body perforation under tail
362	Animal, quadruped	Head, slit mouth, pointed ear
402	Animal, quadruped	Body, pointed leg, perforation through body
991	Animal, quadruped	Perforation through body
992	Human	Base and part of rod
1079	Animal, quadruped	Head, ear
1086	Animal, quadruped	Hind end, tail
1129	Human, head	Flat, slit eyes, pinched nose
1148	Rod	Ends broken

Total 17   1 Unknown   4 Human   10 Animal   2 Rod

Spit No.	Type	Description
ROOM 17		
1040	Animal, quadruped	Hind end, leg

Spit No.	Type	Description
ROOM 18		
39	U	Appendage
44	Rod	Tapered end
55	U	Appendage
81	Human, head	Pinched nose, side missing
93	U	Appendage
146	U	Appendage
155	Animal, quadruped	Pointed leg
157	Rod	Ends broken
164	Human, head	Pinched nose, lip
167	U	Appendage
179	U	Appendage
192	Human, head	Pinched nose, slit eyes
233	Animal, quadruped	Tip of nose, legs missing
264A	U	Appendage
264B	U	Appendage
468	U	Appendage
469	Base	Circular
472	Rod	Ends broken
1057	Animal, quadruped	Hind end, tail
1060	Rod	Tapered end
1061A	U	Appendage
1061B	U	Appendage
1063	U	Appendage
1257	U	Appendage

Total 24   13 Unknown   3 Animal   3 Human   4 Rod   1 Base

Spit No.		Type		Description
ROOM 19				
45		U		Appendage
73		Animal, quadruped		Hind end, rear legs
88		Animal, quadruped		Perforation under tail
123		Animal, quadruped		Hind end, tail
124		Human, female torso		Tips of breasts missing
125		U		Appendage
126		U		Appendage
139		Animal, quadruped		Head, nose missing
476		Animal, quadruped		Head, end of ears, part of nose missing
478		Rod		Ends broken
Total	10	3 Unknown	5 Animal	1 Human 1 Rod
ROOM 23				
1073		U		Appendage
1074		Human		Base and torso
Total	2	1 Unknown	1 Human	
ROOM 38				
53		Animal, quadruped		Half of body perforation
56		Rod		Ends broken
57		Rod		Ends broken
Total	3	1 Animal	2 Rod	
ROOM 40				
1206		Human		Base and torso
1209A		U		Appendage
1209B		U		Appendage
1214		Human, complete		Base, rod, head concave, pinched nose
1225		Animal, quadruped		Body, leg missing
1232		Animal, quadruped		Dog, legs missing
1233		Human, head		Flat, small pinched nose
1238		Animal, quadruped		Body, perforation through body
1239		Human, head, long neck		Long nose, reed or grass impression
1246		U		Appendage
1252		Human, head w/neck		Slightly concave, no face
1305		Human , head		On long rod, pinched nose
1310		Animal, quadruped		Head, mouth open
1313		Animal, quadruped		Head missing
1590		Human, head		Flat, nose missing
1669		Animal, quadruped		Perforation through body
1671		Animal, quadruped		Perforation through body
1675		Rod		Tapered end
1676		Animal, quadruped		One leg

Spit No.	Type	Description
ROOM 40 (continued)		
1680	Animal, quadruped	Body
1684	Human, head	Slightly concave in back, pinched nose, neck
1686	Rod	Ends broken
1688	Rod	Tapered ends
1690	Human, head	Flat, broken nose
1692	Rod	Ends broken
1693	Animal, quadruped	Body
1695	Base	Circular
1697	Animal, quadruped	Body, tail
1700	Human, head	Flat, no face
1701	Animal, quadruped	Head, eyes, nose
1702	Human, head	Flat, pinched nose
1703	Animal, quadruped	Ears
1704	Animal, quadruped	Head with long neck
1705	Rod	Tapered end
1706	Human, head	Concave, pinched nose, neck
1707	Human, female	Torso with breasts, base
1708	Animal, quadruped	Body
1713	Rod	Ends broken
1714	Animal, quadruped	Head, slit mouth, one ear
1715	Animal, quadruped	Head with ears
1717	Human, head	Flat, pinched nose
1718	Rod	Ends broken
1719	Rod	Ends broken
1720	Animal, quadruped	Body, tail
1722	Animal, bird	Complete
1723	Animal, quadruped	Slit mouth, ears broken
1725	Human, head	Concave, pinched nose
1726	Rod	Tapered end
1727	Rod	Ends broken
1729	Human	Crudely made
1730	Human, female	Torso, pointed breasts
1904	U	Appendage
1910	U, curved	Tapered end
1918	U	Possible base
Total 54	6 Unknown 20 Animal	17 Human 10 Rod 1 Base

APPENDIX C
VOLCANIC ROCK SOURCING

As indicated in Chapter 6 a large proportion of the chipped stone tools from Coyote Ruin are of a black or green volcanic rock. In order to characterize this material and to try to determine where it came from eight artifacts and two bedrock samples were selected by A. L. Christenson and sent to the Berkeley XRF Lab for analysis (Table C1). The report on the results follows.

Table C1. Samples Submitted for XRF Analysis.

Sample #	Provenience	Item	Geology
Artifact 1	R18, L4, SPIT 75	drill, black	
Artifact 2	R18, L7, SPIT 730	flake scraper, green	
Artifact 3	R14, vandal soil, SPIT 335	reworked projectile point, gray	
Artifact 4	R27, L2, Bag 30	hammerstone, green	
Artifact 5	R27, L1, Bag 24	flake, black	
Artifact 6	R27, L1. Bag 24	flake, green	
Artifact 7	R27, L3, Bag 22	flake, green	
Artifact 8	R27, L3, Bag 8	flake, green	
Bedrock 1	T15N R1E S22 SE, UTM Z12 386590E 3836029N (NAD 27)		Indian Hills volcanics
Bedrock 2	UTM Z12 394554E 3837142N (NAD 27)		mining test pit in what is probably dacite of Burnt Canyon

BERKELEY ARCHAEOLOGICAL

XRF LAB

Phoebe Hearst Museum of Anthropology
103 Kroeber Hall
University of California
Berkeley, CA 94720-3712

A WAVELENGTH X-RAY FLUORESCENCE ANALYSIS OF INTERMEDIATE TO SILICIC VOLCANIC ARTIFACTS FROM AZ N:7:293 (ASM), NORTHERN ARIZONA

by

M. Steven Shackley, Ph.D.
Director

Report Prepared for

Dr. Andrew Christenson
Prescott, Arizona

for the

Yavapai Chapter
Arizona Archaeological Society

13 April 2001

INTRODUCTION

The geochemical analysis here of seven artifacts from AZ N:7:293 (ASM) and two source rock samples is the first study of volcanic rock artifacts in northern Arizona. The analysis is considered inconclusive generally due to the small source standard sample size. None of the artifacts are likely from the Indian Hills Volcanics (Sample 1), although the remainder of the samples could be either derived from the second source standard from Burnt Canyon or procured from rock of similar magmatic origin.

ANALYSIS AND INSTRUMENTATION

All samples were analyzed whole with little or no formal preparation. The results presented here are quantitative in that they are derived from "filtered" intensity values ratioed to the appropriate x-ray continuum regions through a least squares fitting formula rather than plotting the proportions of the net intensities in a ternary system (McCarthy and Schamber 1981; Schamber 1977). Or more essentially, these data through the analysis of international rock standards, allow for inter-instrument comparison with a predictable degree of certainty (Hampel 1984).

The trace element analyses were performed in the Department of Geology and Geophysics, University of California, Berkeley, using a Philips PW 2400 wavelength x-ray fluorescence spectrometer using a LiF 200 crystal for all measurements. This crystal spectrometer uses specific software written by Philips (SuperQ/quantitative) and modifies the instrument settings between elements of interest. Practical detection limits have not been calculated for this new instrument, but the variance from established standards is shown in Table 1. Sample selection is automated and controlled by the Philips software. X-ray intensity Kα-line data with the scintillation counter were measured for elements manganese (Mn), iron as total iron (Fe), titanium (Ti), rubidium (Rb), strontium (Sr), yttrium (Y), zirconium (Zr), and niobium (Nb). X-ray intensities for barium (Ba) were measured with the flow counter from the Lα-line. Trace element intensities were converted to concentration estimates by employing a least-squares calibration line established for each element from the analysis of international rock standards certified by the National Institute of Standards and Technology (NIST), the US Geological Survey (USGS), Canadian Centre for Mineral and Energy Technology, and the Centre de Recherches Pétrographiques et Géochimiques in France (Govindaraju 1994). Specific standards used for the best fit regression calibration for elements Ti through Nb include G-2 (basalt), AGV-1 (andesite), GSP-1 and SY-2 (syenite), BHVO-1 (hawaiite), STM-1 (syenite), QLM-1 (quartz latite), RGM-1 (obsidian), W-2 (diabase), BIR-1 (basalt), SDC-1 (mica schist), TLM-1 (tonalite), SCO-1 (shale), all US Geological Survey standards, and BR-N (basalt) from the Centre de Recherches Pétrographiques et Géochimiques in France (Govindaraju 1994).

The data from the SuperQ software were translated directly into Excel™ for Windows software for manipulation and on into SPSS™ for Windows for statistical analyses. In order to evaluate these quantitative determinations, machine data were compared to measurements of known standards during each run. The results of the analysis of RGM-1 a rhyolite standard and BHVO-1 an olivine basalt standard analyzed during this study is included in Table 1, and indicates that instrument precision for the elements measured is high (Govindaraju 1994). Further information on the laboratory instrumentation can be found at: http://obsidian.pahma.berkeley.edu/ and Shackley (1998a). Trace element data exhibited in Table 1 are reported in parts per million (ppm), a quantitative measure by weight (see also Figures 1 and 2). Sample N7293-4 was too large to fit in the sample cups and was not analyzed.

GEOCHEMICAL RESULTS AND SUMMARY

Non-destructive analysis of non-glassy rocks by x-ray fluorescence spectrometry is always hazardous (Weisler 1993, 1997; Weisler and Sinton 1997). The elemental variability in these crystalline volcanics due to post emplacement alteration, and simply the variability inherent in non-glassy volcanics hinders confident source assignment.

That being said, IF the variability of the Burnt Canyon source rock is as great as the artifacts clustered around it as shown in the two biplots of four elements, then there is a good probability that these artifacts are derived from that source. The artifacts very likely are not from the Indian Hills source. One source standard is generally not sufficient to establish the elemental variability within a source (see Shackley 1998b).

REFERENCES CITED

Govindaraju, K.
  1994 1994 Compilation of Working Values and Sample Description for 383 Geostandards. *Geostandards Newsletter* 18 (special issue).

Hampel, Joachim H.
  1984 Technical Considerations in X-ray Fluorescence Analysis of Obsidian. In *Obsidian Studies in the Great Basin*, edited by R.E. Hughes, pp. 21-25. Contributions of the University of California Archaeological Research Facility 45. Berkeley.

McCarthy, J.J., and F.H. Schamber
  1981 Least-Squares Fit with Digital Filter: A Status Report. In *Energy Dispersive X-ray Spectrometry*, edited by K.F.J. Heinrich, D.E. Newbury, R.L. Myklebust, and C.E. Fiori, pp. 273-296. National Bureau of Standards Special Publication 604, Washington, D.C.

Schamber, F.H.
  1977 A Modification of the Linear Least-Squares Fitting Method which Provides Continuum Suppression. In *X-ray Fluorescence Analysis of Environmental Samples*, edited by T.G. Dzubay, pp. 241-257. Ann Arbor Science Publishers.

Shackley, M. Steven
  1998a Geochemical Differentiation and Prehistoric Procurement of Obsidian in the Mount Taylor Volcanic Field, Northwest New Mexico. *Journal of Archaeological Science* 25:1073-1082.

1998b Chemical Variability and Secondary Depositional Processes: Lessons from the American Southwest. In *Archaeological Obsidian Studies: Method and Theory*, edited by M.S. Shackley, pp. 83-102. Advances in Archaeological and Museum Science 3. Kluwer Academic/Plenum Press, New York.

Weisler, Marshall I.
1997 Prehistoric Long-Distance Interaction at the Margins of Oceania. In *Prehistoric Long-Distance Interaction in Oceania: An Interdisciplinary Approach*, edited by M.I. Weisler, pp. 149-172. New Zealand Archeological Association Monograph 21. Auckland.

Weisler, Marshall I., and John. M. Stinton
1997 Towards Identifying Prehistoric Interaction Systems in Polynesia. In *Prehistoric Long-Distance Interaction in Oceania: An Interdisciplinary Approach*, edited by M.I. Weisler, pp. 173-193. New Zealand Archeological Association Monograph 21. Auckland.

Table 1. Elemental concentrations for archaeological samples from AZ N:7:293 (ASM). All measurements in parts per million (ppm).

Sample	Mn	Ti	Fe_2O_3	Rb	Sr	Y	Zr	Nb	Ba	Source
SOURCE 1	271	1962	12259	44	74	64	276	13	1463	Indian Hills
SOURCE 2	1290	3052	61636	96	214	43	191	10	809	Burnt Canyon
N7293-1	2274	3162	31255	57	170	33	200	10	1363	undetermined
N7293-2	3786	4199	72029	3	295	31	121	6	183	undetermined
N7293-3	868	5098	32956	62	683	16	114	21	1311	undetermined
N7293-5	311	2126	19820	30	112	44	230	11	395	undetermined
N7293-6	2099	10999	125574	47	369	41	125	6	986	undetermined
N7293-7	507	3202	35708	34	236	23	129	10	501	undetermined
N7293-8	989	2906	35561	79	333	42	193	10	1011	undetermined
RGM H-1	378	2724	18799	145	103	24	217	9	810	standard
BHVO-1	1583	25983	141690	10	404	27	177	20	122	standard

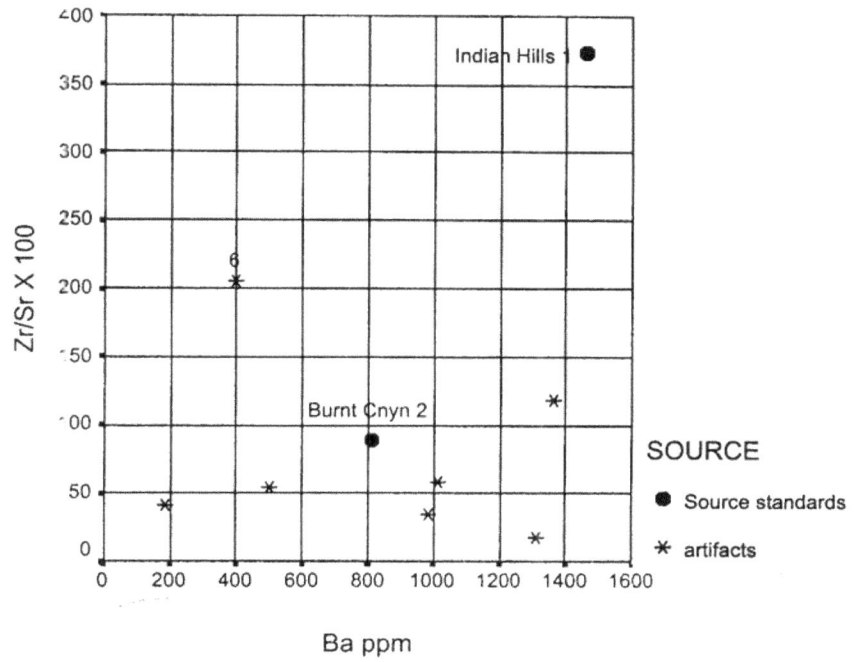

Figure 1. Zr/Sr and Ba biplot of source standards and artifacts.

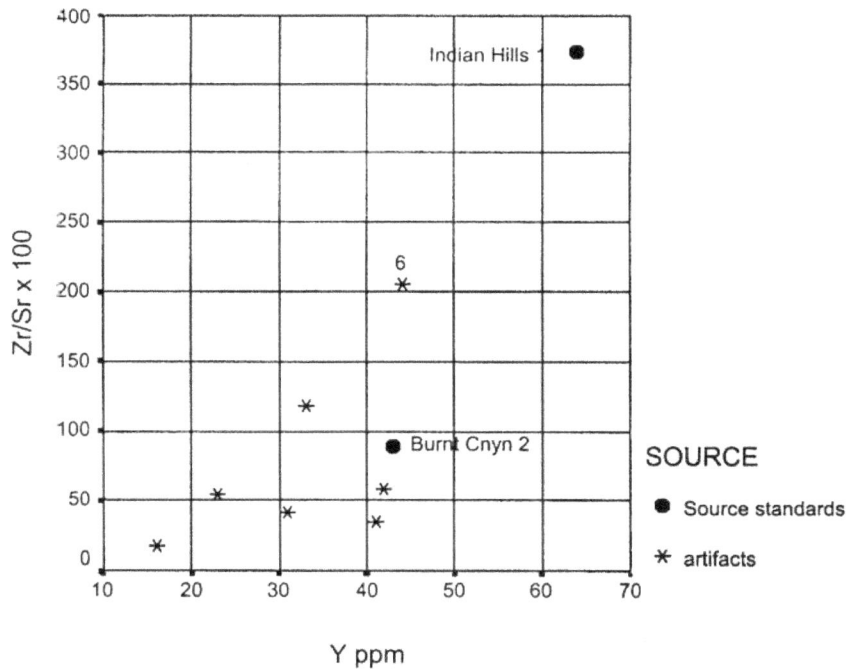

Figure 2. Zr/Sr and Y biplot of source standards and artifacts.

Appendix D
FLOTATION ANALYSIS DATA

Table D1. Raw data from completely analyzed flotation samples.

Context and Provenience	Volumes: Sample (lt. frac.) [charc.][1]	Carbonized Plant Remains	Uncarbonized Plant Remains	Other Material
Room 2 1.30–1.40 m BGS; 0–10 cm Above Floor (burned room)	1.00 l (33.0 ml) [20.0 ml]	**NON-WOODY REMAINS** 34 Cheno-am Seed Frags. 49 *cf.* Cheno-am Seed Frags. 1 *Chenopodium* Seed 4 *cf. Descurainia* Seed Frags. 2 Indet. Seed Frags. 1 *Lepidium* Seed 1 *Mentzelia* Seed Frag. 2 Misc. Endosperm Frags. 9 Misc. Round Fibers 1 *Mollugo* Seed Frag. 2 Monocot *cf.* Poaceae Culm Frags. 6 *Sporobolus*-Type Grains **WOOD CHARCOAL** 3 *cf. Larrea tridentata* 3 *cf. Quercus*	1 *Amsinckia* Seed 47 Cheno-am Seeds Frags. (5 light tan) 76 *cf.* Cheno-am Seeds 42 *Chenopodium* Seeds 1 Cylindropuntia Seed 3 Cylindropuntia Seed Frags. 3 *cf.* Cylindropuntia Seed Frags. 7 *cf. Descurainia* Seeds 2 Dicot Leaves 2 *Eragrostis* Type Florets 51 *Eragrostis* Type Grains 1 *Euphorbia* Seed 2 Indet. Fruit/Seed Frags. 6 Indet. Seed Frags. 44 *Mentzelia* Seeds 16 *Mentzelia* Seed Frags. 2 *Mollugo* Seeds 3 *Mollugo* Seed Frags. 1 Monocot *cf.* Poaceae Blade Frag. 1 Monocot *cf.* Poaceae Culm Frag. (HF) 10 Poaceae Florets 1 Poaceae Floret Frag. Numerous Poaceae Glumes, Lemmas, and Paleas 5 *cf.* Poaceae Grain Frags. 3 Poaceae Spikelets 4 *Portulaca* Seeds 1 *Setaria* Type Fertile Floret 1 Solanaceae *cf. Physalis* Seed 3 *Sporobolus* Type Grains 1 *Suaeda* Seed 2 *Trianthema portulacastrum* Seeds	1 Ant (winged) 3 Chipped Stone Microflakes (obsidian) (HF) 1 Faunal Bone 17 Faunal Bone Frags. (7 burned) (HF) 1 Fire-Altered Rock (HF) 1 Insect Case Numerous Insect Exoskeleton Frags. Numerous Insect-Sized Fecal Pellets 374 Macrospores[2] 5 Macrospore Clusters 7 Rodent-sized Fecal Pellets 1 Turquoise Frag. (HF)

Context and Provenience	Volumes: Sample (lt. frac.) [charc.][1]	Carbonized Plant Remains	Uncarbonized Plant Remains	Other Material
Room 14 1.30 m BGS Levels 1& 2 Between 1st & 2nd Floors (burned room)	1.60 l (141.5 ml) [127.4 ml]	**NON-WOODY REMAINS** 4 *cf. Agave* Caudex Frags. (randomly oriented CaO frags.) 1 *Agave* Round Fiber Bundle with Epidermis (TR; CaO) (HF) 131 *Agave* Fibers (TR; 114 CaO) 553 *cf. Agave* Fibers (CaO)[2] 3 *cf. Agave* Round Fiber Bundles (CaO) 1 *cf. Arctostaphylos* Fruit Frag. 141 Cheno-am Seed Frags. (2 caramelized) 87 *cf.* Cheno-am Seed Frags. 22 *Chenopodium* Seeds (6 reticulate surface, round in plan view, no margin; 16 similar but with smooth surfaces) 4 *Cycloloma* Seeds 10 *cf. Cycloloma* Seed Frags. 1 *cf. Descurainia* Seed Frag. 1 *Eragrostis* Type Grain 2 *cf. Hordeum* Grain Frags. 4 Indet. Fruit Frags. (3 HF) 67 Indet. Seed Frags.[2] 1 *Juniperus* Branchlet Frag. 1 *cf. Lagenaria* Rind Frag. 3 *Mentzelia* Seeds 6 Misc. D-Shaped Fibers (5 CaO) 25 Misc. Endosperm Frags. 10 Misc. Flat Fibers (8 CaO) 32 Misc. Frags. (CaO) 380 Misc. Round Fibers (1 HF)[2] 2 Misc. Round Fiber Bundles 8 Monocot Stem Frags. (parallel veins) 3 *Nolina* Leaf Frags. (with leaf margins) 8 *cf. Nolina* Leaf Frags. 2 *Opuntia* Seed Frags. 4 *cf. Opuntia* Embryo Frags. (1 HF) 91 *Papaver somniferum* Seeds 1 Poaceae Culm Frag. (with node) 8 Poaceae Grain Frags. 1 Poaceae *cf. Phragmites* Culm Frag. (with node) 15 *Portulaca* Seeds 11 *Portulaca* Seed Frags. 1 *Sporobolus* Type Grain 1 *cf. Suaeda* Seed Frag. 6 *Zea mays* Cupules (1 HF) 12 *Zea mays* Cupule Frags. (1 HF) 15 *cf. Zea mays* Cupule Frags. 16 *Zea mays* Glume Frags. 12 *cf. Zea mays* Glume Frags. 6 *Zea mays* Kernel Frags. 7 *cf. Zea mays* Kernel Frags. (2 HF) **WOOD CHARCOAL** 5 *cf. Quercus*	1 *Amsinckia* Seed Frag. 11 Asteraceae Achene Frags. 1 Cheno-am Seed 19 Cheno-am Seed Frags. 8 *cf.* Cheno-am Seed Frags. 28 *Chenopodium* Seeds (smooth, round in facet view, no margin) 2 *cf. Descurainia* Seeds 1 *cf. Descurainia* Seed Frag. 2 Dicot Leaves 2 *Eragrostis* Type Grains 3 *Erodium* Fruit Frag. (1 HF) 4 *Euphorbia* Seeds 2 *Euphorbia* Seed Frags. 3 Indet. Fruit Frags. 33 Indet. Seed Frags. (1 HF) 1 *cf. Larrea tridentata* Leaf Frag. (HF) 3 *Mentzelia* Seeds 2 *Mentzelia* Seed Frags. 2 *cf. Mentzelia* Seed Frags. 3 *Mollugo* Seeds 5 *Mollugo* Seed Frags. 6 Monocot *cf.* Poaceae Blade Frags. (2 HF) 3 Monocot *cf.* Poaceae Culm Frags. 2 Poaceae Culm Frag. (1 HF) 3 Poaceae Glumes/Paleas/ Lemmas 1 Poaceae Rachis Joint Frag. 10 *Portulaca* Seeds 5 *Portulaca* Seed Frags. 1 *Sporobolus* Type Grain 4 *cf. Sporobolus* Grain Frags. 1 *cf. Trianthema portulacastrum* Seed Frag.	1 Burned Insect Exoskeleton Frag. 6 Ceramic Sherds (HF) 11 Ceramic Sherdlets (HF) 1 Charred Insect-Sized Fecal Pellet Frag. 2 Chipped Stone Flakes (HF) 9 Chipped Stone (HF) Microflakes (6 obsidian) (HF) 18 Faunal Bones (4 burned) (1 vert., 2 phalanges, 1 long bone) (4 HF) 218 Faunal Bone Frags. (87 burned) (204 HF) 3 Fire-Altered Rocks (HF) 3 Insect Cases 11 Insect Case Frags. Numerous Insect Exoskeleton Frags. Numerous Insect-Sized Fecal Pellets 1,069 Macrospores[2] 6 Macrospore Clusters 3 Red Resin Globules (*cf.* Creosotebush Lac)(HF) 37 Rodent-Sized Fecal Pellets 1 Shell Frag. (HF) 3 Snail Shells (2 *Gastrocopta* Type, 1 *Helisoma* Type)

222

Context and Provenience	Volumes: Sample (lt. frac.) [charc.][1]	Carbonized Plant Remains	Uncarbonized Plant Remains	Other Material
Room 17 Grid S10,E10 Unit S8, E16 0.70 m BGS	2.20 l (7.0 ml) [4.0 ml]	**NON-WOODY REMAINS** 4 *Agave* Fibers (TR; CaO) 6 *cf. Agave* Fibers (round; CaO) 1 *Atriplex* Fruiting Bractlet Frag. 11 Cheno-am Seed Frags. (1 caramelized) 6 *Chenopodium* Seeds 11 *Chenopodium* Seed Frags. 1 Indet. Fruit/Seed Frag. 24 Indet. Seed Coat Frags. 14 Indet. Seed Frags. 1 *Mentzelia* Seed 2 Misc. Endosperm Frags. 4 Misc. Frags. (CaO) 6 Misc. Round Fibers 2 *Portulaca* Seed Frags. 1 *Sporobolus* Type Grain Frag. 1 Unknown Seed 1 *cf. Zea mays* Glume Frag. 1 *Zea mays* Kernel Frag. 1 *cf. Zea mays* Kernel Frag. **WOOD CHARCOAL** (none identifiable)	8 Indet. Fruit/Seed Frags. 8 Indet. Seed Frags. 8 *Mentzelia* Seed Frags. 1 *Sporobolus* Type Grain	2 Burned Animal Epidermis Frags. (probably reptile) 3 Chipped Stone Microflakes (2 obsidian) (HF) 2 Faunal Bone (1 burned) (1 HF) 15 Faunal Bone Frags. (9 burned) (13 HF) 13 Insect Exoskeleton Frags. 16 Insect-Sized Fecal Pellets 1 Insect Wing Frag. (HF) 28 Macrospores 3 Macrospore Clusters 1 Rodent-Sized Fecal Pellet
Room 17 Ash Pit 0.84 m BGS	1.35 l (10.5 ml) [9.0 ml]	**NON-WOODY REMAINS** 9 *Agave* Fibers (TR; 5 CaO) 1 *cf. Agave* Fiber (round; CaO) 4 Cheno-am Seed Frags. (1 caramelized) 5 *cf.* Cheno-am Seed Frags. 1 *Chenopodium* Seed 14 Indet. Seed Frags. 22 Misc. Endosperm Frags. 3 Misc. Flat Fiber (2 CaO) 5 Misc. Round Fibers 1 Monocot *cf.* Poaceae Culm Frag. 2 *Sporobolus* Type Grains 1 *Zea mays* Cob Frag. 1 *Zea mays* Cupule Frag. 1 *cf. Zea mays* Cupule Frag. 1 *Zea mays* Glume Frag. 2 *cf. Zea mays* Kernel Frags. **WOOD CHARCOAL** 1 Gymnosperm	1 Indet Seed Frag. 1 Indet. Seed Coat Frag. (HF) 1 *Mentzelia* Seed 1 *Mentzelia* Seed Frag. 1 *Portulaca* Seed 1 *Sporobolus* Type Grain Frag.	1 Ceramic Sherd (HF) 14 Faunal Bone Frags. (8 burned) (13 HF) 1 Fire-Altered Rock (HF) 5 Insect Exoskeleton Frags. 1 Insect-Sized Fecal Pellet 270 Macrospores[2] 7 Macrospore Clusters 8 Rodent-Sized Fecal Pellets
Room 17 0.98 m BGS 8 cm Thick Ash Lens at Bed Rock	3.45 l (54.5 ml) [46.0 ml]	**NON-WOODY REMAINS** 106 Agave Fibers (TR; 65 CaO) 1 *Agave* Round Fiber Bundle (TR; CaO) 119 *cf. Agave* Fibers (round, CaO) 1 *cf. Agave* Round Fiber Bundle (CaO) 13 Cheno-am Seed Frags. (1 caramelized) 14 *cf.* Cheno-am Seed Frags. 1 *Echinocereus* Seed 2 Indet. Fruit Frags. (HF) 78 Indet. Seed Frags.	2 Asteraceae Achenes with Pappus (HF) 2 Aveneae Tribe (*cf. Trisetum*) Florets with Awns and Bristles 1 Cheno-am Seed Frag. (white) 1 Indet. Fruit Frag. (HF) 2 Indet. Inflorescence Frags. 2 Indet. Seed Frags. (*Opuntia*?) 7 *Mentzelia* Seeds 42 *Mentzelia* Seed Frags. 2 Monocot *cf.* Poaceae Blade Frags.	1 Ant 2 Burned Animal Epidermis Frags. (Reptile?) 4 Ceramic Sherds (HF) 3 Chipped Stone Flakes (HF) 6 Chipped Stone Microflakes (5 obsidian) (5 HF) 89 Faunal Bone Frags. (45 burned) (82 HF) 20 Fire-Altered Rocks (HF)

Context and Provenience	Volumes: Sample (lt. frac.) [charc.][1]	Carbonized Plant Remains	Uncarbonized Plant Remains	Other Material
		23 Misc. D-Shaped Fiber (17 CaO)	10 Monocot *cf.* Poaceae Blade and Culm Frags. (HF)	3 Insect Cases
		84 Misc. Endosperm Frags.	2 Monocot *cf.* Poaceae Culm Frags. (1 HF)	22 Insect Exoskeleton Frags.
		16 Misc. Flat Fibers (12 CaO)	1 Poaceae Floret	Numerous Insect-Sized Fecal Pellets
		37 Misc. Frags. (CaO)	3 *cf. Sporobolus* Type Grain Frags.	2 Insect Wings
		1,502 Misc. Round Fibers[2]		1,263 Macrospores[2]
		4 Misc. Round Fiber Bundles		181 Macrospore Clusters
		1 Misc. Spiral Twist		Numerous Rodent-Sized Fecal Pellets
		2 *Portulaca* Seeds (1 caramelized)		2 Snail Shells
		4 *Portulaca* Seed Frags.		
		1 *Zea mays* Cupule		
		18 *Zea mays* Cupule Frags.		
		14 *cf. Zea mays* Cupule Frags.		
		1 *cf. Zea mays* Embryo Frag.		
		6 *cf. Zea mays* Glume Frags.		
		3 *Zea mays* Kernel Frags.		
		3 *cf. Zea mays* Kernel Frag. (1 HF)		
		WOOD CHARCOAL		
		1 *cf. Quercus*		
Room 17 Below Groundstone Artifact; Floor at 1.50 m BGS	6.00 l (234.0 ml) [117.0 ml]	**NON-WOODY REMAINS**	13 *Amaranthus* Seeds	3 Ants (1 HF)
		139 *Agave* Fibers (TR; 102 CaO)	9 *Amaranthus* Seed Frags.	1 Azurite Nodule (HF)
		109 *cf. Agave* Fibers (round; CaO)	22 *Amsinckia* Fruits	8 Ceramic Sherds (HF)
		1 AZ U:9:24 (ASU) Unknown A	1 *Amsinckia* Fruit and Stem	9 Ceramic Sherdlets (HF)
		36 Cheno-am Seed Frags. (2 caramelized)	12 *Amsinckia* Seeds	2 Charred Insect-Sized Fecal Pellets
		39 *cf.* Cheno-am Seed Frags.	2 *Amsinckia* Seed Frags.	3 Charred Termite Pellets
		3 *Chenopodium* Seeds	1 *cf. Amsinckia* Seed Frag.	2 Charred Termite Pellet Aggregates
		12 *Chenopodium* Seed Frags.	1 Angiospermae Anther	2 Charred Termite Pellet Frags.
		12 *Cycloloma* Seed Frags.	9 Asteraceae Achenes (1 *cf. Lactuca*)	4 Chipped Stone Flakes (HF)
		2 *Descurainia* Seeds	1 *cf.* Asteraceae Achene Frag.	33 Chipped Stone Microflakes (20 obsidian) (HF)
		5 *cf. Descurainia* Seed Frags.	1 Aveneae Tribe Floret (*cf. Trisetum*) (HF)	6 Faunal Bones (1 burned) (5 HF)
		8 Indet. Fruit/Seed Frags. (3HF)	2 *Bromus* Type Fertile Florets	233 Faunal Bone Frags. (120 burned) (223 HF)
		163 Indet. Seed Frags.[2]	52 Cheno-am Seed Frags.	14 Fire-Altered Rocks (HF)
		1 *Juniperus* Branchlet Frag.	32 *cf.* Cheno-am Seed Frags.	1 *Gastrocopta* Type Snail Shell
		1 *Mentzelia* Seed	176 *Chenopodium* Seeds	6 Insect Cases
		8 Misc. D-Shaped Fibers (2 CaO)	4 *Chenopodium* Seed Frags.	2 Insect Case Frags.
		81 Misc. Endosperm Frags.[2]	1 *Cryptantha* Seed	Numerous Insect Exoskeleton Frags.
		10 Misc. Flat Fibers (6 CaO)	1 *Descurainia* Seed	Numerous Insect-Sized Fecal Pellets
		19 Misc. Frags. (CaO)	3 Dicot Leaf Frag. (1 HF)	1 Insect Wing
		194 Misc. Round Fibers	4 *Elymus* Type Florets	1,983 Macrospores[2]
		2 Misc. Spiral Twists	66 *Eragrostis* Type Grains	34 Macrospore Clusters[2]
		3 Monocot *cf.* Poaceae Culm Frags.	3 *cf. Eragrostis* Type Grain Frags.	100 Rodent-Sized Fecal Pellets (5 HF)
		1 Monocot *cf. Phragmites* Culm Frag.	1 *cf. Eriogonum* Fruit	6 Shell Frags. (1 nacreous, 4 snail) (HF)
		3 *Portulaca* Seeds	4 *Erodium* Spiral Twists	
		2 *Sporobolus* Type Grains	1 *Erodium cicutarium* Fruit	
		6 *cf. Sporobolus* Type Grain Frags.	6 *Erodium cicutarium* Fruit Frags.	
		4 *Zea mays* Cupule Frags.	1 *Erodium cicutarium* Seed	
		3 *cf. Zea mays* Cupule Frags.	1 *Euphorbia* Seed Frag.	
		1 *Zea mays* Glume Frag.	9 Hordeae Tribe Florets	
		1 *Zea mays* Kernel Frag.	3 Indet. Fruit Frags.	
		3 *cf. Zea mays* Kernel Frags.	1 Indet. Fruit/Seed Frag.	
		WOOD CHARCOAL	28 Indet. Seed Frags.	
		1 *Pinus ponderosa* Type	31 *Mentzelia* Seed Frags.	
		5 *cf. Quercus*	69 *Mollugo* Seeds	
			15 *Mollugo* Seed Frags.	
			242 Monocot *cf.* Poaceae Blade Frags. (4 HF)[2]	
			83 Monocot *cf.* Poaceae Culm	

Context and Provenience	Volumes: Sample (lt. frac.) [charc.][1]	Carbonized Plant Remains	Uncarbonized Plant Remains	Other Material
			Frags. (2 HF)[2]	
			20 *Opuntia* Seed Frags.	
			1 *Physalis* Seed	
			1 *cf. Pinus* Cone Frag.	
			6 Poaceae Culm Frags. (1 HF)	
			17 Poaceae Florets (3 *cf. Bromus*-type) (3HF)	
			1 *cf.* Poaceae Floret Frag.	
			1 Poaceae Glume/Palea Lemma	
			3 Poaceae Grains (small, round)	
			6 *cf.* Poaceae Grain Frags.	
			1 Poaceae Rachis Joint Frag.	
			2 Poaceae Spikelets	
			35 *Portulaca* Seeds	
			15 *Portulaca* Seed Frags.	
			1 Solanaceae *cf. Physalis* Seed Frag.	
			3 *Sphaeralcea* Seeds	
			47 *Sporobolus* Type Grains	
			21 *cf. Sporobolus* Type Grain Frags.	
			5 *Trianthema portulacastrum* Seed Frags. (HF)	
			1 *Verbena* Nutlet	

Context and Provenience	Volumes: Sample (lt. frac.) [charc.][1]	Carbonized Plant Remains	Uncarbonized Plant Remains	Other Material
Room 22 1.35–1.45 m BGS	4.30 l (210.0 ml) [21.0 ml]	**NON-WOODY REMAINS** 2 Agave Fibers (TR; 1 CaO) 2 Cheno-am Seeds (2 popped; 1 reticulate) 1 Cheno-am Seed Frag. 1 *cf.* Cheno-am Seed Frag. 3 Indet. Fruit/Seed Frags. 9 Indet. Seed Frags. 3 Misc. Round Fibers 3 Misc. Spiral Twists 1 Monocot *cf. Phragmites* Culm Frag. (small piece) 1 *Portulaca* Seed Frag. 5 *Zea mays* Cupule Frags. 2 *cf. Zea mays* Glume Frags. (1 HF) **WOOD CHARCOAL** 7 *Pinus ponderosa* Type	2 *Amsinckia* Seeds 1 Angiospermae Anther Aggregate 9 Asteraceae Achenes (4 with pappus) 1 Asteraceae Achene Frag. 11 Aveneae Tribe (*cf. Trisetum*) Florets with Awns and Bristles (5 HF) 3 Boraginaceae *cf. Lappula* Seeds 9 *Bromus* Type Florets 14 *Bromus* Type Grains 2 *Bromus* Type Grain Frags. 7 Cheno-am Seed Frags. 2 *cf.* Cheno-am Seed Frags. 13 *Chenopodium* Seeds (smooth surf., round in facet view, no margin) 236 *Cryptantha* Seeds (1 HF) 1 *cf. Cryptantha* Seed 1 *Cryptantha* Seed Frag (HF) 4 *cf. Cryptantha* Seed Frags. 12 *Descurainia* Seeds 4 *cf. Descurainia* Seeds 8 *cf. Descurainia* Seed Frags. 63 *Eragrostis* Type Grains 23 *Eragrostis* Type Grain Frags. 3 *cf. Eragrostis* Type Grain Frags. 21 *Erodium* Fruits 53 *Erodium* Fruit Frags. 10 *cf. Erodium* Fruit Frags. 16 *Erodium* Seeds (1 HF) 7 *Erodium* Seed Frags. (2 HF) 5 *cf. Erodium* Seed Frag. 1 *Erodium* Spiral Twist (HF) 1 *Erodium cicutarium* Fruit (HF) 1 *Euphorbia* Seed Frag. 24 Indet. Fruit Frags. 3 Indet. Fruit/Seed Frags. 34 Indet. Seed Frags. 12 *Malva* Seeds 1 *Malva* Seed Frag. 1 *Mentzelia* Seed 15 Misc. Spiral Twists 101 Monocot *cf.* Poaceae Blade Frags. (21 HF) 92 Monocot *cf.* Poaceae Culm Frags. (13 HF) 2 *Opuntia* Seed Frags. (round in plan view) 70 Poaceae Florets (6 possibly *Bromus* Type, HF) 3 *cf.* Poaceae Floret Frags. 4 Poaceae Glumes/Paleas/Lemmas 11 *Portulaca* Seeds 1 Solanaceae *cf. Physalis* Seed 13 *Sphaeralcea* Seeds 2 *cf. Sphaeralcea* Seed Frags. 77 *Sporobolus* Type Grains 9 *cf. Sporobolus* Type Grain	2 Beetles 3 Ceramic Sherds (HF) 4 Ceramic Sherdlets (HF) 1 Charred Rodent-Sized Fecal Pellet 4 Chipped Stone Flakes (HF) 17 Chipped Stone Microflakes (6 obsidian) (16 HF) 4 Faunal Bones (all unburned) (3 HF) 33 Faunal Bone Frags. (28 burned) (HF) 14 Fire-Altered Rocks (HF) 4 Insect Cases 2 Insect Case Frags. (HF) Numerous Insect Exoskeleton Frag. (1HF) Numerous Insect-Sized Fecal Pellets (112 HF) 4,216 Macrospores[2] 3 Macrospore Clusters 4 Red Resin Globules (*cf.* creosotebush lac) 1 Rodent-Sized Fecal Pellet (1 HF) 5 Shell Frags. (HF) 1 Wasp

Table D2. Raw data from partially analyzed flotation samples.

Context and Provenience	Volumes: Sample (lt. frac.) [charc.][1]	Carbonized Plant Remains	Uncarbonized Plant Remains	Other Material
Room 5 Outside Wall 0.55 m BGS	5.0 l	**NON-WOODY REMAINS** 2 Indet. Nut/Seed Frags. (HF) 1 Monocot *cf. Phragmites* Culm Frag. (node frag.) (HF) 1 *Zea mays* Embryo Frag. (HF) 2 *cf. Zea mays* Cupule Frags. (HF) 2 *cf. Zea mays* Glume Frags. (HF) 1 *Zea mays* Kernel Frag. (HF) 1 *cf. Zea mays* Kernel Frag. (HF)	2 *Amsinckia* Seeds (HF) 4 Monocot *cf.* Poaceae Blade Frags. (HF) 1 Monocot *cf.* Poaceae Culm Frag. (HF)	2 Ceramic Sherds (HF) 6 Ceramic Sherdlets (HF) 5 Chipped Stone Flakes (HF) 25 Chipped Stone Microflakes (HF) 6 Faunal Bones (2 burned) (HF) 220 Faunal Bone Frags. (79 burned) (HF) 7 Fire-Altered Rocks (HF) 1 Probable Broom Brsitle (HF) 4 Shell Frags. (HF)
Room 14 1.40 m BGS Between 2nd & 3rd Floors (burned room)	2.00 l	**NON-WOODY REMAINS** 8 Indet. Fruit/Seed Frags. (HF) 1 Monocot *cf. Phragmites* Blade Frag. (HF) 2 *cf. Prosopis* Seed Frags. (HF) 1 *Zea mays* Cupule Frag. (HF) 3 *cf. Zea mays* Cupule Frags. (HF) 1 *cf. Zea mays* Kernel Frag. (HF)	3 Indet. Inflorescences (*Larrea*?) (HF) 1 *cf. Larrea tridentata* Leaf Frag. (HF) 14 Monocot *cf.* Poaceae Blade Frags. (HF)	11 Ceramic Sherds (HF) 5 Ceramic Sherdlets (HF) 5 Chipped Stone Flakes (HF) 22 Chipped Stone Microflakes (HF) 13 Faunal Bones (2 burned) (HF) 272 Faunal Bone Frags. (160 burned) (HF) 8 Fire-Altered Rocks (HF) 1 Shell Bead (HF) 14 Shell Frags. (HF)
Room 18 0–20 cm Above Floor	6.00 l	**NON-WOODY REMAINS** 1 *cf. Agave* Fiber (round; CaO) (HF) 1 *Arctostaphylos* Seed Aggregate (HF) 2 Indet. Nut/Seed Frag. (HF) 1 Misc. Endosperm Frag. (HF) 1 Misc. Flat Fiber (CaO) 2 *cf.* Poaceae Grain Frags. (*Hordeum*?) (HF) 2 *Zea mays* Cupule Frags. (HF) 1 *cf. Zea mays* Cupule Frag. (HF) 1 *Zea mays* Glume (HF) 1 *Zea mays* Kernel Frag. (HF) 3 *cf. Zea mays* Kernel Frags. (HF)	1 *cf.* Brassicaceae Fruit Frag. (HF) 1 *cf. Celtis* Nutlet Frag. (white) (HF) 4 *Erodium* Spiral Twists (HF) 5 Monocot *cf.* Poaceae Blade Frags. (HF) 4 Monocot *cf.* Poaceae Culm Frags. (HF)	28 Ceramic Sherds (HF) 19 Ceramic Sherdlets (HF) 10 Chipped Stone Flakes (HF) 276 Chipped Stone Microdebitage (231 obsidian) (HF) 3 Chipped Stone Shatter (HF) 32 Faunal Bones (8 burned) (HF) 1184 Faunal Bone Frags. (649 burned) (HF) 47 Fire-Altered Rocks (HF) 1 Insect Wing (HF) 5 Rodent-Sized Fecal Pellets (HF) 5 Shell Frags. (HF) 5 Turquoise Frags. (HF)

Notes for Table D1 and D2: (HF) - Recovered from heavy fraction (all other material is from the light flotation fraction). [1]Abbreviations: (lt. frac.) - Total Light Flotation Fraction Volume; [charc.] - Wood Charcoal Volume in Light Fraction; Dicot - Dicotyledonae; CaO - white styloid crystals present; Frag. - Fragment; Frags. – Fragments; Indet - Indeterminate; Misc. - Miscellaneous; Monocot - Monocotyledonae; TR - Trough-shaped cross section. [2]Estimated number. "Numerous" is defined as more than 50 parts per liter.

APPENDIX E
FAUNAL DATA

Table E1. Taxonomic summary of the surface unit in the north quadrant.

Class/ Order	Genus and Species	Burned/ Calcined	Cut	Gnawed	NISP /MNI
Mammalia/ Lagomorpha	*Lepus californicus* (Black-tailed Jackrabbit)			1	3/1
	Sylvilagus audubonii (Desert Cottontail)	1			13/2
Mammalia/ Rodentia	*Cynomys gunnisoni* (Gunnison's Prairie Dog)			2	10/3
	Spermophilus variegates (Rock Squirrel)				5/2
Reptilia/ Squamata	*Crotalus atrox* (Western Diamondback Rattlesnake)				4/1

Table E2. Taxonomic summary of Test Pit 1.

Class	Genus and Species	Burned/ Calcined	Cut	Gnawed	NISP/ MNI
Mammalia/ Rodentia	*Cynomys gunnisoni* (Gunnison's Prairie Dog)				1/1
	Thomomys bottae (Botta's Pocket Gopher)				1/1

Table E3. Taxonomic summary of Test Pit 2.

Class/ Order	Genus and Species	Burned/ Calcined	Cut	Gnawed	NISP/ MNI
Mammalia/ Artiodactyla	*Odocoileus hemionus* (Mule Deer)	1/1			5/1
	Antilocapra Americana (Pronghorn)		2		2/1
Mammalia/ Carnivora	*Canis latrans* (Coyote)				1/1
Mammalia/ Lagomorpha	*Sylvilagus audubonii* (Desert Cottontail)				2/2
Mammalia/ Rodentia	*Cynomys gunnisoni* (Gunnison's Prairie Dog)				1/1
	Sciurus arizonensis (Arizona Gray Squirrel)				2/1

Table E4. Taxonomic summary of Room 2.

Class/ Order	Genus and Species	Burned/ Calcined	Cut	Gnawed	NISP/MNI
Mammalia/ Artiodactyla	*Odocoileus hemionus* (Mule Deer)	1			6/4
Mammalia/ Carnivora	*Canis latrans* (Coyote)				1/1
Mammalia/ Lagomorpha	*Lepus californicus* (Black-tailed Jackrabbit)			8	33/11
	Sylvilagus audubonii (Desert Cottontail)	2/1		8	141/21
Mammalia/ Rodentia	*Cynomys gunnisoni* (Gunnison's Prairie Dog)				46/16
	Eutamias dorsalis (Cliff Chipmunk)				4/2
	Neotoma albigula (White-throated Woodrat)			1	11/4
	Sciurus arizonensis (Arizona Gray Squirrel)				6/4
	Spermophilus variegates (Rock Squirrel)			1	2/1
	Thomomys bottae (Botta's Pocket Gopher)				5/4

Table E5. Taxonomic summary of Room 5.

Class/ Order	Genus and Species	Burned/ Calcined	Cut	Gnawed	NISP/ MNI
Mammalia/ Artiodactyla	*Odocoileus hemionus* (Mule Deer)			1	4/2
Mammalia/ Lagomorpha	*Lepus californicus* (Black-tailed Jackrabbit)	4		7	13/4
	Sylvilagus audubonii (Desert Cottontail)	15		9	79/11
Mammalia/ Rodentia	*Cynomys gunnisoni* (Gunnison's Prairie Dog)	5		5	26/6
	Neotoma albigula (White-throated Woodrat)				4/4
	Sciurus arizonensis (Arizona Gray Squirrel)	5/2			14/3
Aves/ Falconiformes	*Acipter cooperii* (Cooper's Hawk)				1/1
Aves/ Passeriformes	*Corvus brachyrhynchos* (American Crow)				1/1

Table E6. Taxonomic summary of Room 14.

Class/ Order	Genus and Species	Burned/ Calcined	Cut	Gnawed	NISP/ MNI
Mammalia/ Artiodactyla	*Odocoileus hemionus* (Mule Deer)	7/2		5	34/5
Mammalia/ Carnivora	*Felis rufus* (Bobcat)				1/1
Mammalia/ Lagomorpha	*Lepus californicus* (Black-tailed Jackrabbit)	7		6	48/10
	Sylvilagus audubonii (Desert Cottontail)	7		27	153/22
Mammalia/ Rodentia	*Cynomys gunnisoni* (Gunnison's (Prairie Dog)			7	53/16
	Neotoma albigula (White-throated Woodrat)			3	18/9
	Sciurus arizonensis (Arizona Gray Squirrel)			3	23/8
	Spermophilus variegates (Rock Squirrel)				5/4
Aves/ Galliformes	*Callipepla californica* (California Quail)				2/2

Table E7. Taxonomic summary of Room 17.

Class/ Order	Genus and Species	Burned/ Calcined	Cut	Gnawed	NISP/ MNI
Mammalia/ Artiodactyla	*Cervus Canadensis* (Elk)				2/2
	Odocoileus hemionus (Mule Deer)	4		9	28/8
Mammalia/ Carnivora	*Canis latrans* (Coyote)				2/2
	Canis familiaris (Dog)				1/1
	Felis rufus (Bobcat			1	3/1
	Felis concolor (Mountain Lion)				1/1
	Vulpes sp. (Fox)				1/1
Mammalia/ Lagomorpha	*Lepus californicus* (Black-tailed Jackrabbit)	2		4	40/12
	Sylvilagus audubonii (Desert Cottontail)	6/2	1	4	105/14
Mammalia/ Rodentia	*Cynomys gunnisoni* (Gunnison's Prairie Dog)			12	68/13
	Neotoma albigula (White-throated Woodrat)	2		2	14/5
	Peromyscus sp. (Deer Mouse)				1/1
	Sciurus arizonensis (Arizona Gray Squirrel)	1		1	19/10
	Spermophilus variegates (Rock Squirrel)				1/1
Mammalia	*Thomomys bottae* (Botta's pocket gopher)			1	7
Aves/ Columbiformes	*Zenaidura macroura* (Mourning Dove)				2
Aves/ Falconiformes	*Buteo jamaicensis* (Red-tailed Hawk)				4
	Circus cyaneus (Northern Harrier)				1
Aves/ Galliformes	*Callipepla gambelii* (Gambel's Quail)				3

Table E8. Taxonomic summary of Room 18.

Class/ Order	Genus and Species	Burned/ Calcined	Cut	Gnawed	NISP/ MNI
Mammalia/ Artiodactyla	Cervus Canadensis (Elk)	/1		1	3/2
	Odocoileus hemionus (Mule Deer)	7	1	15	46/13
	Antilocapra Americana (Pronghorn)				1/1
Mammalia/ Carnivora	Felis rufus (Bobcat)	1/1			10/6
	Felis concolor (Mountain Lion)				
	Vulpes sp. (Fox)				1/1
	Taxidea taxus (American Badger)				1/1
Mammalia/ Lagomorpha	Lepus californicus (Black-tailed Jackrabbit)	17/3		17	98/24
	Sylvilagus audubonii (Desert Cottontail)	25/2		65	448/56
Mammalia/ Rodentia	Cynomys gunnisoni (Gunnison's Prairie Dog)	8		23	172/172
	Eutamias dorsalis (Cliff Chipmunk)				1/1
	Neotoma albigula (White-throated Woodrat)	3		3	35/19
	Peromyscus sp. (Deer Mouse)				3/2
	Sciurus arizonensis (Arizona Gray Squirrel)	7		6	115/33
	Sigmodon arizonae (Arizona Cotton Rat)				9/4
	Spermophilus variegates (Rock Squirrel)			1	8/5
	Thomomys bottae (Botta's Pocket Gopher)				6/5
Aves/ Cuculiformes	Geococcyx californianus (Roadrunner)				1/1
Aves/ Falconiformes	Buteo jamaicensis (Red-tailed Hawk)				4/3
Aves/ Galliformes	Callipepla gambelii (Gambel's Quail)				2/2
Aves/ Passeriformes	Aphelocoma californica (Western Scrub-jay)				1/1
	Pica hudsonii (Black-billed Magpie)				1/1
	Tyto alba (Barn Owl)				1/1
Reptilia/ Squamata	Crotalus atrox (Western Diamondback Rattlesnake)				2/2
	Pituophis catenifer (Gopher Snake)				28/2
Osteichthyes	Bony Fishes				2/2

Table E9. Taxonomic summary of Room 19.

Class/ Order	Genus and Species	Burned/ Calcined	Cut	Gnawed	NISP/MNI
Mammalia/ Artiodactyla	*Odocoileus hemionus* (Mule Deer)	1			7/2
Mammalia/ Carnivora	*Felis rufus* (Bobcat)				3/2
Mammalia/ Lagomorpha	*Lepus californicus* (Black-tailed Jackrabbit)		1	4	19/7
	Sylvilagus audubonii (Desert Cottontail)	22		11	70/15
Mammalia/ Rodentia	*Cynomys gunnisoni* (Gunnison's Prairie Dog)	1		3	24/10
	Neotoma albigula (White-throated Woodrat)			1	3/2
	Sciurus arizonensis (Arizona Gray Squirrel)			2	12/4
	Spermophilus variegates (Rock Squirrel)	1			1/1
Aves/ Galliformes	*Callipepla gambelii* (Gambel's Quail)				1/1
Reptilia. Squamata	*Crotalis atrox* (Western Diamondback Rattlesnake)				1/1
Osteichthyes	Bony Fish				2/1

Table E10. Taxonomic summary of Room 23.

Class/ Order	Genus and Species	Burned/ Calcined	Cut	Gnawed	NISP/ MNI
Mammalia/ Artiodactyla	*Odocoileus hemionus* (Mule Deer)			1	1/1
Mammalia/ Lagomorpha	*Lepus californicus* (Black-tailed Jackrabbit)	4		2	9/5
Mammalia/ Rodentia	*Neotoma albigula* (White-throated Woodrat)			1	2/1

Table E11. Taxonomic summary of Room 28.

Class/ Order	Genus and Species	Burned/ Calcined	Cut	Gnawed	NISP/ MNI
Mammalia/ Artiodactyla	*Odocoileus hemionus* (Mule Deer)				4/1
	Antilocapra Americana (Pronghorn)	/1			5/2

234

Table E12. Taxonomic summary of Room 29.

Class/ Order	Genus and Species	Burned/ Calcined	Cut	Gnawed	NISP/ MNI
Mammalia/ Lagomorpha	*Lepus californicus* (Black-tailed Jackrabbit)				1/1
	Sylvilagus audubonii (Desert Cottontail)				1/1

Table E13. Taxonomic summary of Room 38.

Class/ Order	Genus and Species	Burned/Calcined	Cut	Gnawed	NISP/ MNI
Mammalia/ Lagomorpha	*Lepus californicus* (Black-tailed Jackrabbit)				9/4
	Sylvilagus audubonii (Desert Cottontail)	1		1	11/5
Mammalia/ Rodentia	*Cynomys gunnisoni* (Gunnison's Prairie Dog)				4/4

Table E14. Taxonomic summary of Room 40.

Class/ Order	Genus and Species	Burned/ Calcined	Cut	Gnawed	NISP/ MNI
Mammalia/ Artiodactyla	*Odocoilues hemionus*	127/22	3	25	357/16
	Antilocapra Americana (Pronghorn Antelope)	1/11	3	12	50/8
Mammalia/ Carnivora	*Canis latrans* (Coyote)				22/4
	Felis rufus (Bobcat)	4			13/4
	Felis concolor (Mountain Lion)				7/4
Mammalia/ Lagomorpha	*Lepus californicus* (Black-tailed Jackrabbit)	91/3	4	17	565/39
	Sylvilagus audubonii (Desert Cottontail)	268/2	1	29	1610/85
Mammalia/ Rodentia	*Cynomys gunnisoni* (Gunnison's Prairie Dog)	74/1	1	19	536/50
	Microtus mexicanus				1/1
	Neotoma albigula (White-throated Woodrat)	6			39/7
	Spermophilus variegates (Rock Squirrel)	24		15	305/37
	Zapus princes (Western Jumping Mouse)				1/1
Aves/ Cuculiformes	*Geococcyx californianus* (Roadrunner)				2/2
Aves/ Cuculiformes	*Buteo jamaicensis* (Red-tailed Hawk)				1/1
Reptilia/ Squamata	*Crotelus atrox* (Western Diamondback Rattlesnake)				1/1
	Pituophis catenifer (Gopher Snake)				2/2

APPENDIX F
MUSEUM OF NORTHERN ARIZONA SITE CARD

Note that site map location and elevation are wrong. Compare with Figure 2. Card size is reduced to 83%, so scale is incorrect.

MNA 14549   <u>AUSTIN ARCHAEOLOGICAL SITE SURVEY</u>   March 10-12, 1976

EMILIENNE site   -   Hilltop pueblo

Location: T15N R1E Sec.9 (NE¼ NE¼ SW¼ to   2½ miles N of the junction og
                             (NW¼ NW¼ SE¼   roads 89-A and 642.Private land
            (Margery E.Hofstra 235 Madison St., State College,Pa.16801)

Maps: Prescott Valley Az N 7.5" USGS and FS No.A-204

Condition: Severely vandalized

Environment: Granite/schist butte; catclaw,mountain oak, other low bushes

Nearest water: Seasonally in creeks ½ mile NW or 3/4 mile east

Drainage: Arroyos to west vanish in Lonesome Valley; east:Coyote Creek to
                                   Yaeger Wash to Agua Fria River

Arable land: On high creek banks to east

Artifacts: Broken metate,sundry stone tools; obsidian,quartz,chips and flakes

Potsherds: Gray, black-on-gray, white, orange-red, fugitive red (?)

Photos: 14 color slides

Description: The main pueblo was at least two stories high,with a 2' wide
causeway east of rooms 1 to 4,ending near the 5499' high point of
the natural rock base. No crawlways were observed between the many
rooms. There are 12 rooms in the pueblo and 11 outlying rooms
probably one-storey high. The butte is 80' N-S by 50' and the
occupied area above 5470' is 150' by 80'.

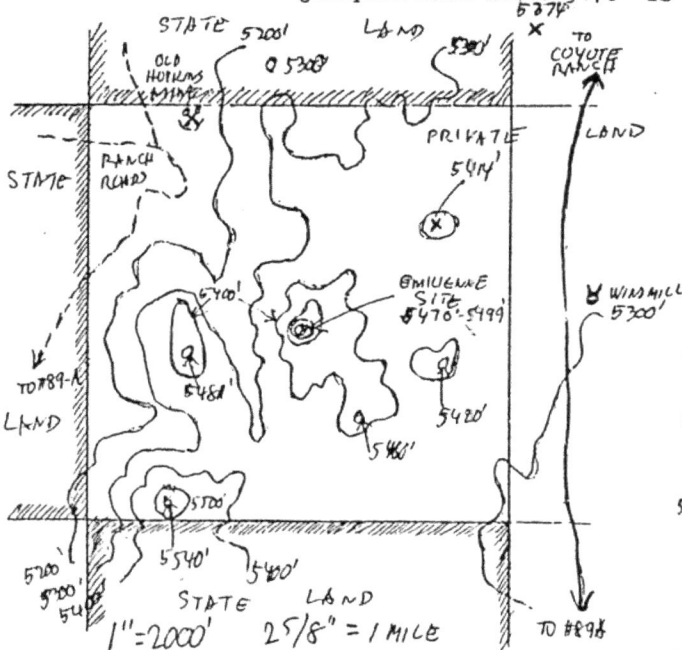

EMILIENNE PUEBLO

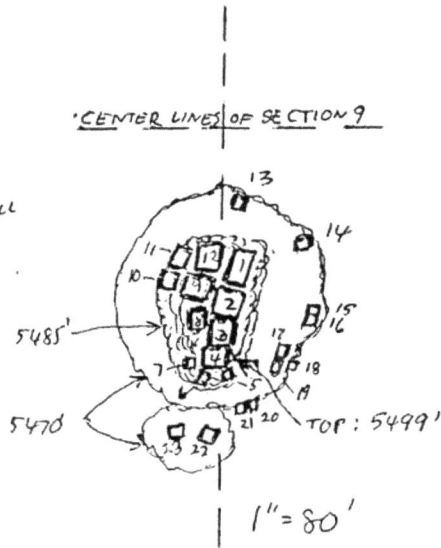

CENTER LINES OF SECTION 9

1"=80'

1"=2000' 25/8"=1 MILE

APPENDIX G
RADIOCARBON DATE INFORMATION

CALIBRATION OF RADIOCARBON AGE TO CALENDAR YEARS

(Variables: C13/C12=-11:lab. mult=1)

Laboratory number:	Beta-170324
Conventional radiocarbon age:	820±80 BP
2 Sigma calibrated result: (95% probability)	Cal AD 1030 to 1300 (Cal BP 920 to 650)

Intercept data

Intercept of radiocarbon age with calibration curve:	Cal AD 1230 (Cal BP 720)
1 Sigma calibrated result: (68% probability)	Cal AD 1160 to 1280 (Cal BP 790 to 670)

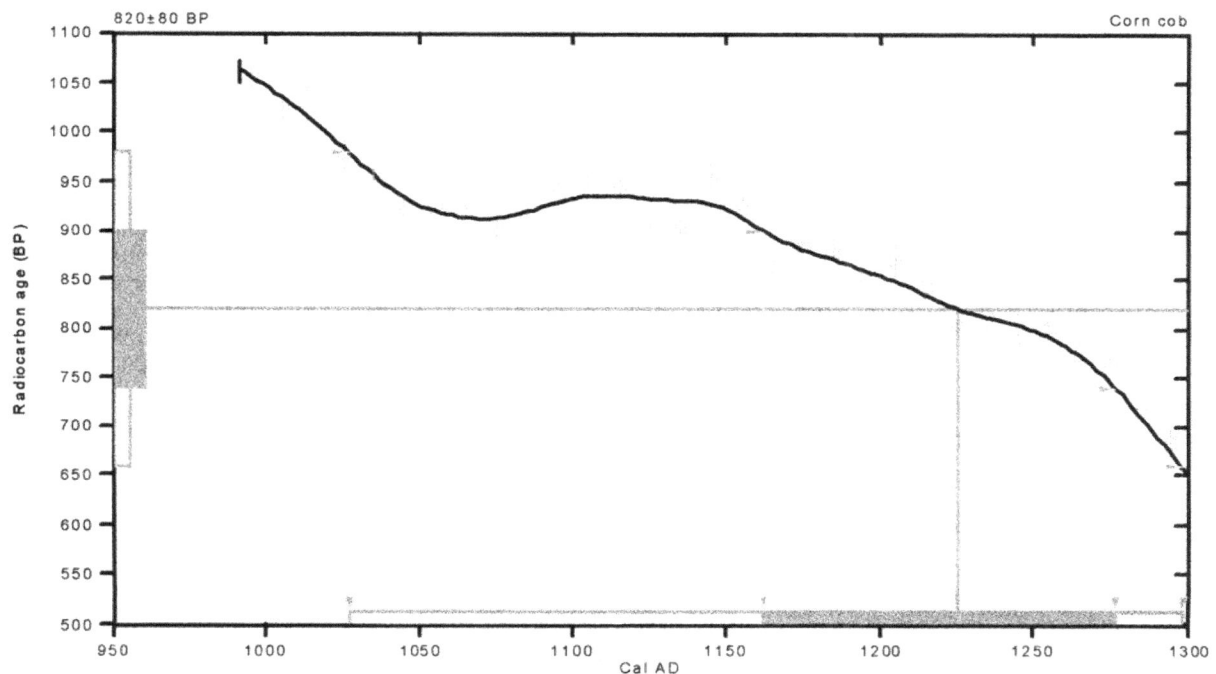

820±80 BP   Corn cob

References:
Database used

Calibration Database
Editorial Comment
    Stuiver, M., van der Plicht, H., 1998, Radiocarbon 40(3), pxii-xiii
INTCAL98 Radiocarbon Age Calibration
    Stuiver, M., et. al., 1998, Radiocarbon 40(3), p1041-1083
Mathematics
A Simplified Approach to Calibrating C14 Dates
    Talma, A. S., Vogel, J. C., 1993, Radiocarbon 35(2), p317-322

Beta Analytic Inc.

4985 SW 74 Court, Miami, Florida 33155 USA • Tel: (305) 667 5167 • Fax: (305) 663 0964 • E-Mail: beta@radiocarbon.com

CALIBRATION OF RADIOCARBON AGE TO CALENDAR YEARS

(Variables: est. C13/C12=-25:lab. mult=1)

Laboratory number:	Beta-157738
Conventional radiocarbon age[1]:	550±60 BP
2 Sigma calibrated result: (95% probability)	Cal AD 1300 to 1450 (Cal BP 650 to 500)

[1] C13/C12 ratio estimated

Intercept data

Intercept of radiocarbon age with calibration curve:	Cal AD 1410 (Cal BP 540)
1 Sigma calibrated results: (68% probability)	Cal AD 1320 to 1350 (Cal BP 630 to 600) and Cal AD 1390 to 1430 (Cal BP 560 to 520)

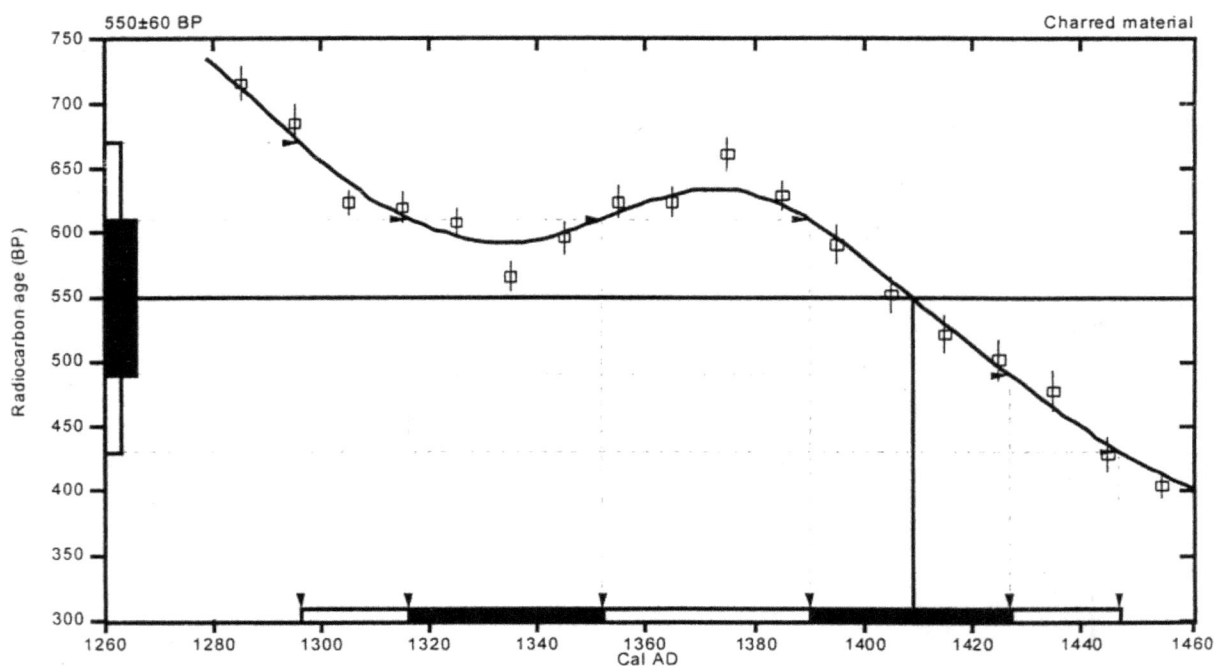

550±60 BP   Charred material

Radiocarbon age (BP) vs Cal AD

References:
  Database used
    INTCAL98
  Calibration Database
  Editorial Comment
    Stuiver, M., van der Plicht, H., 1998, Radiocarbon 40(3), pxii-xiii
  INTCAL98 Radiocarbon Age Calibration
    Stuiver, M., et. al., 1998, Radiocarbon 40(3), p1041-1083
  Mathematics
  A Simplified Approach to Calibrating C14 Dates
    Talma, A. S., Vogel, J. C., 1993, Radiocarbon 35(2), p317-322

Beta Analytic Radiocarbon Dating Laboratory

4985 S.W. 74th Court, Miami, Florida 33155 • Tel: (305)667-5167 • Fax: (305)663-0964 • E-Mail: beta@radiocarbon.com

APPENDIX H
ARTIFACTS FROM COYOTE RUIN IN ARIZONA STATE MUSEUM DATABASE

Recorded by A. L. Christenson in 1999.

Table H1. Coyote artifacts in ASM database.

Gila Pueblo #	Item	Provenience[a]	Description	Size in mm (LxWxT)
		Old Coyote		
GP 39262	Prescott B/G bowl	"?2.+."	geometric design interior; oxidized exterior, reduced interior; abundant silver mica. See Figure 27	144x245
GP 39263	Verde Brown (?) bowl	"No. 1.+."	oxidized	148x277
GP 39264	Verde Brown bowl			
GP 39265	unknown bowl	"Lower House No. 5"	helmet-shaped; buff (?) slip, interior; oxidized	45x91
GP 39266	unknown jar (destroyed by Gila Pueblo <1951)			
GP 39267	Verde Red jar	"Lower House No. 6"	recurved rim; red slip exterior oxidized	115x125; 77 (orifice)
		New Coyote		
GP 39246	tabular knife (2)			
GP 39247	handstone			
GP 39248	mano			
GP 39249	mano (2)			
GP 39250	axe (2)			
GP 39251	maul			
GP 39252	shaft smoother (2)			
GP 39253	metate			
GP 39254	stone artifact			
GP 39255	stone anvil	"Coyote Ranch"	coarse sandstone or quartzite; grooved	97x51
GP 39256	stone slab			
GP 39257	tabular knife			
GP 39258	bone awl		split ungulate long bone	128
GP 39259	shell frog pendant frag.	on house mound		
GP 39260	Leupp (?) B/W	"2 [in circle]"; i.e. Room 2	dipper/small bowl, loop handle; See Figure 24	52x133
GP 39261	unknown bowl	probably contained above item	smudged	
GP 41557	"figurine" frag.		both ends missing; reduced; pit on one side, possible incised line on other	42x16x12
GP 41558	animal figurine frag.		quadruped missing head and legs; oxidized; medium-coarse temper	38x26x29
GP 41559	human figurine frag.		missing corners of head and lower body; scratches next to nose	53x33x14
GP 41560	figurine (?)		cylindrical with missing ends and appendages	31x18

[a] information from Simmons' paper labels or report

APPENDIX I
BURIALS FROM "OLD" COYOTE

The following information is summarized from Simmons (n.d. c) where the nine burials (11 individuals) from the "Old" part of the site are described. As discussed elsewhere (Christenson 2008b: 12.6) he gained his knowledge of aging and sexing skeletons from a number of sources. At this early stage in his career of digging he only speculated about the sex of one burial, although he thought that the child was a girl, with the charcoal under the associated sherd being symbolic of the role of woman that she would perform in the new world! Note that seven of the eight burials had the burial pottery on the left side.

Table I1. Summary of Old Coyote burials.

No.	Age, Sex	Orientation of Head	Depth (in.)	Pottery Grave Goods	Stone Grave Goods	Other Characteristics
1	Adult	E	30	"red" bowl (10 7/8 in. dia.) rt. side of head	grooved sandstone in rt. hand	"anchored" with large stones over limbs and abdomen
2	Adult	E	28	B/G bowl (10 in. dia.) at lt. hand	"ceremonially shaped" obsidian arrowhead near lt. shoulder; red stone disk with 37 turquoise inlay flakes - "red sun in blue sky"	"anchored" with stones
3a	Adult	E	30			found under 3B; "anchored" with stones
3b	Child	NE	24	B/G sherd inverted over charcoal on lt. side		on top of 3a
4	Adult	E	30	"red" bowls inverted at lt. hand		"anchored" with stones
5	Adult, F?	E	36	two small pinch pot bowls (3 1.2 & 4 ½ in. dia. at lt. hand		
6	Adult	E	30	"olla" (5 ¼ in. dia.) lt. of head		
7	Adult	E	48	"olla" (6 ¾ in. dia.) lt. of head		"anchored" with stones
8a	Adult	W	14			boulders over body and head; in abandoned pit house
8b	?	?	?			decayed
9	?	?	?	B/G bowl frags. (8 in. dia.) to lt. of leg		decayed; in pit house that was abandoned after burial

APPENDIX J
PROJECT PARTICIPANTS

SITE WORKERS	LAB WORKERS
Grant Brown	Ben Bailey
Joanne Cline	Ruth Barth
Judy Cummings	Bob Beck
(McCormick)	Joanne Cline
Shelia DeWoskin	Andy Christenson
Del Everett	Jim Christopher
Mark Holt	Judy Cummings
Ginger Johnson	(McCormick)
Pete Lepescu	Leon DeKing
Dick Lord	Frankie Edel
John Midkiff	Cat Euler
Vern Neal	Sue Ford
Jack Papke	Pat Glascow
Warren Parks	Gloria Grimditch
Jim Roberts	Joanne Grossman
Sue Sheffield	Robert Grossman
Laurie Small	Betty Higgins
Mary Spall	Fran Hunold
Charlie Steger	Darwin James
Jim Steinke	Ginger Johnson
Joe Vogel	Susan Jones
Sue Weiss	Liz King
Tom Weiss	Irene Komadina
Mark Ziem	Fred Kraps
Wendell Zipse	Pete Lepescu
	Paul Long
	Betty Loveland
	Margery Mason
	Warren Mason
	Lannie McDonald
	Mavi Melin
	Lonnie Morgan, Jr.
	Mary Moore
	Carol Panlaque
	Debbie Quells
	John Rollo
	Ron Robinson
	Trisha Rude
	Judy Stoycheff
	Laurie Small
	Doris Theriault
	Joe Vogel

APPENDIX K
SITE MAP SECTIONS

The site map for Coyote Ruin was divided into twelve numbered sections as shown below. You can photocopy pages 248 to 259 and assemble them using this image as a guide to produce a map measuring 24 inches wide and 21 inches tall.

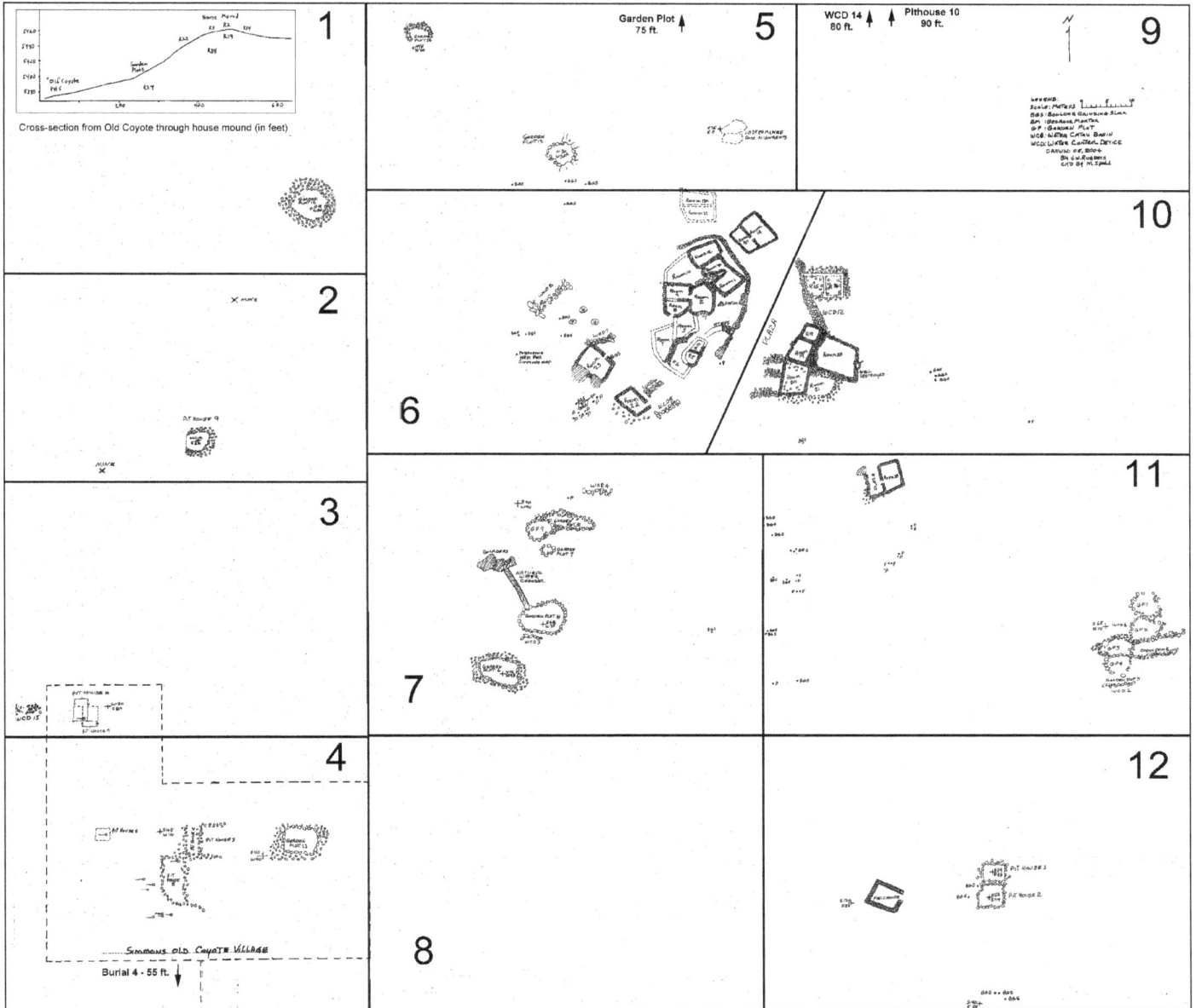

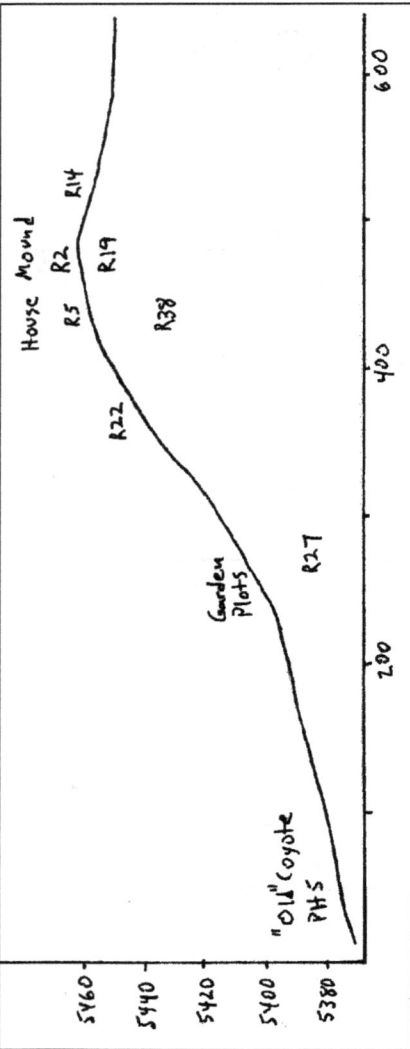

Cross-section from Old Coyote through house mound (in feet)

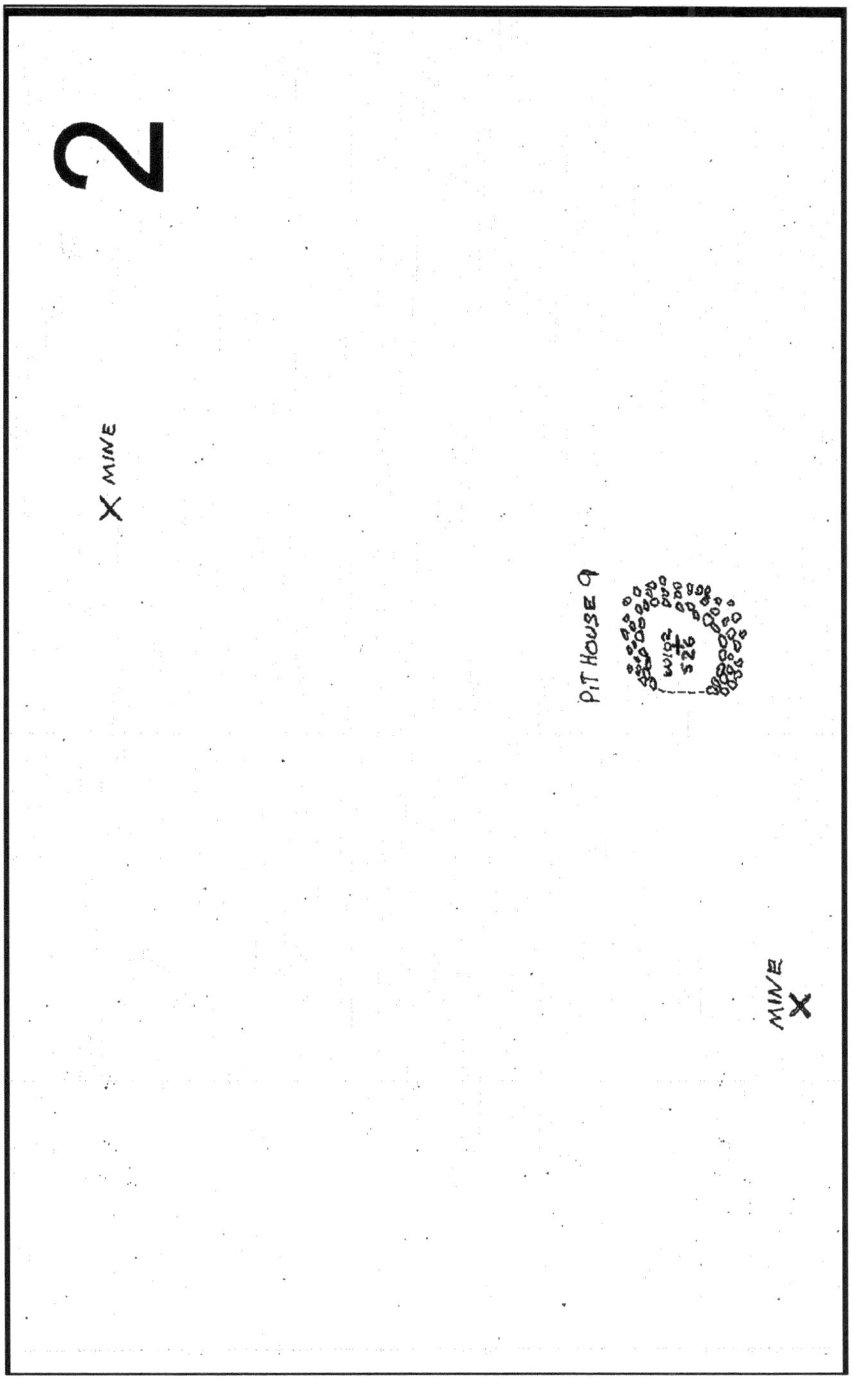

X MINE

PIT HOUSE 9

N10W
S26

MINE
X

3

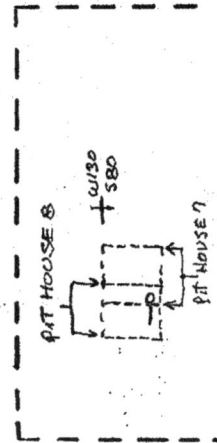

PIT HOUSE 8

+ W130
+ S80

PIT HOUSE 9

210. 04800
010. 000 0
010. 000 0

WCD 15

4

GARDEN
PLOT 11

SILO +
WALL

SILO +
WALL

PIT HOUSE 3

PIT HOUSE 4

PIT
HOUSE
5

PIT HOUSE 6

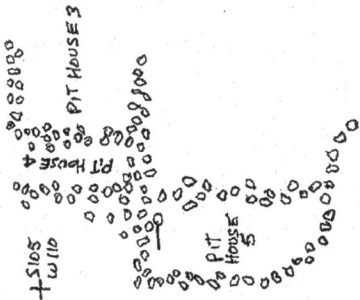

Simmons Old Coyote Village

Burial 4 - 55 ft.

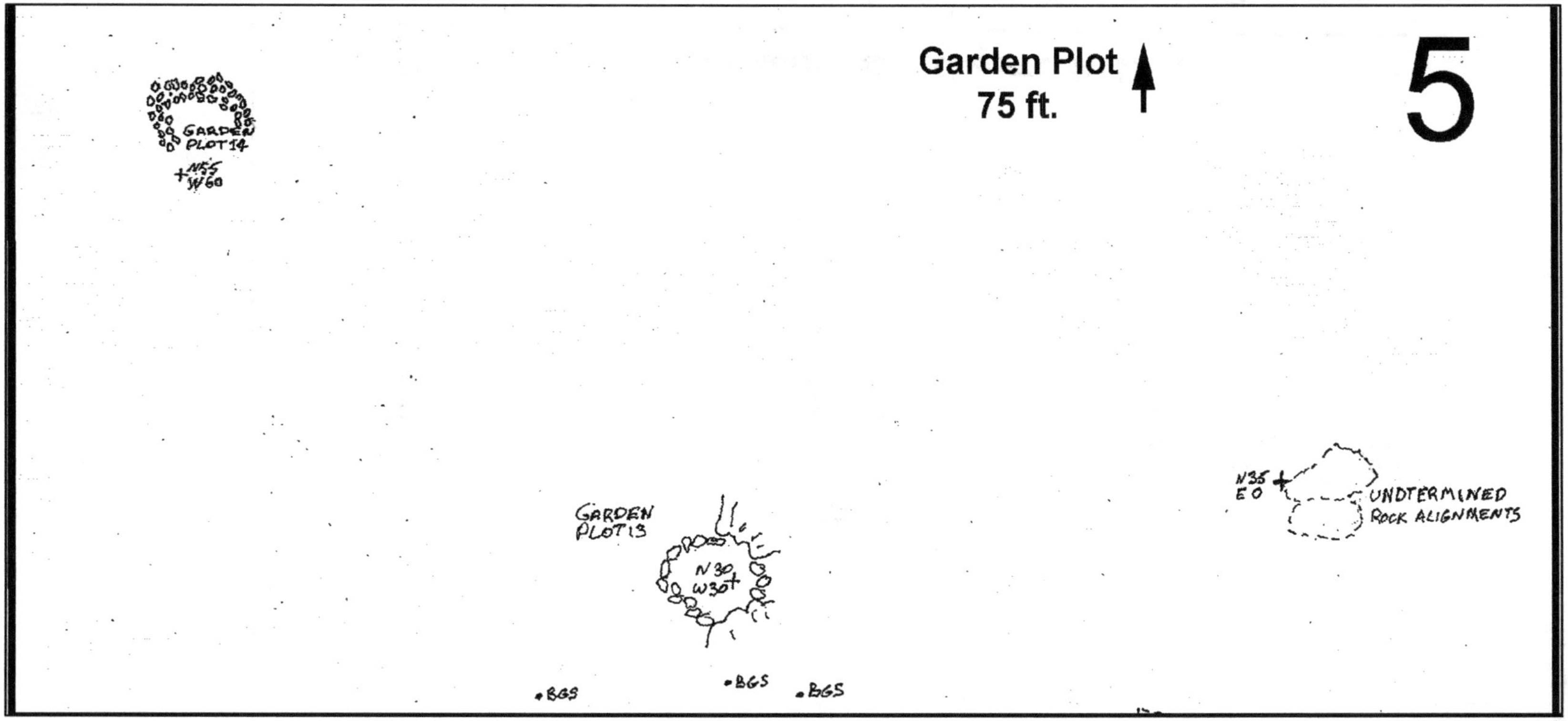

Garden Plot
75 ft.

5

UNDETERMINED
ROCK ALIGNMENTS

N35
E0

GARDEN
PLOT 13

N35
W30

•B6S

•B6S

•B6S

•B6S

GARDEN
PLOT 14

N35
W60

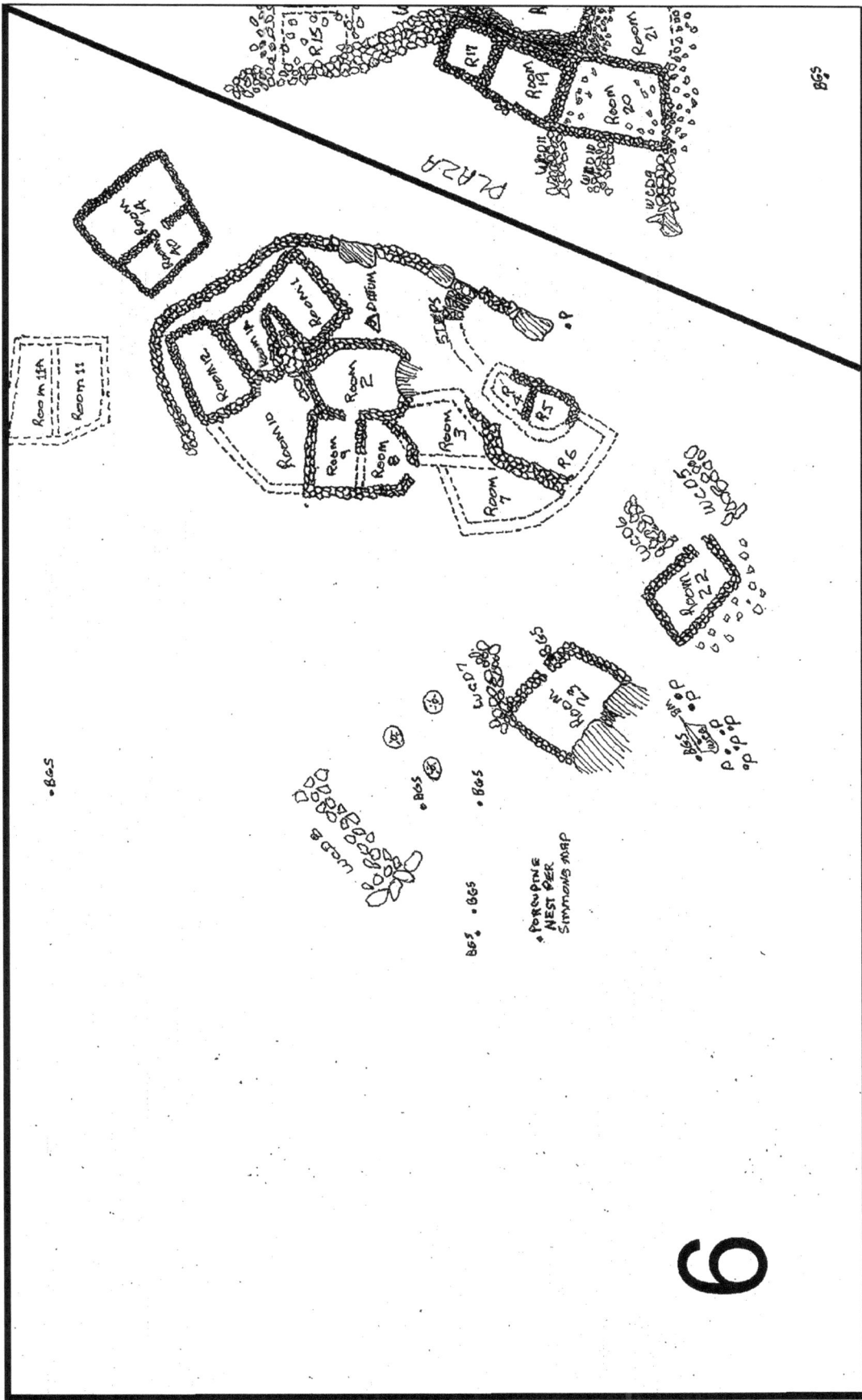

PLAZA

R15

R17

Room 18

Room 20

Room 21

WCD11

WCD08

Room 11A

Room 11

Room 10

Room 12

Room 2

Room 3

Room 9

Room 8

Room 7

Room 4

DATUM

STEPS

P

R

R5

R6

WCD05

WCD06

Room 22

WCD07

Room 23

BGS

Room

PORCUPINE
NEST PIER
SIMMONS MAP

BGS

6

WCD4

•P

GARDEN PLOT 10

GARDEN PLOT 9

GARDEN PLOT 7

+ S40 W40

NATURAL WATER CHANNEL

BOULDERS

GARDEN PLOT 8

+ S68 W35

WCD3

GARDEN PLOT 6

+ S74 W63

GGS

7

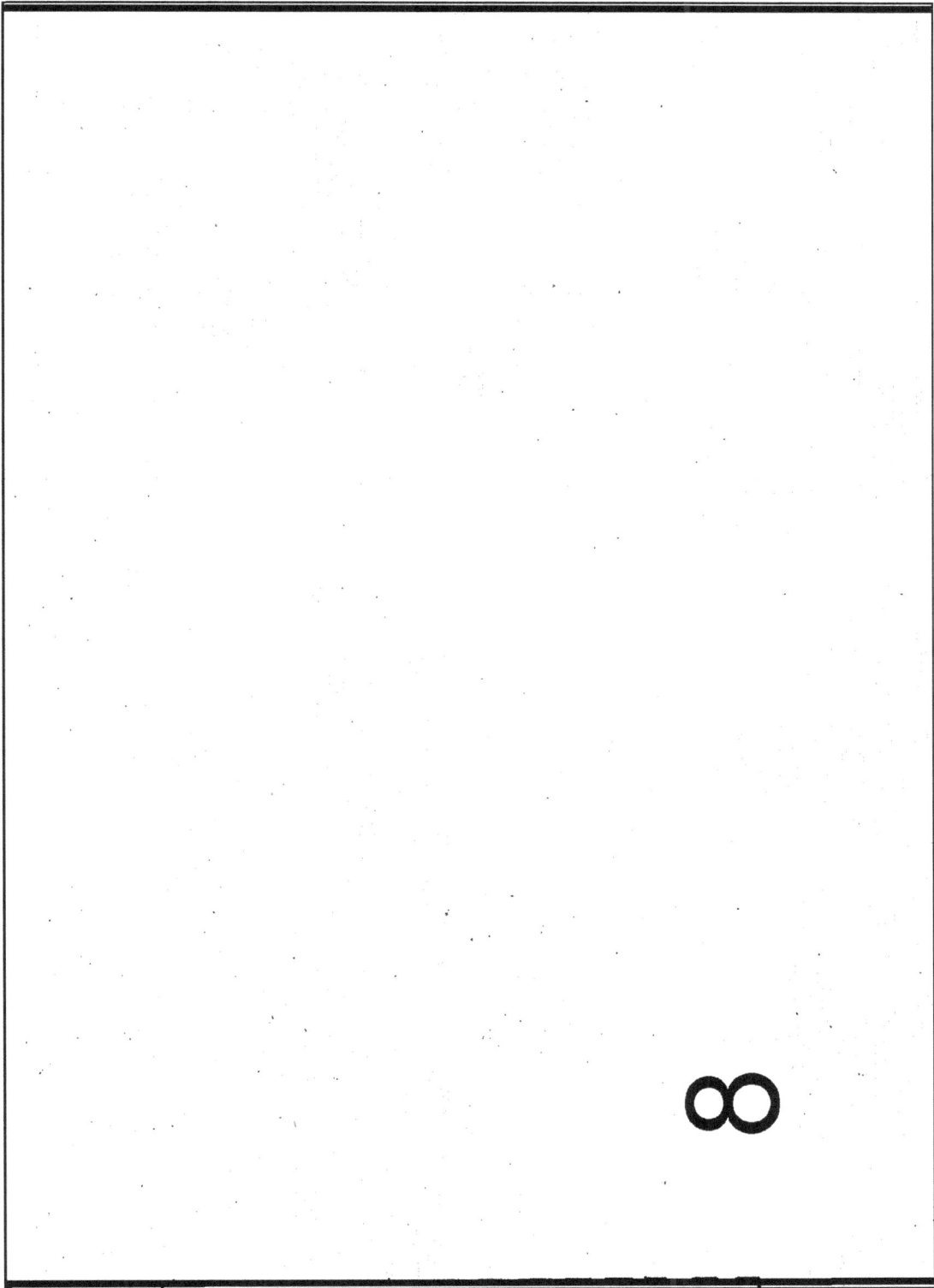

8

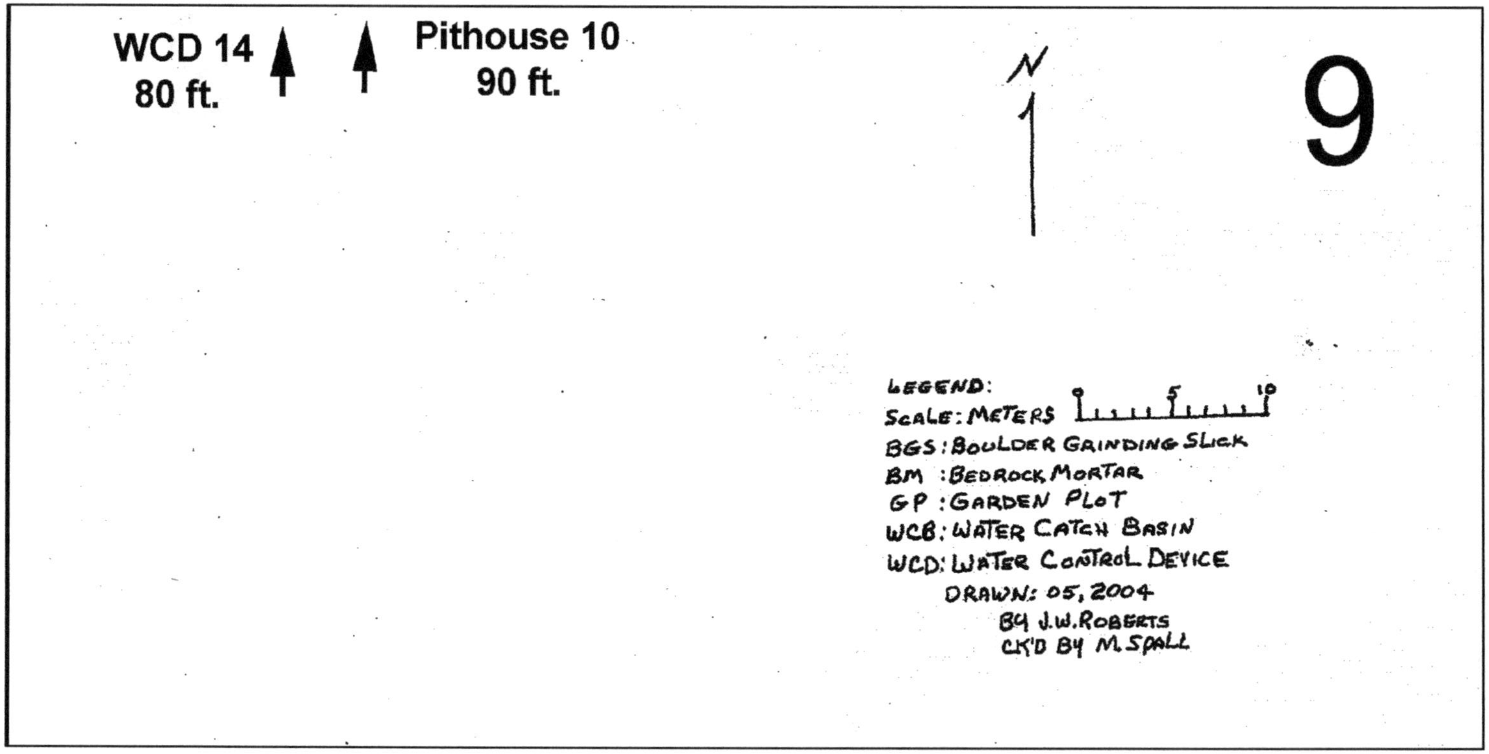

WCD 14
80 ft.

Pithouse 10
90 ft.

N

9

LEGEND:
SCALE: METERS
BGS: BOULDER GRINDING SLICK
BM : BEDROCK MORTAR
GP : GARDEN PLOT
WCB: WATER CATCH BASIN
WCD: WATER CONTROL DEVICE

DRAWN: 05, 2004
BY J.W. ROBERTS
CK'D BY M. SPALL

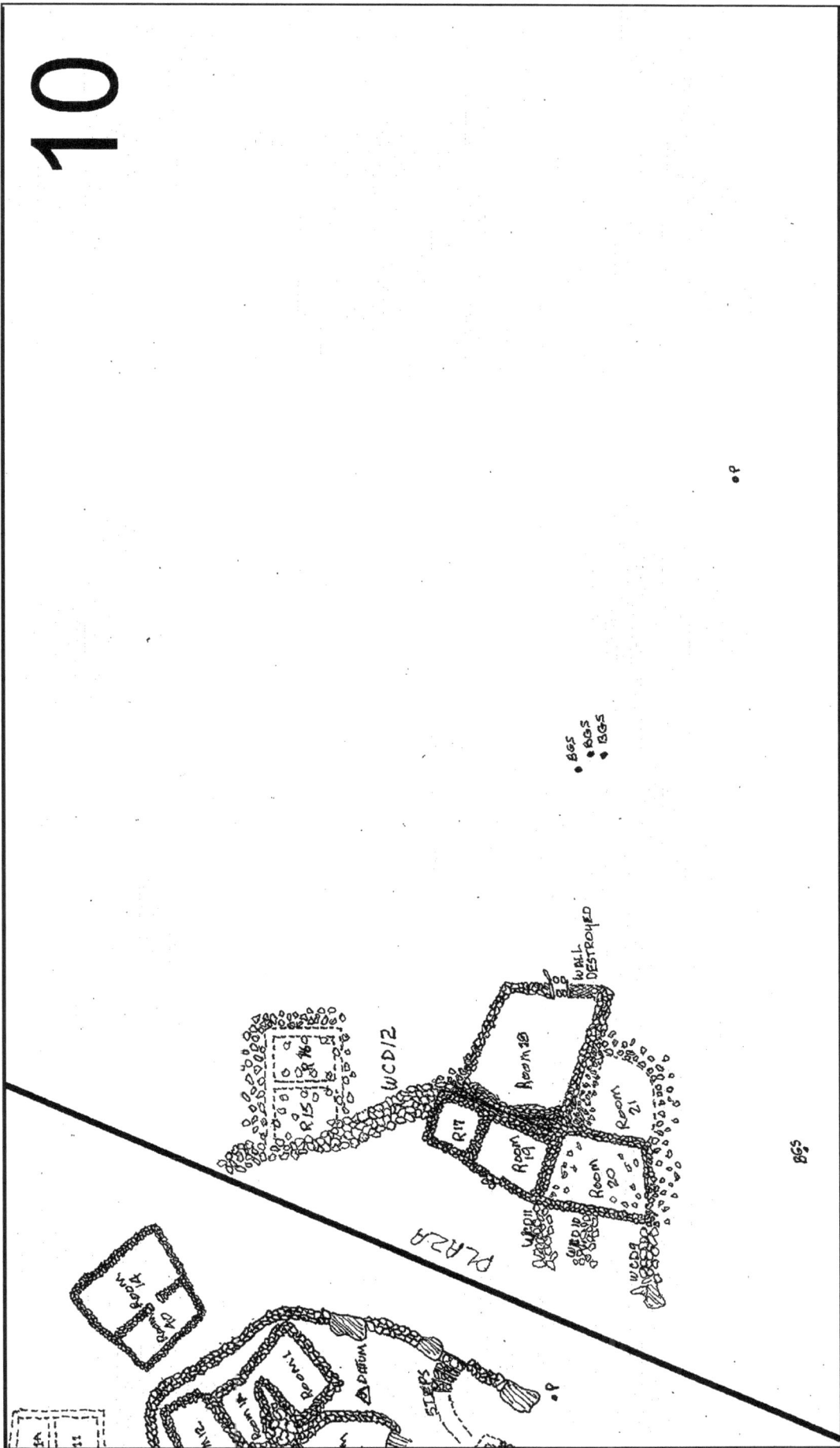

WCD/2

RISQUOR /16

RIT

Room 19

Room 18

WALL DESTROYED

Room 12

Room 20

WCD8

PLAZA

Room 14

TWOP

DATUM

STEPS

BGS

BGS

BGS

BGS

•P

•P

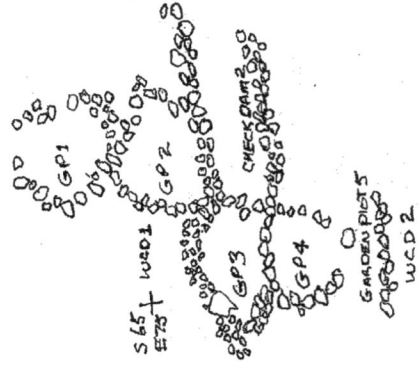

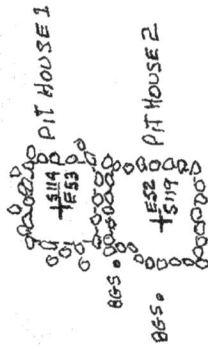

PIT HOUSE 1

S114
E53

PIT HOUSE 2

E52
S119

BGS

BGS

BGS

BGS ● ● BGS

● BGS

S140
E 50

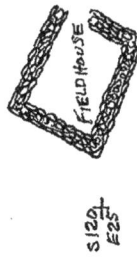

FIELD HOUSE

S120
E25

REFERENCES CITED

Adams, E. Charles
2002   *Homol'ovi: an Ancient Hopi Settlement Cluster.* University of Arizona Press, Tucson.

Adams, Karen R.
1994   Criteria for Identification of Archaeological Plant Specimens, Including Wood Charcoal. Appendix A in *The Roosevelt Rural Sites Study, Volume 3: Changing Land Use in the Tonto Basin,* edited by Richard Ciolek-Torrello and John R. Welch, pp. A-1–A.10. Technical Series No. 28. Statistical Research, Inc., Tucson.

Ahler, Stanley A.
1992   Use-phase Classification and Manufacturing Technology in Plains Village Arrowpoints. In *Piecing Together the Past: Applications of Refitting Studies in Archaeology,* edited by J. L. Hofman and J. G. Enloe, pp. 36-62. BAR International Series 578.

Ahlstrom, Richard V. N.
1985   The Interpretation of Archaeological Tree-ring Dates. Ph. D. dissertation, University of Arizona, Tucson.

Alger, Norman T.
1968   Perkins Pueblo and Tuzigoot - A Cultural Comparison of Two Pueblo IV Sites. Draft M. A. Thesis, Arizona State University, Tempe.

Ambler, J. Richard
1983   Northern Kayenta Ceramic Chronology. In *Archaeological Investigations in the Rainbow City Area, Navajo Mountain, Utah,* edited by P. R. Geib, J. R. Ambler, M. M. Callahan, and H. C. Fairley, pp. 24-66. Northern Arizona University Archaeological Report 576.

Anderson, Duane
1999   *All That Glitters: The Emergence of Native American Micaceous Art Pottery in Northern New Mexico.* SAR Press, Santa Fe.

Anderson, Keith M.
1992   *Tuzigoot Burials.* Western Archeological and Conservation Center, Publications in Anthropology 60.

Anduze, Richard A., Thomas N. Motsinger, and James M. Potter
2003   *Prehistory in West Prescott, Arizona.* Anthropological Research Paper No. 9. SWCA, Inc., Environmental Consultants, Phoenix.

Arnold, Dean E.
1985   *Ceramic Theory and Cultural Process.* Cambridge University Press, Cambridge.

Ascher, Robert
1968   Time's Arrow and the Archaeology of a Contemporary Community. In *Settlement Archaeology,* edited by K. C. Chang, pp. 43–52. National Press Books, Palo Alto.

Austin, Ken
2000   The Mountain Patayan People of West-Central Arizona. In *Archaeology in West-Central Arizona: Proceedings of the 1996 Arizona Archaeological Council Prescott Conference,* edited by T. N. Motsinger, D. R. Mitchell, and J. M. McKie, pp. 63-74. Sharlot Hall Museum Press, Prescott.

Bailey, Douglass W.
2005   *Prehistoric Figurines: Representation and Corporeality in the Neolithic.* Routledge, London.

Baker, William E. and T. N. Campbell
1959   Metal Projectile Points from the Oklahoma Panhandle and Vicinity. *Bulletin of the Oklahoma Anthropological Society* 7:51-54.

Bancroft, Hubert Howe
 1888   *The History of the Pacific States, vol. 12 - Arizona and New Mexico 1830-1888.* The History Co., San Francisco.

Barnett, Franklin
 1970   *Matli Ranch Ruins: A Report of Excavation of Five Small Prehistoric Indian Ruins of the Prescott Culture in Arizona.* Museum of Northern Arizona Technical Series No. 10.

 1973   *Lonesome Valley Ruin in Yavapai County, Arizona.* Museum of Northern Arizona Technical Series No. 13.

 1974   *Excavation of Main Pueblo at Fitzmaurice Ruin: Prescott Culture in Yavapai County, Arizona.* Museum of Northern Arizona Special Publication, Flagstaff.

 1975   *Excavation of a Lower Room at Fitzmaurice Ruin (NA 4031).* Yavapai College, Prescott.

 1978   *Las Vegas Ranch Ruin - East and Las Vegas Ranch Ruin - West: Two Small Prehistoric Indian Culture Ruins in West Central Arizona.* Museum of Northern Arizona Bulletin 51.

 1981   *These Were the Prehistoric Prescott Indians: A History of the Tenure of These Pioneers in Arizona.* Yavapai Chapter, Arizona Archaeological Society, Prescott.

Barth, C. Arthur and Joanne S. Cline
 1999   Shell Artifacts. In *The Sundown Site, NA16385: A Prescott Area Community*, pp. 89-92. The Arizona Archaeologist No. 30. Arizona Archaeological Society, Phoenix.

Bartlett, Katharine
 1939   A Prehistoric "Mine" of Red Argillite, Resembling Pipestone, near Del Rio, Arizona. *Museum Notes* 11(12): 75-78.

Benitez, Alexander V.
 1999   Refining 14th Century Jeddito Yellow Ware Chronology and Its Distribution in Central Arizona. M. A. Thesis, University of Texas, Austin.

Baty, Roger M.
 n.d.   Discussion and Interpretation of JC-AZ-2 Artifacts. MS on file, Smoki Museum, Prescott.

Beals, Ralph L., George W. Brainerd, and Watson Smith
 1945   *Archaeological Studies in Northeast Arizona: A Report on the Archaeological Work of the Rainbow Bridge-Monument Valley Expedition.* University of California Publications in American Archaeology and Ethnology 44(1).

Beck, Bob
 2005   Basket Impressed Pottery. In *Data Recovery at 22 Sites in the Stone Ridge Development, Prescott Valley, Yavapai County, Arizona,* edited by B. L. Leonard and C. K. Robinson, pp. 8.105-109. Soil Systems Publications in Archaeology No. 23.

Belden, George P.
 1870   *Belden, the White Chief, or Twelve Years Among the Wild Indians of the Plains.* C. F. Vent, Cincinnati.

Benson, Lyman
 1969   *The Cacti of Arizona,* 3d. ed. University of Arizona Press, Tucson.

Bequaert, Joseph C. and Walter B. Miller
 1973   *The Mollusks of the Arid Southwest, with an Arizona Check List.* University of Arizona Press. Tucson.

Blan, Linda M. (editor)
 2006   *Archaeological Investigations at Four Sites, YAV-22, 43, 74, and 75, within the Phase IV, Lease 200 Project Area on the Yavapai-Prescott Indian Tribe Reservation, Prescott, Yavapai County, Arizona.* Yavapai-Prescott Indian Tribe, Prescott.

Bohrer, Vorsila L.

1986 Guideposts in Ethnobotany. *Journal of Ethnobiology* 6(1):27–43.

1987 The Plant Remains from La Ciudad, a Hohokam Site in Phoenix. In *Specialized Studies in the Economy, Environment, and Culture of La Ciudad,* edited by Jo Ann E. Kisselburg, Glen E. Rice, and Brenda L. Shears, pp. 67–179. Anthropological Field Studies No. 20. Office of Cultural Resource Management, Department of Anthropology, Arizona State University, Tempe.

Bostwick, Todd W. and H. Young

2000 Four Prehistoric Copper Bells from the Prescott Region, Arizona. In *Archaeology in West-Central Arizona: Proceedings of the 1996 Arizona Archaeological Council Prescott Conference,* edited by T. N. Motsinger, D. R. Mitchell, and J. M. McKie, pp. 75-80. Sharlot Hall Museum Press, Prescott.

Braatz, Timothy

2003 *Surviving Conquest: A History of the Yavapai Peoples.* University of Nebraska Press, Lincoln.

Brand, Donald

1938 Aboriginal Trade Routes for Sea Shells in the Southwest. *Association of Pacific Coast Geographers Yearbook* 4:3-10.

Brennan, T.C. and A.T. Holycross

2006 *A field guide to amphibians and reptiles in Arizona.* Arizona Game and Fish Department. Phoenix.

Breternitz, David A.

1966 *An Appraisal of Tree-Ring-Dated Pottery in the Southwest.* Anthropological Papers of the University of Arizona, No. 10, University of Arizona Press, Tucson.

Brodhead, Michael J.

1973 Elliot Coues and the Apaches. *The Journal of Arizona History* 14:87-94.

Brown, David E.

1994 Great Basin Conifer Woodland. In *Biotic Communities: Southwestern United States and Northwestern Mexico*, edited by David E. Brown, pp. 52–57. University of Utah Press, Salt Lake City.

Brown, David E., and Charles H. Lowe

1994 *Biotic Communities of the Southwest* (map). University of Utah Press, Salt Lake City.

Brown, Marie E.

1994 Site 442-48: Faunal Assemblage. In *Across the Colorado Plateau: Anthropological Studies for the Transwestern Pipeline Expansion Project,* vol. XIII, pp. 198-207. OCA/Maxwell Museum, Albuquerque.

Bryant, Douglas D.

1982 Lithic Analysis of Projectile Points from Yerba Buena, Chiapas, Mexico. *Lithic Technology* 11:21-28.

Burgh, Robert F.

1959 Ceramic Profiles in the Western Mound at Awatovi, Northeastern Arizona. *American Antiquity* 25(2):184-202.

Cardew, Michael

1969 *Pioneer Pottery.* St. Martin's Press, New York.

Carrillo, Charles M.

1997 *Hispanic New Mexican Pottery: Evidence of Craft Specialization 1790-1890.* LPD Press, Albuquerque.

Castetter, Edward F.

1935 *Ethnobiological Studies in the American Southwest, I. Uncultivated Native Plants Used as Sources of Food.* The University of New Mexico Bulletin No. 266, Biological Series 4(1). University of New Mexico Press, Albuquerque.

Castetter, Edward F., Willis H. Bell, and Alvin R. Grove
1938 *Ethnobiological Studies in the American Southwest, VI. The Early Utilization and the Distribution of Agave in the American Southwest.* The University of New Mexico Bulletin No. 3355, Biological Series 5(4). University of New Mexico Press, Albuquerque.

Catlin, George
1844 *Letters and Notes on the Manners, Customs, and Conditions of the North American Indians.* London (1973 reprint by Dover Publications, New York).

Caywood, Louis R.
1936 Fitzmaurice Ruin. In *Two Pueblo Ruins in West Central Arizona,* by E. H. Spicer and L. R. Caywood, pp. 87-115. University of Arizona Bulletin, Social Science Bulletin No. 10.

Caywood, Louis R. and Edward H. Spicer
1935 *Tuzigoot: The Excavation and Repair of a Ruin on the Verde River near Clarkdale, Arizona.* National Park Service.

Chapman, John and Bisserka Gaydarska
2007 *Parts and Wholes: Fragmentation in Prehistoric Context.* Oxbow Books, Oxford.

Chenault, Mark L.
1993 Microartifact Recovery from Hohokam Floors. In *In the Shadow of South Mountain: The Pre-Classic Hohokam of La Ciudad de Los Hornos,* ed. by M. L. Chenault, R. V. N. Ahlstrom, and T. N. Motsinger, pp. 531-556. SWCA Archaeological Report No. 93-30.

2002 The Microarchaeology of Hohokam Floors. In *Culture and Environment in the American Southwest: Essays in Honor of Robert C. Euler,* ed. By D. A. Phillips, Jr. And J. A. Ware, pp. 89-112. SWCA Anthropological Research Paper No. 8.

Chenault, Mark L. and John D. Cater
1993 Looking for Flakes in All the Wrong Places: Testing Kiva Floors at Yellow Jacket. In *Why Museums Collect: Papers in Honor of Joe Ben Wheat,* ed. By M. S. Duran and D. T. Kirkpatrick, pp. 39-50. Archaeological Society of New Mexico Paper 19.

Christenson, Andrew L.
1986a Projectile Point Size and Projectile Aerodynamics: An Exploratory Study. *Plains Anthropologist* 31:109-128.

1986b Reconstructing Prehistoric Projectiles from Their Stone Points. *Journal of the Society of Archer Antiquaries* 29:21-27.

1987 Projectile Points: Eight Millennia of Projectile Change on the Colorado Plateau. In *Prehistoric Stone Technology on Northern Black Mesa, Arizona.* SIU-C Center for Archaeological Investigations Occasional Paper No. 12.

1993 Archaeological Testing at Five Sites in a Proposed Housing Subdivision (Dynamite Hill North) in Tuba City. CSWTA, Inc., Tuba City.

1994 A Test of Mean Ceramic Dating Using Well-dated Kayenta Anasazi Sites. *Kiva* 59:297-317.

1995 Non-Buffware Decorated Ceramics and Mean Ceramic Dating. In *Roosevelt Community Development Study, Volume 2: Ceramic Chronology, Technology, and Economics,* edited by James M. Heidke and Miriam T. Stark, pp. 85-132. Center for Desert Archaeology Anthropological Papers 14. Tucson.

1997a Mean Ceramic Dating of Several Prescott Area Sites. In *The Neural Site. NA 20788,* edited by Joanne E. Grossman, pp.69-75. Yavapai Chapter, Arizona Archaeological Society, Prescott.

1997b Neural Site (NA 20788) Chipped Stone. In *The Neural Site, NA 20788,* edited by J. E. Grossman. Yavapai Chapter, Arizona Archaeological Society, Prescott.

1997c Side-notched and Unnotched Arrowpoints: Assessing Functional Differences. In *Projectile Technology,* edited by Heidi Knecht, pp. 131-142. Plenum Press, New York.

1999 Ceramic Analysis: Technological Variation at the Groseta Ranch Road Site and Tuzigoot Ruin. In *Archaeological Investigations in the Vicinity of the Groseta Ranch Road Site (Sites AZ N:8:40 through AZ N:8:43[ASM]: Tuzigoot Phase Southern Sinagua Field House Localities in Northeastern Yavapai County, Arizona,* by S. M. Kwiatkowski, pp. 79-97. ARS Project Report 97:61.

2000 Petrographic Analysis of Sands, Self-tempered Clays, and Prehistoric Ceramics from the Prescott Area. In *Archaeology in West-Central Arizona: Proceedings of the 1996 Arizona Archaeological Council Prescott Conference,* edited by T. N. Motsinger, D. R. Mitchell, and J. M. McKie, pp. 155-163. Sharlot Hall Museum Press, Prescott.

2003 Petrographic Analysis of Sherd and Sand Samples. In *Prehistory in West Prescott, Arizona,* prepared by R. A. Anduze, T. N. Motsinger, and J. M. Potter, pp. 145-153. SWCA Anthropological Research Paper No. 9.

2005a Ceramic Artifacts. In *Data Recovery at 22 Sites in the StoneRidge Development, Prescott Valley, Yavapai County, Arizona,* pp. 8.1 to 8.995, edited by Banks L. Leonard and Christine K. Robinson. Soil Systems Publications in Archaeology No. 23. Phoenix.

2005b Description of the Fitzmaurice Ceramic Series. In *Data Recovery at 22 Sites in the StoneRidge Development, Prescott Valley, Yavapai County, Arizona,* edited by Banks L. Leonard and Christine K. Robinson, pp. 8.97 to 8.102. Soil Systems Publications in Archaeology No. 23. Phoenix.

2005c Petrographic Analysis. In *Data Recovery at 22 Sites in the StoneRidge Development, Prescott Valley, Yavapai County, Arizona,* edited by Banks L. Leonard and Christine K. Robinson, pp. 8.111-8.121. Soil Systems Publications in Archaeology No. 23. Phoenix.

2005d J. W. Simmons, Archaeologist of Central Arizona. In *Inscriptions: Papers in Honor of Richard and Nathalie Woodbury,* ed. by R. N. Wiseman et al. Archaeological Society of New Mexico 31, pp. 21-44.

2005e Petrographic Analysis of Pottery Presumed to Have Been Made by the Yavapai - Tizon Wiped and Orme Ranch Plain. MS in possession of the author.

2006a Petrographic Analysis of Sherds. In *Archaeological Investigations at Four Sites, YAV-22, 43, 74, and 75, within the Phase IV, Lease 200 Project Area on the Yavapai-Prescott Indian Tribe Reservation, Prescott, Yavapai County, Arizona,* edited by Linda M. Blan., pp. 58-66. Yavapai-Prescott Indian Tribe, Prescott.

2006b Observations on the Production of Prescott Black-on-gray. MS in possession of the author.

2007a Stone Artifacts from Pueblo Poniente. In *The Terrazona Archaeological Project: Investigations in a Portion of Pueblo Poniente, AZ T:11:164 (ASM), a Hohokam Site in Southwestern Phoenix, Maricopa County, Arizona,* by T. E. Wright et al., pp. 143-172. Pueblo Grande Museum Occasional Papers No. 8. Phoenix.

2007b Aesthetics of Prescott Black-on-gray Pottery. Paper given at Historic Preservation Partnership Conference, Prescott.

2008a Prescott Gray Ware from Upper Burro Creek, Yavapai, County, Arizona. In *Prescott to Perry Mesa: 4,000 Years of Adaptation, Innovation, and Change in Central Arizona,* edited by C. K. Robinson, C. D. Breternitz, and D. R. Mitchell, pp. 10.1-10.9. Sharlot Hall Museum Press, Prescott.

2008b King's Ruin Burials. In *Prescott to Perry Mesa: 4,000 Years of Adaptation, Innovation, and Change in Central Arizona,* edited by C. K. Robinson, C. D. Breternitz, and D. R. Mitchell, pp. 12.1-12.16. Sharlot Hall Museum Press, Prescott.

2008c Ceramic Analysis, T:4:308, 310, and 312. Report on Cahava Springs, PaleoWest, Phoenix.

2009 Lithic Analysis, YAV 34/35 and 82 (Connector Road). Draft report for Yavapai-Prescott Indian Tribe, Prescott.

2010 Lithic Analysis, YAV 77. Report for Yavapai-Prescott Indian Tribe, Prescott.

2012a Stone Artifact Analysis. In *Archaeological Excavations at the Northwestern Edge of La Plaza, a Hohokam Village Site in Tempe, Arizona,* ed. By Eric S. Cox and A.E. Rogge, pp. 9.1-9.49. URS Cultural Resources Report 2012-11(AZ). Phoenix.

2012b Two Traditions of Pottery Making in the Verde Valley. Paper presented at the Inaugural Biennial Verde Valley Archaeology Symposium, Camp Verde.

in prep. Ceramic Analysis. In West Side Road report, Yavapai-Prescott Indian Tribe, Prescott.

City of Prescott
2003 *Parks and Recreation Map.* Map posted on the Internet at www.cityofprescott.net.

Clark, John E.
1986 Another Look at Small Debitage and Microdebitage. *Lithic Technology* 15(1):21-33.

1991a Flintknapping and Debitage Disposal among the Lacandon Maya of Chiapas, Mexico. In *The Ethnoarchaeology of Refuse Disposal,* ed. By E. Staski and L. D. Sutro, pp. 63-78. Arizona State University Anthropological Research Papers No. 42.

1991b Modern Lacandon Lithic Technology and Blade Workshops. In *Maya Stone Tools: Selected Papers from the Second Maya Lithic Conference,* ed. By T. R. Hester and H. J. Shafer, pp. 251-265. Prehistory Press, Madison.

Cline, Joanne S.
1997 Faunal Analysis. In *The Neural Site: NA 20788,* by Robert E. Grossman, pp. 55-58. Yavapai Chapter, Arizona Archeological Society, Prescott.

Cline, Joanne S. and Earl Cline
1983 *The Storm Site, NA 13407: Excavation of Two Small Prescott Culture Ruins.* The Arizona Archeologist No. 18. Arizona Archeological Society, Phoenix.

Colton, Harold S.
1939 *Prehistoric Culture Units and Their Relationships in Northern Arizona.* Museum of Northern Arizona Bulletin No. 17.

1941a Prehistoric Trade in the Southwest. *Scientific Monthly* 52(4): 308-319.

1941b *Winona and Ridge Ruin, Part II, Notes on the Technology and Taxonomy of the Pottery.* Museum of Northern Arizona Bulletin No. 19, Flagstaff.

1949 The Prehistoric Population of the Flagstaff Area. *Plateau* 22(2):21-25.

1955 *Pottery Types of the Southwest, Wares 8A, 8B, 9A, 9B.* Museum of Northern Arizona Ceramic Series 3A, Flagstaff.

1956 *Pottery Types of the Southwest, Wares 5A, 5B, 6A, 6B, 7A, 7B, 7C.* Museum of Northern Arizona Ceramic Series 3C, Flagstaff.

1958 *Pottery Types of the Southwest, Wares 14, 15, 16, 17, 18.* Museum of Northern Arizona Ceramic Series 3D, Flagstaff.

Colton, Harold S. and Lyndon L. Hargrave
1937 *Handbook of Northern Arizona Pottery Wares.* Bulletin No. 11. Museum of Northern Arizona, Flagstaff.

Cordell, Linda S., David E. Doyel, and Keith W. Kintigh
1994 Processes of Aggregation in the Prehistoric Southwest. In *Themes in Southwest Prehistory,* edited by G. J. Gumerman, pp. 109-133. School of American Research Press, Santa Fe.

Cosner, Aaron J.
1951 Arrowshaft-straightening with a Grooved Stone. *American Antiquity* 17:147-148.

Crotty, Helen K.

1983   *Honoring the Dead: Anasazi Ceramics from the Rainbow Bridge-Monument Valley Expedition.* UCLA Museum of Cultural History Monograph Series No. 22.

Cummings, Linda Scott, and Kathryn Puseman

1995   Pollen and Macrofloral Analysis at Site AZ N:8:27 (ASM). In *Archaeological Investigations at Three Prehistoric Sites Along State Route 69 Between Mayer and Dewey, Yavapai County, Arizona,* edited by Douglas R. Mitchell, pp. 63–72. Archaeological Report No. 95-114. SWCA, Inc., Environmental Consultants, Phoenix.

Cummings, Linda Scott, Kathryn Puseman, and Thomas E. Moutox

2003   Pollen and Macrofloral Analyses. In *Prehistory in West Prescott, Arizona,* prepared by Richard A. Anduze, Thomas N. Motsinger, and James M. Potter, pp. 121–131. Anthropological Research Paper No. 9. SWCA, Inc., Environmental Consultants, Phoenix.

Cushing, Frank Hamilton

1920   *Zuni Breadstuff.* Indian Notes and Monographs vol. 8.

Dawe, Bob

1997   Tiny Arrowheads: Toys in the Toolkit. *Plains Anthropologist* 42:303-318.

DeBoer, Warren R.

1983   The Archaeological Record as Preserved Death Assemblage. In *Archaeological Hammers and Theories,* edited by J. A. Moore and A. S. Keene, pp. 19-36. Academic Press, New York.

DeLorme Mapping

1993   *Arizona Atlas and Gazetteer,* 1st ed. DeLorme Mapping, Freeport, Maine.

DeWitt, Ed, Victoria Langenheim, Eric Force, R. K. Vance, P. A. Lindberg, and R. L. Driscoll

2008   *Geological Map of the Prescott National Forest and the Headwaters of the Verde River, Yavapai and Coconino Counties, Arizona.* USGS Scientific Investigations Map 2996.

Doelle, William H., David A. Gregory, and Henry D. Wallace

1995   Classic Period Platform Mound Systems in Southern Arizona. In *The Roosevelt Community Development Study: New Perspectives on Tonto Basin Prehistory,* edited by M. D. Elson, M. T. Stark, and D. A. Gregory, pp. 385-440. Anthropological Papers No. 15, Center for Desert Archaeology.

Dohm, Karen

1990   Effect of Population Nucleation on House Size for Pueblos in the American Southwest. *Journal of Anthropological Archaeology* 9: 201-239.

Dosh, Steven G.

1987   Iron Springs Land Exchange Archaeological Testing Project, Yavapai County, Arizona. Museum of Northern Arizona, Flagstaff.

Douglas, Charles L., and Margaret Jean Whitman

1974   Analysis of Faunal Remains. In *Excavation of the Main Pueblo at Fitzmaurice Ruin: Prescott Culture in Yavapai County, Arizona,* by Franklin Barnett, pp. 46-49. Museum of Northern Arizona Special Publication. Flagstaff.

Douglass, Amy A.

1990   *Prehistoric Exchange and Sociopolitical Development in the Plateau Southwest.* Garland Publishing, Inc., New York.

Duering, Walter Thomas

1969   The Classic Period Hohokam with Reference to the Sinagua, Salado, and Prescott Branches. Appendix A - A Probable Prescott Branch Site on the Lower Agua Fria River. http://www.stockmorehouse.com/reports/hohokam/ch000_69.htm

Ellis, Christopher J.

1997   Factors Influencing the Use of Stone Projectile Tips: An Ethnographic Perspective. In *Projectile Technology,* edited by

H. Knecht, pp. 37-74. Plenum Press, New York.

Elson, Mark D. and James N. Gundersen
1992   The Mineralogy and Sourcing of Argillite Artifacts: A Preliminary Examination of Procurement, Production, and Distribution Systems. In *The Rye Creek Project: Archaeology in the Upper Tonto Basin, Vol. 2: Artifact and Specific Analyses,* edited by Mark D. Elson and Douglas B. Craig. pp. 429-462. Center for Desert Archaeology Anthropological Papers No. 11.

Euler, Robert C.
1958   *Walapai Culture History.* Unpublished Ph.D. dissertation, Department of Anthropology, University of New Mexico, Albuquerque.

1978   Comments. In *Proceedings of the 1973 Hohokam Conference,* edited by D. E. Weaver, Jr., S. S. Burton, and M. Laughlin, pp. 22. Center for Anthropological Studies, Contributions to Anthropological Studies No. 2. Albuquerque.

1982   Ceramic Patterns of the Hakataya Tradition. In *Southwestern Ceramics: A Comparative Review,* ed. by A. H. Schroeder, pp. 53-69. The Arizona Archaeologist No. 15. Arizona Archaeological Society, Phoenix.

Euler, Robert C. and Henry F. Dobyns
1962   Excavations West of Prescott, Arizona. *Plateau* 34:69-84.

Fewkes, J. W.
1896   Pacific Coast Shells from Prehistoric Tusayan Pueblos. *American Anthropologist* (old series) 9:359-367.

1912   Antiquities of the Upper Verde River and Walnut Creek Valleys, Arizona. In *Twenty-eighth Annual Report of the Bureau of American Ethnology, 1906-1907,* pp. 181-220. Government Printing Office, Washington, D.C.

1927   Archaeological Field-Work in Arizona. *Smithsonian Miscellaneous Collections* 78(7):207-232.

Fish, Paul R. and Godfrey Whiffen
1967   Arizona N:4:6 (ASU), The Excavation of an Early Pueblo III Site near Perkinsville, Arizona. MS on file, School of Human Evolution & Social Change, Arizona State University, Tempe.

Fladmark, K. R.
1982   Microdebitage Analysis: Initial Considerations. *Journal of Archaeological Science* 9: 205-220.

Flenniken, J. Jeffrey and Anan W. Raymond
1986   Morphological Projectile Point Typology: Replication Experimentation and Technological Analysis. *American Antiquity* 51:603-614.

Fontana, Bernard L.
1966   An Archaeological Survey of the Cabeza Prieta, Arizona. MS on file, Arizona State Museum Library and Archives, Tucson.

Fontana, Bernard L., William J. Robinson, Charles W. Cormack, and Ernest E. Leavitt, Jr.
1962   *Papago Indian Pottery.* University of Washington Press, Seattle.

Forde, C. Daryll
1931   Hopi Agriculture and Land Ownership. *Journal of the Royal Anthropological Institute* 61: 357-405.

Formby, D. E.
1986   Pinto-Gypsum Complex Projectile Points from Arizona and New Mexico. *The Kiva* 51:99-125.

Fowler, Don D. and John F. Matley
1979   *Material Culture of the Numa: The John Wesley Powell Collection, 1867-1880.* Smithsonian Contributions to Anthropology No. 26.

Frampton, Fred P.
1978   Analysis of Potsherds and Ceramic Wares. In *Las Vegas Ranch Ruin - East and Las Vegas Ranch Ruin - West: Two Small Prehistoric Indian Culture Ruins in West Central Arizona*, by F. Barnett, pp. 52-64. Museum of Northern Arizona Bulletin 51.

Franceschi, Vincent R., and Harry T. Horner, Jr.
1980   Calcium Oxalate Crystals in Plants. *The Botanical Review* 46(4):361–427.

Franklin, Hayward H.
1980   *Excavations at Second Canyon Ruin, San Pedro Valley, Arizona.* Arizona State Museum Contribution to Highway Salvage Archaeology in Arizona No. 60.

Gamble, Lynn H. and Chester D. King
2011   Beads and Ornaments from San Diego: Evidence for Exchange Networks in Southern California and the American Southwest. *Journal of California and Great Basin Anthropology* 31(2): 155-178.

Gasser, Robert E.
1977   The Relationship of Plant Ecology and Plant Remains to Prehistoric Subsistence in Copper Basin. Appendix B in *Archaeology in Copper Basin, Yavapai County, Arizona: Model Building for the Prehistory of the Prescott Region*, by Marvin D. Jeter, pp. 295–321. Anthropological Research Paper No. 11. Arizona State University, Department of Anthropology, Tempe.

Gifford, E. W.
1933   Northeastern and Western Yavapai Myths. *The Journal of American Folk-Lore* 46:347-415.

1936   *Northeastern and Western Yavapai.* University of California Publications in American Archaeology and Ethnology 34(4):247–354. University of California Press, Berkeley.

Gilbert, B. Miles
1980   *Mammalian Osteology.* Modern Printing Company, Laramie, Wyoming.

Gilbert, B. Miles, Larry D. Martin, Howard G. Savage
1996   *Avian Osteology.* Missouri Archeological Society, Columbia.

Gladwin, Winifred and Harold S.
1930   *The Western Range of the Red-on-Buff Culture.* Gila Pueblo Medallion Papers 5.

1934   *A Method for Designation of Cultures and Their Variations.* Medallion Papers No. 15. Gila Pueblo, Globe.

Gladwin, Harold S., Emil W. Haury, E. B. Sayles and Nora Gladwin
1937   *Excavations at Snaketown Material Culture.* Reprinted in 1965 for the Arizona State Museum by University of Arizona Press, Tucson.

Goodman, John
1998   Common Cartridge Case and Shotshell Base Headstamps. In Late Historic Artifacts Field Recording and Dating Guide. Complied for Workshop on Historic Artifact Identification, Arizona Archaeological Council, Phoenix, May 29.

Gould, Frank W.
1951   *Grasses of the Southwestern United States.* University of Arizona Press, Tucson.

Gratz, Kathleen and Donald C. Fiero (editors)
1974   Agua Fria - Verde River Brownware Conference. Museum of Northern Arizona, Flagstaff.

Grossman, Joanne E. (editor)
1997   *The Neural Site, NA 20788.* Yavapai Chapter, Arizona Archaeological Society, Prescott.

Grossman, Robert E.
2000   The Neural Site: A Late Prescott Area Site. In *Archaeology in West-Central Arizona: Proceedings of the 1996 Arizona Archaeological Council Prescott Conference,* edited by T. N. Motsinger, D. R. Mitchell, and J. M. McKie, pp. 81-89. Sharlot Hall Museum Press, Prescott.

Hackbarth, Mark R., E. Margaret MacMinn-Barton, and Robert J. Miller
1993   Osteological and Mortuary Analyses of the SCFAP Burials. In *Classic Period Occupation on the Santa Cruz Flats: The Santa Cruz Flats Archaeological Project,* edited by T. K. Henderson and R. J. Martynec, part II, pp. 541-577. Northland Research, Flagstaff.

Hanson, James Austin
1975   *Metal Weapons, Tools, and Ornaments of the Teton Dakota Indians.* University of Nebraska Press, Lincoln.

Hard, Robert J.
1990   Agricultural Dependence in the Mountain Mogollon. In *Perspectives on Southwestern Prehistory,* edited by P. E. Minnis and C. L. Redman, pp. 135-149. Westview Press, Boulder.

Hargrave, Lyndon L.
1970   *Mexican Macaws: Comparative Osteology and Survey of Remains from the Southwest.* Anthropological Papers of the University of Arizona No. 20.

1974   Identification of Bird Bones. In *Excavation of Main Pueblo at Fitzmaurice Ruin: Prescott Culture in Yavapai County, Arizona,* by Franklin Barnett, pp. 49-50. Museum of Northern Arizona Special Publication. Flagstaff

1978   Identification of Bird Bones. In *Las Vegas Ranch Ruin - East and Las Vegas Ranch Ruin – West: Two Small Prehistoric Prescott Indian Culture Ruins in West Central Arizona,* by Franklin Barnett, pp. 21-22. Museum of Northern Arizona Bulletin No. 51. Flagstaff.

Harper, Marshall Kevin
1998   Prescott Gray Ware: A Stylistic Approach. M. A. Thesis, Northern Arizona University, Flagstaff.

Haury, Emil W.
1976   *The Hohokam: Desert Farmers & Craftsmen.* University of Arizona Press. Tucson.

Hayden, Julian D.
1970   Of Hohokam Origins and Other Matters. *American Antiquity* 35: 87-93.

Hays-Gilpin, Kelley Ann and Mary-Ellen Walsh-Anduze
1997 Prescott Ceramic Conference Results. *Arizona Archaeological Council Newsletter* 21(1):2-3.

2001   *Ceramic Manual 2001: Prescott Gray Ware.*   http://jan.ucc.nau.edu/swpottery/PRESCOTT/PGW.htm   Northern Arizona University, Flagstaff.

Hevly, Richard H.
1978   Summary of Faunal Remains. In *Las Vegas Ranch Ruin – East and Las Vegas Ruin – West: Two Small Prehistoric Prescott Indian Culture Ruins in West Central Arizona,* By Franklin Barnett, p. 22, 76. Museum of Northern Arizona Bulleting No. 51. Flagstaff.

Higgins, Elizabeth S.
1997   Analysis of the Ceramic Collection. In *The Neural Site, NA 20788,* edited by Joanne Grossman, pp.19-53. Yavapai Chapter, Arizona Archaeological Society, Prescott.

1999a   Ceramics: Pottery. In *The Sundown Site, NA 16385: A Prescott Area Community,* pp. 25-54. The Arizona Archaeologist No. 30. Arizona Archaeological Society, Phoenix.

1999b   Human Burials: Feature Descriptions. In *The Sundown Site, NA 16385: A Prescott Area Community,* pp. 125-142. The Arizona Archaeologist No. 30. Arizona Archaeological Society, Phoenix.

2000   The Neural Site: A New Look at Prescott Tradition Ceramics in *Archaeology in West-Central Arizona: Proceedings of the 1996 Arizona Archaeological Council Prescott Conference,* edited by Thomas N. Motsinger, Douglas R. Mitchell, and James M. McKie, pp.165-176. Sharlot Hall Museum Press, Prescott.

2003   Artifact Analysis: Ceramics. In *Life and Death Along Willow Creek: AZ N:7:163 (ASM),* edited by Paul V. Long, Jr. and Linda M. Blan, pp. 39-51. YCAAS Occasional Paper Number 11, Yavapai Chapter, Arizona Archaeological Society, Prescott.

Hodgson, Wendy C. and Liz Slauson
1995   *Agave delamateri* (Agavaceae) and its Role in the Subsistence Patterns of the Pre-Columbian Cultures in Arizona. *Haseltonia* No. 3, pp. 130-140.

Hoffman, Charles M.
1997   Alliance Formation and Social Interaction during the Sedentary Period: A Stylistic Analysis of Hohokam Arrowpoints. Ph. D. dissertation, Arizona State University, Tempe.

Hoffmeister, Donald F.
1986   *Mammals of Arizona.* University of Arizona Press. Tucson.

Holloway, Richard G., and Gavin H. Archer
1999   Botanical Analysis. In *Archaeological Investigations Along Pioneer Parkway, Yavapai County, Arizona,* by Gavin H. Archer, Andrew L. Christenson, Dawn M. Greenwald, and Richard G. Holloway, pp. 74–93. Cultural Resource Report No. 99-76. SWCA, Inc., Environmental Consultants, Tucson.

Horton, Sarah L.
1994   Excavation of Lynx Creek Ruin: A Study of Architectural Differentiation. M. A. Thesis, Northern Arizona University, Flagstaff.

Horton, Sarah and Noel Logan
1993   Testing Excavations at Three Sites for Lynx Creek Ranch Estates, Prescott Valley, Arizona. Southwest Environmental Consultants, Sedona.

Howard, Ann Valdo
1993   Marine Shell Artifacts and Production Processes At Shelltown And the Hind Site. In *Shelltown And The Hind Site A Study of Two Hohokam Craftsman Communities In Southeastern Arizona, V*ol. 1., edited by William S. Marmaduke and Richard J. Martynec, pp. 321-448. Northland Research, Inc. Flagstaff.

Howell, David H.
1940   Pipestone and Red Shale Artifacts. *American Antiquity* 6(1):45-62.

Huckell, Bruce B.
1982   *The Distribution of Fluted Points in Arizona: A Review and an Update.* Arizona State Museum Archaeological Series 145. Tucson.

Huckell, Lisa W.
2005   Macrobotanical Remains. In *Data Recovery at 22 Sites in the StoneRidge Development, Prescott Valley, Yavapai County, Arizona,* edited by Banks L. Leonard and Christine K. Robinson, pp. 11.1–11.97. Publications in Archaeology No. 23. Soil Systems, Inc., Phoenix.

Hull, Kathleen L.
1987   Identification of Cultural Site Formation Processes Through Microdebitage Analysis. *American Antiquity* 52:772-783.

Jackson, A. T.
1943   Indian Arrow and Lance Wounds. *Bulletin of the Texas Archeological Society* 15:38-65.

James, Edwin
    1823   *Account of an Expedition from Pittsburgh to the Rocky Mountains, Performed in the Years 1819, 1820.* Longman, Hurst, Rees, Orme, and Brown, London.

James, George W.
    1908 (1972)   *Indian Basketry.* Dover Publications, New York.

James, Kathleen G.
    1974   Analysis of Potsherds and Ceramic Wares, in *Excavation of the Main Pueblo at Fitzmaurice Ruin,* by Franklin Barnett, pp 106-129, Museum of Northern Arizona Special Publication, Flagstaff.

James, Steven R.
    2003   Hunting and Fishing Patterns Leading to Resource Depletion. In *Centuries of Decline during the Hohokam Classic Period at Pueblo Grande,* edited by D. R. Abbott, pp. 70-81. University of Arizona Press, Tucson.

Jeter, Marvin D.
    1977   *Archaeology in Copper Basin, Yavapai County, Arizona: Model Building for the Prehistory of the Prescott Region.* Anthropological Research Paper No. 11. Arizona State University, Department of Anthropology, Tempe.

Johnson, Ginger
    1995   *A View of Prehistory in the Prescott Region.* Author, Prescott.

    1996   *The Bonnie Site, NA 15810.* Yavapai Chapter, Arizona Archaeological Society, Prescott.

    1998   *Stricklin Forest Park Site, AZ:N:7:63 - NA 25778.* Yavapai Chapter, Arizona Archaeological Society, Prescott.

Johnson, Paul C.
    1980   An Analysis of Animal Remains from Alder Wash Ruin (AZ BB:6:9) and the Dos Bisnagas Site (AZ BB:6:6). In *The Peppersauce Wash Project* by W. Bruce Masse. MS on file, Arizona State Museum Library and Archives, University of Arizona, Tucson.

Jones, Volney H.
    1945   Plant Materials. In *Archaeological Studies in Northeast Arizona,* by R. L. Beals, G. W. Brainerd, and W. Smith, pp. 159-163. University of California Publications in American Archaeology and Ethnology 44 (1).

Justice, Noel D.
    2002   *Stone Age Spear and Arrow Points of the Southwestern United States.* Indiana University Press, Bloomington.

Kamp, Kathryn A. and John C. Whittaker
    1999   *Surviving Adversity: The Sinagua of Lizard Man Village.* University of Utah Anthropological Papers No. 120.

Kamp, Kathryn A., Nichole Timmerman, Gregg Lind, Jules Greybill, and Ian Natowsky
    1999   Discovering Childhood: Using Fingerprints to Find Children in the Archaeological Record. *American Antiquity* 64:309-315.

Kearney, Thomas H., and Robert H. Peebles
    1960   *Arizona Flora*, 2d. ed. University of California Press, Berkeley.

Keeley, Lawrence H.
    1996   *War before Civilization: The Myth of the Peaceful Savage.* Oxford University Press, New York.

Keen, A. Myra
    1984   *Sea Shells of Tropical West America. Marine Mollusks From Baja California to Peru.* Stanford University Press. Stanford.

Keepax, Carole A.
1977 Contamination of Archaeological Deposits by Seeds of Modern Origin with Particular Reference to the Use of Flotation Machines. *Journal of Archaeological Science* 4:221–229.

Khera, Sigrid and Patricia S. Mariella
1983 Yavapai. In *Handbook of North American Indians, Volume 10 - Southwest,* edited by A. Ortiz, pp. 38-54. Smithsonian Institution, Washington.

Kelly, Isabel
1978 *The Hodges Ruin a Hohokam Community in the Tucson Basin.* Anthropological Papers of the University of Arizona Number 30. University of Arizona Press. Tucson.

Kohler, Timothy A.
1989 Introduction. In *Bandelier Archaeological Excavation Project: Research Design and Summer 1988 Sampling,* edited by T. A. Kohler, pp. 1-12. WSU Department of Anthropology Reports of Investigations 61.

Kojo, Yasushi
1991 Rethinking Methods and Paradigms of Ceramic Chronology. Ph. D. dissertation, University of Arizona, Tucson.

Krieger, Medora H.
1965 *Geology of the Prescott and Paulden Quadrangles, Arizona.* USGS Professional Paper 467.

Kroeber, Alfred L.
1925 *Handbook of the Indians of California.* Bureau of American Ethnology Bulletin 78.

1939 *Cultural and Natural Areas of Native North America.* University of California Publications in American Archaeology and Ethnology Vol. 38.

Kwiatkowski, Scott M.
2004 The Prehistory of Central and West-Central Arizona: A View from the Yavapai-Prescott Indian Tribe. Paper presented at the Arizona Archaeological Council fall meeting, Tucson.

Lally, Joe and A. J. Vonarx
2011 Fire: Accidental or Intentional? An Archaeological Toolkit for Evaluating Accident and Intent in Ancient Structural Fires. In *Contemporary Archaeologies of the Southwest,* edited by W. H. Walker and K. R. Venzor, pp. 157-171. University Press of Colorado, Boulder.

Lambert, Ruth E.
1998 Ceramic Wares and Types: Assessing H. S. Colton's Ceramic Concepts. In *Unit Issues in Archaeology: Measuring Time, Space, and Material,* edited by A. F. Ramenofsky and A. Steffen, pp. 147-162. University of Utah Press, Salt Lake City.

Latta, Frank F.
1949 *Handbook of Yokuts Indians.* Kern County Museum, Bakersfield.

Laylander, Don
2006 The Regional Consequences of Lake Cahuilla. *San Diego State University Occasional Archaeological Papers* 1:59-77.

LeBlanc, Steven A.
1999 *Prehistoric Warfare in the American Southwest.* University of Utah Press, Salt Lake City.

Lehr, J. Harry
1978 *A Catalogue of the Flora of Arizona.* Desert Botanical Garden, Phoenix.

Leonard, Banks L.
2005 Conclusions and Application of the Research Design. In *Data Recovery at 22 Sites in the StoneRidge Development, Prescott Valley, Yavapai County, Arizona,* Vol. 3, edited by Banks L. Leonard and Christine K. Robinson, pp. 15.1-15.81. Soil Systems Publications in Archaeology No. 23. Phoenix.

Leonard, Banks L. and Cory D. Breternitz
2005   Other Treatment and Preservation Issues. In *Data Recovery at 22 Sites in the StoneRidge Development, Prescott Valley, Yavapai County, Arizona,* Vol. 3, edited by Banks L. Leonard and Christine K. Robinson, pp. 14.1-14.19. Soil Systems Publications in Archaeology No. 23. Phoenix.

Leonard, Banks L., and Christine K. Robinson
2005   *Data Recovery at 22 Sites in the StoneRidge Development, Prescott Valley, Yavapai County, Arizona,* edited by Banks L. Leonard and Christine K. Robinson. Soil Systems Publications in Archaeology No. 23. Phoenix.

Lightfoot, Kent G.
1979   Food Redistribution among Prehistoric Pueblo Groups. *The Kiva* 44: 319-339.

Lindsay, Alexander J., Jr.
1969   The Tsegi Phase of the Kayenta Cultural Tradition in Northeastern Arizona. Ph. D. dissertation, University of Arizona, Tucson.

Linford, Laurence D.
1979   *Archaeological Investigations in West-Central Arizona: The Cyprus-Bagdad Project.* Arizona State Museum Archaeological Series 136. Tucson.

Lockett, Hattie G.
1933   *The Unwritten Literature of the Hopi.* University of Arizona Social Science Bulletin 2. Tucson.

Logan, Noel and Sarah Horton
1994   Archaeological Excavations at the Campground Site, AR-03-09-03-276, Granite Basin, Prescott National Forest. Southwestern Environmental Consultants, Sedona.

Long, Paul V., Jr., Faye T. Long, and Linda M. Blan
2008   *The Piñon Oaks Site Complex: Data Recovery at Six Prescott Culture Sites, Prescott, Arizona.* MARS Research Paper No. 1.

Mabry, Jonathan B.
2005   Diversity in Early Southwestern Farming and Optimization Models of Transitions to Agriculture. In *Subsistence and Resource Use Strategies of Early Agricultural Communities in Southern Arizona,* edited by Michael W. Diehl, 113-152. Anthropological Papers No. 34. Center for Desert Archaeology, Tucson.

MacDonald, Douglas H. and Barry S. Hewlett
1999   Reproductive Interests and Forager Mobility. *Current Anthropology* 40:501-523.

Macnider, Barbara S., Richard W. Effland, Jr., and George Ford
1989   *Cultural Resources Overview: The Prescott National Forest.* Archaeological Consulting Services Cultural Resources Report No. 50.

Madsen, John H.
1999   A Del Rio Argillite Pipe from the Marana Platform Mound. In *The Sundown Site, NA16385: A Prescott Area Community,* pp. 209-211. The Arizona Archaeologist 30. Arizona Archaeological Society, Phoenix.

Mallery, Garrick
1881   Sign Language among the North American Indians. In *First Annual Report of the Bureau of Ethnology,* pp. 263-552. Government Printing Office, Washington.

Martin, Alexander C., and William D. Barkley
1961   *Seed Identification Manual.* University of California Press, Berkeley.

Martin, John F.

1973   On the Estimation of the Sizes of Local Groups in a Hunting-Gathering Environment. *American Anthropologist* 75:1448-1468.

Matthews, W., C. A. I. French, T. Lawrence, D. F. Cutler, and M. K. Jones

1997   Microstratigraphic Traces of Site Formation Processes and Human Activities. *World Archaeology* 29:281-308.

Mauseth, James D.

1988   *Plant Anatomy*. The Benjamin/Cummings Publishing Company, Menlo Park.

McGregor, John C.

1943   Burial of an Early American Magician. *Proceedings of the American Philosophical Society* 86(2):270-298.

McKie, James M.

2000   A Brief Look at "Prescott Tradition" Site Variation and Settlement in Ponderosa Pine Habitats of the Upper Hassayampa River Area. In *Archaeology in West-Central Arizona: Proceedings of the 1996 Arizona Archaeological Council Prescott Conference,* edited by T. N. Motsinger, D. R. Mitchell, and J. M. McKie, pp. 111-117. Sharlot Hall Museum Press, Prescott.

McKusick, Charmion R.

2001   *Southwest Birds of Sacrifice*. The Arizona Archaeologist No. 31. Arizona Archaeological Society, Phoenix.

McOmie, A. M.

1918   *Dry-farming in Arizona*. University of Arizona, College of Agriculture, Agricultural Experiment Station Bulletin 84. Tucson.

Medicine Crow, Joe

1978   Notes on Crow Indian Buffalo Jump Traditions. *Plains Anthropologist* 14:249-253.

Michelsen, Ralph C.

1967   Pecked Metates of Baja California. *Masterkey* 41:73-77.

Miksicek, Charles H.

1986   Plant Remains from the Tanque Verde Wash Site. In *Archaeological Investigations at the Tanque Verde Wash Site: A Middle Rincon Settlement in the Eastern Tucson Basin*, by Mark D. Elson, pp. 371–394. Anthropological Papers No. 7. Institute for American Research, Tucson.

Minnis, Paul E.

1981   Seeds in Archaeological Sites: Sources and Some Interpretive Problems. *American Antiquity* 46(1):143–152.

1987   Identification of Wood from Archaeological Sites in the American Southwest. I. Keys for Gymnosperms. *Journal of Archaeological Science* 14:121–131.

Mitchell, Douglas R. and Tom Motsinger

2010   *Archaeological Investigations at Willow Lake Ruin, Prescott, Arizona*. PaleoWest Technical Report No. 08-21.

Montero, Laurene G.

1993   The Chipped Stone Assemblage from the Santa Cruz Flats. In *Classic Period Occupation on the Santa Cruz Flats: The Santa Cruz Flats Archaeological Project,* edited by T. K. Henderson and R. J. Martynec, vol. II, pp. 313-362. Northland Research, Flagstaff.

Montgomery, Barbara Klie

1993   Ceramic Analysis as a Tool for Discovering Processes of Pueblo Abandonment. In *Abandonment of Settlements and Regions; Ethnoarchaeological and Archaeological Approaches,* edited by C. M. Cameron and S. A. Tomka, pp. 157-164. Cambridge University Press, Cambridge.

Morris, Percy A.
1966   *A Field Guide To Shells Of the Pacific Coast And Hawaii, Including Shells of the Gulf of California.* Houghton Mifflin Company. Boston

Motsinger, Thomas N.
2000   Ceramic Figurines at the Hassayampa Ruin and Simmons' "Groom Creek Effigy Culture." In *Archaeology in West-Central Arizona: Proceedings of the 1996 Arizona Archaeological Council Prescott Conference,* edited by T. N. Motsinger, D. R. Mitchell, and J. M. McKie, pp. 145-154. Sharlot Hall Museum Press, Prescott.

Motsinger, Thomas N., Douglas R. Mitchell, and James M. McKie
2000   A Prescott Primer: Introduction to the Archaeology and the Conference. In *Archaeology in West-Central Arizona: Proceedings of the 1996 Arizona Archaeological Council Prescott Conference,* edited by T. N. Motsinger, D. R. Mitchell, and J. M. McKie, pp. 1-11. Sharlot Hall Museum Press, Prescott.

Mueller, James W. and Daniel Schecter
1970   Analysis of Ceramic Wares. In *Matli Ranch Ruins: A Report of Excavation of Five Small Prehistoric Indian Ruins of the Prescott Culture in Arizona,* by Franklin Barnett, pp. 80-89. Museum of Northern Arizona Technical Series No. 10.

Munson, Patrick J., Paul W. Parmalee, and Richard A. Yarnell
1971   Subsistence Ecology of Scovill, a Terminal Middle Woodland Site. *American Antiquity* 36(4):410–431.

Murray, Priscilla
1980   Discard Location: The Ethnographic Data. *American Antiquity* 45:490-502.

Nabokov, Peter
1981   *Indian Running: Native American History & Tradition.* Ancient City Press, Santa Fe.

Neily, Robert B. (editor)
2006   *The Willow Lake Site: Archaeological Investigations in Willow & Watson Lakes Park, Prescott, Arizona.* Logan Simpson Design Technical Reports in Prehistory No. 1.

Nelson, Ben A., Timothy A. Kohler and Keith W. Kintigh
1994   Demographic Alternatives: Consequences for Current Models of Southwestern Prehistory. In *Understanding Complexity in the Prehistoric Southwest,* edited by G. J. Gumerman and M. Gell-Mann, pp. 113--146. Addison-Wesley, Reading, Massachusetts.

Nelson, Margaret C.
1986   Chipped Stone Analysis: Food Selection and Hunting Behavior. In *Short-Term Sedentism in the American Southwest: The Mimbres Valley Salado,* by B. A. Nelson and S. A. LeBlanc, pp, 141-176. University of New Mexico Press, Albuquerque.

Nelson, Richard S.
1991   *Hohokam Marine Shell Exchange and Artifacts.* Arizona State Museum Archaeological Series 179. Tucson.

Neusius, S. W. and C. J. Phagan
1983   Patterns of Large and Small Game Procurement among the Dolores Anasazi: A. D. 600-950. Paper presented at the Second Anasazi Symposium, Farmington.

North, Chris
2008   The Prescott Frontier: Sociopolitical Organization in the Prescott Culture Area of West-Central Arizona. In *Prescott to Perry Mesa: 4,000 Years of Adaptation, Innovation, and Change in Central Arizona,* edited by C. K. Robinson, C. D. Breternitz, and D. R. Mitchell, pp. 13.1-13.12. Sharlot Hall Museum Press, Prescott.

Nuzhnyi, Dmitri
1990   Projectile Damage on Upper Paleolithic Microliths and the Use of Bow and Arrow Among Pleistocene Hunters in the Ukraine. In *The Interpretative Possibilities of Microwear Studies,* edited by B. Graslund, pp. 113-124. Aun 14, Uppsala.

Odell, George H. and Frank Cowan
1986   Experiments with Spears and Arrows on Animal Targets. *Journal of Field Archaeology* 13:195-212.

Olsen, Stanley J.,
1964   Mammal Remains from Archeological Sites, Part 1 – Southeastern and Southwestern United States. Papers of the Peabody Museum of American Archaeology and Ethnology 56(1). Cambridge, Massachusetts.

Ozbal, Rana
2000   Microartifact Analysis: Tell Kurku Excavations: Preliminary Report. *Anatolica* 26:49-55.

Parker, Kittie F.
1972   *An Illustrated Guide to Arizona Weeds.* University of Arizona Press, Tucson.

Pase, Charles P., and David E. Brown
1994a Rocky Mountain (Petran) and Madrean Montane Conifer Forests. In *Biotic Communities: Southwestern United States and Northwestern Mexico,* edited by David E. Brown, pp. 43–48. University of Utah Press, Salt Lake City.

1994b Interior Chaparral. In *Biotic Communities: Southwestern United States and Northwestern Mexico,* edited by David E. Brown, pp. 95–99. University of Utah Press, Salt Lake City.

Peterson, Jane D.
1994   Chipped Stone. In *The Pueblo Grande Project, vol. 4: Material Culture,* edited by M. S. Foster, 49-118. Soil Systems Publications in Archaeology No. 20.

Peterson, Roger Tory and Edward L. Chalif
1973   *A Field Guide to Mexican Birds.* Houghton Mifflin Company, Boston, Massachusetts.

Phillips, Bruce G.
1998   Botanical Analyses. In *Life Along Big Bug Creek in the Early Years: The SR 69 Cordes Junction to Mayer Archaeological Project,* compiled by Walter R. Punzmann, Margerie Green, Lourdes Aguila, and Amy Phillips, pp. 343–360. Cultural Resource Report No. 105. Archaeological Consulting Services, Ltd., Tempe.

Pilles, Peter J., Jr.
1996   The Pueblo III Period along the Mogolllon Rim: The Honanki, Elden, and Turkey Hill Phases of the Sinagua. In *The Prehistoric Pueblo World, A. D. 1150-1350,* edited by M. A. Adler, pp. 59-72. University of Arizona Press, Tucson.

Pilles, Peter J., Jr. and James McKie
1998   Conquest, Replacement, or Transition? - The Prehistoric and Protohistoric Period Yavapai in Central Arizona. Paper presented at the conference "The Transition from Prehistory to History in the Southwest," Albuquerque.

Plog, Fred
1975   Demographic Studies in Southwestern Prehistory. In *Population Studies in Archaeology and Biological Anthropology: A Symposium,* edited by Alan C. Swedlund, pp. 94-103. Society for American Archaeology Memoir 30.

Punzmann, Walter R., Margerie Green, Lourdes Aguila, and Amy Phillips, compilers
1998   *Life Along Big Bug Creek in the Early Years: The SR 69 Cordes Junction to Mayer Archaeological Project.* Cultural Resource Report No. 105. Archaeological Consulting Services, Ltd., Tempe.

Purcell, David E.
2010   Three Sides to a Ceramic Tradition: The View from Big Black Mesa. Paper presented at the Pecos Conference, Silverton, Colorado.

Pyszczyk, Heinz
1999   Historic Period Metal Projectile Points and Arrows, Alberta, Canada: A Theory for Aboriginal Arrow Design on the Great Plains. *Plains Anthropologist* 44:163-187.

Rau, Charles
1876   *The Archaeological Collections of the U. S. National Museum in Charge of the Smithsonian.* Smithsonian Contributions to Knowledge 287, vol. 11(4).

Raup, James W.
1976   Some Experiments with Replica Projectile Points used as Arrow Points. *The APE: Experimental Archaeology Papers* 4:281-303.

Rea, Amadeo M.
1978   Identification of Bird Bone. In *Las Vegas Ranch Ruin – East and Las Vegas Ruin – West: Two Small Prehistoric Prescott Indian Culture Ruins in West Central Arizona,* by Franklin Barnett, p. 76. Museum of Northern Arizona Bulleting No. 51. Flagstaff.

1981   Resource Utilization and Food Taboos of Sonoran Desert Peoples. *Journal of Ethnobiology* 1(1):69-83.

1998   *Folk Mammology of the Northern Pimas.* University of Arizona Press, Tucson.

Reid, J. J.
1973   Growth and Response to Stress at Grasshopper Pueblo, Arizona. Ph.D. dissertation, University of Arizona, Tucson.

Rodgers, James B. and Donald E. Weaver, Jr.
1990   Preliminary Testing Report and Data Recovery Research Plan for Six Archaeological Sites along State Route 69 Near Dewey in Yavapai County, Arizona. Plateau Mountain Desert Research, Flagstaff.

Rogers, Malcolm J.
1928   Remarks on the Archaeology of the Gila River Drainage. *Arizona Museum Journal* 1(1):21-24.

Rose, Martin R.
1994   Long Term Drought Reconstructions for the Lake Roosevelt Region. In *The Roosevelt Rural Sites Study, Volume 3: Changing Land Use in the Tonto Basin,* edited by R. Ciolek-Torrello and J. R. Welch, pp. 311-359. Statistical Research Technical Series No. 28.

Rosen, Arlene Miller
1986   *Cities of Clay: The Geoarchaeology of Tells.* University of Chicago Press, Chicago.

1989   Ancient Town and City Sites: A View from the Microscope. *American Antiquity* 54: 564-578.

Rosenthal, E. Jane, Douglas R. Brown, Marc Severson, and Roberta M. Hagaman
1978   *The Quijotoa Valley Project.* Cultural Resources Management Division Western Archeological Center, National Park Service, Tucson.

Rye, Owen S.
1981   *Pottery Technology: Principles and Reconstruction.* Taraxacum, Washington.

Schroeder, Albert H.
1953   Notched Stones in Southwestern Sites. *American Antiquity* 19: 158-160.

1975   *The Hohokam, Sinagua, and the Hakataya.* IVCMS Occasional Paper no. 3.

Seeman, Mark F.
1985   Craft Specialization and Tool Kit Structure: A Systemic Perspective on the Midcontinental Flint Knapper. In *Lithic Resource Procurement: Proceedings from the Second Conference on Prehistoric Chert Exploitation,* edited by S. C. Vehik, pp. 7-36. Southern Illinois University, Center for Archaeological Investigations, Occasional Paper 4. Carbondale.

Seymour, Gregory R.
1997   A Reevaluation of Lower Colorado Buff Ware Ceramics: Redefining the Patayan in Southern Nevada. M. A. Thesis, University of Nevada, Las Vegas.

Shackley, M. Steven
2005   *Obsidian: Geology ands Archaeology in the North American Southwest.* University of Arizona Press, Tucson.

Shafer, Harry J.
2003   *Mimbres Archaeology at the NAN Ranch Ruin.* University of New Mexico Press, Albuquerque.

2006   Extended Families to Corporate Groups: Pithouse to Pueblo Transformation of Mimbres Society. In *Mimbres Society,* edited by V. S. Powell-Marti and P. A. Gilman, 15-31. University of Arizona Press, Tucson.

Shepard, Anna O.
1956   *Ceramics for the Archaeologist.* Carnegie Institution of Washington Publication 609.

Sherwood, Sarah C.
2001   Microartifacts. In *Earth Sciences and Archaeology,* edited by P. Goldberg, V. T. Holliday, and C. R. Ferring, pp. 327-351. Kluwer Academic/Plenum Publishers, New York.

Shott, Michael J.
1997   Stones and Shafts Redux: The Metric Discrimination of Chipped-Stone Dart and Arrow Points. *American Antiquity* 62:86-101.

Sibley, David Allen,
2003   *The Sibley Field Guide to Birds of Western North America.* Alfred A. Knopf, Inc., New York.

Simmons, J. W.
n.d. a   An Introduction to the Williamson Valley Series. MS on file, Arizona State Museum Library and Archives, A-20. Tucson.

n.d. b   The Yavapai Culture (Yavapai County Arizona). MS on file, Arizona State Museum Library and Archives A-50. Tucson.

n.d. c   Jerome:8:6, Old Coyote Ruin. MS on file, Arizona State Museum Library and Archives A-31, pp. 130-142. Tucson.

1931   The Black on Grey Culture of Western Yavapai County. *Yavapai Magazine* 21(10): 12-13, 16.

1937   Lonesome Valley Ruins. Prepared for Arizona WPA Writers' Project. MS on file, Arizona State Musum Archives, A-36. Tucson.

Simonis, Donald E.
2000   Western Prescott and Cohonina Traditions. In *Archaeology in West-Central Arizona: Proceedings of the 1996 Arizona Archaeological Council Prescott Conference,* edited by T. N. Motsinger, D. R. Mitchell, and J. M. McKie, pp. 195-203. Sharlot Hall Museum Press, Prescott.

Small, Laura Ann
2010   Spatial Distribution of Prescott Gray Ware. M. A. Thesis, Northern Arizona University, Flagstaff.

Smith, Marion F., Jr.
1985   Toward an Economic Interpretation of Ceramics: Relating Vessel Size and Shape to Use. In *Decoding Prehistoric Ceramics,* edited by Ben A. Nelson, pp. 254-309. Southern Illinois University Press, Carbondale.

South, Stanley
1972   Evolution and Horizon as Revealed in Ceramic Analysis in Historical Archaeology. *The Conference on Historic Site Archaeology Papers 6(2):71-116* (reprinted in *Method and Theory in Historical Archaeology*, by Stanley South, pp.201-235. Academic Press. New York.)

1977   Archaeological Pattern Recognition: An Example from the British Colonial System. In *Conservation Archaeology,* edited by M. B. Schiffer and G. J. Gumerman, pp. 427-477. Academic Press, New York.

Spicer, Edward H.
1936 King's Ruin. In *Two Pueblo Ruins in West Central Arizona,* by E. H. Spicer and L. R. Caywood, pp. 5-85. University of Arizona Bulletin, Social Science Bulletin No. 10.

Stephen, Alexander M.
1936 *Hopi Indian Journal.* Columbia Contribution to Anthropology 23.

Stevanović, Mirjana
1997 The Age of Clay: The Social Dynamics of House Destruction. *Journal of Anthropological Archaeology* 16: 334-395.

Stockel, H. Henrietta
1995 *The Lightning Stick: Arrows, Wounds, and Indian Legends.* University of Nevada Press, Reno.

Taylor, Alison
2008 Aspects of Deviant Burial in Roman Britain. In *Deviant Burial in the Archaeological Record,* edited by Eileen M. Murphy, pp. 91-114. Oxbow Books, Oxford.

Teague, Lynn S.
1998 *Textiles in Southwestern Prehistory.* University of New Mexico Press, Albuquerque.

Thomas, David Hurst
1978 Arrowheads and Atlatl Darts: How the Stones Got the Shaft. *American Antiquity* 43:461-472

Thorpe, Richard and Geoff Brown
1985 *The Field Description of Igneous Rocks.* Open University Press, Buckingham.

Tower, D. B.
1945 *The Use of Marine Mollusca and Their Value in Reconstructing Prehistoric Trade Routes in the American Southwest.* Papers of Excavators Club 2(3).

Town of Chino Valley
2003 *Town of Chino Valley 2003 General Plan.* Plan posted on the Internet at www.chinoaz.net.

Town of Prescott Valley
2004 *Prescott Valley, AZ, Street Map.* Map posted on the Internet at www.pvaz.net.

Tringham, Ruth
2000 The Continuous House: A View from the Deep Past. In *Beyond Kinship: Social and Material Reproduction in House Societies,* edited by R. A. Joyce and S. D. Gillespie, pp. 115-134. University of Pennsylvania Press, Philadelphia.

Turney, Omar A.
1929 *Prehistoric Irrigation in Arizona.* Arizona State Historian, Phoenix.

USDA Forest Service
1974 *Seeds of Wood Plants in the United States.* Agriculture Handbook No. 450. Washington, D.C.

Upham, Steadman
1978 Final Report on Archaeological Investigations at Chavez Pass Ruin: The 1978 Field Season. Report on file at Coconino National Forest, Flagstaff.

1988 Archaeological Visibility and the Underclass of Southwestern Prehistory. *American Antiquity* 53:245-261.

1994 Nomads of the Desert West: A Shifting Continuum in Prehistory. *Journal of World Prehistory* 8(2):113-167.

Van Keuren, Scott, Susan L. Stinson, and David R. Abbott
1997 Specialized Production of Hohokam Plain Ware Ceramics in the Lower Salt River Valley. *Kiva* 63:155-175.

Van West, Carla R. and Jeffrey H. Altschul

1994 Agricultural Productivity and Carrying Capacity in the Tonto Basin. In *The Roosevelt Rural Sites Study, Volume 3: Changing Land Use in the Tonto Basin,* edited by R. Ciolek-Torrello and J. R. Welch, pp. 361-435. Statistical Research Technical Series No. 28.

1997 Environmental Variability and Agricultural Economics along the Lower Verde River, A.D. 750-1450. In *Vanishing River: Landscapes and Lives of the Lower Verde Valley,* edited by S. M. Whittlesey, R. Ciolek-Torrello, and J. H. Altschul, pp. 337-392. SRI Press, Tucson.

Varien, Mark D., William D. Lipe, Michael A. Adler, Ian M. Thompson, and Bruce A. Bradley

1996 Southwestern Colorado and Southeastern Utah Settlement Patterns: A.D. 1100 to 1300. In *The Prehistoric Pueblo World, A. D. 1150-1350,* edited by M. A. Adler, pp. 86-113. University of Arizona Press, Tucson.

Vehik, Susan C.

1977 Bone Fragments and Bone Grease Manufacturing: A Review of Their Archaeological Use and Potential. *Plains Anthropologist* 22:169-182.

Waddell, William

1986 *Ethnobotany of the Northeastern Yavapai.* Unpublished M.S. thesis, Department of Botany, Northern Arizona University, Flagstaff.

Wagner, Gail E.

1982 Testing Flotation Recovery Rates. *American Antiquity* 47(1):127–132.

Walker, James

1983 Argillite Mine Pueblo. Arizona, Archaeological Sites Planning Study, Phase I. Arizona Conservancy. MS on file at State Historic Preservation Office (SHPO), Phoenix.

Wallace, Dwight

1989 Functional Factors of Mica and Ceramic Burnishing. In *Pottery Technology,* edited by Gordon Bronitsky, pp. 33-39. Westview Press, Boulder.

Wallace, Henry D.

1995 Decorated Buffware and Brownware Ceramics. In *The Roosevelt Community Development Study, Vol. 2: Ceramic Chronology, Technology, and Economics,* edited by J. M. Heidke and M. T. Stark, pp. 19-84. Center for Desert Archaeology Anthropological Paper No. 14.

Walsh, Mary-Ellen and Andrew L. Christenson

2003 Ceramic Artifact Analysis: An Examination of Technological Variation in Prescott Gray Ware. In *Prehistory in West Prescott, Arizona,* by R. A. Anduze, T. N. Motsinger, and J. M. Potter, pp. 47-72. SWCA Anthropological Research Paper No. 9.

Waters, Michael R.

1992 *Principles of Geoarchaeology: A North American Perspective.* University of Arizona Press, Tucson.

Weaver, Donald E., Jr.

1996 Early Prescott Culture Settlements in the Dewey Area. Paper presented at the Prescott Archaeology Conference, Prescott.

Weed, Carol S.

1970 Two Twelfth Century Burials from the Hopi Reservation. *Plateau* 43(1): 27-38.

Weed, Carol S. and Albert E. Ward

1970 The Henderson Site: Colonial Hohokam in North Central Arizona: A Preliminary Report. *The Kiva* 36(2):1-12.

Wendt, G. E., P. Winlelaar, C. W. Wiesner, L. D. Wheeler, R. T. Meurisse, A. Leven, and T. C. Anderson

1976 *Soil Survey of Yavapai County, Arizona, Western Part.* USDA Soil Conservation Service and Forest Service.

West, Steven M.
1992 Temper, Thermal Shock, and Cooking Pots: A Study of Tempering Materials and Their Physical Significance in Prehistoric and Traditional Cooking Pottery. Master's Thesis, Department of Materials Science and Engineering, University of Arizona, Tucson.

Westfall Deborah and Marvin D. Jeter
1977 The Ceramics of Copper Basin. In *Archaeology in Copper Basin, Yavapai County, Arizona, Model Building for the Prehistory of the Prescott Region,* by Marvin D. Jeter, pp 376-389. Arizona State University Anthropological Research Paper No. 11, Tempe.

White, Gilbert F., David J. Bradley, and Anne U. White
1972 *Drawers of Water: Domestic Water Use in East Africa.* University of Chicago Press, Chicago.

Whittaker, John
1987 Making Arrowpoints in a Prehistoric Pueblo. *Lithic Technology* 16:2-12.

Wilcox, David R.
1975 A Strategy for Perceiving Social Groups in Puebloan Sites. In *Chapters in the Prehistory of Eastern Arizona, IV,* by Paul S. Martin et al., pp. 120-159. Fieldiana: Anthropology 65.

Wilcox, David R., Donald Keller, and David Ortiz.
2000 Long-Distance Exchange, Warfare, and The Indian Peak Ruin, Walnut Creek, Arizona. In *Archaeology in West-Central Arizona: Proceedings of the 1996 Arizona Archaeological Council Prescott Conference,* edited by Thomas N. Motsinger, Douglas R. Mitchell, and James M. McKie, pp. 119-143. Sharlot Hall Museum Press, Prescott.

Wilcox, David R., Gerald Robertson, Jr., and J. Scott Wood
2001 Antecedents to Perry Mesa: Early Pueblo III Defensive Refuge Systems in West-Central Arizona. In *Deadly Landscapes: Case Studies in Prehistoric Southwestern Warfare,* edited by Glen E. Rice and Steven A. LeBlanc, pp. 109–140. University of Utah Press, Salt Lake City.

Wilcox, David R. and Terry Samples
1992 The Wagner Hill Ballcourt Community and Indian Peak Ruin: Revised Permit Report of the 1990 MNA/NAU/Oberlin Archaeological Field School and Subsequent Studies. Museum of Northern Arizona, Flagstaff.

Wilcox, David R., Joseph P. Vogel, Tom Weiss, Sue Weiss, and Neil Weintraub
2008 The Hilltop Defensive and Communication Systems of the Greater Prescott Area, A. D. 1100 to 1275, and Their Cohonina Neighbors. In *Prescott to Perry Mesa: 4,000 Years of Adaptation, Innovation, and Change in Central Arizona,* edited by C. K. Robinson, C. D. Breternitz, and D. R. Mitchell, pp. 16.1-16.39. Sharlot Hall Museum Press, Prescott.

Willey, Gordon R., and Philip Phillips
1958 *Method and Theory in American Archaeology.* University of Chicago Press, Chicago.

Wood, J. Scott
1987 *Checklist of Pottery Types for the Tonto National Forest.* The Arizona Archaeologist No. 21. Arizona Archaeological Society, Phoenix.

Wyeth, Nathaniel J.
1851 Indian Tribes of the South Pass of the Rocky Mountains; The Salt Lake Basin; The Valley of the Great Saaptin, or Lewis' River, and the Pacific Coasts of Oregon. In *Historical and Statistical Information Respecting the History, Condition and Prospects of the Indian Tribes of the United States,* part 1, by H. R. Schoolcraft, pp. 204-228. Lippincott, Grambo and Co., Philadelphia.

www.ingramcontent.com/pod-product-compliance
Lightning Source LLC
Chambersburg PA
CBHW081357270326
41930CB00015B/3332